The Ends of Performance

THE ENDS
OF
PERFORMANCE

Edited by

Peggy Phelan

and

Jill Lane

NEW YORK UNIVERSITY PRESS
New York and London

NEW YORK UNIVERSITY PRESS
New York and London

© 1998 by New York University

Chapter 16 from *TDR/The Drama Review* 40, no. 2 (T150-Summer 1996): 60–70. © 1996 New York University and the Massachusetts Institute of Technology

Library of Congress Cataloging-in-Publication Data
The ends of performance / edited by Peggy Phelan and Jill Lane.
p. cm.
Includes bibliographical references and index.
ISBN 0-8147-6646-3 (cloth : acid-free paper). — ISBN
0-8147-6647-1 (paper : acid-free paper)
1. Theater. 2. Anthropology. 3. Arts. 4. Semiotics and the
arts. I. Phelan, Peggy. II. Lane, Jill, 1967– .
PN2041.A57E53   1997
792—dc21   97-33733
                CIP

New York University Press books are printed on acid-free paper, and their binding materials are chosen for strength and durability.

Manufactured in the United States of America

10 9 8 7 6 5 4 3 2 1

Contents

Moving the Body Politic

Performance in the Field

Making New Bodies

Another End

Acknowledgments

We would like to thank Amanda Barrett, Ph.D., Candidate in Performance Studies and codirector of the First Annual Performance Studies Conference in New York City. The energy, intelligence, and vision she brought to the conference also illuminate much of the work in this volume. We are grateful to Tanya Augsburg for arranging Orlan's presentation at the conference and grateful to Michel Moos and Tanya for their fine translation of Orlan's text. We truly appreciate the assistance of David Moos and Kelli Saunders of SIPA Press for helping us locate and reprint the photographs of Orlan's performances. Donna McAdams was extremely kind in granting permission to reprint her photos of Deb Margolin, as was Tom Raufffenbart in granting us permission to reprint several of David Wojnarowicz's images. Jackie Allen and Branislav Jakovljevic helped expedite the process, and we are grateful to them for helping make our work lighter. Eric Zinner and Despina Papazoglou Gimbel, from New York University Press, have been level-headed, encouraging, and superbly efficient in all our encounters. Special thanks are due to Ted Ziter for his constant support. Peggy gratefully acknowledges Jill's excellent work on the index.

This book is dedicated to our teacher, friend, and colleague James Ndukaku Amankulor, in whose memory we also dedicated the first performance studies conference. He was among the very finest of scholars, whose work on African performance was and is a model of intercultural knowing. His untimely death in 1995 has left the field and our lives inestimably poorer.

Finally, our deepest gratitude is to the contributors of this book for so generously sharing their exceptional writing and for so graciously attending to the long process of editing. We are honored to present their work in this volume and thank each of them for taking part.

ONE

Introduction: The Ends of Performance

Peggy Phelan

Prelude

One history of the genesis of this collection declares the First Annual Performance Studies Conference held in New York in March 1995 the progenitor. In this history, we retrospectively interpret what we were up to almost two years ago when we planned the conference, "The Future of the Field." This version of history has the advantage of allowing me to make claims as grand as these: *In consultation with Jill Lane and Amanda Barrett, two brilliant graduate students in the Department of Performance Studies, Tisch School of the Arts, New York University, we decided that the best way to organize the program would be to present an argument about both the history and the future of the academic discipline.* But the security of this narrative in relation to an event as sprawling as a five-hundred-person conference is hardly reliable. Not only is my own memory imperfect, self-aggrandizing, and distorting, the conference planning had many features of trauma—a sharp sense of latency and a realization that what we were swimming in was rarely ever clear water.[1] By invoking trauma to describe voluntary conference planning I do not mean to minimize the serious psychic and political consequences of coercive traumatic experiences. But I do mean to suggest that the gap between the controlled, well-mapped plan and the event's messier unfolding makes it extremely difficult to view the relationship between the conference and this volume in a straightforward way.

Moreover, to declare the conference the origin of the book is to make a link between the two events that the conference as a whole tried to question. To yoke writing to the belated summary of the event that has passed restricts both the potential futures of that writing and the ineluctable desire to be lost for which many live events live. Moreover, if this book were designed as the "collected papers" of the conference, it would implicitly function as a theatre script for a performance. In editing this volume, we have tried both to retain some of the verve and energy of the 1995 conference and to extend and enrich several themes that the conference pointed to but could not fully explore.

For me personally, the relationship between helping organize a conference and helping edit a book was a vexed one right from the start. Before agreeing to serve as the conference director, I had several stern conversations with my various selves that went something like this:

Peggy, the worrier: "*Are you crazy? If you have time to burn, why not edit an anthology? It will last much longer, will have a wider readership, and will be a better use of your particular skills than organizing another conference. For God's sake, you are a writer. Stop hiding from that, sit down, and write.*"

Peggy, the querulous: "*Books, books, books. Yes, you are a writer, but the fact is, you have been teaching for a long time. In your classes and your writing you drone on and on about the value of live events, the incredible force of people agreeing to be in the same time and space for the same purpose. And then when you can help bring such an event together, you say, 'go edit a book.' What kind of hypocrite are you?*"

Peggy, the dreamer: "*Could you do a conference as a living anthology? A conference that worked like a book with a real argument, a conference that actually moved the field forward? A conference that presupposed, rather than argued for, the discipline's acceptance of interculturalism, feminism, antiracism, anticolonialism, and antihomophobia? A conference that showcases the work you really love?*"

Peggy, the worrier: "*O God, once the idealistic dreamer is in on it, I know I lose. But let me say this emphatically: you have to have two or three independent graduate assistants; you need the support of the senior scholars in the field, and the energy of the most exciting work of graduate students. Otherwise, you'll waste a year of your life and achieve nothing but migraines.*"

Of course our conversations with ourselves are never so clear, but perhaps this conveys the general conflict. My part in this book is, in a certain sense, the querulous dreamer's thank you to the worrier.

Act One

The 1995 conference was a follow-up to a 1990 conference held in New York to celebrate the ten-year anniversary of the Department of Performance Studies at Tisch. Behind the beginning, then, an earlier beginning. The temporality we wanted to stage during "The Future of the Field" moved both forward and backward. We hoped that the 1995 conference, billed as "the first annual" event, would celebrate and critique the rapid institutionalization of the field. Northwestern University's Performance Studies Department had agreed to host "the second annual," and we were willing to wager that a two-year commitment would produce a third. All such living arguments rely on narratives, mythologies, folklore, and rituals that reveal both the internal and external boundaries of any community. Given our own psychic, physical, and discursive relations to the field and its particular departmental manifestation in New York, we were necessarily emboldened and blinded by those boundaries. These boundaries convey, above all, a historical narrative.

One potent version of the history of performance studies is that the field was born out of the fecund collaborations between Richard Schechner and Victor Turner. In bringing theatre and anthropology together, both men saw the extraordinarily deep questions these perspectives on cultural expression raised. If the diversity of human culture continually showed a persistent theatricality, could performance be a universal expression of human signification, akin to language?[2] If performance communities continually made themselves into mini-cultural ensembles, how did their rules and responses reflect larger cultural imperatives? If ritual were to be understood as a piece of theatre, how would the definition of theatre need to be revised? Was "theatre" an adequate term for the wide range of "theatrical acts" that intercultural observation was everywhere revealing? Perhaps "performance" better captured and conveyed the activity that was provoking these questions. Since only a tiny portion of the world's cultures equated theatre with written scripts, performance studies would begin with an intercultural understanding of its fundamental term, rather than enlisting intercultural case studies as additives, rhetorically or ideologically based postures of inclusion and relevance.

This is the story that surrounded me when I first began teaching in the Department of Performance Studies at Tisch in 1985. I was immediately fascinated by the idea that two men gave birth. I had heard the same story about psychoanalysis, although instead of Schechner and Turner, the fathers were called Freud and Breuer, or sometimes Freud and Fliess. I liked these stories a lot. But I cannot say I truly believed them. Nothing in my own understanding of how ideas worked or of how births happen would allow me to. But something in the story appealed to me.

When I first began reading Turner's and Schechner's work I was struck by its generosity and porousness, its undisguised desire to be "taken up." Such an open solicitation is a feature of much work written by white academic men of their generation, but there was something more to it than that. It has the urgency of a telephone ringing; it says, "answer me, add to me, take me with you." I was jealous of their staggering energy (charts and maps and field notes and a thousand airplane trips), and I was envious of some of Schechner's oddly poetic sentences. But I was also a little suspicious of their ease, their sense that all could be understood if we could only see widely and deeply enough. Even at my young age, or perhaps because of my age, I did not share their confidence, their enthusiastic faith. But I was impressed and found their language infectious. Before long I was using Turner's "liminality" and Schechner's "not not" as if they were the "mom" and "dad" of my infant speech. Theirs was the work that first framed the field for me, but it was other work that sustained me and provoked me to write. This anthology is an attempt to highlight some of that work, to explain why I think these "points of contact"—to take up Schechner's inviting phrase—can sustain the field in the next century. But I get ahead of myself.

As the institutionalization of performance studies spread throughout the eighties (sometimes under other names) in the United States and internationally, the openness of the central paradigm sometimes made it seem that performance studies was (endlessly?) capable of absorbing ideas and methods from a wide variety of disciplines. This openness allowed performance studies to avoid the dead-end recitations of "hail to the chief" that most disciplines demand, and perhaps more radically, to escape the conventions of methodological allegiance to a particular field's system of knowledge. In the eyes of its adherents, performance studies was able to combine new work in critical theory, literary studies, folklore, anthropology, postcolonial theory, theatre studies, dance theory, and feminist and queer studies while forging a new intercultural epistemology.

But institutionalization is hardly ever benign, and one could easily tell the story of the consolidation of the discipline of performance studies in a much less flattering manner. Many people (including some of my own inner voices) did tell me such stories, but I'll use the conditional here to muffle echoes and because I love the guilty. To wit: one could accuse the discipline of practicing some of the very colonialist and empire-extending arts it had critiqued so aggressively. One could argue that performance studies was a narrow, even small-minded, version of cultural studies. One could say that performance studies had so broad a focus precisely because it had nothing original to say. One could suggest that the famous "parasitism" of J. L. Austin's linguistic performative was actually a terrific description of performance studies itself. One could even argue that the whole discipline was created as a reactionary response to the simulations and virtuality of postmodernism; a discipline devoted to live artistic human exchange could easily be taken up by the universities in the eighties precisely because its power as a vital form of culture exchange had been dissipated. A new discipline formed just in time to commemorate a dead art would be in keeping with the necrophilia of much academic practice.

But each of these (conditional) claims misses what I believe are the most compelling possibilities realized by performance studies. While theatre and anthropology certainly played a central role in the generative disciplines of performance studies, other "points of contact" have also had exceptional force in the field. Moreover, many of these points of contact are instrumental to "the future of the field," not because theatre and anthropology have "ended" but because the function and force of those disciplines have been so thoroughly revised in the past two decades—for reasons that far exceed the relative strengths and weaknesses of academic inquiry at all. If indeed we are entering a new intercultural "global village," then we must begin to imagine a post-theatrical, post-anthropological age. Such a post-age, like all postage, is reinscribed, written over, as the very condition of the post's arrival (see Ulmer).

But to arrive, one might think, is to begin. Why then begin with the ends of performance? Looking at performance and writing about those visions are the means by which I approach my truest ends—to love what rationalism says is phantasmatic, to imagine and realize, however tentatively and momentarily, a world elsewhere. To join in the grand chorus of "ends" serenading the end of this century is to note the symptomatic impulse to consolidate and leave behind our not quite brave island. The new century, like Miranda's new world, looks brave precisely because we are not yet in it. In transposing and transcribing "the future of the field" into "the ends of performance," I mean to indicate the congenial, albeit often secret, relation between futures and ends. During the conference, Orlan, a contemporary French performance artist who employs plastic surgery as a way to underline the transformative imperatives of the physical and psychic dimension of time, offered us the slogan "Remember the Future." For the future is the stage, that grand canopy that drapes and folds our most unspeakable desires, the stage that promises to dramatize our pasts, to enact them in such a way that we might begin to understand them, to touch them, to know them, to become intimate with them. Those pasts that we have still not encountered we label "ends" so that we might one day reach them. For we know that there is no future that remains untouched by the whispering pass of our many pasts.

In my dream a thousand people wait backstage to participate in an outdoor talent night. At the very end of the line is a little girl in a Superman costume. But whereas he wore a big S on his broad chest, she has a P across her skinny torso. She seems to move up as the awful performers do their talent and exit the stage, but she remains forever last on line. I keep asking her what her talent is and she always replies, "Tap." Time passes and she remains there at the end of the line, not speaking unless I demand it, and even then she only mutters that tiny word, "Tap." When I wake I spell out all the letters in the dream, good girl Freudian that I am: S P T A P. And then I'm off and running: Spat. Jack Spratt. Platter Clean. S.P. Spinal tap. E.S.P., what I'm always wishing I were having, P.S., the abbreviation for "performance studies"; P.S., the abbreviation for "postscript," for the age that follows print and post; stamp, pat, Joe Papp, pap smear, pee, little p-ness, until I see with that horrifying clarity of a fist in my face: P A S T. Tap as time passes into the past. We can resolve trauma by putting time in order, by allowing it to pass into the past. This is a dream about the heroic act of belief in a recoupable past, my endless dream of the girl who knew, who holds the secret, who will someday claim the stage after all these parading impostors, my performing selves, finally move off the stage. This is what it means to believe in the future.

The dramatization of the past in the present is related to both Freud's term for psychoanalytic understanding, *nachträglichkeit*, "afterwardness" or deferred action, and Schechner's understanding of performance as "twice behaved behavior." For Freud, *nachträglichkeit* indicated the retrospective account that reinterprets the past in such a way that what had been repressed by the unconscious can be joined with consciousness. The querulous dreamer can join the worrier here in the "afterwardness" of the conference, retrospectively interpret the gap wrought by the difference between the plan and the event, and rename it *The Ends of Performance*. The interpretation of the conference could not occur at the time of its unfolding because the very fulsomeness of its enactment short-circuited our interpretative capabilities. Freud understood that curing the traumatic symptom required a lot of talking afterward. Talking after the event, post-talking, the often tedious recitations of events and sequences, rehearses the tongue for trickier, less sequential psychic acts. For talking after often means "talking over," and in that performance one might be able to discern what consciousness overlooked during the event's unfolding. This talking after and talking over is where the curative interpretation occurs within psychoanalysis: in the rehearsing of the event that has passed, the analyst and the analysand learn how to play the past when it happens again in the future. Performance studies as a discipline has, until recently, been in the first part of this process: the careful recitation of the facts of the event. It is only recently that the field has given sharper attention to curative interpretations, to the affective and ideological consequences of performance events. It is these consequences that the essays in this volume articulate. Such interpretations, which are always reinterpretations, are also what I most hope will become the future of the field and the truest end of performance—truest in the sense that they help us move past the time of the diagnosis and bring about, enact, give us the time of the cure.

Act Two

> At the end point, when the velvet whisper of the final curtain's enveloping dark is about to absorb us all, when we find ourselves in this century's last lumbering act, when we have reached the end of the road, the end of the way we once lived and thought, spoke and prayed, dreamed and died, why act a part, why make a move? Why write or read?

Print culture has heaved its last gasp, the heralding angels of the virtual proclaim.[3] This was also said about the pencil upon the commodification of the office computer, but I still find myself tucking sticks of yellow-colored lead behind my ear, in my mouth, across the pages that sail across my desk. These gestures are not nostalgic; they are sometimes quick, often careless, occasionally calculating. But for me they remain necessary acts, functions I cannot do without. In the same way, books for me are also necessary acts, events of making, reading, longing, learning. Creating performances and writing about those performances require acts of critical and creative imagination; both contend with the imperatives carried by "the act."

Thinking of performance in the expanded field of the electronic paradigm requires that we reconsider the terms that have been at the contested center of performance studies for the past decade: simulation, representation, virtuality, presence, and above all, the slippery indicative "as if." The electronic paradigm places the "as if" at the foundation of a much-hyped "global communication," even while it asks us to act "as if" such a network would render phantasmatic race, class, gender, literacy, and other access differentials. While the connections between the theatricality and performance elements of the electronic paradigm have been much discussed, there is a more transformative way performance studies can illuminate the hazards and hopes of the new technologies. The electronic paradigm as an epistemic event represents something more than a new way to transmit information; it redefines knowledge itself into that which can be sent and that which can be stored. To put it another way, knowledge in the electronic age is post-able and preservable information. Performance studies, precisely because it has struggled so rigorously with the perils of preservation and the treacheries of transmission, is alert to the Net's potential to flatten and screen that which we might want most to remember, to love, to learn. We have created and studied a discipline based on that which disappears, art that cannot be preserved or posted. And we know performance knows things worth knowing. As the electronic paradigm moves into the center of universities, corporations, and other systems of power-knowledge, the "knowing" that cannot be preserved or posted may well generate a mourning that transcends the current lite Luddite resistance to technology. Who knows? *("No comment," says the dreamer, while the worrier goes out for a smoke.)*

Part of what performance knows is the impossibility of maintaining the distinction between temporal tenses, between an absolutely singular beginning and ending, between living and dying. What performance studies learns most deeply from performance is the generative force of those "betweens." In the time between when he shot himself and when he died (about forty-three hours), Vincent Van Gogh painted his last, and to my eyes, most extraordinary painting, *Crows over a Wheat Field under Threatening Skies*.[4] *Between Theater and Anthropology,* Schechner's powerful primer for performance studies, is a manual for igniting the space "between" two dominant discourses. If we are now approaching a "post" relationship to theatre and anthropology, we must remember that the post we tear into every day rarely contains telegrams announcing our terminal end point. Rather than burying print culture, the electronic paradigm mimics it, carries its rules and graphics into another zone, extending the domain of print, and more perniciously, inflating English as the coin of the virtual realm. These acts of conquest and transcription are interesting not because we need to be reminded of the violence and illusionary seductions of colonialist and capitalist enterprises, but because they illustrate again the strange temporal economy in which we live. What we carry in our "post" is a series of transpositions, transcriptions, transfigurations. Our current "post" signals the difficulty of the end ever arriving at its true ending, or of remaining singular, fixed, gone.

And so, like Didi and Gogo, we go on.

Act Three

If the past is something we encounter in the future tense of our yet to be realized interpretation, we must realize the cast of that retemporizing. One of the most alarming features of the discourse of the new technologies, for example, is its tendency to repress the existence of previous technologies. Yelling, "I'm new, I'm new," this new discourse, like most born-again devotees, forgets the technologies that preceded it and helped bring it into being. In the discourse of the new technologies, performance tends to be seen as atechnological, rather than as a complex technology refined across cultures and across history. Thus, in an electronic and mechanical age, it is increasingly difficult to notice the sophisticated technologies always already at play in live performance and theatre. Pointing to the brave new world of the electronic episteme, we do well to "remember the future." It's right behind us, still breathing. We've been here many times before. It used to be called the rehearsal room.

If we accept Schechner's claim that performance is "twice behaved behavior," we must then ask, what is the force of that repetition? How does performance studies illuminate the project of historiography, the effort to rehearse the event that is gone but still radiating meaning to someone (if only the laboring historian) who is removed in time from its "first" unfolding? Rosalind Krauss has demonstrated that there is no original until the copy is operative. Thus, the meaning of originality is dependent on the copy, the forgery, the counterfeit. What then do we mean when we move from the behavior of the rehearsal room to the behavior of the performance? To frame an act "behavior" is to engage in a highly technological semiotics of movement; it is, in other words, to execute a rigorous mental "behavior" we might call "reading the performative." As Schechner has often pointed out, "twice behaved behavior" gets to be called "behavior" because it is performed much more than twice. This mimicry and iteration is the place where performance and performativity intersect.

I was often grounded for bad behavior, for acting out, for misbehaving. I did the same thing many times, pushing the pulse of the authorities assigned to discipline my errant behavior. Each time I misbehaved, however, I thought of it as the first time. The thrill and excitement, the delicious freedom of refusing, made each act new to me, if not to those compelled to watch me. If someone had told me then that I was repeating myself in these sometimes dangerous inquiries into myself, I would have laughed. Part of what kept me at my bad behavior was the belief that with each act I was breaking new ground, lifting ever more surely the curtain of civility draped over my life, a curtain I feared was designed to muffle me forever.

I had, like so many girls raised in the United States, a facility for mimicry. I would watch the people paid to watch me and show them themselves as seen on the body and in the voice of a bratty, skinny, long-haired white girl. As my mimicry became more polished, I could feel the rage it produced more precisely. I was interested in how closely I could calculate the act and its effect. I practiced in my room, in front of my mirror, on my bicycle, in swimming pools. I performed for myself and against them. I even tried to rehearse imitating myself in case any of the watchers tried to imitate me. The true end of my rehearsal of self-mimicry was to exhibit no reaction, to act as if my projected watchers-turned-performers had not acted at all. When they did not act me out, I began to think they were depriving me of my most spectacular performance, and in the distorting logic of young girls, their refusal to imitate me accelerated my imitations of them. I was hoping that they would become infected by my will to copy. But they remained immune.

Performance and performativity are braided together by virtue of iteration; the copy renders performance authentic and allows the spectator to find in the performer "presence." Presence can be had only through the citation of authenticity, through reference to something (we have heard) called "live." Perhaps the relationship between performance, performativity, and performance studies might best be expressed as "a way of happening, a mouth." When W. H. Auden wrote that about poetry in his elegy for W. B. Yeats, he was trying to survive what he himself had just said: "For poetry makes nothing happen." Like Austin struggling and failing to find a speech act that is not performative, Auden tries to posit the notion that poetry, despite its anti-making, its resistant productivity, survives because it manages to fill its modest home "in the valley of its making," in the deep lozenge of the throat's dark, almost formless cavity. As the Beckett of *Not I* also knew, mouths "happen" as they speak. Mouths happen *to* speak and that is what performance and poetry strive to remain alive to, even while mourning the unavoidability of that forgetting. Performing the conventions of poetic elegy that require the rehearsal of the poet's end, Auden complies with this statement: "But for him it was his last afternoon as himself," by which Auden also means it was Yeats's last afternoon by himself. For death remakes the public poet as social icon (or social outcast). The signifier "Yeats" will become the means by which the living modify "the words of a dead man." Thus, as Auden puts it, in the act of death the poet necessarily "became his admirers." This transformative becoming is both the usual order of owning or possessing the memory of the dead, as in, Yeats now belongs to his readers. More profoundly though, Auden means the line to suggest the way the dead embellish, add to the living. In the same way I might say "pink becomes you," Auden suggests that Yeats, in death, becomes his readers and makes them "better."

This transformative becoming is the almost always elegiac function of performance theory and writing, if not performance itself. Our admiration for performance tempts us beyond our reason to make it ours, for better or for worse. The challenge before us is to learn to love the thing we've lost without assimilating it so thoroughly that it becomes us rather than remaining itself.

What lies before the field of performance studies is precisely a discipline: a refusal to indulge the killing possessiveness too often bred in admiration and love. The lessons we most need to learn are lessons in mourning without killing, loving without taking. This is the end toward which performance aims. Even though I lack the means to attain it, some of my truest ends are to try to dream it into being.

Act Four

The essays here tell a story that continues the conversation begun during "The Future of the Field," albeit in a different key and with several new interlocutors. Conceiving of performance studies as a project of historiography illuminates the rich task of the historian who tries to restage a drama that is behind us for someone who necessarily encounters that past in the future of its unfolding. This is precisely the space in which the performance historian lives. In the section entitled "Writing History/Performing Memory," Joseph Roach, Jill Lane, and Robert Sember think through the politics of desire that animates periods that have preceded our own. They remind us again how central the question of desire is to our own understanding and interpretation of cultural events. While Roach is interested in bringing together the history of theatrical performance recorded in Pepys's diary with the performances of everyday life he also recorded, Roach is most interested in analyzing the relationship between history, memory, and deaths. Roach's inquiry is most animated by memories that cross the grave: that transformative crossing is what gives memory its performative force for historiography. While Roach, contending with the prodigious Pepys, celebrates the performative force of memory, Lane explores the performative force of colonial power and its performance in acts of war and writing. Analyzing the conquest of New Mexico and the first recorded history of that event, she considers the violence enacted in the strategic alternations between historical memory and amnesia, between staging history and writing the present. Sember, on the other hand, is interested in evoking psychoanalysis, often mistakenly dubbed an "ahistorical" methodology, as one way to understand what histories our bodies do and do not carry. Reading Freud's essay on mourning, Sember offers us a way to see David Wojnarowicz's extraordinary photography in relation to the performative force of an HIV diagnosis. Insisting that mourning occurs on both sides of the death drive, Sember outlines a redemptive vision of Wojnarowicz's controversial *Sex Series*. Slyly including a reading of John's Gospel, Sember also prohibits the devastatingly violent divisions between Christian fathers and HIV-positive men that has haunted the reception of Wojnarowicz's work since the artist's public tango with Cardinal John O'Connor in New York and the Reverend Donald Wildmon in Ohio. In all three essays, very careful attention is given to legible and preserved histories. The implicit assumption in each essay is that such legible history, however smudged or watermarked it might initially appear, demands, perhaps even creates, its own spectator/reader/witness. This faith in legibility is part of what motivates their own desire to write, to make marks now about then, to answer back in the language of the present and thereby suture active memory to the performance of history. Consciousness of the enormity of this desire, I believe, is part of what informs the project of performative writing.

What exactly does it mean to write performatively? For Della Pollock, performative writing is "precisely not a matter of formal style." It is an inquiry into the limits and possibilities of the intersections between speech and writing. Pollock's essay evokes what it names; it maps a territory not yet seen. This is the lesson of performance itself—the ability to realize that which is not otherwise manifest. Performative writing seeks to extend the oxymoronic possibilities of animating the unlived that lies at the heart of performance as a making.

One of the places many of us frequently perform is the classroom. Eve Kosofsky Sedgwick offers us several scenarios, directions for staging pedagogical encounters that reverberate beyond the theatre of the university. Not content with passive reading, Sedgwick explores what some consequences of a performative education might be. At once specific and grounded in her own pedagogical practice, Sedgwick's syllabi also function as a musical score for a composition of your own devising.

Theresa M. Senft is also interested in testing the consequences of what a performative education might offer. Senft weaves an aching narrative about her mother's death around the performative possibilities of spare body parts, newly composed medical and mechanical bodies. A keening, resistant instance of the limitations and consolations of the new electronic paradigm, Senft's own essay is a kind of shunt that connects her language both to her dead mother and to her living language, offering us a modem that gives us access to a world wide enough to dream and die in.

Mady Schutzman considers the tragic-comedy of contemporary advertising in her performative writing. Schutzman is interested in the hysteria of copying and the copying of hysteria. Tracing the history from Charcot's wildly self-replicating performances of hysteria to advertising, Schutzman performs a new form of identification and disidentification with the imitative images that so thoroughly saturate our cultural symbolic.

Amanda Denise Kemp's essay is a text for (and from) performance. Voicing a series of questions about "the Black body," which is to say her African American woman's body as it moves through Johannesburg, by way of Mississippi and Evanston, Kemp imaginatively performs a travel log, a new form of "field notes." Implicitly she works to show the way much "academic" writing stops short of a chronicle of affect; it tends not to post the information that most deeply galvanizes the investments we make in performing and reciting. Employing multiple voices and characters, the method of Kemp's essay works to fuse the critical imagination central to both performance and theory.

Kemp's essay helps set the stage for the direct political confrontations considered in the section "Moving the Body Politic." Doris Sommer and

Diana Taylor's two essays (conceived and written to be read together) offer a duet that underscores the difficulty of saying and speaking interculturally in a world economy that rarely if ever stages conversations on neutral platforms. Examining the orthographic, political, and psychic possibilities of the longing in national belonging, Sommer and Taylor extend the stage of the performative speech act and illuminate some of its most contested political dimensions. Taylor and Sommer insist that performances of identity reflect, as Sommer puts it, "a range of staggered be-longings, desired, virtual, but wisely and prophylactically unconsummated connections." Such performances are above all movements between and across, restless movements rather than secure arrivals.

Randy Martin animates different aspects of what we might call a kinesthetic epistemology. He is interested in how social movements are configured as physical movements and how such configurations illuminate the distinctions between social theory and practice. Arguing that there is a distinction between staging crisis and succumbing to it, Martin suggests that the concept of agency that is often missing in theories of social movements might be revitalized by using performance as a model of collective movement. Placing performance at the center of social theory allows mobilization to become a political possibility.

Such border crossings may be easier for scholars than performers. In the section "Performance in the Field," the authors consider more directly the disciplines in which they find themselves. As Marcia B. Siegel brilliantly points out in her reading of the Arlene Croce–Bill T. Jones debacle, institutionalized voices of authority can have a harrowing effect on the movements of performers. Thinking through the politics of dance criticism with refreshing candor, Siegel usefully reminds us that "classical ballet was cultivated by, about, and for the ruling classes of Europe. . . . [I]t is a political as well as a theatrical imagining of a particular kind, one that encompasses only one segment of the world most of us know or would like to know." Arguing that Croce was defending that world in her essay for the *New Yorker,* Siegel provides a fascinating reading of the interests that amplify Croce's voice and the interests that make Jones's *Still/Here* a dance popular enough to launch a national tour.

If the Croce version of dance has led to a kind of rigidity in some forms of dance scholarship, the politics at work in some forms of art history has led Jane Blocker to consider the possibility that actual immobility might have a peculiarly interesting force for performance studies. Blocker analyzes the ways Kenneth Patchen's physical confinement informed the writing and painting he made while largely confined to his bed. Blocker vigorously challenges art history to rethink the relationship between "still lives" and performative making.

Perhaps no one's work has had a more galvanizing effect on performance theory in recent years than Judith Butler's. Jon McKenzie astutely traces the ways Butler assimilated and revised the work of Turner and Schechner in formulating her notion of gender performances. Moving "between theater and anthropology" and philosophy, McKenzie offers the most compelling non-psychoanalytic response to Butler's work that I've seen. Noting the extraordinary consequences of rendering the extraordinary normative, both McKenzie and Butler help render philosophy a more politically useful interlocutor than it sometimes seemed to be in the not too remote past.

Jamer Hunt's search for Sylvia (Bataille) Lacan is an ebullient but critical exposure of disciplines, including performance studies, that rely too much on the native informant. Hunt's almost comic attempts to "connect" with his subject are a poignant illustration of the drama that the ethnographer is sometimes tempted to repress rather than stage in the composition of scholarship. Hunt's focus on his unsuccessful attempts to meet with Sylvia Lacan also emphasize the rehearsals we enact, and the scripts we write, well before we spontaneously meet one another "live."

May Joseph skillfully analyzes the work of Britain's leading Black British feminist playwrights. Drawing on postcolonial theory and critical legal theory, Joseph unravels the intricate nexus of social pressures and institutional practices that simultaneously create and deny a viable socio-legal position for Black British women. In the process, Joseph deepens contemporary conversations on "underrepresented" voices in the theatre, challenging theatre scholars to reconsider the complexity of that "representation" in political, social, as well as aesthetic terms.

In the section entitled "Making New Bodies," Tanya Augsburg's extremely useful contextualization of Orlan's concerns as an artist prior to her most recent performances of plastic surgery allows us to begin to see Orlan's work in something other than its highly mediated and sensationalized frame. Alert to the ethics of radical performance acts, Augsburg does not shy away from engaging in a multivalent conversation with Orlan's controversial work. Orlan's own "Intervention" reveals the artist's aim to rethink the temporality and force of the white woman's body "at the threshold of a world for which we are neither mentally nor physically ready." Orlan's surgical performances reveal, with chilling penetration, what it means to give the body to art and what it means to summon and observe such giving in the age of technological commodification of the art object. Dazzling and upsetting, Orlan's performances expose our desire to live with silent saints, mute sacrificial objects whose unbounded beauty will somehow redeem us. Refusing to be silent, Orlan redesigns her body in order to show us a little more clearly where we suture the human and the machine, the woman and her body, the dream and the act. Working at the threshold between Artaud's "body without organs," Lacanian psychoanalysis, and feminist body art, Orlan's "interventions" reconstruct the limits of skin and the limits of performance as an inquiry into self-dramatization and spectatorial voyeurism. Watching Orlan's video documentation of her surgery, seeing the scalpel that inscribes her facial tissue, I begin to understand what French feminists meant by *écriture féminine*. But Orlan's work is harrowing to me. Brave. Bold. Bound up in the revolting economy of the art object. What I remember is blood crawling across the screened image of her skin the way Van Gogh's paint moves across the threatening skies of his last canvas. While it is true that the surgeon holds the knife/pen, Orlan is clearly the *auteur* of this act (see figure 1.1). Her face is "in process," a set of quotations, citations of "beautiful" faces. As writing, Orlan's performances remind us that the body is not coherent; only reading practices—in their broadest performance—make them beautiful, sick, well, living, or dying. The weight of art history's looking relations, the economy of the gaze that governs the encounter between the beholder and the object, creates a seam that enfolds the look I bring to Orlan's performance. I cannot tell if that seam is an embrace or a scar. I am tempted to take comfort in the "both/and" and to simply declare that Orlan's performances are both an embrace and a scar. But to do so would remove me too quickly from the ethical pivot in which these cuts suspend me. Does the pleasure I take in the image of her oozing blood suggest that I asked for this sacrifice? Does Orlan's commodification of her bodily fluids as 'holy relics' in the violent economy of the art world render the spiritual dimensions of her work insincere? These questions continue to ooze long after Orlan's blood stops seeping.

While Orlan's performances are blasphemously literal, Deb Margolin's are devoutly phantasmatic. Piling up a network of connections between characters who invent characters, Margolin's performance text composes a riveting fantasy in which the notion of "extermination" is a remapping of place and time, rather than an extinction of it. Cut free from the boundaries of a mortal body, cast out of a novel for not being quite the "right"

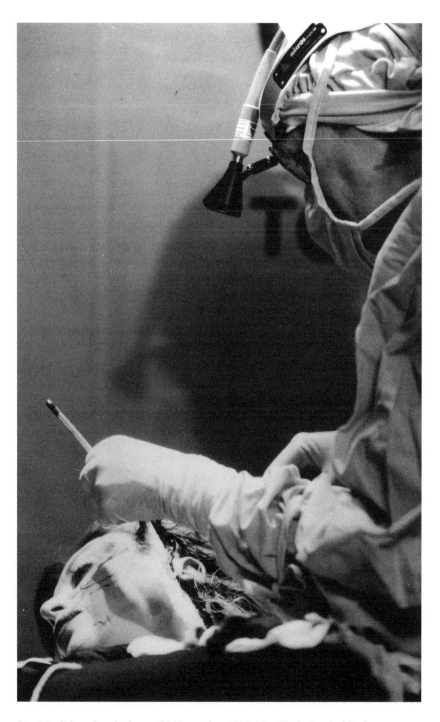

Fig. 1.1. Orlan, *Omniprésence,* 21 November 1993. New York, *Surgical Performance, no. 7.* Photo by Vladimir Sichov; by permission of Orlan and SIPA Press.

character, the voices Margolin sets in motion here are voices I hope will whisper to me when I can no longer remember the plot of this field. Margolin's "Of Bugs, Mice, and Women" underlines the indivisibility of performance and performativity. While Auden reminds us that poetry is "a way of happening, a mouth," Margolin shows us what happens to that mouth as it grows into the flickering stage lights that expose its endless performance deep in "the valley of its making."

Finally, Richard Schechner concludes the volume by taking us back to the original question of the field. Bluntly asking, "what is performance studies anyway?" Schechner intimates a different version of the history and the future of the field from the one I offer here. Such a recasting is a necessary part of what I hope this field performs, the rehearsal after the performance: twice behaved behavior that erases the distinction between then and now, original and copy, past and present, me and you.

Act Five

Of course these essays are not a composite picture of the field. *The Ends of Performance* attempts to map a world that we have not yet seen. Cast toward the future behind us and the past in front of us, these essays imagine a reader who is tolerant of a hundred different definitions of the term "performance," and curious about the stories such an overly burdened word might tell us about the performances enacted then, now, and a little later on, in your hands and eyes. Indebted to the intersections between theatre and anthropology, these essays also illuminate what I take to be some of the most promising forms of investigation into worlds elsewhere, indicative investigations for which performance studies lives.

> As we approach the millennium and pick our way through the litter of "ends" every-where strewn about the stage of this age, I hope these essays help illuminate the fact that such recitations of endings, including of course this one, are themselves perfor-mances—acts that both solicit and resist the notion of an end at all. Plural and un-ending, The Ends of Performance *charts several paths across the drama of time. I hope this book, taken as a whole, also makes vivid why performance studies can be a compellingly amorous discipline. All we know about the end is the urgent need for the cure by love. Maybe if they are shaken properly, held in the right light, some-thing of how we might invent such a cure might fall like fairy dust from the words and worlds assembled here. If not, well, maybe someday you will write a better book. Hope so. If so, please post it to me.*

NOTES

1. See Cathy Caruth (1995) on trauma's latency.
2. See Herbert Blau, "Universals of Performance" (1990).
3. See Sue-Ellen Case (1995) for a representative example.
4. For a full reading of the painting in relation to performance, see Peggy Phelan, "Not Surviving Reading" (1997).

WORKS CITED

Austin, J. L. *How to Do Things with Words*. 2d ed. Cambridge: Harvard University Press, 1975.

Blau, Herbert. "Universals of Performance; or Amortizing Play." In *By Means of Performance: Intercultural Studies of Theatre and Ritual*, ed. Richard Schechner and Willa Appel, 250–72. Cambridge: Cambridge University Press, 1990.

Butler, Judith. *Bodies That Matter*. New York: Routledge, 1994.

Caruth, Cathy. *Trauma: Explorations in Memory*. New York: Routledge, 1995.

Case, Sue-Ellen. "Performing Lesbians in the Space of Technology: Part I." *Theatre Journal* 47.1 (1995).

Krauss, Rosalind. *The Originality of the Avant Garde and Other Modernist Myths*. Cambridge: Massachusetts Institute of Technology Press, 1985.

Phelan, Peggy. "Not Surviving Reading." *Narrative* 5.1 (1997): 77–87.

Schechner, Richard. *Between Theater and Anthropology*. Philadelphia: University of Pennsylvania Press, 1985.

Turner, Victor. *From Ritual to Theatre: The Human Seriousness of Play*. New York: PAJ Publications, 1982.

Ulmer, Gregory. "The Object of Post-Criticism." In *The Anti-Aesthetic: Essays on Postmodern Culture*, ed. and intro. Hal Foster, 83–110. Port Townsend, WA: Bay Press, 1983.

WRITING HISTORY/PERFORMING MEMORY

TWO

History, Memory, Necrophilia

Joseph Roach

We speak so much of memory because there is
so little of it left.

—Pierre Nora

On the afternoon of Shrove Tuesday, February 23, 1669, Samuel Pepys, clerk of acts to the Navy Board, violated the corpse of Katherine of France, Henry V's queen. Pepys proudly recounted this act of *lèse majesté* in his remarkable diary. As the frank repository of so many of the theatre-loving clerk's observations and adventures, *The Diary of Samuel Pepys* has long provided theatre historians with their most valued eyewitness accounts of plays, players, playgoers, and playhouses during the decade that began with the Restoration of King Charles II in 1660. But the reports that Pepys makes on the performance of his daily life—and by the word *performance* in this context I mean the kinesthetic and vocal embodiment of social memory and self-invention—are often no less theatrical than his accounts of the stage. They certainly can be more uncannily revealing, most emphatically so in the diarist's self-congratulatory memoir of fondling and kissing on the lips the partially mummified remains of Queen Katherine, the "queen of all, Katherine" of Shakespeare's *Henry V,* which were then on display by special arrangement at Westminster Abbey.

On the cusp of the most intimate of memories and the most public of historical events, this bizarre entry in *The Diary of Samuel Pepys* introduces a way of thinking about performance that discloses an urgent but often disguised passion: the desire to communicate physically with the past, a desire that roots itself in the ambivalent love of the dead.

Mnemosyne, the goddess of memory, is, after all, mother to the Muses. In the daily ritual of Pepys's inscriptions there occurs a kind of secular devotion to memory. By its protocols, the diarist transcribes the sounding lyre of Terpsichore, representing the purposive actions of diurnal social performance, onto the many-layered palimpsest of Clio's silent scroll. The terms in which I want to understand this ritual—memory, history, and necrophilia—underscore my view that the most promising approach to the history of performance resides in the history of memory itself. Since the seventeenth century at least, the relationship between history—as the archival record of events—and memory—as the transmission of tradition through performance—has been as troubled as the relationship between the living and the dead. Historians record that social and material relations with the dead underwent a fundamental change during the European Enlightenment (Curl, Ragon), a change that French historian Pierre Nora locates in the substitution of what he calls "places of memory" *(lieux de mémoire)*, the artificial sites of the modern production of national and ethnic memories, for "environments of memory" *(milieux de mémoire)*, the behavioral retentions of unscripted tradition, in which the dead, taking the form of ghosts and ancestral spirits, once participated more actively. As Jacques Le Goff sums up in *History and Memory*, "While the living have at their disposal an increasingly rich technical, scientific, and intellectual memory, memory seems to turn away from the dead" (85). Standing on the divide between history and memory, the dead and the living, Pepys ironically enacted a sensuous physicality of human continuity, a gestural Dance of Death that folded the erotic into nostalgia, what Georges Bataille, in *Erotism: Death and Sensuality*, terms the "paradoxical experiences of plethora and swoon" (104).

In this regard, Pepys's Shrovetide visit to the tombs of Westminster Abbey in the company of his family staged an exemplary performance. Mrs. Pepys and he were entertaining out-of-town cousins, including Barbara (Bab) and Betty Pepys, aged twenty and eighteen respectively, who hailed from provincial Impington and to whom the shows of London beckoned. Having been disappointed by the postponement of the opening of Thomas Shadwell's *Royal Shepherdess* at the Duke's playhouse, the party settled on an alternative entertainment, as the diarist proudly recounts:

> Therefore I now took them to Westminster Abbey and there did show them all the tombs, very finely, having one with us alone (there being other company this day to see the tombs, it being Shrove Tuesday); and there we did

see, by perticular favour, the body of Queen Katherine of Valois, and had her upper part of her body in my hands. And I did kiss her mouth, reflecting upon it that I did kiss a Queen, and that this was my birthday, 36 year old, that I did first kiss a Queen. (Pepys 9:456–57)

Among the antiquarian delights stimulated by this performance must be numbered the diarist's pleasure in writing down its particulars. Queen Katherine died in 1437 at the age of 36, precisely the age of Samuel Pepys on the day of his assignation with her remains 232 years later. In the dialectic of history and memory, this was a significant encounter, one acted out, as if on a stage, in the most sacred shrine of English national memory by one of its most prurient blabbermouths.

The clerk of acts found quite a leading lady. As the daughter of Charles VI of France, Katherine lived within a polity that Benedict Anderson in *Imagined Communities* calls "dynastic" (19–22). Henry V of England insisted on marrying her as part of the price of peace after Agincourt. Their son became Henry VI. Widowed early, Katherine married Owen Tudor. Their grandson became Henry VII. As an important functionary in a nascent bureaucracy of the seventeenth-century nation-state, Samuel Pepys, by contrast, lived within a polity that emerged from the decline, in Anderson's words, of "the automatic legitimacy of sacral monarchy" (21). The turbulent history of events between Katherine's reign and Pepys's career is weirdly embodied by the restless perambulations of her corpse. It is more subtly (dis)embodied by the slow transformation of the abbey itself from an environment of memory, in Nora's sense of hallowed corporeal tradition, to a touristic place of memory, which contains "the rituals of a society without ritual" (Nora 12). When Queen Katherine's sepulcher in the Lady Chapel was disturbed by renovations ordered by Henry VII, her body was placed in a coffin with a removable lid at the east end of the Confessor's Chapel at the side of the tomb of Henry V. There she remained on view by "especiall favour" until at least the mid-eighteenth century, her most recent reburial dating from 1878 (Pepys 9:457n). By the time Pepys handled the fragile segments of this macabre heirloom, the torso had become detached from the pelvis and legs.

To say, however, as Pierre Nora does, that modernity creates a society without ritual is to underestimate the expanding power of the quotidian rites of secular society—institutional, familial, and recreational. On the day of the Pepys family outing in 1669, the stage of the Duke's theatre and the tombs of the abbey offered the early modern celebrants two different but related versions of what Polonius might call historical-pastoral drama, either one of which would serve to make more memorable their London holiday. The pastoral play, as exemplified by such oxymorons as "royal shepherdess," stages the erotic possibilities of social inversion. The historical play, here put on by Pepys himself, usurps the place of Henry V on the stage most sacred to English dynastic memory, the place where all English kings save Edward V went to be crowned and the place where many others were buried. Osculation with the corpse of a queen of England, performed by an upwardly mobile commoner on the festive, calendrical coincidence of Shrovetide (Mardi Gras) and his birthday, locates in a specific anecdote tensions between history and memory, the individual and the state. On the one hand, the partially preserved corpses of kings and queens, no less than the effigies fabricated to symbolize the immortality of their "body politic," insist on their physical as well as their spiritual presence among the living. On the other hand, the self-inventing carnivalesque of Pepys's necrophilic performance transforms the *milieu de mémoire* of dynastic tradition into a version of what contemporaries like Charles Gildon knew as the "Mimic State" of the English theatre (*Life of Betterton* 10). Here actors, perhaps the prototypical modern subjects, stood in for kings.

In *Cities of the Dead: Circum-Atlantic Performance,* I have explored the ways the royal effigy and the performance of cultural memory are closely cognate in both theory and practice. Such a convergence of practices, embodied in Pepys's act of raising Queen Katherine's mummified lips to his own, activates the semantic network of a complex word:

> Normal usage employs the word *effigy* as a noun meaning a sculpted or pic-
> tured likeness. More particularly it can suggest a crudely fabricated image of a
> person, commonly one that is destroyed in his or her stead, as in hanging or
> burning *in effigy*. When *effigy* appears as a verb, though that usage is rare, it
> means to evoke an absence, to body something forth, especially something
> from the distant past (*OED*). *Effigy* is cognate to *efficiency, efficacy, efferves-
> cence,* and *effeminacy* through their mutual connection to ideas of producing,
> bringing forth, bringing out, and making. (Roach 36)

The key point here is that beyond ostensibly inanimate effigies fashioned from wood or cloth there are more elusive but also more powerful effigies fashioned from flesh. Such effigies are made by performances. They consist of a set of actions that hold open a place in memory. A theatrical role, for instance, like a stone effigy on a tomb, has a certain longevity in time, but its special durability stems from the fact that it must be re-fleshed at intervals by the actors or actresses who step into it, condensing the complex erotics of memory into a singularly tangible object of desire. As such, the living effigy, the actor, functions as a fetishized substitute for the corpse. And as such, the stage functions as a *lieu de mémoire* on which modernity presents what it calls "period revivals," necrophile spectacles from the high canon that Nora could have been describing when he wrote of "moments of history torn away from the movement of history, then returned; no longer quite life, not yet death, like shells on the shore when the sea of living memory has receded" (12).

Pepys, whose stolen backstage kisses from pretty actresses made his diary notorious (Pepys 8:27–28), took particular note of the player-queens. Shakespeare's *Henry V* was not the stage version of the betrothal of Katherine of France performed during Pepys's lifetime, but the diarist's delight that he "did kiss a Queen" resonates equally in the one that he did see enacted, the version in rhymed couplets by Roger Boyle, Earl of Orrery. In it Mary Betterton ("Ianthe") played Katherine, for whose hand King Henry V, played by Henry Harris, and Owen Tudor, played by the great Thomas Betterton, are rivals. Pepys records his enthusiasm for the play and the production, with but one significant reservation:

> And to the new play at the Duke's house, of *Henery the 5th*—a most noble play, writ by my Lord Orery; wherein Batterton, Harris, and Ianthes parts are most incomparably wrote and done, and the whole play the most full of heighth and raptures of wit and sense that ever I heard; having but one incongruity or what did not please me in it—that is, that King Harry promises to plead for Tudor to their mistress, Princess Katherine of France, more then when it comes to it he seems to do; and Tudor refused by her with some kind of indignity, not with the difficulty and honour that it ought to have been done in to him. (Pepys 5:240–41)

Here Pepys sides with the self-fashioning new man in his morganatic wooing of Katherine. The Elizabethan historian Raphael Holinshed, one of Shakespeare's and Orrery's sources, put a transgressive spin on this liaison, recording that Katherine, on the death of Henry V, "being yoong and lustie, following more hir owne wanton appetite than fréendly counsell, and regarding more priuate affection than princelike honour, tooke to husband priuilie a galant gentleman and a right beautifull person, indued with manie goodlie gifts both of bodie & mind, called Own Teuther" (Holinshed 3:190). Perhaps the careerist Clerk of Acts Samuel Pepys identified himself with Owen Tudor. He certainly insisted on the dignity and honor required by the fact of the ultimate succession of the House, which Holinshed puffed up with a spurious genealogy, styled as "descended of the noble linage and ancient line of Cadwallader last king of the Britains" (3:190).

Onstage, in the spectacular living memory of Restoration theatrical performance, the physical production of Orrery's *Henry V* attempted to make a point with emphasis similar to Pepys's. The producers did so by casting the sympathetic Betterton as Owen Tudor and by costuming the royal effigies in a most remarkably authentic, if anachronistic, way. King Charles II, the duke of York, and the earl of Oxford were somehow persuaded to loan their actual coronation robes to the theatre for this production. The old prompter John Downes records that whereas Harris as Henry V wore the duke of York's suit and William Smith as Burgundy wore Oxford's, King Charles's own robes were assigned to Betterton, an unrealistic but powerfully symbolic anticipation of the eventual ascent of the Tudor (and perforce the Stuart) line (*Roscius Anglicanus* 52, 61).

One necessary preliminary to that ascent was the marriage contracted (or extorted) by King Henry V with Katherine of France. In Shakespeare's version, the warrior king woos (or coerces) the young princess through a translator, speaking in broken French but with unremitting purpose. As in Samuel Pepys's manipulation of the corpse, the king's triumph turns on a kiss, but a kiss that he explicitly performs on her silent lips as a prerogative of self-fashioning:

> *King Henry:* It is not a fashion for the maids in France to kiss before they are married, would she say?
> *Alice: Oui, vraiment.*
> *King Henry:* O Kate, nice customs cur'sy to great kings. Dear Kate, you and I cannot be confin'd within the weak list of a country's fashion. We are the makers of manners, Kate; and the liberty that follows our places stops the mouths of all find-faults, as I will do yours, for upholding the nice fashion of your country in denying me a kiss; therefore patiently and yielding. *[Kissing her]*. You have witchcraft in your lips, Kate; there is more eloquence in a sugar touch of them than in the tongues of the French council; and they should sooner persuade Harry of England than a general petition of monarchs. (*Henry V*, V.ii.265–79)

Katherine maintains a deathly stillness through this speech and thereafter: the witchcraft is in her unspeaking lips; like Pepys's in the Abbey, Henry's vanity requires no response. Onstage in effigy, Katherine, once "yoong and lustie," becomes a voiceless vessel of collective memory, as in life her body became the vehicle for dynastic succession and national destiny, only to be reinhabited by actresses from Mary Betterton to Emma Thompson as a mortified souvenir, putrefying Muse to the "makers of manners" in succeeding generations.

I am arguing here that the necrophilic impulse on which Pepys acted in Westminster Abbey serves the ends of performance in a particular way. It seeks to preserve a sense of the relationship with the past by making physical contact with the dead. It uses the word *effigy* as a verb. Before the eyes of his wife and family members, Pepys struck a bargain with the dead, one through which their tangible presence among the living could be performed. Like Shakespeare's Henry V before him, he sealed that bargain with a stolen kiss. Like the performance of Orrery's or Shakespeare's histories, he parlayed what can be known of history into what can be experienced, however phantasmally, as memory.

The next day, February 24, 1669, it was back to the office for Pepys, "doing of much business" (Pepys 9:458). Business for Pepys meant helping invent the bureaucratic apparatus of the modern state, first as clerk of acts and eventually as the king's secretary for admiralty affairs. At both work and leisure, then, the relationship between memory and history was a matter of performance in the name of—and even in the place of—the sovereign. In this effort of imagining the future, effigies continued to exert their considerable charm, as they still do today in the tradition-bearing (and tradition-inventing) form of "makers of manners" of many kinds— beauty queens, carnival queens, queens for a day, drag queens, welfare queens, queens of the silver screen, and now the queen of hearts. In assessing the significance of these messengers, communicating between the imagined past and the no less fantastic present, historians of performance must reckon more boldly with Mnemosyne. Even in death—especially in death—she has witchcraft in her lips.

WORKS CITED

Anderson, Benedict. *Imagined Communities: Reflections on the Origin and Spread of Nationalism.* 1983. Rev. ed., London: Verso, 1991.

Bataille, Georges. *Erotism: Death and Sensuality.* 1957. Trans. Mary Dalwood. San Francisco: City Lights Books, 1986.

Curl, James S. *A Celebration of Death: An Introduction to Some of the Buildings,*

Monuments, and Settings of Funerary Architecture in the Western European Tradition. New York: Scribner's, 1980.

Downes, John. *Roscius Anglicanus; or, An Historical Review of the Stage.* 1706. Ed. Judith Milhous and Robert D. Hume. London: Society for Theatre Research, 1987.

Gildon, Charles. *The Life of Mr. Thomas Betterton, the Late Eminent Tragedian.* London: Printed for Robert Gosling, 1710.

Holinshed, Raphael. *Chronicles of England, Scotland, and Ireland.* 6 vols. 1577–86. Reprint, London: J. Johnson, 1808.

Le Goff, Jacques. *History and Memory.* Trans. Steven Rendall and Elizabeth Claman. New York: Columbia University Press, 1992.

Nora, Pierre. "Between Memory and History: *Les Lieux de Mémoire.*" *Representations* 26 (spring 1989): 7–25.

Pepys, Samuel. *Diary.* Ed. Robert Latham and William Mathews. 11 volumes. Berkeley: University of California Press, 1976.

Ragon, Michel. *The Space of Death: A Study of Funerary Architecture, Decoration, and Urbanism.* Trans. Alan Sheridan. Charlottesville: University Press of Virginia, 1983.

Roach, Joseph. *Cities of the Dead: Circum-Atlantic Performance.* New York: Columbia University Press, 1996.

THREE

Seeing Death:

The Photography of

David Wojnarowicz

Robert Sember

<blockquote>
If you want to endure life, prepare yourself for
death.

—Sigmund Freud, "Thoughts for the Times on
War and Death"
</blockquote>

In May 1991, the New York photographer David Wojnarowicz, suffering
from AIDS-related illnesses, visited Chaco Canyon in the New Mexico
desert. A national historical park, Chaco contains hundreds of partially
excavated stone ruins attributed to the Anasazi, the ancestors of the native
peoples that today live in the pueblos of the Southwest (Lekson et al.
1988). Wojnarowicz was accompanied on this journey by his close friend
and fellow photographer, Marion Scemama, who helped him shoot a final
self-portrait.

Imitating the ruins in the canyon, Wojnarowicz buried himself in the
desert sands, leaving only his face exposed.[1] The photograph (fig. 3.1)
shows him almost completely submerged. His eyes are closed and his lips
slightly parted. Small pebbles and fine sand collect around his eyes and in
the cleft of his chin, giving the impression that he is either about to sink
completely below the sands or has just risen to the surface; the direction
of his movement is unclear. The stillness of the photograph perpetuates
this uncertainty by fixing him in time and place—the moment of the
crossing of a boundary between earth and air, dark and light, past and
future. This unsettling stillness continues a primary conceit of Wojnaro-

Fig. 3.1. David Wojnarowicz, *Untitled,* 1993. Gelatin-silver print, 28 x 28". Courtesy of P.P.O.W., New York. Reproduced with the permission of the estate of David Wojnarowicz.

wicz's art: the activation of the resonance of what exists below the surface reality.

From a young age, Wojnarowicz was positioned to question convention, what he calls the "Other World . . . the brought-up world; the owned world. The world of coded sounds: the world of language, the world of lies" (1991c: 87–88). Born in 1954 into a violent suburban New Jersey family that broke apart when he was very young, Wojnarowicz lived periodically as a homeless hustler in New York and traveled extensively in the United States and occasionally in Europe. In the late 1970s, with the help of the photographer Peter Hujar, with whom he lived in New York City's East Village, he devoted himself to writing, photography, painting, film-making, and performance.[2]

Most of Wojnarowicz's work was made in the context of the AIDS epidemic. The loss of Hujar and numerous other friends to AIDS, and Wojnarowicz's own diagnosis and illness are primary subjects of his work.[3] The results are not conventionally autobiographical, however. Infection initiates an enraged confrontation (conducted through his work) with the "Other World." In "Postcards from America: X Rays from Hell" (1991d) he explains that the rage is "really about the fact that WHEN I WAS TOLD THAT I'D CONTRACTED THIS VIRUS IT DIDN'T TAKE ME LONG TO REALIZE THAT I'D CONTRACTED A DISEASED SOCIETY AS WELL" (114, emphasis in original).

While Wojnarowicz's AIDS writings and images result from this social diagnosis and the "altered" vision following from infection, they also initiate a sustained investigation of how perception itself is implicated in the creation of the "Other World." His infection, therefore, prompts a recognition of both the invented quality of reality and the fact that convention disguises the mechanism of its production. It is the presence of death that compels this deconstructive function of his work and it is his altered vision, what I wish to call the vision of infection, that permits him to undertake the labor it requires.

Infected Vision 1

Infection changed Wojnarowicz's experience of the world, giving the impression that "the rest of [his] life [was] being unwound and seen through a frame of death" (1991d: 113). This process of unwinding, with all its mechanical and regressive resonances, raises important questions about the relationship between the body and perception. Wojnarowicz offers in his writings a phenomenological analysis of the vision of infection that documents the function of sight within the borders of death. In doing so he invites us to consider the intersection between biology and time. He selects photography as a metaphor for this intersection:

> When I move my eyes very slowly from left to right while sitting still, I can feel and hear a faint clicking sensation suggesting that vision is made up of millions of tiny stills as in transparencies. Since everything is generally in movement around us, then vision is made up of millions of "photographed" and recalled pieces of information. (1991b: 53)

By suggesting that sight is a "photographic" moment in a sequence of images created from a movement through or across space, Wojnarowicz enters into what is now a well established debate about the link between perception and apparatus. Crucial to these debates is an analysis of time.

Time, Wojnarowicz's construction of vision implies, does not follow the image sequence exactly. To begin with, the "photographed" quality of perception suggests that the external image is empirically no less real than the image "taken" with the eye; in fact, the "photograph" may very well precede, even tutor, perception. More precisely, the perceptual moment is a repetition and recollection.[4]

Vision is constructed or developed, then, when image and memory are brought together, each in its own time. This temporal contact mirrors the mechanical process Wojnarowicz outlines, in which two surfaces, so to speak, the eye and the object, both in motion, pass across each other. Vision occurs at the point of contact between perception and memory. When one is faced with death, however, this construction seems to fall apart, or become "unwound." Writing of the state of infection, Wojnarowicz illustrates this dynamic by presenting a juxtaposition, frequently found in his work and certainly evident in the last self-portrait, between the interior of the psyche and the exterior landscape. When a person is infected, it is as if "the entire landscape and horizon is pulling away from you in reverse order," he writes, "to spell out a psychic separation" (quoted in Lippard 1994: 8). Infected vision, I suggest, bears witness through its frame of death to this perceptual technology. With infection, the illusion that vision is an immediate and present experience is lost; we are "cured" of the blindness that permits us to see things as present. What, then, is seen through infection and how?

Wojnarowicz's theorizing suggests that living within the frame of death and seeing with the eyes of infection enable him to perceive, perhaps even initiate, the liquefaction of the image and the illusion of presence. That is, this vision provokes a disappearance. In a figure reminiscent of the Chaco portrait, he describes how anticipated loss "sets into trembling the subtle water movements of shadows, like lines following the disappearance of a man beneath the surface of an abandoned lake" (1991c: 10).[5] We shall return to this abandoned, patterned surface in a moment.

While infected vision may set the present in motion, it also enables Wojnarowicz to see outside the conventional time of perception. That is, he may experience the broken line of still images without having memory thread them into a sequence that gives the appearance of presence. Infection opens time so that the image does not evidence the present but functions as an opening to the past and the future. Tutored in this way of seeing, Wojnarowicz may perceive, in addition to the visible, the necessary disappearance measured in the currents of motion and time that run beneath the image. For the most part we forget and are therefore blind to this disappearance in our acts of vision. By disturbing the surface of the image, however, Wojnarowicz focuses his eyes precisely on this moment of disappearance. This refocusing is powerfully realized in the disappearances that line the surface of the image of Wojnarowicz's submersion in the abandoned Chaco desert.

In July 1992, a little over a year after the trip to Chaco, Wojnarowicz died in New York City of complications from AIDS-related illnesses. The Chaco portrait, however, is dated 1993, suggesting that it was printed after his death and seen only by those who survive him. This dramatizes how our witnessing of his death is doubled by the shifting time of the image: we see his death from before and after. Death, therefore, effects a cleavage in the photographic moment. While the record of a moment, the image splits the instant to recall a past when Wojnarowicz was still alive while also projecting a future when he will be dead. Thus the photograph contains a second moment in addition to the one visible in the image. This second moment narrates Wojnarowicz's movement toward death.

The doubling also occurs in the actual production of the photograph, which too may have bridged the moment of his dying. While the negative was created when Wojnarowicz was alive, the development—the second exposure and submersion in the developing and fixing fluids—of the photograph may not have come until after his death. The second flash of light needed to produce the positive photographic image recalls the first flash and since this image anticipates the death of its author, this photographic recollection takes on a prophetic function. The light promises only death. This effect emerges at the point where the image of Wojnarowicz and the photograph's surface touch in a chemical fixing of time.

The portrait presents an allegory of the relation between body and vision. Recalling the moment when he learned of his infection, Wojnarowicz comments that "the first minute after being diagnosed you are forever separated from what you had come to view as your life or living, the world outside the eyes. The calendar tracings of biological continuity get kind of screwed up" (quoted in Lippard 1994: 18). By juxtaposing the "view of life" with the "calendar tracings of biological continuity," he draws attention to a distinction between the view outside the eye and the view within. Infection, in altering the time of the body, appears then to replace one vision with another. I will call this intervention the prophetic touch, a light touch, for it looks forward to death.

The realization of this in-sight is clearly summarized in the Christian narrative of prophecy, death, and resurrection. Particularly striking in Christ's return is the need for both visual and physical evidence of his death and his survival. That is, belief in the resurrection is a function of both touch and sight. In anticipating his death, Jesus himself establishes this link in his miraculous cure of a blind man.[6] The "cure" is effected through a combination of fluid, sand, touch, and light, the very substances that merge in the Chaco portrait. Christ's touch produces a temporal effect similar to the one outlined above. In John 9:1–10, it is written that

> [When he saw the blind man, Jesus said,] "We must work the works of Him
> who sent me. . . . As long as I am in the world, I am the light of the world."
> As he said this, he spat on the ground and made clay of the spittle and
> anointed the man's eyes with the clay, saying to him, "Go wash in the pool
> of Siloam [which means sent, the past tense of send]." So he went and
> washed and came back seeing. [Jesus was not there when the blind man re-
> turned and when asked] "Where is he?" [by those who knew him when he
> had been blind] he said, "I do not know."

It would be possible to weave from this account a lesson in the blindness of faith, for although able to see, the "healed" man is unable to see the one thing he is asked, where is the "light" that healed.

Restoring sight, however, may not have been the only purpose of this miracle, which is what Diderot (1966 [1749]) implies in his essay "Letter on the Blind for the Use of Those Who See," when he relates how divinity may be found in a touch. "Place your hands upon the body," he urges, "and there you will sense the divinity that resides in the admirable mechanism of your own organs" (20). Consequently, if we are unable to "see" the light we should feel for it across the body, retracing and refinding a recollection of the creator's touch. Thus, for the blind man of John's Gospel, the miracle of sight is the memory of a touch; the miracle is as much in the memory as in the sight.[7]

The cure effected by Christ's touch comes at a price, however, for it brings with it the anticipation of loss. Diderot warns of this when he observes that "Though [the sighted] have more pleasure in life, the blind have much less regret at the thought of death" (1966 [1749]: 17). The consequence of sight is the intensification of mourning, an anticipatory mourning. The prophetic promises an absence and initiates a detachment, or unraveling, of memory from vision. This is, as I have suggested above, a falling away of presence. The prophetic touch transforms the body into an opening that we call mourning, the recollection of the past in order to negotiate loss and death.

Photographs are particularly powerful mourning surfaces because of the temporal contradiction that lies at their heart. They perform both an evidential—frequently mistaken for a truthful—and an aporetic function,[8] that is, they suggest that objects are present while simultaneously confirming their absence. Benjamin (1980) names this paradox the "aura," a temporal haze clouding "the indiscernible place in the condition of that long past minute where the future is nesting, even today, so eloquently that we looking back can discover it" (203). The aura is closely related to death, as Benjamin confirms when he refers to the condition of photographic time as *uberleben*, a term de Man (1986) translates as "liv[ing] beyond your own death in a sense" (85). In this beyond, the photograph returns to our sight a moment that has been, yet it also "doubts" the loss by "living" its afterlife.[9]

Benjamin's reading ultimately emphasizes the endurance of the image, its eternal future, not its disappearance, and in that sense favors the hope that resides in the past. The photograph is able to survive the loss of its original object, which affords it an independence that Benjamin names hope. In viewing Wojnarowicz's Chaco portrait, however, I am drawn to his closed eyes and the (unlocatable) moment of death around which the temporality of the photograph is structured. The image suggests a refusal to see, to open his eyes, to accept the cure, to believe in hope. The line drawn between the world beyond the eyes and the vision within, the infected vision, is tenaciously held. It is the unseen that concerns me most in this image: what does Wojnarowicz perceive within as he lies in the Chaco sands, eyes closed?

Seeing Death

I am led to suggest that this photograph was Wojnarowicz's attempt to create an image of his dying. If true, this undertaking is performed in the doubled sites/sights defined above—the subject of the image (Wojnaro-wicz submerged) and the image as a point in time. That is, the moment of "crossing over" is performed by both Wojnarowicz and the photograph. What, though, is the connection between these deaths? Is it indeed possible to see one's own death? And further, is it possible for an image to die?

My questions touch on concerns that Freud explored in an essay written shortly after the beginning of the First World War, "Thoughts for the Times on War and Death" (1957 [1915]). In this desperate text, a response to the extraordinary presence of death, Freud confronts a psychic blind spot that echoes the one I encounter in Wojnarowicz's closed eyes. For Freud, this blindness is a manifestation of the impotence he clearly feels in the face of war. His frustration comes in response to the realization that "in the unconscious every one of us is convinced of his own immortality." Therefore, he continues, "it is indeed impossible to imagine our own death; and whenever we attempt to do so we can perceive that we are in fact still present as spectators" (289).

Death, as the ultimate form of negativity, has no place in the uncon-scious; thus we are enabled to support an illusion of immortality. Freud's text works to dismantle this illusion by qualifying life as essentially an effect of death. He wishes to remove death from the abstraction that makes the literal costs of war as inconceivable as they are inevitable. "People really die; and no longer one by one, but many, often tens of thousands, in a single day," he writes. "The accumulation of death puts an end to the impression of chance" (1957 [1915]: 291).

Freud conducted his inquiry from the position of a spectator of the deaths of "tens of thousands." Through his writing we are witness to his struggle and his admittedly failed attempt to identify with or fully empa-thize with the dead via a successful imaging of his own death. In his attempt to learn lessons about survival from the destruction of the war, Freud asserts the need to bring death into the proximity of life; not only can death no longer be denied, we must be "forced to believe in it" (1957 [1915]: 291). The reward of this belief is the experience of a life that has "recovered its full content." Thus, the fullness of life is contingent on the contemplation of its future loss. A proximity to death, Freud suggests, has the paradoxical effect of enhancing our ability "to endure" the demands that come with living. The necessity to endure the risk of death within life is a difficult formula to bear in this time of AIDS, for it reflects a psychic correlation to "wars" that are almost impossible to survive even when held at the distance of spectatorship.

In his pursuit of a means to articulate the fullness of death, Freud appears to conclude that the greater our proximity to death, the more literal our spectatorship of the presence of death in our daily lives, the less effective our tools of representation. In fact, these technologies may be counterproductive. In order to enhance life, we seek

> in the world of fiction, in literature and in the theater compensation for what has been lost in life. There we still find people who know how to die. . . .
> [Yet] in the realm of fiction we find the plurality of lives which we need. We die with the hero with whom we have identified ourselves; yet we survive him, and are ready to die again just as safely with another hero. (291)

Despite the predominance of violence and death in our art, it is not dying that we encounter. Instead, through our repeated survival of narratives of death, it is our sense of immortality that is enhanced. Representation appears to repeat the very failure of the unconscious we need to redress.

In the face of the failure of the figurative to approximate the literalness of death, Freud turns his attention to the task of interrupting the seamless surface of the psychic figure, which too appears to stage only safe deaths. Breaking the surface, however, requires that we undertake extensive and frequently painful psychic work. In other words, psychoanalysis reminds us that we are required to remember. This is directed toward halting the repetitions that simultaneously mark and inhibit memory. Psychic work, in that it moves toward the past in order to attend to the requirements of the future, resembles the doubling active in Wojnarowicz's portrait. The temporal ambiguity evident in this work and managed through the figure of death can only, I wish to suggest, be inferred from the rhythms of recollection. Like Wojnarowicz, memory seems to rest "blindly" in time.

The paradox of psychoanalytic labor is that our search for a relationship to the deaths of others begins with a search for our own deaths. In addition to entailing a working through time, this project also cuts a path across the topography of the psyche defined by the dichotomy between self and other. It is a journey directed toward the moment and place where loss has inscribed a boundary within the self. As Lacan has taught us, the perceptual image plays a crucial role in the inscription of this temporal/spatial boundary and the loss it initiates. The assumption of the image of the other is the first experience of the limit of the self. Lacan (1977 [1949]) hints at the loss in this moment, which he describes as the "assumption of the armor of an alienating identity, which will mark with its rigid structure the subject's entire mental development" (4). The laying down of psychic time and psychic space is impossible without this limit.

The Limit

Wojnarowicz undertakes a number of substitutions within the Chaco portrait that enable him to play across the photographic paradox of presence and absence, past and future, and to engage in the excavation of the moment. He forges most particularly a clear relationship between himself and the location, which, in its position as a national historical site, suggests a past for which we have no clear narratives. Without a "history," the ruins are both disturbingly present and uncomfortably silent. They too lie at the border we are inclined toward thinking of as the moment of death, the place where history shifts into nature. The history of Chaco, written into the crumbling ruins, may be brought to a halt by the discoveries of historical fact or may break loose from the thread of memory that would fix them within a historical sequence. These are the tensions between myth and fact, and nature and history that trouble our epistemologies. This is part of the unraveling Wojnarowicz describes, a falling back not only in time but also in form.

In one of his most sustained studies of his relationship to death, the essay "In the Shadow of the American Dream: Soon All This Will Be Picturesque Ruins" (1991b), Wojnarowicz writes of just such a still moment and place:

So what is this feeling of emptiness?
  Maybe it's that the barren landscape becomes a pocket of death because of its emptiness. Maybe the enormity of the cloudless sky is a void reflecting the

mirror-like thought of myself. That to be confronted by space is to be filled like a vessel with whatever designs one carries—but it goes further than these eyes having nothing to distract them as vision does its snake-thing and wiggles through space. There is something in all that emptiness—it's the shape of a particular death that got erected by tiny humans on the spare face of an enormous planet long before I ever arrived, and the continuance of it probably long after I have gone. (42)

Emptiness is predominant in this description. The relationship between Wojnarowicz and the landscape is that of two containers, each holding the emptiness of the other. Each is the "shape of a particular death" in much the same way that the kivas at Chaco are filled with an enigmatic silence.[10]

Wojnarowicz explicitly states that this sense of death is a shape that extends beyond the reach of vision. The photograph images this in the pose he has adopted—with eyes closed, mouth open, he bears a formal resemblance to the landscape. Submerged in the sands, Wojnarowicz has seen his life unwind to the point where he marks little more than a fold in the surface, a boundary between two vessels. This crude form constitutes the most basic distinguishing mark of the self in psychoanalytic terms and calls our attention to the elementary drama of Lacan's mirror stage, which "projects the formation of the individual into history" as a spatial form (1977 [1949]: 4).

Once again we are presented with how this history is articulated by the double action of eye and hand. Laplanche (1976) specifies these two developments as "the visual perception allowing an apprehension of the body as a separate object" and "tactile perceptions, the cutaneous surface having a quite particular role by virtue of the fact that the subject can explore his own body through it with another part of his body, the skin being perceived simultaneously from within and from without" (81–82). In its simplest form, the boundary of the self is identified as a sack of skin. Because of this boundary, a distinction between the self and other is formed, allowing for the later experiences of love and loss. In both instances, the occurrence of a boundary entails a profound identification with the other as both separate yet related to the self. Resemblance is crucial to separation. In its extreme situations, such as passionate love or intense loss, the boundary threatens to dissolve and we are returned to the ancient history in the self and its rudimentary formations.

"When I put my hands on your body on your flesh I feel the history of that body." This is the opening sentence of a text incorporated into a piece (fig. 3.2) Wojnarowicz made in 1990 after he had lost a number of friends to AIDS and when he himself had been diagnosed with AIDS. This is undoubtedly one of the most piercing images of mourning produced in the AIDS crisis, not least because of its daring exploration of the intimate bond between death and sex: in the text layered over the skeletons, Wojnarowicz tells of making love. With the hindsight of the archivist, I also see in the image of these skeletons, exposed by the delicate brushing of the archaeologist's tools, a promise of the later, posthumous photograph where he lies, eyes closed, half exposed in the desert sand, an ambiguous artifact inviting our interpretations. The image will be read by either eye or hand and if Christ is turned against the eyes of time, Wojnarowicz, in this work, harnesses the promise of touch in order to undertake an archaeology of his future.

The excavation is conducted in the sexual exchange between lovers. Wojnarowicz finds that in loving, the other pours through his hands, unraveling a double ribbon of recollection and anticipation. The lesson of love in the age of AIDS is that the body in love is on the threshold of time, evacuated through a wound impossible to suture: "When I put my hands on your body on your flesh. . . . I see the flesh unwrap from the layers of fat and disappear. I see the fat disappear from the muscle. . . . I see the organs gradually fade into transparency, leaving a gleaming skeleton . . . that slowly revolves until it becomes dust." His lover's body flows through his hands like sand through the chiasmic narrowing of an hourglass.

And like an hourglass that has been turned, the text shifts at its center point and Wojnarowicz reciprocates the flow of his lover: "If I could attach our blood vessels in order to anchor you to . . . this present time, I would. If I could open your body and slip up inside your skin and look out your eyes and forever have my lips fused with yours I would." Emptied out, the other becomes an imaginary repository for Wojnarowicz's own body. And it fits like a glove. With a gesture that is at once powerfully sexual and achingly melancholic, Wojnarowicz slips into the sack of the other, hoping to reverse the dissolution his touch has precipitated, and attempting to close the hole in time. Such uninhibited intercourse within the AIDS crisis, for those of us who are literate with the epidemic's choreography of surfaces, may be a deadly proposition. Wojnarowicz does not conceal this

Fig. 3.2. David Wojnarowicz, *When I Put My Hands on Your Body,* 1990. Gelatin-silver print and silk-screened text on museum board, 26 x 38". Courtesy of P.P.O.W., New York. Reproduced with the permission of the estate of David Wojnarowicz.

threat and its particular resonance within the gay community. We see this in the skeletons coupled in the lower left corner of the picture. They do not lie face to face, but illustrate, rather, the position of anal penetration Wojnarowicz would have to assume to enter his lover in the way he does, to penetrate him to the point where they see with the same eyes.[11]

In his gloss on the theory of mourning, Pontalis (1978) explains that "an object [is] incorporated into the shell, the container of the ego; [it is] a process, therefore, that is intrapsychic and whose teleological purpose has been said to be to 'kill the dead' " (183). Wojnarowicz, it appears, has inverted the structure of mourning, positioning himself in the shell of the other. In this inversion he directly engages the psychic threat that mirrors the physical one established by AIDS. At the point at which Wojnarowicz could be expected to accomplish the work of mourning, when, in Freud's words, "a deference for reality gains the day," he has moved into the phantasmatic world of the mourning ego and the lost object—he has also, quite literally, positioned himself for death.

Given the temporal structure of mourning, this is also a move into the past, establishing a Janus-like perception over time. The grammar of this relation could resemble the way time is turned back on itself in the narrative of the miracle of the blind man who has always already been sent. Wojnarowicz teaches us that this is, in fact, the grammar and vision of infection: "When I found out [I was HIV-positive]," he explained, "I felt this abstract sensation, something like pulling off your skin and turning it inside out and then rearranging it so that when you pull it back on it feels like what it felt like before, only it isn't and only you know it" (quoted in Lippard 1994: 18).

Infected Vision 2

In a set of eight photomontages dating from 1988 to 1989, Wojnarowicz gives us a glimpse of what it is like to be separated from "the world outside the eyes" and to see "in reverse order" through the doubled eyes of infection. He also attempts, in this work, to have the image engage the same confrontation with death he undertook in his regressive identification with his lover. These photographs, among the most important of "post-diagnosis" (the term is his) pieces, are gathered under the brief title *The Sex Series* with a dedication to the photographer Marion Scemama, who took the photograph of David buried in the sands of Chaco Canyon (fig. 3.3).[12]

The works have a simple, repetitive composition. Predominantly landscapes printed in the negative, they are constructed from found images. It appears that the subject of motion links a number of the images; the eight are bound together by the fact that they are all deathly still, phantoms hallowed by the negative light. Inset into each of these landscapes are medallion-shaped images taken from pornographic slides and films. Three of the eight pieces contain a more complex set of discs showing, in addition to the pornographic images, blood cells seen under a microscope, police at ACT-UP demonstrations, and images of Saint Sebastian, and a man in a hospital bed.

By far the most striking—and strangely, least commented on—charac-

Fig. 3.3. David Wojnarowicz, *Untitled*, from *The Sex Series*, 1988–89. Gelatin-silver prints, 20 x 24". Courtesy of P.P.O.W., New York. Reproduced with the permission of the estate of David Wojnarowicz.

teristic in the series is the use of the negative. While the images listed above are not insignificant, I would argue that the negative is Wojnarowicz's primary subject and that his principal material is the history of the surface of the photograph, which he strips away as he did the surfaces of the lover's body in *When I Put My Hands on Your Body*. That gesture—the past, present, and future peeling away in his cupped hands—is a precise realization of how AIDS has intensified the temporal structures shared by both mourning and sex and explains the significance of the title of the series—*The Sex Series*. The composition also appears to explicitly mimic the photographic aura defined by Benjamin in that it holds one moment in the other.

By printing in the negative, Wojnarowicz continues the theme of the inversion initiated in the reversal of his own bodily surface when he converted from negative to positive. By printing in the negative, he is precipitating, at the surface of the photograph, a movement in the horizon that pulls "away from you in reverse order to spell out a psychic separation." *The Sex Series,* then, releases from light the same complexes of vision and touch I have outlined above.

If we look below these twilight, frozen images to the skeleton of the pieces, we see the rush of time that photography has always envied in the world and that is the locus of its desire. It is at the corners of the inserts that we can begin peeling away at the surface of the photographic objects themselves. Those openings are like apertures that shuddered open for a moment of light, a fleeting chemical contact, and the images they contain, bodies in a point of contact, are recollections of that touch. Barthes has established that this recollection is the very essence of the photograph— in a blink, light is transformed into memory, the true subject of the photograph is "the lacerating emphasis of the *noeme* ('that-has-been')" (1981: 32). When the negative is exposed, however, the dissolve that Wojnarowicz documented in the earlier piece occurs at the level of the photographic surface.

Photographs are awash with time, which brings to the surface the memory of contact. This should remind us of how the blind man, touched, develops sight by bathing in the waters of Siloam. Wojnarowicz does not conceal this photographic unconscious, he makes it the subject of his infected vision, ultimately finding in the reverse order of the negative a psychic separation, pocketing himself in the phantasmic sack of light that is the negative—the "ego" of the image. In this performative image, then, he may possibly "imagine" his own death. In one of his last works, *Untitled,* 1992 (fig. 3.4), in which he appears empty-handed, he confesses, "I am all emptiness and futility . . . a carbon copy of my form. I can no longer find what I'm looking for outside of myself . . . my head is glass and my eyes have stopped being cameras. . . . I am looking for the aperture of complete and final emptiness."

In suggesting that the negative is the latent subject of the image, I hope to fashion a response to Freud's idea that the unconscious has no place for death. The formula "the unconscious does not know the negative" should be understood in this way: It does not know the negative, because it is the negative, which is in opposition to the supposedly full positivity of life. And it is the negative to the extent that its very constitution, as a heterogeneous system, is correlative to the loss, absence, and negation of the object

Fig. 3.4. David Wojnarowicz, *Untitled,* 1992. Gelatin-silver print and silk-screened text, 38 x 26". Courtesy of P.P.O.W., New York. Reproduced with the permission of the estate of David Wojnarowicz.

of satisfaction. This is brought to visibility by the inverting vision of infection.

In times of death, Freud suggests, we are stripped of the "later accretions of civilization" (1957 [1915]: 299) like ruins stripped by an archaeologist, and are thus able to remember a past in which we may discover the desire for our own deaths as well as the deaths of others. To "survive" these desires we may, for a time, need to inhabit the position of the ancient objects we have both lost and destroyed. That is, we must find a way to image, as ourselves, the interior time and space of our psyches. David Wojnarowicz's infected vision maps one such in-sight.

NOTES

I wish to thank Peggy Phelan for her extraordinary guidance through these first stages of my relationship to the work of David Wojnarowicz. Tom Rauffenbart has been more than generous in providing me access to David's archive; without his permission to reprint some of David's photographs, this essay would be greatly diminished. A comforting and stimulating companion in this work is Mysoon Rizk, who has gently reminded me of the basics of art history and criticism. Radz Subramaniam and David Gere have both read this piece in earlier drafts and given much appreciated advice.

1. While not the subject of this paper, the significance of Chaco to Wojnarowicz warrants further commentary. Believed to date from around A.D. 900 to 1130–1180, the Chaco settlements lay at the confluence of an elaborate network of ancient roads that extended thousands of miles to the south and north, a network still visible from the tops of the mesas in the region. These traces form a geography of the "prehistory" of the United States, a frequent subject of Wojnarowicz's work. His selection of Chaco as the site for his self-portrait continued his political and mythical search for an exit from the rigid confines of contemporary reality. Frequently, in his search he experienced a continuity between his body and the landscape through which he was traveling, perceiving each moment as an opening into an extended time. While archaeologists have no conclusive explanation for the decline of Chaco and the Anasazi culture, it is clear that the region was depopulated in a very short time, suggesting a period of terrible hardship, upheaval, and death. The echoes of such disaster in the silence of the ruins offer a provocative parallel to Wojnarowicz's apocalyptic images of life within the AIDS epidemic.

2. His work was exhibited in the 1991 Whitney Biennial and is in the collection of the Museum of Modern Art (MOMA). He was a major figure in the

downtown art scene of the 1980s, but remains relatively unknown outside the art world. He achieved national media prominence in 1989 when an AIDS exhibition at Artist's Space in New York City was defunded by the NEA because of a piece Wojnarowicz wrote for the catalogue about Cardinal O'Connor's stand on sexuality and condom distribution. A year later, his successful court case against the Reverend Donald Wildmon also received extensive media coverage as one of the signature events in the so-called culture wars.

A major retrospective of his work at the New Museum of Contemporary Art in Soho is planned for January 1999. For examples of his work, see Blinderman 1990, the exhibition catalogue from the University Galleries of Illinois State University, and *Aperture,* no. 137, titled *Brush Fires in the Social Landscape* (1994), devoted entirely to Wojnarowicz's work.

3. Wojnarowicz was diagnosed HIV-positive in 1987, the year Peter Hujar died of AIDS.

4. See Phelan (1993, 1997) on the temporalities of photographic and cinematic images and their relationship to truth. Her chapter in *Mourning Sex,* entitled "Infected Eyes: Dying Man with a Movie Camera, *Silverlake Life: The View from Here*" (1997) has prompted many of the questions that have directed my reading of Wojnarowicz's AIDS work.

5. This image is presented in the essay "Loosing the Form in Darkness" (1991c), in which Wojnarowicz laments the loss inherent in sight. It is suggestive that this discussion occurs in response to his recollections of public sex encounters.

6. This discussion of Jesus is prompted in part by Wojnarowicz's use of images of Christ in his work. He gathered many of these images while traveling in Mexico, Puerto Rico, and the U.S. Southwest. They feature prominently in his film and video work, most notably the video accompaniment to his performance piece *ITSOFOMO (In the Shadow of Forward Motion).* Christ also appears in a work that Reverend Wildmon objected to, *Untitled (Jean Genet)* (1989). The work is a xerox collage in which a portrait of Jean Genet, placed in the foreground and hallowed, is juxtaposed with an image of Christ shooting up. In the court deposition, Wojnarowicz explains that he wished to illustrate that Christ would have had compassion for the injecting drug users that many vilified in the time of AIDS. This compassion is expressed through identification.

7. For Jesus, however, this memory confirms his relation to death. From the Gospels we learn that Jesus was troubled by touch; memory and sight combine on the surface of both body and image in a prophetic touch. If touched, Jesus must then likely remember. In his case he is required to remember the future, what is to come in fulfillment of the prophecy. This temporal structure is particularly clear in this miracle, for Jesus, who has been sent, in turn sends the blind man to wash in the waters of "Sent," or the curative waters of the Past. The

parallels with the photographic body are striking; it too retrieves the past through touch and submersion.

8. For discussions of doubt and truth in the photographic image, see Barthes 1981 and 1985, Benjamin 1980 [1931], Phelan 1993, and Sontag 1989.

9. This contradictory function is reminiscent of the mourning process, which also holds the image as a confirmation of loss and evidence of its continuation. Mourning work is in many ways the resolution of this "perceptual" problem as recollections are decathected and the image settles fully into the past. De Man emphasizes this resolution in his writing when he explains that "the image belongs not to the life of the original, the original is already dead . . . [it] belongs to the afterlife of the original, thus assuming and confirming the death of the original" (1986: 85). I wish to stay for a time with the lack of clarity that comes with a greater belief in the referent or original than de Man would permit. That is, I wish to explore the image's melancholic aspects.

10. Kivas are architectural structures common to almost all of the Anasazi buildings. Large, circular chambers, usually wholly or partly underground, they are believed to have functioned as the site for much of the communal activity of the settlements. Their hollowness only emphasizes the loneliness that Wojnarowicz experienced in the years following his diagnosis.

11. See Bersani's discussion (1995) of Genet for an elaboration of the aggressive and dissolving effects of homosexual sex. Bersani suggests that this ascetic aspect of homosexual desire is a site for a radical rethinking of the politics of identity.

12. In an interview, Marion Scemama explained that the title of the series developed as a response to an exhibition in Paris on human sexuality that included little on gay or lesbian sexuality. Angered by what he perceived as censorship and homophobia, Wojnarowicz set about creating the work.

WORKS CITED

Barthes, Roland. *Camera Lucida,* trans. Richard Howard. New York: Hill and Wang, 1981.
———. "On Photography." In *The Grain of the Voice: Interviews, 1962–1980.* New York: Farrar, Straus and Giroux, 1985.
Benjamin, Walter. "A Short History of Photography." In *Classic Essays on Photography,* ed. Alan Trachtenberg. New Haven: Leet's Island Books, 1980 [1931].
Bersani, Leo. *HOMOS.* Cambridge: Harvard University Press, 1995.
Blinderman, Barry, ed. *Tongues of Flame.* New York: D.A.P./Distributed Art Publishers, 1990.
de Man, Paul. *The Resistance to Theory.* Minneapolis: University of Minnesota Press, 1986.

Diderot, Denis. "Letter on the Blind for the Use of Those Who See." In *Diderot's Selected Writings,* ed. and trans. Lester G. Crocker. New York: Macmillan, 1966 [1749].

Freud, Sigmund. "Thoughts for the Times on War and Death." In *The Standard Edition of the Complete Psychological Works of Sigmund Freud,* ed. and trans. James Strachey in collaboration with Anna Freud. Vol. 14. London: Hogarth Press, 1957 [1915].

———. "Mourning and Melancholia." In *Collected Papers,* ed. and trans. Joan Riviere. Vol. 4. New York: Basic Books, 1959 [1917].

———. "Negation." In *The Standard Edition of the Complete Psychological Works of Sigmund Freud,* ed. and trans. James Strachey in collaboration with Anna Freud. Vol. 19. London: Hogarth Press, 1961 [1923].

Lacan, Jacques. "The Mirror Stage as Formative of the Function of the I as Revealed in Psychoanalytic Experience." In *Ecrits: A Selection,* ed. and trans. Alan Sheridan. New York: Norton, 1977 [1949].

Laplanche, Jean. *Life and Death in Psychoanalysis,* trans. Jeffrey Mehlman. Baltimore: Johns Hopkins University Press, 1976.

Lekson, Stephen H., Thomas C. Windes, John R. Stein, and James W. Judge. "The Chaco Canyon Community." *Scientific American* 259, no. 1 (1988): 100–109.

Lippard, Lucy R. "Passenger on the Shadows." *Aperture,* no. 137 (fall 1994): 6–25.

Ortiz, Simon J. "What We See: A Perspective on Chaco Canyon and Pueblo Ancestry." In *Chaco Canyon: A Center and Its World,* ed. Mary Wachs. Santa Fe: Museum of New Mexico Press, 1994.

Phelan, Peggy. *Unmarked: The Politics of Performance.* New York: Routledge, 1993.

———. *Mourning Sex: Performing Public Memories.* New York: Routledge, 1997.

Pontalis, J.-B. "On Death-Work in Freud, in the Self, in Culture." In *Psychoanalysis, Creativity, and Literature,* ed. Alan Roland. New York: Columbia University Press, 1978.

Sontag, Susan. *On Photography.* New York: Doubleday, 1989.

Wojnarowicz, David. "Being Queer in America: A Journal of Disintegration." In *Close to the Knives: A Memoir of Disintegration.* New York: Vintage Books, 1991a.

———. "In the Shadow of the American Dream: Soon All This Will Be Picturesque Ruins." In *Close to the Knives: A Memoir of Disintegration.* New York: Vintage Books, 1991b.

———. "Loosing the Form in Darkness." In *Close to the Knives: A Memoir of Disintegration.* New York: Vintage Books, 1991c.

———. "Postcards from America: X Rays from Hell." In *Close to the Knives: A Memoir of Disintegration.* New York: Vintage Books, 1991d.

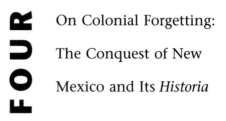

FOUR

On Colonial Forgetting:
The Conquest of New
Mexico and Its *Historia*

Jill Lane

The prestige that could only derive from the
written word thus began its portentous career
across the American continent.
—Angel Rama, *The Lettered City*

The conquest of New Mexico has been so perfectly forgotten it is worth remembering. It has not been forgotten due to any lack of consequence; for the peoples of New Mexico its consequences were grave and irrevocable. Not banal, uninteresting, or too typical, the conquest was literally derivative. To achieve its ends, it restaged key signifying patterns and tropes of earlier conquests that, by 1598 were readily available for reuse. In New Mexico, conquest met its end: the expedition crossing the Rio del Norte "discovered" not the lands or peoples of New Mexico (already "discovered" some decades before), but rather the limits of its own paradigm. In the story of New Mexico, then, we will find the discourse of conquest migrating toward and disguising itself in a new practice of writing, a movement dramatized in the exchanges and substitutions between the so-called last conquistador, Don Juan de Oñate, and his soldier-turned-historian, Gaspar de Villagrá, whose 1611 *Historia de la nuevo Mexico [sic]* offered a "true" eyewitness account of the 1598 conquest.

The prologue to Villagrá's *Historia,* a pindaric ode written by a royal scribe in Madrid, honors both the conqueror and the historian. Of the conqueror, the poem sings,

Oñate sought the ancient land
From whence the Aztec came,
A new Mexico at hand
Wherein to gain his fame. . . .
Another Cortés, brave, discreet,
A new Columbus here.[1]

Following the spirit of Villagrá's text, the verse unabashedly pens a hope that Don Juan de Oñate will stand in the annals of history among the "greatest" conquistadors and New World explorers. It traces a genealogy of conquest fame: Oñate enters a "new" Mexico to redraw the boundaries of the Spanish empire, which were drawn by Cortés before him, in turn drawn by Columbus before him. He is last in a long line of conquistadors, and thus stands first on the expanding frontier of empire.

The historian Gaspar de Villagrá figures in this military genealogy, but only by corollary, having served as captain under Oñate's command: "In light of such a flame / Villagrá has won his fame." While Oñate served the Crown as a "true soldier" brandishing his "bloody sword," Villagrá has rendered an equally important service by exchanging his own sword for the "worthy pen":

Though each passing day and year
Ravage and burn and cut and sear
The marks he left will perish not.
(Villagrá 39)

The marks of the sword, like that of passing days, are so many cuts and ravages; the mark of the pen, in turn, can render those ravages immutable. In the historical text, the cuts and ravages take on the character of scars, discursively ordered into a text to be read and remembered by posterity. Thus the conqueror and the historian of New Mexico, wielding sword and pen on the far border of empire, assume complementary roles: through their combined efforts, the boundary and meaning of empire are re-membered anew.

But Oñate and Villagrá lost the wager with history. Who now remembers the deeds of this New Mexican conquest, as heroic or otherwise? Who reads the *Historia,* as they still do *El Cid* or *La Araucana?*[2] In spite or because of the twin efforts of the sword and the pen, the conqueror and the historian of New Mexico are little remarked in North or Central American cultural memory. To the contrary, rather than doubly seal and commemorate their future glory, the alliance between these acts of war and these acts of writing instead reveal and figure their own forgetting.

A Trope

The sword and the pen: a grand trope of medieval Europe, a particular trope of the Spanish Golden Age (think of Cervantes), from which emerges a remarkable nexus of interrelated acts of war and writing that make up the world of Spanish conquest. We know that the cataclysms of Spanish "discovery" and conquest in the New World occasion furious circulation between the projects of war and the projects of writing: both mutually inform and advance New World carto-graphy, New World ethno-graphy, New World historio-graphy. These projects, in turn, are marked not by their "newness," but rather by their consistent attempts to account for the incommensurability of the "New" with recourse to known formulations of the "Old"—hence through acts of both war and writing, "Anahuac" becomes "New Spain." For Michel de Certeau, the "discovery" and "conquest" are themselves a greater project of writing: "the conqueror will write the body of the other and trace there his own history. . . . This is *writing that conquers*. It will use the New World as if it were a blank, 'savage' page on which Western desire will be written" (1988 xxv). Here the sword is already a kind of pen, inscribing the narrative of Spanish empire onto the body of the land and its peoples; here the pen is already a kind of sword, violently reinscribing the newly discovered land and peoples of America into the book of empire.

Between the sword and the pen of Spanish conquest lies a complex range of performative acts and rhetorical postures, both warlike and writerly, that advance, restage, and seal Castilian rule in new territory, thereby perpetuating and reinventing Spanish empire across time and space. Among them we find, for example, the reading of the (in)famous *Requerimiento,* the inscriptions of the name of the monarch on solitary rocks, the planting and unfurling of the royal standard, the ceremonies attending the Acts of Vassalage and Obedience, the forced participation of indigenous peoples in "pedagogical" religious dramas, and so on.[3] Together, these acts make up a complex economy of inscription that circulates the performative force through which empire is produced, maintained, articulated, and enacted.

The Story of the Conquest

Like many tales of Spanish conquest in the Americas, the story of the conquest of New Mexico fully engages the discourse of the "New," marked by origin myths and providential beginnings. The northbound movement of the New Mexican conquest thus posits a "zero point" or starting point in time that enables its ritual repetition through space.[4] In New Mexico, Oñate hopes to find the legendary Seven Cities, supposedly founded by Spanish bishops exiled centuries before from Muslim Spain. If the bishops were once forced out of a vanquished Spain by the Moors, the now victorious kingdom will answer that exile not only by finding these diasporic Spanish peoples in the land of a new "infidel," but also by moving the very boundaries of empire so as to embrace them once again. With each new discovery across the Atlantic, the projected location of those cities had progressively moved from the Antilles to the Western Indies to Mexico, and now was believed to be in the territory of New Mexico (Junquera 14; Hammond 1979, 20–33). Thus the conquest of New Mexico is formulated in part as a quest for the source of legend, the answer to an originary exile. The ever vanishing origin seduces the conquistador farther and farther north, taking Oñate as far north as Wichita, in present-day Kansas, before colonial authorities force him back.

This story of conquest implies too a narrative of new discovery, of travel beyond the cartographically mapped, the empirically known. Crossing the northern frontier of New Spain marked by the Rio del Norte (today the Rio Grande), Oñate and Villagrá enter "vast and solitary plains where foot of Christian never trod before" (Villagrá 125), and together initiate a new chapter in Spanish conquest. Moreover, while Oñate seeks a "new" Mexico, Villagrá figures this Mexico not as a copy of the first, but as its origin: "It is a well-known fact that the ancient Mexican races, who in ages past founded the city of Mexico, came from these regions" (42). Oñate seeks not just new territory for the crown of Spain, but the very origin of Aztec greatness. In a calculated reversal, Villagrá implies that it was Cortés, rather than Oñate, who found the "new" and "copied" Mexico. Here Oñate becomes the "Christian Achilles," for whom alone was reserved the privilege of discovering the Seven Cities of their forefathers, and of conquering the "original" Mexican lands, in this "the most hidden portion of the earth" (Villagrá 41, 72).

The conquest of New Mexico, like those before and after, thus engages grand performative tropes: Oñate travels north both to seek and to stage there a new Mexico, a new Spain: a warlike "theatre" that engages a complicated mix of the metaphoric and the literal, the make-believe and the belief-made-real (see Taussig). Here empire departs to the land of the other, understood as the mythical space of origin, to repeat itself there. Unlike the discourses of travel and discovery, the logic of conquest does not allow for return. In the case of the Spanish kingdom of Castile, expansion entails the continual ostension and reproduction of the body politic in conquered lands, in a centuries-long tradition that dates to the *reconquista* of Muslim territory in the Iberian Peninsula. The Castilian Crown does not treat conquered territories as either colonies or trading outposts, but as the prolongation of the kingdom itself.[5]

Thus the founding, the (re)making, of a new Spain requires a grammar of performative gestures: the *Requerimiento* is perhaps its most famous instance. Read on the horizon of New Mexican land (otherwise Pueblo territory), this speech act, in which Don Juan de Oñate claims possession of the lands in the name of the king, is performative: for the Spanish, it enacts what it enunciates. While we can read this practice cynically, it is nonetheless compelling (and strange indeed) that this single act of reading aloud not only establishes the "legal" and "moral" grounds for any and all future Spanish contact, warfare, settlement, missionary activity, and commerce among the Pueblos and in New Mexican land, but also—within the Spanish conquest imaginary—fundamentally reconstitutes the status and meaning of that land and its peoples in relation to the Spanish Crown. An act such as the *Requerimiento* is, to borrow Derrida's language on the sacred source of law, a "founding and justifying moment" that institutes law as performative force, "not in the sense of law in the service of force . . . servile and thus exterior to the dominant power," but rather as force itself, "a more internal, more complex relation with what one calls force, power or violence" (Derrida 941). In an overdetermined (gross) ritual invocation of the "sacred" source of imperial expansion, the *Requerimiento* literally and figuratively rereads, reads to, and writes a new place, New Mexico, in this founding gesture. This writerly performance does not ceremonially seal the victories of warfare: it enacts and initiates the founding violence of conquest itself.

Conquest Imitation

The story of the conquest of New Mexico is not one of origins or providential beginnings; it is, rather, the story of the decadence of the Spanish conquest imagination, a markedly baroque conquest in the twilight of the Spanish Golden Age. The conquest of New Mexico is haunted everywhere by ghosts of conquest past. By 1598, the whole rhetoric of New World discovery has suffered profound erosion. Well over a century after the first voyage of Columbus, and two generations after Cortés's entry into Tenoctitlán, Spanish discovery and conquest in the Americas are no longer a discourse of the new. The New World folds over, doubling itself: Oñate's citations derive not from the "Old" world, but from the New; he founds not a new Sevilla, nor a new Córdoba, but a new Mexico.

By 1598, another form of "writing" has entered and profoundly altered the economy of conquest: the discourse of law. In 1519, Cortés brashly sets his ships to sail against his orders, and proceeds with an unauthorized and generally improvised spectacular expedition on the continent. In 1598, Oñate sets out to conquer New Mexico under the watchful auspices of the Crown and in accordance with a meticulously detailed legal contract that took no less than four years of bureaucratic wrangling in royal courts to settle. Decades of Spanish settlement in the Americas had generated an expansive administrative bureaucracy, which stipulated precise conduct of encounter and conquest, enforced by a growing body of law, notably the New Laws of 1542, and later the so-called Ordinances of Discovery of 1573. The pen and the sword dance a new configuration: Oñate's contract is meticulously reviewed, edited, and modified by the viceroy, literally written over with marginal citations of ordinances and relevant articles that allow or prohibit his proposed conduct in New Mexico.[6] In addition, Oñate is made to read and sign a certified copy of "Instructions"—a kind of conquest handbook, a long list of dos and don'ts.[7] By 1598, no conquest expedition leaves without a royal scribe and notary, so that all conquest behavior can be carefully recorded, monitored, documented. Thus, while Oñate is theoretically embarking on a "new" discovery into the great "unknown," his every move there is allowed to be neither new nor unknown; each is already written and sealed by legislative authority.

Even beyond the proscriptions of this colonial administration, the acts of conquest themselves have become increasingly codified, and have developed a taxonomy of repeatable behaviors. The actions of conquest here have all the trappings of what Richard Schechner might call "restored behavior" (35). Historians find Cortés's conquest of the Aztecs remarkable as the birth of an entire paradigm of conquest behavior. Tzvetan Todorov comments that Cortés "crystallizes into a unique type of behavior elements hitherto . . . disparate. Once the example is set, it spreads with impressive speed" (99).[8] Richard Trexler similarly understands Cortés's conquest as the self-conscious model for what he calls "military theatre" in the Americas: "Soldiers acted, crafting events for their subsequent performance by imitators" (191). Don Juan de Oñate, the "new" Cortés setting out to claim a "new" Mexico, is precisely one of those imitators. By 1598, tropes of conquest have very much become "twice-behaved" (Schechner 36), and constantly mediate their status as "revivals" against their desire for the glory of the "new."

Conquest under Erasure

The story of the conquest of New Mexico is not about beginnings or repetitions: it is about the end of conquest. By 1598, a curious thing has occurred in colonial New Spain: conquest has disappeared. The 1573 Ordinances of Discovery make this clear: "Discoveries are not to be called conquests. Since we wish them to be carried out peacefully and charitably, we do not want to use the term 'conquest' to offer any excuse for the employment of force or causing injury to the Indian" (in Hanke 1973, 112). The ordinances mark a profound change in the relation between the monarch and the class of nobles who served as conquistadors. A brief comparison between the first laws governing conquest activity in 1513 and the 1573 ordinances is revealing. In 1513, the Laws of Burgos instituted the practice of forcibly relocating and splintering native communities by "giving" the Indians in "allotments" *(repartimientos)* to conquistadors to labor on their *encomiendas*. This practice was justified on the grounds that, since Indians were "by nature . . . inclined to idleness and vice," proximity to their Spanish masters would promote their learning; they would "profit" by "observing the conduct of the Spaniard" (in Parry 336–37). But by 1573, the conquistadors' conduct is, it seems, no longer exemplary, and is instead a contagious model of vice. Now it is the Spaniard, under the influence of the very *word* "conquest," whose proximity to the Indian might elicit "the employment of force or the causing of injury." In 1513, military success in acts of conquest offered the aspiring noble advancement in a prestige economy of honor and wealth transplanted from reconquest Spain: the successful conquistador garnered advanced title and status of his family name, and earned wealth in the form of land and the servitude of the conquered. "Conquest" as a term, a strategy, and a practice served the interests of the nobility and the Crown alike. By 1573, that prestige economy has been seriously curbed by the monarch, whose interests are no longer served by the all-too-evident brutality of conquest. Quite apart from the unwelcome publicity of the growing Black Legend, the monarch's finances are now better served by consolidating the exploitation of the vast and yielding mineral wealth in Mexico and Peru. His favor thus falls away from the conquistador and toward the colonial administrator. The conquistador/noble thus operates in a crippled economy of honor, an economy disabled by the suppression of that central node—conquest—through which prestige is reproduced and circulated.

The language of Oñate's contract and instructions carefully circles around the linguistic place where conquest might once have lived. His mission is to "discover" and "take possession" of the land to spread the holy faith. Instead of "conquering" Indians, he will "pacify" and "reduce" them (*DJO* 42, 65). These discursive moves are, of course, strategic. The ordinance mandates "pacification" while effacing the Spanish aggression that would provoke the Indian resistance in the first place. The monarch re-dresses the unspeakable brutality of conquest by making conquest itself unnameable. Whatever is designated by the word "conquest" is thus removed to another unidentified place, so that the empire can reimagine (or discover) itself without violent agency.

To occupy the space of the conquistador in this "post-conquest" moment is to inhabit deeply contested terrain: the conqueror is rigorously produced and molded by the state, only to be as rigorously erased by the same. Both Oñate and Villagrá are confronted with the same dilemma: how to enact the unnameable conquest of New Mexico. The related enactments of soldier and historian produce a peculiar inversion of normative expectation. The soldier enacts the "new" conquest by performing history, by restoring and restaging the behaviors of those who produced conquest when it was still named and valued as such. Only by repeating and revisiting that past does this conquest come into its own present. The historian, in turn, produces the New Mexican conquest *as a conquest* for the first time; the writing of the history does not so much record events as discursively activate them in a frame hitherto absent and disallowed. For Villagrá, writing history is the practice through which he can name and advance a conquest that has been silenced; for Oñate, restoring history is the practice through which he advances a conquest without giving it that name. For both men, nothing less than their coherent social identity is at stake: under the distracted watch of the monarch, they operate not so much for the ir future remembrance as for their very presence.

Ramón Gutiérrez has argued that Oñate's strategies are guided by the knowledge that seventy-five years after Cortés's conquest of the Aztecs, the indigenous peoples of New Mexico had heard of that devastating defeat. Therefore, he claims, Oñate devises his own conquest strategies in order to "fix in the Indian mind that their own subjugation in 1598 [is] identical to the Aztec's submission in 1523" (48).[9] It seems more plausible that these strategies operate to fix that idea in the *Spanish* mind, impressing on the Spaniards that their own conquest of New Mexico is of the same nature and order as that of Cortés, and as such, is a "true" conquest in spite of its appellation in the contract.

That Oñate's own retinue should resemble that of Cortés, then, is not coincidental. Like Cortés before him, he flies a standard featuring Our Lady of the Remedies. He invites exactly twelve Franciscan friars to play a similar role and function in the "spiritual conquest" of New Mexico as that of the famed Franciscan "Twelve Apostles" in Mexico.[10] In his contract, Oñate even insists on gaining possession of a New Mexican woman to act as "a second Malinche" (*DJO* 48, 321), acting for him as indispensable advocate and translator as that first Malinche had for Cortés.[11] Restaging key signifying patterns of earlier conquests, this conquest assembles and enacts its own genealogical history, offering a Mannerist rendition of Cortés's conquest, now restaged in another Mexico.

Oñate's official *entrada* into the territory is celebrated by "a sermon, a great ecclesiastical and secular celebration, a great salute and rejoicing, and, in the afternoon, a *comedia*" (*DJO* 315).[12] The *comedia* is of particular interest here, as it literally restages a central performative episode of Cortés's conquest of Tenoctitlán. Villagrá is the only witness to offer an account of the drama: "This drama pictured the advent of the friars to New Mexico. We saw the priests coming to this land, kindly received by the simple natives, who reverently approached on bended knee and asked to be received into the faith, being baptized in great numbers" (129). This "plot" finds its power in its historical referent: it reenacts the arrival of the "Twelve Apostles of the Indies" in Mexico in 1524. Trexler writes that the Twelve Apostles "joined Cortés in a theatrical greeting that became the visual image *par excellence* of the spiritual conquest" (191). Cortés had assembled many native *caciques* to witness his greeting of the twelve friars. He fell to his knees, and in this posture kissed the hand and hem of each Franciscan. Cortés then ordered the *caciques* to do likewise, thus enacting a pedagogical lesson for them that would be recorded and repeated thereafter: they would kneel before the friars as they would before the Christian god, and they would do so every time their communities greeted friars in the future. Trexler reminds us that "paintings of the event were hung in churches across New Spain and the different conquistadors . . . taught their Indians far and wide to welcome the friars as they saw Cortés welcoming the Apostles in the pictures" (192). This paradigmatic gesture was similarly repeated in royal and religious *entradas* into New Spain, and reenacted as the "plot" of countless dramas.

Written for the occasion by one of the captains and performed by soldiers, this New Mexican *comedia* serves to thematize both the historical precedent and future goal of the conquest for the members of the expedition. Restaging the first arrival of Franciscans on American soil, the scene positions their project in the legacy of spiritual conquest. While it sets forth only the evangelizing mission, conforming therefore to the dictates of the Ordinances of Discovery, it does so first by referencing the action of Cortés, the "great" conquistador of New Spain. As this was a very common "plot" in missionary drama of New Spain, we can be quite confident that the role of Cortés/conquistador would have been enacted; either Oñate himself or an actor-soldier acting in his place would have played the role.[13] Through this *comedia*, then, Oñate is able to act both in the name of the monarch and, more importantly, in the image of Cortés.

Following the *comedia,* Oñate delivers the *Requerimiento.* We remember that the Catholic monarchs in 1512 had mandated the reading of the *Requerimiento* upon entry into the land to be conquered, to systematize and articulate royal claims on new territory and its peoples as grounds for just war. By 1598, the *Requerimiento* has been substantially edited. More text is devoted to its evangelical mandate and mission and less to threats of war. Here Oñate cannot quite repeat Cortés. But the many conquests enacted by Cortés's generation have been distilled into this "new-improved" text; the *Requerimiento* signals a continual bureaucratization of warfare, which does not so much replace conquest as displace and defer it.[14] Once these words are spoken, the land and all its peoples thereafter belong to Spain; all future Indian resistance could be, would be, and indeed was interpreted as treasonous—a violation of this *Requerimiento*—and punished accordingly.

When the Spaniards proceed to enter the Pueblos to "enforce" the Act of Possession, it is accompanied by the very conquest-violence that the ordinances theoretically prohibit:

Our provisions were exhausted fifty leagues before we reached the first settle-ments. We were in such extreme need that the governor [sent] men ahead to the first pueblos with eighty pack animals to bring maize. . . . although it was against the wishes of the natives and to their great grief. . . . Because of this and other annoyances, the Indians fear us so much that, on seeing us ap-proach . . . they flee to the mountains, abandoning their homes, and so we take whatever we wish from them. (*DJO* 609–10) [15]

Note that Oñate *himself*, arriving well after his men, does not "conquer"; following the wanton pillage and brutal "annoyances" of his soldiers, he instead "invites" the terrorized Indians to appreciate the Christian mission of the visitors, and asks them to participate in the official Acts of Vassalage and Obedience (a reading of an even more edited version of the *Requeri-miento*). If the Pueblo Indians show no visible signs of resistance through-out this ceremony, the conquistador concludes that they thereby "demon-strate" their "willingness" to be subjects of the king (*DJO* 340).

The key performative gesture that punctuates and seals the "act of vassalage" for the Spanish is, of course, the one originally developed by Cortés: after the speech, the Indians are made to kneel before the friars. For each Pueblo, Oñate instructs the *caciques* that to demonstrate "their desire to offer obedience to God and the King, they should fall on their knees, as a sign that it [is] indeed true and as proof of vassalage and submission, and kiss the hand of the father commissary, in the name of God" (*DJO* 340).[16] Oñate relies on this historically charged gesture to seal his (non)conquest and to enact his own authority. The Spaniards, not the Pueblo Indians, understand the dense historical significance of the role Oñate plays: Oñate acts in the name of the king but in the image of Cortés. The fissure between name and image, a mark of dissonance between the monarch and his conquistador-subject in these late days of Spanish con-quest, is precisely the fissure Oñate's behavior works to suture. By 1598 reenacting Cortés seems the only way Oñate might imagine (or discover) himself a "rightful" conquistador in the terms of the now bankrupt econ-omy of honor through warfare.

Conquering History

If we turn to Villagrá's *Historia* of these events, the first thing we note is that he ignores (or forgets) this provenance of prior conquests. Villagrá's opening pages establish the operative fiction of his task. Neither historian nor poet by profession, the soldier becomes both "more in response to the sense of duty I feel than in confidence of my ability" (35). Villagrá figures his monarch as the cause and the effect of both the conquest and its historical retelling: "Most Christian Philip," he begins, "You are the Phoenix of New Mexico, newly produced and come forth from the burning flames and embers of most holy faith" (41); here the monarch is born anew through the conquest of New Mexico just as New Mexico is born anew through the king's rule. This soldier-poet is, it seems, driven by the mandate of history itself: to borrow an analysis from Louis Marin, the monarch "makes history, but it is history that is made in what he does, and the same time his historian, by writing what he does, writes what must be written" (42).

Michel de Certeau suggests that any historical operation refers to a relation between a social *place* (a milieu, a profession), a "scientific" *practice* (a discipline), and the construction of a *writing* (a literature) (1988, 57). At a minimum, Villagrá's practice entails recording "heroic" events of the recent conquest, and the place is the seat of empire; addressed to and written for the monarch, the writing commemorates "with faithful zeal" the advance of empire effected in his name. His writing takes the form of a heroic epic poem following the Spanish historico-literary tradition of telling conquest history in epic form, dating as far back as *El Cid* and as recently as Alonso de Ercilla's *La Araucana* in 1589, which no doubt served as the model for the *Historia*. *La Historia de la nuevo México [sic]* is thus created not only for the monarch but also to safeguard the heroism of his compatriots, which "if left to . . . the mercy of passing years will be sacrificed on the altars of time" (35).

Yet we already suspect this operation of a deeper fiction. Judging from the many official inquiries and reviews following Oñate's settlement in the Pueblos, one can see that the New Mexican conquest has in no way impressed the king. Official inquiries reveal that the land is of "extreme sterility" and that "it will not render any benefit to the king our lord" (*DJO* 684). The poet records the "heroic deeds" not because they are memorable, but because they have already been forgotten. If the king is reborn in the conquest of New Mexico, it is not through the events of 1598, but through the textual staging of conquest in Villagrá's 1609 *Historia*.

Villagrá's *Historia* thus makes itself in the gap left open by the discursive erasure of "conquest" and its incomplete replacement with "discovery." The writing does not travel with Oñate to discover the "hidden portion of the earth" of New Mexico; it uses that travel to reach and rediscover the hidden place of conquest. Unlike other narratives of American conquest, Villagrá's text generally resists the heterologic impulse to speak about the "other." Instead the text obsessively follows the Spaniards, and in turn provides a remarkable ethnologic record of Spanish military culture. For example,

> They [the soldiers] are all expert in the art of cooking. They wash and bake, in short provide everything for their needs, from the wood they burn to the salt with which they season their food. They are expert in the art of tilling the soil. Every hour of the day you might find them clothed in shining steel as though they were encased in solid bronze. (178)

The kind of ethnographic detail normally reserved for the record and study of "other" cultures is here used in the service of his own. But apparently, Villagrá has no confidence that the monarch recognizes this particular military culture *as* his own; the conquistador has, in a manner of speaking, become "other" to his king.

Like the earlier epics *El Cid* and *La Araucana,* the epic poem, with its linear teleology, allows Villagrá to stage the conquest according to a particular conception of historical reality: "The victors experience history as a coherent, end-directed story told by their own power" (Quint 9). But unlike *La Araucana,* epic history is not the point of departure, but rather, the desired destination. Like Oñate before him, Villagrá relies on a historically charged conquest genre to reinvest his conquest with heroic significance. The *Historia* charts a discursive epic journey where the heroism and high moral character of the conquistadors will be progressively "discovered" by its privileged reader, the monarch. The literary frame of a perilous journey is constant throughout: "Worthy Sir, we have embarked upon our voyage and are now upon the high seas. Land has disappeared from sight, and our safety now depends upon the course we take and the management of our ship. Hearken well to my words that nothing may be lost which otherwise might prove of value from this voyage" (72). King and poet are "brought to safety," of course, by the secure and wise leadership of Oñate and his captains. Each canto is framed by a moral lesson that prompts the king to read each episode "properly." Endless platitudes, maxims, and other moralizing observations riddle the text; Villagrá takes no chance that the king will fail to appreciate the wisdom and virtue of the Spanish soldiers at every moment in the tale. The text becomes a lesson book on military heroism, virtue, and honor. The *Historia,* I suggest, is a countertext to the very Ordinances of Discovery.

But how indeed can a poet-soldier justify lecturing to his king on the matter of morals? Above all other narrative strategies, the fundamental authority of his text appeals not to the classics, nor to the persuasiveness of the epic model of history, but to the provenance of his authorial voice. Here Villagrá capitalizes on another trope of New World writing: the appeal to eyewitness experience. As Pagden writes, "It is the 'I' who has seen what no other being has seen who alone is capable of giving credibility to the text" (89). Having no other claim to authority, Villagrá stakes the authority of his heroic tale first and last on his status as *witness:* "Hearken, O mighty King, for I was witness of all that I here relate!" (42). As Pagden also remarks, New World writings are repeatedly punctuated by what Michel de Certeau has called the modalities of witnessing ("It was obvious," "It was evident," etc.) (Pagden 89; de Certeau 1986, 68). In Villagrá's text, these markings strategically and progressively move the *place* of his writing from the royal court, where the king has authority, beyond the frontier of empire, well beyond the prescriptions of colonial authorities and prescribed behaviors, to a place where only the eyewitness can tell the "true" history of the glory of conquest. It is only here in the new place of this writing, finally, that the conquest of New Mexico is enacted in the terms of conquest that Villagrá so desperately wants remembered. The practice of "recording" this history, then, allows the soldier-historian to "treasure" and "remember" not the past conquest of New Mexico in 1598, but the very meaning and function of conquest in the present.

Villagrá's own concluding remarks already foretell the eventual failure of their efforts. The poet is perhaps ironic, perhaps nostalgic, perhaps bitter, when he appeals, "O ye who seek renown in battle, remember it is well that ye be not too mighty with your tongue; better yet that you wield a sword with prowess! Take heed from this story!" (193). But what is the moral of this story? Does not the writing of this history itself tell us that this soldier has chosen to be mighty with his tongue where he could not be with his sword? Elsewhere the poet speaks conquest's own eulogy: "Through history those men are heroes whose deeds have been given proper recognition by the historian's pen" (35). He already senses that the pen does not render the glory of the sword immutable; in this historical moment, the pen takes up a work that the sword itself cannot perform. Thus while the old prestige economy of conquest may momentarily enter into its present here, it does so at the expense of its own practice: mandated out of existence by the monarch, the performance of Spanish conquest finds its refuge, and later a final resting place, in a practice of writing.

When the epic is reviewed by the royal censors in 1609, it seems at first to succeed on Villagrá's terms. The censor Professor Espinel writes, "The verses are many and though lacking in imagination and poetical worth, are a true and connected history" (Villagrá 269). However, in 1614, Villagrá is charged and found guilty with a crime related to his participation in the conquest of New Mexico. The poet-soldier had apparently taken up writing in New Mexico once before, prior to his *Historia:* "From that place he wrote a letter to the viceroy of Spain, praising the high quality, richness, and fertility of the provinces of New Mexico, when the opposite is true, as it is a sterile and poor land" (*DJO* 1116).[17] Villagrá's writing is found guilty, in other words, of lacking truth and offering far too much imagination. Oñate, in turn, is also tried and found guilty of brutality in New Mexico at the battle of Ácoma. In the end, the law exiles both men from the New Mexico they "conquered," and both die stripped of their desired military honors. Despite Oñate and Villagrá's attempts to invoke performatively in act and word the "honor" of conquest, the final word rests with the royal court of law, whose discourse cannot afford to speak the violence of conquest, even as it benefits from its practice.

NOTES

I am grateful to Ted Ziter, Erin Hurley, Joseph Roach, Peggy Phelan, and Robert Potter for thoughtful commentary on earlier versions of this work.

1. Gaspar de Villagrá, *History of New Mexico, 1610,* trans. Gilberto Espinosa (Los Angeles: Quivira Society, 1933), 38. Despite losses in translation, I will cite the 1933 Quivira Society English translation throughout. The verse structure of the *Historia* is one loss: the translation is in prose. The pindaric ode quoted above was translated in verse.

2. Beatriz Pastor Bodmer doesn't even mention Villagrá's *Historia* in her study of Spanish accounts of exploration and conquest in the New World. She assumes the genre of conquest writing is effectively over after publication of *La Araucana,* in 1589.

3. See Greenblatt 1991, Seed, Todorov 146–49 for more extended analyses of the *Requerimiento* and acts of taking possession.

4. Debray 27. Debray discusses the "primary determinants" of time and space in the founding of national societies, arguing that any community requires (1) a delimitation in time, or the assignation of origins (the Temple), and (2) delimitation within an enclosed space (the Ark). It seems to me that unlike the "nation," empire uses the assignation of origins to renegotiate and expand its delimitation in space, or in his terms, that the "Temple" always travels on the "Ark."

5. See Sánchez-Albornoz.

6. See "Contract of Don Juan de Oñate for the Discovery and Conquest of New Mexico," in Hammond (1953, 42–57). Hammond's collection and translation of the official documents, writings, and letters associated with Don Juan de Oñate will hereafter be referenced in this text as *DJO*.

7. See "Instructions to Don Juan de Oñate, October 21, 1595," *DJO* 65–68.

8. Cortés himself owed many of his strategies to the reconquest of Muslim Spain, which was coming to an end during his childhood. See H. B. Johnson, 3–31. Nevertheless, Cortés's devastation of Tenoctitlán emerges in both contemporary accounts and in our historical memory as the paradigmatic tale of Spanish conquest, in part, no doubt, *because* he was so widely imitated.

9. See Gutiérrez for a fascinating discussion of the parallels between Oñate's conquest and that of Cortés; it initially motivated this reading. Also see Hammond (1979, 25).

10. Oñate begins with twelve friars. Only ten appear to have accompanied him as far as New Mexico.

11. According to Oñate's letters, she had been abducted from Pant-ham-ba Pueblo during Castaño de Sosa's unauthorized travel into New Mexico in 1590. From available evidence, it seems that her role was none so illustrious as her model: well into the expedition, Oñate complained that "she does not know the language or any other in New Mexico, nor is she learning them" (*DJO* 321).

12. From the official "Itinerary of the Expedition."

13. Gutiérrez claims that Oñate definitely played the role of Cortés and that Indians actually participated in this drama (49). While this is probable, I have found no evidence to confirm it.

14. This new *Requerimiento* no longer authorized the enslavement of Indians. But this conduct is not therefore ended, only re-moved: the "improved" Ordinances of Discovery in 1573, for example, recommend that if the Indians are not cooperative, the preachers "should ask for their children under the pretext of teaching them and keep them as hostages" (in Hanke 1973, 114).

15. From the letter of Captain Velasco to the viceroy, March 22, 1601.

16. See *DJO* 337–62 for the official records of the Acts of Obedience and Vassalage by the Indians in each of the Pueblos. Each varies slightly, but all end with this gesture of submission.

17. From the "Conviction of Oñate and his Captains, 1614."

WORKS CITED

Debray, Régis. "Marxism and the National Question." *New Left Review*, no. 105 (Sept.–Oct. 1977): 25–41.

de Certeau, Michel. *Heterologies: Discourse on the Other.* Trans. Brian Massumi. Minneapolis: University of Minnesota Press, 1986.

———. *The Writing of History.* Trans. Tom Conley. New York: Columbia University Press, 1988.

Derrida, Jacques. "Force of Law: The 'Mystical Foundation of Authority.' " *Cardozo Law Review* 11, nos. 5–6 (July/August 1990): 919–1046.

Greenblatt, Stephen. *Marvelous Encounters: The Wonder of the New World.* Chicago: University of Chicago Press, 1991.

———, ed. *New World Encounters.* Los Angeles: University of California Press, 1993.

Gutiérrez, Ramón A. *When Jesus Came, the Corn Mothers Went Away: Marriage, Sexuality and Power in New Mexico, 1500–1846.* Stanford: Stanford University Press, 1991.

Hammond, George P. *Don Juan de Oñate and the Founding of New Mexico.* Santa Fe: El Palacio Press, 1927.

———. *Don Juan de Oñate, Colonizer of New Mexico.* Vols. 1 and 2. Santa Fe: University of New Mexico Press, 1953.

———. "The Search for the Fabulous in the Settlement of the Southwest." In *New Spain's Far Northern Frontier: Essays on Spain in the American West, 1540–1821,* ed. David J. Weber. Albuquerque: University of New Mexico Press, 1979.

Hanke, Lewis, ed. *History of Latin American Civilization: Sources and Interpretations.* Vol. 1, *The Colonial Experience.* Boston: Little, Brown, 1993.

———. *Latin America: A Historical Reader.* Boston: Little, Brown, 1973.

———. "The 'Requerimiento' and Its Interpreters." *Revista de Historia de America* 1 (March 1938): 25–34.

Johnson, H. B., ed. *From Reconquest to Empire: The Iberian Background to Latin American History.* New York: Knopf, 1970.

Junquera, Mercedes. Introduction to *Historia de Nuevo México,* ed. Mercedes Junquera. Madrid: Historia 16, 1989.

Marin, Louis. *Portrait of the King.* Trans. Martha M. Houle. Minneapolis: University of Minnesota Press, 1988.

Pagden, Anthony. "*Ius et Factum:* Text and Experience in the Writings of Bartolomé de Las Casas." In *New World Encounters,* ed. Stephen Greenblatt, 85–100. Los Angeles: University of California Press, 1993.

Parry, John H., and Robert G. Keith, eds. *New Iberian World.* Vol. 1, *The Conquerors and the Conquered.* New York: Times Books, 1984.

Pastor Bodmer, Beatriz. *The Armature of Conquest: Spanish Accounts of the Discovery of America, 1492–1589.* Trans. Lydia Longstreth Hunt. Stanford: Stanford University Press, 1992.

Quint, David. *Epic and Empire: Poetics and Generic Form from Virgil to Milton.* Princeton: Princeton University Press, 1993.

Rama, Angel. *The Lettered City*. Ed. and trans. John Charles Chasteen. Durham: Duke University Press, 1996.

Sánchez-Albornoz, Claudio. "The Continuing Tradition of Reconquest." In *From Reconquest to Empire: The Iberian Background to Latin American History*, ed. H. B. Johnson, 41–54. New York: Knopf, 1970.

Schechner, Richard. *Between Theater and Anthropology*. Philadelphia: University of Pennsylvania Press, 1985.

Seed, Patricia. "Taking Possession and Reading Texts: Establishing the Authority of Overseas Empire." In *Early Images of the Americas: Transfer and Invention*, ed. Jerry M. Williams and Robert E. Lewis, 111–47. Tucson: University of Arizona Press, 1993.

Taussig, Michael. "History as Sorcery." In *Shamanism, Colonialism, and the Wild Man: A Study in Terror and Healing*, 366–92. Chicago: University of Chicago Press, 1987.

Todorov, Tzvetan. *The Conquest of America: The Question of the Other*. Trans. Richard Howard. New York: Harper and Row, 1984.

Trexler, Richard C. "We Think, They Act: Clerical Readings of Missionary Theatre in 16th Century New Spain." In *Understanding Popular Culture: Europe from the Middle Ages to the Nineteenth Century*, ed. Steven Kaplan, 189–228. New York: Mouton, 1984.

Villagrá, Gaspar de. *Historia de la Nueva México*. Mexico City: Imprenta del Museo Nacional, 1900.

———. *Historia de Nuevo México*. Ed. Mercedes Junquera. Madrid: Historia 16, 1989.

———. *History of New Mexico, 1610*. Trans. Gilberto Espinosa. Los Angeles: Quivira Society, 1933.

PERFORMATIVE WRITING

FIVE

Performing Writing

Della Pollock

We are all in a position of ravishment—call it
lack, if you must; our only hope for survival—
call it love—being, against all odds and through
all our divisions, to keep on writing.
——Susan Suleiman, *Subversive Intent*

Contemporary discourses of history, culture, and identity seem still to be spinning in "textuality," feeling the loss of reference as a loss of bearings, feeling suddenly, uneasily lifted from ready cartologies of meaning into an Oz-like world not of meaninglessness exactly but of duplicity, doubleness, and simulation. From the eye of this storm, what is/was is always on the verge of becoming something else. Words don't stick. They are "Janus-faced," "fickle," indifferent to discourses of truth and meaning.[1] In language as difference, in language riddled with difference, criticism becomes an exercise in double plays: in pastiche, parody, punning.

But with each turn and return of language, "textuality" seems increasingly to fold in on itself, to turn back on the very act of writing, making it difficult if not impossible to make sense, to make claims, to make meaning, making writing its own object/subject, which duly un/writes itself in every figure and turn, sometimes in cynical pleasure, sometimes in abject horror, leading Julia Kristeva, for instance, to ask, what is there but writing? what is there to do but write?[2]

Kristeva's questions anticipate and exhaust the so-called linguistic turn. In so doing, they also echo earlier questions, the question Theodor Adorno posed in the early sixties, for instance, the question asked by a character in Sartre's play *Morts sans sepulture,* " 'Is there any meaning in life when men exist who beat people until the bones break in their bodies?' " Adorno writes on the edge of referentiality, at once referring the question itself to the atrocities of the Second World War and anticipating, on those grounds, the collapse of both referential and normative meaning systems. With this question, Adorno ushered in a new or "post-" modernism in which the literature of commitment (exemplified for Adorno in the plays of Bertolt Brecht) was particularly suspect. Drenched as it was, Adorno argued, in the discourses of capital, political literature of various kinds focuses in turn on "the question whether any art now has the right to exist; whether intellectual regression is not inherent in the concept of committed literature because of the regression of society."[3] Alternatively, Adorno claimed a narrow and fading aesthetic margin, a space from which, for instance, Beckett's characters might at least underline speech with silence.

In the place of Adorno's dark margin, the last resort of high modernism, is now the debris of walls previously keeping work from play, art from politics, high from low culture, speech from writing, aesthetic from commodity discourses. Out of the resulting inky spillage, out of what we have come to call "textuality" or the sense that all discourse is encompassed within a multilayered, reflexive/reproductive "text," rise questions trembling with imperatives for performance: What words remain to the body made at once abject by history and abstract by textuality? How then can we speak? What is or might be the purview of the writing/performing subject? How might writing break up the regressive reiterations of "textuality"? How might *performative* writing not only speak the surrounding darkness but hail loss and lost pleasure in the place of rank commodification?

Writing between Brecht on the one hand and Beckett on the other, Adorno centers the question of writing in performance, in brutally chastened hopes for embodied, creative counterspeech. I recall Adorno/Brecht here in order, among other things, to recall performative writing to performance, to the arena of corporeal history in which Adorno himself wrote. Sue-Ellen Case has argued that "the critical discourses of speech-act theory and deconstruction ultimately bring the notion of performativity back to their own mode of production: print."[4] Rethinking writing from the twin loci of Adorno and Kristeva challenges an easy identification of performativity with print and the subsequent absorption of performance into textuality as "performativity." At the same time, it refuses an equally easy and equally false distinction between performance and text, performance and performativity/textuality, or, for that matter, performativity and print-textuality.

Rather, at the brink of meaning, poised between abjection and regression, writing as *doing* displaces writing as meaning; writing becomes meaningful in the material, dis/continuous act of writing. Effacing itself twice over—once as meaning and reference, twice as deferral and erasure—writing becomes itself, becomes its own means and ends, recovering to itself the force of action. After-texts, after turning itself inside out, writing turns again only to discover the pleasure and power of turning, of making not sense or meaning per se but making *writing* perform: Challenging the boundaries of reflexive textualities; relieving writing of its obligations under the name of "textuality"; shaping, shifting, testing language. Practicing language. Performing writing. Writing performatively.

I want to explore some of the ways what we have come to call "performative writing" answers discourses of textuality not by recovering reference to a given or "old" world but by writing into a new one. For me, performative writing is not a genre or fixed form (as a textual model might suggest) but a way of describing what some good writing *does*. All good writing isn't and needn't be performative. Nor would all the writers cited here consider their work performative. Performativity describes a fundamentally material practice. Like performance, however, it is also an analytic, a way of framing and underscoring aspects of writing/life. Holding "performative writing" to set shapes and meanings would be (1) to undermine its analytic flexibility, and (2) to betray the possibilities of performativity with the limitations of referentiality.

Unfortunately, performative writing has come to carry its own *faux* referents: stylish, trendy, clever, avant-garde, projecting in turn a kind of new formalism. Performative writing is, for me, precisely not a matter of formal style (especially in the degraded sense of glinting, surface play).[5] It is a discursive practice that—misprisioned—may have disastrous consequences, that may be *bad*—or, for that matter, *good*. The discourses of textuality have removed the veil of innocence from language, drawing us away from questions of what words do or don't mean into the complex problem of *how to mean* in words and yet tend to limit the answer to such questions to the reiteration of social, historical, textual formations. The question thus turns back on itself, deflecting the possibilities for normative critique of the way we write or *do* writing and of what writing *does* that it nonetheless implies.

Performative writing is an important, dangerous, and difficult intervention into routine representations of social/performative life. It has a long and varied history in anthropology, feminist critique, and writing about performance, taking much of its impetus from the cross-disciplinary "break" into poststructuralism.[6] But my aim here is neither to assess the history of performative writing nor to represent performative writing in all its forms and implications, but rather to identify the need to make writing speak *as* writing. To discern possible intersections of speech and writing. To resolve the alienation of meaning and reference within postmodern textualities not by reinscribing presence per se but by making writing exceed its determinations within structures of absence/presence in order to perform a social function. Performative writing spins, to some extent, on the axis of impossible and/or regressive reference and yet out into new modes of subjectivity and even referentiality. Finally, then, I want to read performative claims on textuality for their immanent utopics, for their susceptibility to the democracies of imperfect, inexpert repetition, revision, replay, and remand.

Performance Writing/Writing Performance: One Way In

Several years ago I attended a workshop/conference on writing history. The conference discussions circulated around the rise of "experimental" history writing, the new "narrative history," and what was variously called self-revelation, self-disclosure, and self-reflection in the composition of history.[7] One argument in particular has continued to haunt me. A distinguished feminist historian argued that more "conventional" forms of writing history—the dull but steadfast forms of the academic article and the monograph—were more "democratic" than the new (or renewed) forms of narrative history because they could be taught.[8] As forms of intellectual and cultural capital, they could be relatively easily and equally distributed across social class differentials. And having acquired such conventions and/or plain techniques, anyone could contribute to the formation of social knowledge.

Like my colleague, I was and remain suspicious of a preening avant-gardism in new (history-)writing. I am wary of the extent to which a new/old formalism (even in the form of Brechtian alienation techniques) might divert attention from the subject(s) of history to their fine containers. But my primary response at the time was one of stifled horror. I recall flushing and stiffening at what seemed to me democracy become mediocracy, at the looming sense of democracy as a science of the lowest common denominator, as competency trumping specialty, as random access to generic brands. I recoiled from the gray, undifferentiated space of this democracy. Here, it seemed to me, was the democracy of the Food Lion, Kmart, and superstores everywhere: flatline consumption disguised as purchasing power; democracy turned over to the bland multiplicity of bodies pushing identical carts up and down aisles promising equally bland satisfaction.

In his argument against the "politics of clarity," Henry Giroux decries what he calls the "populist elitism" implicit in such a view. Referring to the often smug tendency to privilege clarity in popular discourses of writing and education (how could anyone with any common sense not be for clarity?), Giroux argues, "clarity becomes a code word for an approach to writing that is profoundly Eurocentric in both context and content"—writing that conforms to presuppositions about standard language use and neglects the historical, political, and cultural specificity of diverse audiences or publics.[9] Claims for such writing assume a correspondence theory of language that effaces questions of voice, style, and difference and "flattens" the relationship between language and audience, refusing not only the endless mediations and negotiations that compose their relationship and the meanings that flow from it, but the recognition of subaltern claims on language use that a more genuinely plural reading/writing democracy would entail. The homogenization of language in the name of clarity tends to cleanse knowledge of "complex discourses or oppositional insights." Giroux argues,

> there is a tendency to perceive members of diverse public cultures as objects rather than subjects, as socially constructed pawns rather than as complex and contradictory human agents who mediate, read, and write the world differently. The politics of such a position often either leads one into the exclusionary territories of Eurocentrism, elitism and colonialism, or into the political dead end of cynicism and despair.[10]

My historian colleague seemed to be arguing, in Giroux's words, for "deepening the possible relations between the discourse of education and the imperatives of a radical pluralized democracy" by availing a wide range of producers of the means of production.[11] Her argument ultimately aimed to return the surplus value of writing to students through access to writing/literature as a set of techniques or tools.[12] Yet her arguments for accessibility and clarity (per Giroux) rest precariously on the romantic assumption that more "artistic" efforts are the privilege of specially gifted sensibilities—of geniuses or real "talents" whose skills are anointed or otherwise bemused. For better or for worse, the argument seems to go, this is another kind of writing, written by "other" kinds of people whose peculiarly uncommon capabilities make them, in turn, peculiarly incapable of performing the role of the common citizen within a democratic culture. Even in its claims for the writer, the argument divides the writer and the artist along lines distinguishing technique and talent, reprivileging technique while reifying its difference from talent.

While enticing, the argument seems to me to fail on two counts: (1) it reduces the agonistic pleasures and possibilities—indeed, the performativities—of democratic exchange (conflict, compromise, dialogue, debate) to equal access, and (2) it reiterates, even in its disavowal, the elitism of nineteenth-century, Anglo-romantic conceptions of the poet/writer, reproducing distrust for artistic, imaginative, and opaque writing, as opposed to allegedly serviceable and clear uses of language, identifying democracy with the latter and refusing or deferring writing that, in effect, as Trinh Minh-ha observes, "does not translate a reality outside itself but, more precisely, allows the emergence of a new reality": writing as the constitutive form of unrealized democracies.[13]

Moving Out

As I consider the problematic appeal of what has come to be called "performative writing," I want not so much to dispel the mystery my historian friend ascribed to the poet/writer as to dissolve the dichotomies on which her argument is built, especially those dividing the historian and the artist, and what are conventionally considered their respectively common and uncommon discourses.

At the same time, I can't entirely abandon the logics of function and effect. Reading Michael Taussig's claims for "writing effectively against terror," for instance, I have to reserve for "good" writing the expectation that it will serve a social function.[14] Its value depends on its effectiveness, on how well it performs within a system animated not only by democratic conflict but by conflict over the nature and aims of democracy. That conflict in turn performs writing as an effect, as a sedimentation in the form of a specific social relation. What I want to call performative writing is thus both a means and an effect of conflict. It is particularly (paradoxically) "effective." It forms itself in the act of speaking/writing. It reflects in its own forms, in its own fulfillment of form, in what amounts to its performance of itself, a particular, historical relation (agonistic, dialogic, erotic) between author-subjects, reading subjects, and subjects written/

read. Performative writing is thus no more and no less formally intelligible than a road sign or a landmark: its styles may be numbered, taught, and reproduced, but its meanings are contextual. It takes its value from the context-map in which it is located and which it simultaneously marks, determines, transforms.

I am left then with what seem contradictory desires: on the one hand, to make a taxonomic dis/play of performative writing in order, among other things, to make performative writing generally available for use; and, on the other hand, to insist on the difficulty of performative writing/ writing performatively. I want to suggest that performative writing is a technique, even a technology, that must and can be commonly deployed, and yet this appropriation of *techne* can be no more merely stylistic or mechanical than it should be instrumental—conclusions, I'm afraid, to which a list/manifesto of performative elements, options, directions may lead. Against both boutique and "how-to" (social-realist) models of performative writing, I want to suggest a third possibility: performative writing as a dynamic response to the extent to which writing and performance have failed each other by withdrawing—whether defensively or by pejorative attribution—into identification with either arcane or apparently self-evident means of knowledge production.

The list that follows assumes a negative case: a kind of writing antithetical to the vitality of performed culture, writing that threatens to dehydrate performance or that subordinates performative temporalities to the spatial and alien(ating) conventions of the (scholarly) "text." As insidious/disappointing as such writing (or the prospect of such writing) may be, it is not in the nature of writing per se to wring the life out of performance—or to remarginalize it within cultures of scholarship. To write performance is not in and of itself to betray it. Rather, it seems to me, the betrayal consists in not writing it, in conceding to the deployment of language against performance and so to the absence/death of performance in processes of knowledge formation. The answer to the claims of textuality on performativity is thus not to write less but to write more: to write in excess of norms of scholarly representation, to write beyond textuality into what might be called social mortalities, to make writing/textuality speak to, of, and through pleasure, possibility, disappearance, and even pain.[15] In other words, to make writing perform.

I offer the following list then with some irony. It is descriptive/prescriptive, practical/theoretical. As itself an excursion into performative writing, it is intended to map directions/directives for performative writing without foreclosing on the possibility that performance may—at any moment—

unhinge or override its claims (assuming that performance, as practice, is never fully in control of its effects). My use of the list form is intentionally hyperbolic: it is meant to yield entry into the discourses of performative writing and simultaneously to indicate its own insufficiencies and instabilities. Directed at once at the loose currency of "performative writing" and rising anxiety about how to define it, how to name *it* once and for all, this list is meant to un/name performative writing, to refuse its recuperation to matters of style and form by positioning definitional claims within a broadly normative framework.

I don't think that performative writing is a matter of "anything goes" or that anyone can do it anymore than "anyone" can write "good" history or that "good" history is not fundamentally a prescriptive category with elaborate implications for evaluation. What follows is then only a suggestive framework for what neither the specially talented nor the evaluatively unreflexive might do in the name of expanding the realm of scholarly representation.

Six Excursions into Performative Writing

1. Performative writing is *evocative*. It operates metaphorically to render absence present—to bring the reader into contact with "other-worlds," to those aspects and dimensions of our world that are other to the text as such by re-marking them. Performative writing evokes worlds that are other-wise intangible, unlocatable: worlds of memory, pleasure, sensation, imagination, affect, and in-sight. Whereas a mimetic/realist perspective tends to reify absent referents in language, thus sustaining an illusion of full presence, a performative perspective tends to favor the generative and ludic capacities of language and language encounters—the interplay of reader and writer in the joint production of meaning. It does not describe, in a narrowly reportorial sense, an objectively verifiable event or process but uses language like paint to create what is self-evidently a *version* of what was, what is, and/or what might be.

What I want to call performative writing (often felt only in a flash or, per Turner, a "flicker")[16] collapses distinctions by which creative and critical writing are typically isolated.[17] It is neither entirely self-constitutive (in the manner of an avowed fiction) nor referential (in the sense of pointing to or revealing a world outside language). It does not entail "going over" into creative writing or excorporating the resources of the creative writer for criticism per se, but hybridizing the very terms by which such claims might be made, suggesting an in-between, "liminoid" field of possibility, a field of hybrid, mixed forms that exceed categorical distinctions in their effort to *make possible,* to make absence present and yet to recover presence from structural, realist mimesis for poesis.

Performative, evocative writing confounds normative distinctions between critical and creative (hard and soft, true and false, masculine and feminine), allying itself with logics of possibility rather than of validity or causality, the scientific principles underlying positivist distinctions between "true" and "false." It shifts the operative social paradigm from the scientific "what if" (what *then?*) to its performative counterpart, "as if" (what *now?*),[18] drawing the reader into a projected im/mediacy that never (mimetically) forgets its own genealogy in performance.

In the poesis of *making possible,* performative writing simultaneously slips the choke hold of conventional (scientific, rational) scholarly discourses and their enabling structures. It moves *with,* operates alongside, sometimes through, rather than above or beyond, the fluid, contingent, unpredictable, discontinuous rush of (performed) experience—and *against* the assumption that (scholarly) writing must or should do otherwise. It requires that the writer drop down to a place where words and the world intersect in active interpretation, where each pushes, cajoles, entrances the other into alternative formations, where words press into and are deeply impressed by "the sensuousness of their referents."[19]

The writer and the world's bodies intertwine in evocative writing, in intimate coperformance of language and experience. Thus, for instance, when Carol Mavor writes with/about the photographs of the maid-of-all-work Hannah Cullwick, collected by the late Victorian poet Arthur Munby, the reader reads with her, seeing what she sees and feeling the subtle press of Cullwick's image on her imagination. The ensuing scene goes beyond both identification and "readerly" productions of Barthes' endlessly open text to engage the reader in a material encounter with the photographs. Mavor locates herself and the reader in the act of taking up the pictures, of removing them from the collector's box stored in the Wren Library at Trinity College, Cambridge. Performing viewing, Mavor fingers an image of Cullwick's rough, working hands, laid open and blackened with soot before her, before our wondering eyes. Their hands, always already mediated by the protocols of looking and being-looked-at, touch. They touch us. In Mavor's hand/eye, the image takes on its own agency. It performs her and through her, us, now caught in a kind of *ménage à trois* of looking/feeling/wanting. Mavor draws us in as the images, in her description, "pop out of their small drawer" and catch her red-handed, in the scene of her own (now our own) desire: "Hannah's big, disconnected hands mirror my own as I fondle the tiny pictures of hard-working woman [*sic*] that have been fetishistically frozen in a lovely miniature museum: a team effort by inspector Munby and the librarians of the Wren library."[20] The image turns back on Mavor, suggesting her own fetishistic enchantment.

And yet in gentle conspiracy with Hannah against their mirror-image — the "team effort" by "inspector Munby" and his curators to keep Hannah closed, her show shut down — Mavor tells the picture from Hannah's point of view: "Hannah took pleasure in blackening her [hands] with grime. And, because simple grime was never enough, Hannah used patches of black lead (that she would spit on) to literally draw on her skin." Mavor evokes in the very shape and feel of her sentences the twin pleasure she and Hannah take in Hannah's dark hands. As if in homage to the maid's desire to write her-self, literally to draw on her skin, inscribing herself as she did with black lead, Mavor draws her reader into the (perverse) pleasures with which she now inscribes the page:

> the portrait of Hannah invites overall fingering. Feel her calluses. Feel the silky brocade fabric with its raised floral design. Feel the leather wrist strap. Imagine what it feels like to wear one. Feel the brush in her hand, in yours. Feel her muscular arms. As Hannah once said about her own hands (to Munby), "They are quite *hard* again — feel."[21]

Fingering, feeling, making us feel: the page is the material stage of Mavor's evocation. She reads/writes in body-time, moving the reader into (e)motion, into what can only be called critical ecstasy (*ex-stasis*) through the performance of her own subjectivity within the scene of reading-writing an image performing. Her performance echoes Hannah's in front of the camera, doubling the urgency with which Hannah displayed her hands in interaction with her reader reading, realizing Hannah's performance now in excess of the frames and boxes that contained it. Mavor brings the act of seeing images taken in the late nineteenth century into the full body of the reader's experience. She does not re-present the photographs as much as she rehearses their claim on the reader/viewer's body-imagination, making it possible for us to know Hannah not *as* different but *in* all of her demanding, resplendent difference.

2. Performative writing is *metonymic*. It is a self-consciously partial or incomplete rendering that takes its pulse from the *difference* rather than the *identity* between the linguistic symbol and the thing it is meant to

represent. It dramatizes the limits of language, sometimes as an endgame, sometimes as the pleasures of playing (*jouissance*) in an endlessly open field of representation. It recognizes the extent to which writing displaces, even effaces "others" and "other-worlds" with its partial, opaque representations of them, not only not revealing truths, meanings, events, "objects," but often obscuring them in the very act of writing, securing their absence with the substitutional presence of words, effectively making absent what mimetic/metaphoric uses of language attempt to make present.

In the ironic turns of its own self-consciousness, metonymic writing thus tends also to displace itself, to unwrite itself at the very moment of composition, opening language to what it is not and can never be. Writing performed *in extremis* becomes unwriting. It un/does itself. Even this phrase—"un/does itself"—is a minor metonymy. It marks the materiality of the sign with the use of a practically unspeakable, non- or counter-presential element of punctuation, an element intelligible only by reference to visual grammatical codes by which a slash or "/" is distinguishable from a "!" or ";", that in its particular use here to divide and double a word—to make the word mean at least two things at once and so to refuse identification with a unitary system of meaning—locates language itself within the medium of print-play. It thus *does* or achieves itself by visually materializing its fixities within print and yet *undoes* that fixity by literally slashing open the word to competition between what Bakhtin considered the "centrifugal" and "centripetal" impulses in languages, the twin strategies of dispersal and containment operative in any word, at any given moment, here dramatized in a "slash."[22]

Exemplified in Derrida's infamous erasure [X], and popularized in Roland Barthes's rampant parentheticals, blank ellipses, and almost sculptural formations of grammar and alphabets (epitomized in the title of his 1975 book, *S/Z*), the metonymics of writing exceed wordplay to encompass Judith Hamera's breathless parataxis and the density with which Bruce Henderson layers camp on camp, as well as the spectral delicacy with which Jane Blocker rehearses the power of representation to rub out the very object it covets.[23] Reflecting on her efforts to write the work of the Cuban American performance artist Ana Mendieta, Blocker notes that she is driven by a sense of loss, by a sense of "just-having-missed" Mendieta before she was killed in 1985:

I read her biographies and histories (what few there are) over and over to convince myself that she is not gone, to repeat the familiar—the story of her life, the story of her exile, the story of her art. I look at the slides, photographs, and films she left behind as though they might point to her presence, but they always only remind me that she has gone.[24]

Metonymic writing is often, as it is here, filled with longing for a lost subject/object, for a subject/object that has disappeared into history or time, and for what, in the face of that disappearance, may seem both the inadequacy and impossibility of evocation. Mendieta's earthworks (grave sites that flame and dwindle into ash, shoreline images that are no sooner inscribed in sand than they are swept away by wave after wave) are devoted to disappearance. They perform the beauty and fragility of life as dying, as gaining its flickering beauty in the process of (always already) disappearing. Centered in that place where life and performance intersect as dying, as disappearance, they moreover tremble with the beauty of life as performance.

Life, death, performance, and disappearance mix and fuse in Mendieta's work, rising to her own mysterious death in 1985. Together, they dare Blocker to go beyond obsession and fetishization, beyond desire to write the "lost" object, to find/fix it in print and so ultimately to deny the quaking essence of Mendieta's work/life, into loss, into transformation and performance. Taking up Peggy Phelan's charge to write "into" disappearance, Blocker characterizes her project as an attempt to move "from a *representation* of loss—history—to an *enactment* of loss—an admission that the story of present absence cannot be sustained."[25] In so doing, she opens her text to performance, to writing as a figure of loss, as a process of *losing* and so *realizing* the performed life.

> The "failure" of history is not meant to suggest that the very discipline in which I am engaged somehow falls short, that it lacks efficacy. Rather, by "failure" I refer to that process whereby history self-destructs, or should I say "self-deconstructs"? I am not yet willing to relinquish the telling of stories, to suggest that as "representations" they are inherently flawed and therefore wrong. What I would like to do is to celebrate their failure; to see that they are finite, that at a certain point, by virtue of repetition, redundancy, or familiarity, they begin to break down. It is this disabling that produces or at least allows for the performative—that effect whereby history is returned to the present, whereby the reader or listener is brought into being by the tale.[26]

For Blocker, history/writing exhausts itself in the pleasures of performance, in its failure to save history from itself, from its return to the present in the being/becoming of the reader reading. As de Certeau has argued, whatever good history writing wins, it does not keep.[27] It gains by losing, by giving itself away—in the double sense of revealing its own materiality and letting go of the object/referent conventionally held tight within a presumably transparent correspondence between the print/symbol and its referent. As Blocker suggests, writing is a metonymy of history that achieves performativity in the production of a reader reading or a surplus of meanings, an ambi/multi-valence of possible, future histories. Blocker suggests an alternative "presence"—one less tied to the nostalgic regimes of symbol-meaning than to the rigors of living in exile, on the edge of death.

In the metonymic display of its own materiality, writing underscores the difference between print-based phenomena and the corporeal, affective, processual temporalities in which they operate, thus actually featuring what they aren't. Metonymic writing invokes the presence of what it isn't, ironically, by elaborating what it is—by either camping on its own forms or running them to the limit or hyperbolizing the symbol-signifier as the figment of print and punctuation. I am reminded of my fourth-grade teacher, Miss Carlson, an image of frothing white hair and skeletal command, who seemed literally to *undertake* the roll. She stood at the front of the room, before the gridlock of our fixed, evenly spaced desks, calling out each name backwards, as it was written on her roll sheet. "Smith, Joe!" she would call out; "Pollock, Della!" She performed *print,* enacting our disciplinary subjection to its forms and expectations, but simultaneously inviting—despite herself—transgression. When the confirmation of presence was not quickly forthcoming, when "Smith, Joe" didn't immediately answer, "Here!" we all turned away from Miss Carlson to *see* who *wasn't there.* We turned toward absence, thrilling to the prospect of Joe's lateness, his possible punishment or truancy: where was he? what exotic, other thing was he doing elsewhere? Turning away from the stiff teacher at the front of the room, we crossed through the law of print-presence into the absent-Imaginary. What had Miss Carlson, despite herself, authorized but this turning away? this giggling, momentary trespass of absence on school territory? Joe (or, for that matter, me, here) was more present in his absence, in being present in name only than he ever was on other days when, careful, polite, looking straight ahead, he guaranteed the connection between word and referent with his bodily presence, with the appropriation of his body to smug confirmation of print's ability to name its object, "Here!"

Marking an absence, metonymic writing also marks itself an active, material signifying process that is neither a prison house nor a fun house, not a place even, but a boundary space, inviting laughter and transformation.[28] It is a space of absence made present in desire and imagination, through which readers may pass like shadows or fiends (or like the kids in my fourth-grade class): tentative, wild, demanding, almost always and never really free.

3. Performative writing is *subjective.* By which I don't mean subject-centered or circling back on the writer/subject in such a way as to enclose the "self" within either narrative or mirror-reflections, or ideologies of humanist individuality or selfhood. This is the aim of many conventional autobiographies whose express purpose is to write a coherent self across time.[29]

Thinking about writing as a material practice, I want to stipulate a more specific sense of the performative self or subjectivity as the performed relation between or among subjects, the dynamic engagement of a contingent and contiguous (rather than continuous) relation between the writer and his/her subject(s), subject-selves, and/or reader(s). Writing that embodies this kind of subjectivity tends to *subject* the reader to the writer's reflexivity, drawing their respective subject-selves reciprocally and simultaneously into critical "intimacy."[30] This process is performative precisely to the extent to which it defines the subject-self in/as the effect of a contingent, corporeal, shifting, situated relation—and so itself as shifting, contingent, contextual—rather than, say, as the end-object of a narrowly autobiographical account or the foundational identity to which "experience narratives" often refer.[31]

I think of this relation as having a particularly erotic dimension, especially as suggested by Susan Suleiman's rereading of Marguerite Duras's novel *The Ravishing of Lol V. Stein,* through Lacan:

> Reading Lacan with Duras, we see emerging the possibility of a psychoanalytic discourse that would not be a discourse of mastery but a discourse of mutual entanglement. . . . Who speaks, or writes, the ravishment of Lol V. Stein? Feminine discourse, which is not always where one expects to find it, reminds us that when it comes back to being human, we are all in a position of ravishment—call it lack, if you must; our only hope for survival—call it love—being, against all odds and through all our divisions, to keep on writing.[32]

Entanglement, ravishment, love, writing: what I want to call performative writing does not project a self, even a radically destabilized one, as much as a relation of being and knowing that cuts back and forth across multiple "divisions" among selves, contexts, affiliations such that, as Elspeth Probyn notes, "the self is not simply put forward, but . . . is reworked in its enunciation."[33]

Reworking the self in its enunciation (as itself the enunciative context of self-making) requires two preliminary moves: first, shifting from *positioning* the self (and so potentially either spatializing and reifying identities or opening identity to Judith Butler's absurd "etc.")[34] to articulating the motive, shaping relations among selves in an ongoing process of (self-) production; and second, shifting from documenting "me" to reconstituting an operative, possible "we."[35] The self that emerges from these shifting perspectives is, then, a possibility rather than a fact, a figure of relation emerging from between lines of difference, moving inexorably "from her experience to mine, and mine to hers," reconstituting each in turn.[36] The performative self is not merely multiple; the multiple self is not in and of itself performative. As Probyn argues, the performative self "is not simply put forward"; it *moves* forward (into survival? democracy?) and between selves/structures, projecting in turn alternative figures of social relation.

In "Stabat Mater," Julia Kristeva emblematizes lines institutionally and materially dividing mother and father tongues, semiotic and symbolic discourses, suggesting typographically their difference and simultaneity:

Christianity is doubtless the most refined symbolic construct in which femininity, to the extent that it transpires through it—and it does so incessantly—is focused on *Maternality*. Let us call "maternal" the

FLASH—instant of time or of dream without time; inordinately swollen atoms of a bond, a vision, a shiver, a yet formless, unnameable embryo. Epiphanies. Photos of what is not yet visible and that language necessarily skims over from afar, allusively. Words that are always too distant, too abstract for this underground swarming of seconds, folding in unimaginable spaces. Writing them down is an ordeal of discourse, like love. What is loving, for a woman, the same thing as writing. Laugh. Impossible. Flash on the unnameable, weavings of abstractions to be torn . . .

ambivalent principle that is bound to the species, on the one hand, and on the other stems from an identity catastrophe that causes the Name to topple over into the unnameable that no one imagines as femininity, non-language or body. Thus Christ, the Son of man, when all is said and done is "human" only through his mother—as if Christly or Christian humanism could only be a materialism (this is, besides, what some secularizing trends within its orbit do not cease claiming their esotericism). And yet, the humanity of the Virgin mother is not always obvious, and we shall see how, in her being cleared of sin, for instance, Mary distinguishes herself from mankind. . . .[37]

But as often as I've turned to this essay, especially for the provocative pleasures of its mother-words, I've also been frustrated by feeling that it tends to objectify rather than mobilize the differences it inscribes. I read it back and forth, up and down, crisscrossing in my reading performance the institutional, material, and discursive lines it draws. And yet I withdraw, tired, finally resting—as does the essay, I think—in the binarism it displays.

Others have tried to engage the double and multiple voices Kristeva invokes by writing past representation into relation through dialogue. But the dialogic form does not in and of itself guarantee performativity. It may or may not work. It may be bad or failed performativity. Indeed, it may backfire egregiously, as it does in the case of Hope Edelman's *Motherless Daughters,* a book I opened thinking about my sister-in-law's recent death and about her eight-year-old daughter, my niece, only to find a letter to the author: "Dear Hope," the book began.[38] I tried to read on, thinking this book has obviously been important to many people, making myself think, "how interesting that she begins with *others'* words"—but couldn't, finally realizing, of course, that where Edelman begins is with a salutation to herself. The gesture at dialogic return functions here as proof of the authority of the narrator. It confirms rather than in any way displaces authorial perspective, bringing the story back to its beginnings in "Hope."[39] I tried to believe that the inkling of a very bad pun here (one that celebrated identity—appropriating "hope" to "Hope" and irony to singularity—rather than difference) was mere projection on my part— until I saw ads for the sequel, a collection of similar letters, called *Letters to Hope.* Here was, it seemed to me, a worst-case per/version of monologue masking as dialogue.

One alternative is to engage dialogue as a drama or interaction among voices divided up into separate characters or selves. With significant exceptions, however, this approach tends to disentangle the multiple voices or subject-selves always already entangled in the production of a performative self.[40] It tends to divide and conquer the production of a performative self, favoring rational distinctions among voices over their erotic entanglement. To the contrary, Nancy Mairs hails a sensual synergy of selves living together in the writing self, calling the writing "self" to the "we" constituted in the pleasures of articulating with a "not-me": "I don't see how anyone engaged in self-representation can fail to recognize in the autobiographical self, constructed as it is in language, all the others whom the writing self shelters. The not-me dwells here in the me. We are one, and more-than-one. Our stories utter one another."[41]

There are few examples of one story folding into another, of one story uttering another, bypassing questions of appropriation altogether to perform the indwelling of Mairs's "not-me" as elegant as Carol Stack's recent book, *Call to Home,* an account of the return of African Americans to an impoverished, rural South in the late seventies and eighties. Stack notes that in early versions of the book she tried to maintain a clear distinction between the stories she heard and the stories she told about them, between her narrative voice and her interpretations of the people with whom she spoke. "But my voice today," she says, "is in part a voice taught to me by the Carolinians who told me their stories; they and I conspired to understand and communicate their experience."[42] Inhabited at once by the people with whom she spoke and the people-readers with whom she is now speaking, Stack's voice shifts unpredictably, almost imperceptibly from one story or narrative key into another.

Like the creek Stack describes in the opening paragraphs of *Call to Home,* which "twists, doubles back and redoubles, and works itself almost into knots, wringing out the territory like anxious knuckles squeezing a sponge," Stack's view "swings out deep and wide, cutting a broad arc." We watch with her as "the ground lifts back and away from a fringe of cypress and gum trees up gently through all the acres of fields" and Pearl's house, "the house where Samuel was born in 1922, where he and Pearl lived their married life and raised their ten children," comes into focus. Moving slowly, Stack takes us along as she reviews the house's minor improvements. She observes, knowing what we will come to know, "There are still children in the house, grandchildren now," as we cross over the threshold and, taught well by Stack's own careful tone and demeanor, reach out a hand to greet our beckoning host: "Pearl," Stack says, "is still Miss Pearl."[43]

Performative subjectivities often begin small—in a daughter's question or a friend's comment.[44] Or simply in the desire to speak frankly, directly to a reader, implying a reader's presence in the evident anticipation of a reply. Beginning in the small, concrete gestures of answering back, performative subjectivities may also rise to the coursing, liturgical uncertainty with which Dick Hebdige remembers "america."

In Hebdige's montage United States, there are no stable selves. They have been evacuated, leaving the landscape, however, redolent with performative subjectivities. Abandoning cartography for memory, spatial analysis for the broken, wanton, post- (pre-?) narrative temporalities of life on the edges of Los Angeles, Hebdige writes an exile's nonstory. He appears in his/story as the author who finally makes himself at home in his own prose, shifting into an "I"-frame, shifting down from "he" to "me," as he finally writes/drives his way past both individuality and alienation toward something like hope, something like love *("call it lack, if you must; our only hope for survival—call it love")*:

> He spent one Christmas alone, in self-inflicted solitary, detached at last after several years in exile from most of the moorings that had tied him to his old life in Britain, and like some latter-day Scrooge, he found himself assailed, of course, by all the ghosts and distant objects he'd mislaid or thrown away to escape to this place. On Christmas day he picked up the phone and called one of his oldest friends in London, the widow of his other oldest friend and he was shocked as always, thanks to fiber-optic technology, by the "fact" she sounded close enough to touch. . . .
>
> . . . she takes the phone into another room so we can talk unimpeded without being overheard by her new family. Within minutes we're talking old times, . . . and it all feels so effortless leaning back two decades into old understandings. . . . It feels so comfortable and right to talk here and now in the present tense across 6,000 miles and an 8 hour time difference, then pause, to wait inside a silence, wait for it to break without having to worry about what's coming next, confident in the knowledge, perhaps fallacious, that the person on the other end is riding every nuance right alongside you and that everything is flowing unimpeded back and forth along the tele-pathic circuitry set up all those years ago in all those hours spent sitting to-gether in the same apartment where she's sitting now, in the hours that passed as we sat there listening to music, smoking, making cups of tea, dis-secting who said what to whom with what effect earlier that evening in the pub, watching the grey London dawn come up, slow and still, over the rain-wet rooftops of the houses opposite.
>
> Suddenly it's time to leave home again and come back here to where I live and as I replace the receiver I catch myself, reflected in the mirror by the man-telpiece, face cracked open in the goofy, oafish, adolescent grin I recognise from ancient schoolboy portraits in the family photo album. Imperceptibly, old London wraps me in its foggy aura and I move about the sunlit California kitchen with the costermonger swagger of a juvenile extra in *Oliver!*, the musi-cal. My accent has slipped so far back down towards its 1950's cockney origin that the attendant at the Arco station, where I stop several hours later to buy gas, cannot understand a single word I'm saying.[45]

4. Performative writing is *nervous*. It anxiously crosses various stories, theories, texts, intertexts, and spheres of practice, unable to settle into a

clear, linear course, neither willing nor able to stop moving, restless, transient and transitive, traversing spatial and temporal borders, linked as it is in what Michael Taussig calls "a chain of narratives sensuously feeding back into the reality thus (dis)enchained."[46] Rather than skittish in the sense of glancing or superficial (or even merely anxious), "nervous" writing follows the body's model: it operates by synaptic relay, drawing one charged moment into another, constituting knowledge in an ongoing process of transmission and transferal, finding in the wide-ranging play of textuality an urgency that keeps what amounts to textual travel from lapsing into tourism, and that binds the traveler to his/her surging course like an electrical charge to its conduit.

Nervous performativity differs from intertextuality generally in its genealogical imperative. It takes its pulse from a specifically Foucauldian sense of history as a discontinuous recurrence of disciplines and practices, of "interpretations" incorporated in history as events. Genealogy must, for Foucault, stage those interpretations. It must make them "appear as events on the stage of historical process." In this way, history introduces discontinuity into experience. Rather than drawing continuous lines or tracking origins, history as genealogy

> divides our emotions, dramatizes our instincts, multiplies our body and sets it against itself. [It] deprives the self of the reassuring stability of life and nature, and it will not permit itself to be transported by a voiceless obstinacy toward a millennial ending. It will uproot its traditional foundations and relentlessly disrupt its pretended continuity.[47]

A Foucauldian genealogy historicizes the body. It records and explicates the history in "what we tend to feel is without history—in sentiments, love, conscience" as well as in their absence, in "the moment when they remain unrealized."[48]

Genealogy writes a body always already written by history. But centered in the body, it also writes that history in breaks and ruptures, not as a text per se but as the story of living bodies always already contesting, at both macro- and micro-political levels, the social texts to which they are otherwise indentured.

Genealogy becomes, in Joe Roach's work, for instance, performance genealogy.[49] Roach tracks the body in/as performance, as the dizzying, "vortical" force and effect of performance across the history of New Orleans race/class cultures. Considering how spectacular procedures are similarly engaged in slave markets, eighteenth-century brothel shows, and contemporary football games, Roach jump-cuts one century and the next, street markets and the Astrodome, focusing, however, per Foucault, on the "singularity of events outside of any monotonous finality." He isolates rather than compresses the different scenes in which spectacle, display, and performance play out their respective power and appeal.[50] With insistent specificity, he splices events, at once displaying the condensation of culture in performance and enacting Foucault's claim that "knowledge is not made for understanding; it is made for cutting."[51]

With similarly cinematic intensity and more explicitly carnivalesque delight, Ruth Bowman crosses nineteenth-century circus and literary romance traditions with 1990s documentary filmmaking. She deposes conventional genre and period distinctions, performing in her own prose/documentary the instability of claims to authenticity and sincerity that have otherwise so often drawn the American imagination into pious complacency.[52] She crosscuts nineteenth- and twentieth-century performance traditions, historiographically performing the very doubleness and duplicity she finds in circus "humbug." Bowman substitutes the dis/continuous play of performance riddling American culture—from P. T. Barnum's American Museum through Nathaniel Hawthorne's novels and Jennie Livingston's *Paris Is Burning*—for the seductions of authenticity and "experience." Like Roach, she decenters the body-self in the very form of her essay, reflecting in the broken continuities of her own text the genealogy of double-selves she writes.

5. Performative writing is *citational.* Operating again at the interstice of writing and performance, and perhaps more narrowly informed by discourses of textuality than other modes of performative writing, citational writing quotes a world that is always already performative—that is composed in and as repetition and reiteration. Citational writing figures writing as rewriting, as the repetition of given discursive forms that are exceeded in the "double-time" of performing writing and thereby expose the fragility of identity, history, and culture constituted in rites of textual recurrence.[53] Judith Butler has argued that performativity at best fails gendered/sexual identity by temporalizing it, by marking its origins in repetition policed to perfection.[54] Identity cannot escape its discursive construction in/as iteration but, through performance, it may exert a counterpressure. It may repeat with a vengeance, making repetition stumble, stutter, driving a wedge into the practices of re/turn (between turn and return), thus at least promising repetition with a *difference.*[55]

Echoing the quotational meta-drama of a Brecht play, citational writing tends toward what Fredric Jameson calls "pastiche"—or parody without the punch, parody worn smooth by repetition, traced through with the failure of Brechtian/modernist irony to overcome postmodern conditions.[56] But staging Butler's failure against Brecht's, citational writing gains a kind of melancholy hopefulness. Repetition isn't all bad. Inevitably imperfect, it is the living sign that reproduction can never be total or absolute. In Judith Hamera's reflections on her reluctance to leave her field sites (in this case, a classical ballet studio) behind, moreover, it is the site of (re)turn, of something like a turn *en pointe,* spinning the disciplinary histories of ballet and scholarship into a unique alliance. Hamera recovers nostalgia (perhaps the ultimate trope of return) as the *excess* of history (its specter and low "other") in what may seem the excessive repetitions, quotations, and citations that constitute her argument:

> Nostalgia has a bad name, admittedly often justifiably. Nostalgia's complicity in the projects of imperialism and salvage ethnography are well known and I will not review them here. But even outside these critiques the press is not good. . . . As those of us who contemplate leaving our [fieldwork] sites—to the extent that such leavetakings are subject to contemplation—as we look for our EXITS and think about getting busy, getting hurt, getting tired, getting out, can we not, instead, imagine an "embodied nostalgia" with a capacity to "engender its own ironies" (Battaglia 78), a slippery, ludic container of/ for ethno-time, one in and through which memory and desire merge their backward glances into an affective alliance with stable limits but multiple, unstable possibilities (Sippl 25)? And could not such an affective alliance beget an ethnographic home place or home story, one thoughtfully, contingently, critically poised at the brink of "stay" and "go," a place or story where, in the words of Jori Graham: "(. . . The hurry [of Time] is stopped) (and held) (but not extinguished) (no)"?[57]

Hamera exemplifies the "embodied nostalgia" to which she appeals. In this passage, among others, quotations mix and overlap. They disappear and spiral, one into another. But who quotes? Who re-cites? Who says "EXITS"? " 'stay' and 'go' "? Who repeats "getting" to exhaustion ("getting busy, getting hurt, getting tired, getting out") and then appeals to the high discourses of "ethno-time," echoing bell hooks on "homeplace," slipping the "I" who wonders into the place of the "we" who imagines an "embodied nostalgia"? Hamera's voice is written over and shot through with quotation, with other voices clamoring to be heard, held in ready equipoise within the "ludic container" of her prose.

Hamera is, it seems, ravished by writing and yet, writing on, quoting on, rewriting, she ravishes writing in turn. You can almost hear her rifling the pages of books beside her as she writes them into her writing, as the surrounding stacks of books threaten to fall. But you don't, they don't. Hamera tunes them all to the rhythm of her own run on/at the keyboard. There is something of a supra-personal, Laurie Anderson performance here; something of an ancient ritual of collective memory. "Hamera" is the one who remembers and desires, through whose body and words are coded the "affective alliance with stable limits but multiple, unstable possibilities" she imagines. "She" becomes the performativity of her prose, becoming her-self in turn in "affective alliance"—in love—with the field subjects/friends she leaves behind.

Citational writing underscores the double movement of quotation. It stages its own citationality, re-*sighting* citation, displaying it in an accumulation of quotations or self-quotation or quotation from beyond the borders of academic prose (such as the Jorie Graham poem Hamera quotes here or the long poem that concludes Linda Alcoff's important reflection on "The Problem of Speaking for Others"),[58] with the primary effect of reclaiming citation for affiliation.

Umberto Eco argues that it is impossible in the postmodern era even to say "I love you" without sounding like you're quoting a Harlequin romance. Quotation is, for Eco, the defining figure of postmodernity. Within its folds, love itself is pre-written. The best we can do is simulate its expression by quoting the quote, double-quoting the romance.[59] On the other hand, as Barthes noted in the late seventies, the language of love is itself a transgression, suggesting (nostalgia for) a time when *eros* wasn't driven out of the marketplace by commodity exchange.[60] At once caught in a web of quotations and pulling at the fine threads in which it is caught, "love" moves through writing as pleasure. It is the urgency with which Hamera remembers both her field subjects and the texts through and against which their relationship is articulated. It is the drama of quoted and quotational texts wrapping themselves around each other in conflict, need, passion, necessity. It is the performance of writing writing, pressing on through hyper-aesthetics and the enclosure of writing within writing, into "affective alliance" with writing itself. In citational performativities, love comes home to language, and language to desire, each renewing itself in the other-texts and other-bodies without which it is nothing.

6. Performative writing is *consequential.* It not only dramatizes J. L. Austin's early distinction between constative and performative utter-

ances—between words that report what other words and people do and words that *do* what other words report (exemplified for Austin—as Eve Kosofsky Sedgwick has made painfully clear—in the difference between the wedding announcement and the wedding vow)—but subsumes the constative into the performative, articulating language generally as an operational means of action and effects.[61] Writing that takes up the performativity in language is meant to make a difference, "to make things happen."[62] Or, as Tania Modleski has argued in defense of Virginia Woolf's beautiful prose, it is rhetorical—although not rhetorical as opposed to beautiful or in the sense of rhetoric as "a suppressive force." It is rhetorical, rather, in the sense of rhetoric "as a *productive* force, and, most definitely and performatively, as *force.*"[63]

But just as performative evocation is not mimetic, and nervous performativities are not only intertextual, so performative writing that is consequential is not broadly rhetorical. It is not the same thing as rhetoric. It recasts rhetoric as a constitutive aesthetic, leading Maurice Charland, for instance, to wonder, "Perhaps critical rhetoric . . . requires a performative moment which seeks to name a new audience and constitute a new *sensus communis.*"[64] Rather than appealing to given audiences or speaking, as Adorno claims Brecht does, in the language of established discursive communities, performative rhetoric names a new public. At least in part through the kind of evocative processes described earlier, it projects new modes of being and relating through its forms, constituting the very norms by which it will be read.[65]

Performative rhetorics are performative to the extent that they operate from within circuitries of reader response. The realities they project assume negotiation. They involve the reader not as the subject/object of persuasion of a given reality claim but as a cowriter, co-constituent of an uncertain, provisional, normative practice. In this light, I think of border-works like bell hooks's *Black Looks* and Simon Watney's *Practices of Freedom,* works that call their readers to perform at the boundary of at least two worlds.[66] I think also of the invitations to risk and conviction that permeate Peggy Phelan's work and of the bardic force with which Dwight Conquergood speaks the past into the future.

As the effect of a social relation and as a mode of cultural, historical action, performative writing throws off the norms of conventional scholarship for an explicit, alternative normativity. It operates by a code of reflexive engagement that makes writing subject to its own critique, that *makes writing* a visible subject, at once making it vulnerable to displacement by the very text/performances it invokes and shoring up its capacity for political, ethical agency. As performance, as writing that stipulates its own performativity, performative writing enters into the arena of contest to which it appeals with the affective investment of one who has been there and will be there at the end, who has a stake in the outcome of the exchange. The writing/subject puts his/her own status on the line not in the debased-Derridean sense of reveling in absence, in the winking spectacle of nakedness to which the emperor is now invited, but in the name of mobilizing *praxis,* breaking the discursive limits of the emperor's stage, and invigorating the dynamics of democratic contest in which the emperor and his new clothes (or lack thereof) are now continually refigured.

In these pages, I have only crossed into the terrain of performative writing, a terrain that seems larger with each step. Writing performatively opens the field of writing to incursion, permeation, multiplicity. It expands the very possibilities for writing to sometimes terrifying proportions. But perhaps more frightening than its size and range is the extent to which performative writing requires its reading, writing, and written subjects to negotiate the claims of its respective forms. Metonymic and consequential currents within performative writing, for instance, may seem incompatible, the former carrying its subject(s) into effacement by time, the latter into action in time. Together they articulate an asymmetry, even a contradiction at the heart of performative writing, a tension—whether construed as oppositional, hierarchical, erotic, practical, or differential—between the reflexive instabilities of poststructural language use and its ethical, political commitments. Critics of poststructuralism have repeatedly wondered where instability stops and commitment begins. Their arguments tend to assume a radical difference between the figural turns of metonymic and directive speech, a difference that implies a necessary, free, and arbitrary choice between endless hermeneutic deferral and material politics. But I would argue—and here, only in the most preliminary terms—that questions of performativity divert the tension between (even the binary/textualist opposition that maintains the distance between) these claims toward *materializing possibility* in and through a kind of writing that is distinctly performative: writing that recognizes its delays and displacements while proceeding as writing toward engaged, embodied, material ends. It is in thus spinning off textuality that I see the mark of a genuinely new politics, a politics that not only refuses to choose between affirmation and reflexivity (or to yield to charges of either rank positivism or wound-licking narcissism) but also refuses to identify writing with either reflexivity or referential affirmation, pursuing it instead as a critical means of bypassing both the siren's song of textual self-reference and the equally dangerous, whorling drain of unreflexive commitment. Performative writing takes its energy from that refusal, and from the moment when such apparent contradictions surge into productivity.

I do not mean to suggest that the tensions between affirmation and reflexivity, speaking and writing, writing and doing, are false or easily resolved. But to give up not only on doing versus writing but on making writing *do* seems to me cynical at best. Much recent literary and cultural critique founders on the corollary assumption that since politics is impossible anyway, then what we are doing anyway is politics.[67] Which has led me to ask in this essay, what are we doing anyway? The struggle to write performance seems to me to give performative writing its depth and value, ethically, politically, and aesthetically. In this struggle at least, performative writing seems one way not only to make meaning but to make writing meaningful.

But what is *it? the student asks again. I repeat, perhaps all too easily, all too pedantically, That's the wrong question: "it" refuses ontological inscription; "it" is a subject formation; "it" won't bear noun-modifiers. But what* is *it? she comes back, the repetition now, finally, proving its excess: she hasn't been asking as much as I've been hearing the wrong question. The question, I realize, echoed through many other forms and places, has less to do with definition than with desire, less to do with wanting to resolve performative writing under the usual rubrics of autobiography (and self-presence), narrative (and closure), reflexivity (and "indulgence"), and rhetoric (or persuasion) than with the palpable appeal of its difference, its aberrant relation to norms of just " 'good writing.' "[68] Performative writing is queer, even in the old, now twisted, now queered sense of "queer" as oddly familiar, strange even in its bent similarity to what's common and known or to what common sense calls "good." Performative writing is an itinerant in the land of good writing. It travels side by side with normative performances of textuality, sometimes even passing for the "same," but always drawing its energy from a critical difference, from the possibility that it may always be otherwise than what it seems.*

What is it that we want when we ask, insistently, over and over, "What is it"? What is it, moreover, that I have deferred until the after-text of this text? A definition, a complete demonstration, maybe. More likely, finally, the same-but-different body of performative writing, slipping now from the evidentiary platform of "examples" to the corridors of an ongoing intermission. Between acts, among inter-acts, I let myself now ask the question the student asked; I perform the student, colleague, friend's question, "What is it?" and find myself now reading writing, writing reading, touching pages touching me, drawing me into mutual desire for—what? what is it for? The question moves as does the writing, forward, into exigency. Performative writing is what it is not in itself but for . . . for what? Turning the page, turning the corner, I have to say, to the extent that it is, it is for relatives, not identities;[69] *it is for space and time; it is for a truly good laugh, for the boundary, banal pleasures that twine bodies in action; it is for writing, for writing ourselves out of our-selves, for writing our-selves into what (never) was and may (never) be. It is/is it for love?*

NOTES

An earlier version of this paper was presented at the Performance Studies Conference, New York University, 23–26 March 1995, as part of the plenary session on "Performative Writing." I am, as ever, indebted to Jane Blocker, Jacquelyn Dowd Hall, Joy Kasson, and Carol Mavor and to Larry Grossberg for invaluable contributions to revisions.

1. Mikhail Bakhtin, *Problems of Dostoevsky's Poetics,* ed. and trans. Caryl Emerson (Minneapolis: University of Minnesota Press, 1984), 202; Homi K. Bhabha, "Introduction: Narrating the Nation," in *Nation and Narration,* ed. Homi K. Bhabha (New York: Routledge, 1990), 3.

2. See, e.g., Julia Kristeva, *Powers of Horror: An Essay on Abjection,* trans. Leon S. Roudiez (New York: Columbia University Press, 1982).

3. Theodor Adorno, "Commitment," trans. Francis McDonagh, in *Aesthetics and Politics,* trans. and ed. Ronald Taylor (London: NLB, 1977), 188.

4. Sue-Ellen Case, "Performing Lesbian in the Space of Technology: Part I," *Theatre Journal* 47.1 (1995): 8.

5. As opposed, for instance, to style as tactical resistance per, e.g., Dick Hebdige, *Subculture: The Meaning of Style* (New York: Methuen, 1979).

6. See Henry M. Sayre, "Critical Performance: The Example of Roland Barthes," in *The Object of Performance: The American Avant-Garde since 1970* (Chicago: University of Chicago Press, 1989), 246–64.

7. It is not within the scope of this essay to review the complexities of new history writing. I would, however, cite two compelling examples: Carolyn Steedman, *Landscape for a Good Woman* (New Brunswick: Rutgers University Press, 1986); and Mary Lowenthal Felstiner, *To Paint Her Life: Charlotte Salomon in the Nazi Era* (New York: Harper, 1994).

8. Carolina Seminar on Gender and History: Workshop on Writing and Re-

sponsibiiity, National Humanities Center, Research Triangle Park, NC, 7 May 1993.

9. Henry A. Giroux, "Language, Power, and Clarity or 'Does Plain Prose Cheat?' " in *Living Dangerously: Multiculturalism and the Politics of Difference* (New York: Peter Lang, 1993) 166.

10. Giroux, 168, citing bell hooks, *Yearning: Race, Gender, and Cultural Politics* (Boston: South End Press, 1990).

11. Giroux, 167.

12. Note alternative models in Tony Bennett, *Outside Literature* (New York: Routledge, 1990); Walter Benjamin, "The Author as Producer," in *Reflections,* ed. Peter Demetz, trans. Edmund Jephcott (New York: Harcourt Brace, 1978), 220–38.

13. Trinh T. Minh-ha, *Woman, Native, Other* (Bloomington: Indiana University Press, 1989), 22; cited in Giroux, 160.

14. Michael Taussig, *Shamanism, Colonialism, and the Wild Man: A Study in Terror and Healing* (Chicago: University of Chicago Press, 1987), 3.

15. See Peggy Phelan, "The Ontology of Performance: Representation without Reproduction," in *Unmarked: The Politics of Performance* (New York: Routledge, 1993), 146–66; and on performance as scholarly representation, see Dwight Conquergood, "Poetics, Play, Process, and Power: The Performative Turn in Anthropology," *Text and Performance Quarterly* 9.1 (1989): 82–88.

16. Per Victor Turner on the liminal moment, *From Ritual to Theatre* (New York: Performing Arts Journal Publications, 1982), 44.

17. See Robert Scholes, "The English Apparatus," in *Textual Power: Literary Theory and the Teaching of English* (New Haven: Yale University Press, 1985), 1–17.

18. On the "subjunctive mood" of ritual, see Turner, 82–84.

19. Michael Taussig, *The Nervous System* (New York: Routledge, 1992), 7.

20. Carol Mavor, *Pleasures Taken: Performances of Sexuality and Loss in Victorian Photographs* (Durham: Duke University Press, 1995), 89–90.

21. Mavor, 91–92.

22. See Mikhail Bakhtin, "Discourse in the Novel," in *The Dialogic Imagination,* ed. Michael Holquist, trans. Caryl Emerson and Michael Holquist (Austin: University of Texas Press, 1981), 259–422.

23. Roland Barthes, *S/Z,* trans. Richard Miller (London: Jonathon Cape, 1975); Judith A. Hamera, " 'Bye Bunheads, Little Feet and Big Red': Leaving Le Studio," paper presented at the national meeting of the Speech Communication Association, 18 November 1995; Bruce Henderson, "Call Me Neely: David Trinidad 'V.O.D.' and the Poetics of Patty Duke," paper presented at the national meeting of the Speech Communication Association, 20 November 1995.

24. Jane Blocker, untitled paper presented at the Performance Studies Conference, New York University, New York, 25 March 1995.

25. Blocker, untitled paper.

26. Blocker, untitled paper; see also Blocker, "Conclusion: Writing toward Disappearance," in *Where Is Ana Mendieta? Identity, Performativity, and Exile* (Durham: Duke University Press, forthcoming).

27. See Michel de Certeau, *The Writing of History*, trans. Tom Conley (New York: Columbia University Press, 1988).

28. This is the space of Cixous's Medusa and Bhabha's "nation." See Hélène Cixous, "The Laugh of the Medusa," *Signs* 1 (1976): 875–93; Bhabha, "Introduction: Narrating the Nation"; and Bhabha, *The Location of Culture* (New York: Routledge, 1994), 145–46.

29. Per, for instance, Homi Bhabha's sense of the performative as a "repetitious, recursive" narrative strategy that operates in tandem with the continuist project of the "pedagogical" not only to constitute the "nation" but to redeem and reiterate it "as a reproductive process." The conventional auto/biography or story of a single life may, like the story of a nation, constitute the self in the "double-time" of (narrative) performance and (historical) pedagogy. Bhabha, *The Location of Culture*, 145.

30. See Diane P. Freedman, Olivia Frey, and Frances Murphy Zauhar, eds., *The Intimate Critique: Autobiographical Literary Criticism* (Durham: Duke University Press, 1993).

31. See Joan Scott, "The Evidence of Experience," *Critical Inquiry* 17.4 (1991): 773–97. See also Donna Haraway, "Situated Knowledges," in *Simians, Cyborgs, and Women: The Reinvention of Nature* (New York: Routledge, 1991), 183–201.

32. Susan Suleiman, *Subversive Intent: Gender, Politics, and the Avant-Garde* (Cambridge: Harvard University Press, 1990), 117–18; note Suleiman's sense that her reading of Lacan is "unorthodox," especially as confirmed and developed by Jane Gallop, *Reading Lacan* (Ithaca: Cornell University Press, 1985). Suleiman, 231.

33. Elspeth Probyn, *Sexing the Self: Gendered Positions in Cultural Studies* (New York: Routledge, 1993), 2. Probyn takes the pulse of her argument from Roland Barthes, *Image-Music-Text*, trans. Stephen Heath (New York: Hill and Wang, 1977), 157.

34. See Judith Butler, *Gender Trouble: Feminism and the Subversion of Identity* (New York: Routledge, 1990), 143; on discourses of positionality, see Adrienne Rich, "Notes toward a Politics of Location (1984)," in *Blood, Bread, and Poetry: Selected Prose, 1979–1985* (New York: Norton, 1986), 210–31.

35. See Probyn, 4: "the possibility of the self rests within a filigree of institutional, material, discursive lines that either erase or can be used to enable spaces in which 'we' can be differently spoken." See also Stuart Hall, "Cultural Identity and Diaspora," in *Identity, Community, Culture, Difference*, ed. Jonathon Rutherford (London: Lawrence and Wishart, 1990).

36. Probyn, 4.

37. Julia Kristeva, "Stabat Mater," in *The Kristeva Reader,* ed. Toril Moi (New York: Columbia University Press, 1986), 161–62.

38. Hope Edelman, *Motherless Daughters: The Legacy of Loss* (New York: Delta, 1994).

39. See Bakhtin, "Discourse in the Novel," esp. 272–75.

40. These include Eve Kosofsky Sedgwick and Michael Moon's dialogic encounter in "Divinity: A Dossier, a Performance Piece, a Little-Understood Emotion," which triangulates the reader in desire that ripples through Moon and Sedgwick's exchange as both comic lack and excess, in Sedgwick, *Tendencies* (Durham: Duke University Press, 1993). See also D. Soyini Madison's performative essay " 'That Was My Occupation': Oral Narrative, Black Feminist Theory, and Performance," *Text and Performance Quarterly* 13.3 (1993): 213–32.

41. Nancy Mairs, *Remembering the Bone House: An Erotics of Place and Space* (Boston: Beacon, [1989], 1995), 11.

42. Carol Stack, *Call to Home: African Americans Reclaim the Rural South* (New York: Basic Books, 1996), xix. As an anthropologist, Stack perhaps represents the best in a long tradition of anthropological contributions to reflexivity in published research, figured most notably in James Clifford and George E. Marcus, eds., *Writing Culture: The Poetics and Politics of Ethnography* (Berkeley: University of California Press, 1986) and its recent rejoinder, Ruth Behar and Deborah A. Gordon, eds., *Women Writing Culture* (Berkeley: University of California Press, 1995). See also Elizabeth Enslin, "Beyond Writing: Feminist Practice and the Limitations of Ethnography," *Cultural Anthropology* 9.4 (1994): 537–68.

43. Stack, 1–2.

44. See Henry Louis Gates's prefatory letter to his daughters in *Colored People* (New York: Knopf, 1994), xi–xvi; and Phelan, "The Golden Apple: Jennie Livingston's *Paris Is Burning,*" in *Unmarked,* 104.

45. Dick Hebdige, "On Tumbleweeds and Body Bags: Remembering America," *Longing and Belonging: From the Faraway Nearby* [an International exhibition curated for the site Santa Fe] Albuquerque, NM: University of New Mexico Press, 1996.

46. Taussig, *The Nervous System,* 7.

47. Michel Foucault, "Nietzsche, Genealogy, History," in *Language, Counter-Memory, Practice,* ed. Donald F. Bouchard (Ithaca: Cornell University Press, 1977), 154. See also Scott, esp. 796–97, on historicizing experience per Foucault.

48. Foucault, "Nietzsche, Genealogy, History," 139–40.

49. Joseph R. Roach, "Slave Spectacles and Tragic Octoroons: A Cultural Genealogy of Antebellum Performance," *Theatre Survey* 33.2 (1992): 167–87.

50. Foucault, "Nietzsche, Genealogy, History," 140.

51. Foucault, "Nietzsche, Genealogy, History," 154.

52. Ruth Laurion Bowman, "Performing Social Rubbish: Humbug and Romance in the American Marketplace," in *Exceptional Spaces: Essays in Performance and History,* ed. Della Pollock (Chapel Hill: University of North Carolina Press, 1997); see also Shannon Jackson, "Performance at Hull-House: Museum, Microfiche, Historiography," in *Exceptional Spaces.*

53. Bhabha, *The Location of Culture,* 145.

54. See Judith Butler, "Bodily Inscriptions, Performative Subversions," in *Gender Trouble,* 128–41, and Butler's qualification in *Bodies That Matter* (New York: Routledge, 1993).

55. Following Mary Russo, *The Female Grotesque: Risk, Excess, and Modernity* (New York, Routledge, 1995), 70: "To put on femininity with a vengeance suggests the power of taking it off."

56. Fredric Jameson, "Postmodernism and Consumer Society," in *The Anti-Aesthetic: Essays on Postmodern Culture,* ed. Hal Foster (Port Townsend, WA: Bay Press, 1983), 111–25.

57. See Hamera, who cites Susan Stewart, *On Longing: Narratives of the Miniature, the Gigantic, the Souvenir, the Collection* (Durham: Duke University Press, 1993); Linda Hutcheon, *A Poetics of Postmodernism: History, Theory, Fiction* (New York: Routledge, 1988); Debbora Battaglia, "On Practical Nostalgia: Self-Prospecting among Urban Trobrianders," in *Rhetorics of Self-Making,* ed. Debbora Battaglia (Berkeley: University of California Press, 1995).

58. See also Michael S. Bowman, "Performing Southern History for the Tourist Gaze: Antebellum Home Tour Guide Performance," in *Exceptional Spaces,* ed. Pollock; Linda Alcoff, "The Problem of Speaking for Others," *Cultural Critique* (winter 1991): 5–32.

59. Umberto Eco, *Postscript to* The Name of the Rose, trans. William Weaver (San Diego: Harcourt, 1984), 67–68.

60. Roland Barthes, *Roland Barthes by Roland Barthes,* trans. Richard Howard (New York: Noonday Press, 1977), 65–66:

> Political liberation of sexuality: this is a double transgression, of politics by the sexual, and conversely. But this is nothing at all: let us now imagine reintroducing into the politico-sexual field thus discovered, recognized, traversed, and liberated . . . *a touch of sentimentality:* would that not be the *ultimate* transgression? the transgression of transgression itself? For, after all, that would be *love:* which would return: but in another place.

See also Bertolt Brecht, "Preface to *Drums in the Night,*" in *Collected Plays,* ed. Ralph Mannheim and John Willett (New York: Vintage, 1971), 1:376–77, on "sex that gives rise to associations."

61. J. L. Austin, *How to Do Things with Words* (Cambridge: Harvard University

Press, 1962). See also Eve Kosofsky Sedgwick's critique of Austin's heterosexual presumption in "Queer Performativity: Henry James's *The Art of the Novel," GLQ* 1 (1993): 2, rehearsed in her introduction, with Andrew Parker, to *Performance and Performativity,* ed. with Andrew Parker (New York: Routledge, 1995).

62. Marianna Torgovnick, introduction to *Eloquent Obsessions: Writing Cultural Criticism,* ed. Marianna Torgovnick (Durham: Duke University Press, 1994), 4.

63. Tania Modleski, *Feminism without Women: Culture and Criticism in a "Postfeminist" Age* (New York: Routledge, 1991), 54. See in general Modleski's discussion in "At the Crossroads: On the Performative Aspect of Feminist Criticism," 45–58.

64. Maurice Charland, "Finding a Horizon and *Telos:* The Challenge to Critical Rhetoric," *Quarterly Journal of Speech* 77 (1991): 77–78.

65. In this way, performative writing remains closely bound up with historical, material traditions of performance, despite, for instance, Sue-Ellen Case's important concern:

> It is confounding to observe how a lesbian/gay movement about sexual, bodily practices and the lethal effects of a virus, which has issued an agitprop activist tradition from its loins, as well as a Pulitzer-prize winning Broadway play (*Angels in America*), would have, as its critical operation, a notion of performativity that circles back to written texts, abandoning historical traditions of performance for the print modes of literary and philosophical scrutiny. (Case, 8)

66. bell hooks, *Black Looks: Race and Representation* (Boston: South End Press, 1992); Simon Watney, *Practices of Freedom: Selected Writings on HIV/AIDS* (Durham: Duke University Press, 1994).

67. I am grateful to Jacquelyn Hall for this succinct formulation.

68. See the e-mail exchange that followed the Performance Studies Conference at New York University, reprinted as "From Perform-l: The Future in Retrospect," *Drama Review* 39.4 (1995): 142–63, esp. Jenny Spencer's questions of 8 April 1995, 158.

69. I was particularly inspired in this regard by Beth Mauldin, unpublished paper for Art 369/Communication Studies 257, spring 1996.

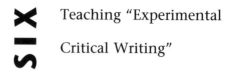 Teaching "Experimental

Critical Writing"

Eve Kosofsky Sedgwick

Course Rationale

The syllabus for the graduate seminar says:

> As the ambitions of literary criticism become more expansive and searching
> under the influence of deconstruction, feminism, Marxism, psychoanalysis,
> popular culture, and liberatory theoretical movements around race, colonial-
> ism, and sexuality, there is increased room for experimentation and reflec-
> tiveness in the modalities of critical writing, as well. This course, itself experi-
> mental, will offer readings and a workshop to help graduate students explore
> and expand the shifting grounds of possibility for their own preprofessional
> and professional writing. Boundaries between genres, between "critical" and
> "creative" writing, between private and public address, between argumenta-
> tion and performance, between individual and collaborative production, and
> between literary and nonliterary texts will be subject to exploration. The ulti-
> mate goal of the class is to prepare students to produce professionally publish-
> able writing that will change the current profile of what is publishable in our
> profession.

I've taught Experimental Critical Writing at both undergraduate and graduate levels. Both work consistently well, and many of the assignments are
appropriate for both levels. With undergraduates, the course works as an
alternative to more generically based creative writing classes. For graduate
students, its main function is to trouble and interrupt the process of
professionalization: to make sure that students at the anxious, rather
numbing preprofessional level will not lose touch with their own writerly
energies.

The point of having frequent, short, tightly framed assignments is to

overcome students' (especially graduate students') inhibitions about exper-
imentation. With only a couple of exceptions, the assignments are organized around very specific formal choices and/or constraints, and students
choose their own subject matter.

As in any workshop, students need explicit advice about how to give
and solicit useful responses. I always ask them not to jump quickly to "I
like . . ." or "I don't like . . . ," but to linger as long as they can at the stage
of "What is the ambition of this piece?" (Other ways to put this include,
"What does the form of this piece know?"—with the implicit addition,
". . . that the reader or even writer may not already know?") Ritually,
there's a silence after someone reads a piece aloud, which I will eventually
punctuate by asking, "So, what's this piece up to?" or sometimes—but
never as a rhetorical question—"How is this piece a response to the assignment?"

How the Course Is Conducted

The class meets weekly for two and a half hours. Because it is run as a
workshop, classes must be small (fifteen students or, preferably, fewer). For
most of the semester, there are weekly assignments involving three to
five pages of writing; collaborative assignments and one or two longer
assignments take two weeks apiece.

All students duplicate and circulate their writing each week. We try to
discuss as many pieces as we can; pieces that aren't read aloud and discussed in class are read at home, and the other workshop members and I
hand back brief written responses to those pieces.

Grading is on the basis of a portfolio handed in at the end of the
semester (revisions of earlier pieces are welcome, but not required), with a
substantial component for workshop participation.

I try to include some time each week for a brief discussion of the
assigned reading, but the clear emphasis is on the students' writing. I do
offer a detailed explanation, at the end of each class, of the rationale for
the next assignment and some possibilities it may offer.

Reading and Performance Elements

The class assignments are often coordinated with readings and performances planned for the semester. (For example, the assignments collected

here reflect a reading series that brought Wayne Koestenbaum and Marilyn Hacker to Duke during one semester.) Last time I taught these classes, I also brought in a performance artist, Eric Dishman, who not only performed, but also ran a two-and-a-half-hour "Performance 101" class/practicum for each of the seminars. This worked so well (especially with the undergraduates) that I plan to do it early in the semester whenever I teach these courses in the future. It not only dramatized many issues of space and address more graphically and memorably than any amount of jawboning could have, but it made vivid to us that verbal meaning isn't the only or necessarily the most powerful form of meaning—even where words are involved.

Sample Assignments

• Performative Utterances

This is always the first assignment on the syllabus: students need to be reminded that their words do something besides being evaluated. The class discussion of this assignment assumes that some of the "performative utterances" will be closer to Austin's model of the explicit performative than others, and uses that fact not to judge students' work, but to begin to map some of the different dimensions of performativity.

In *How to Do Things with Words,* J. L. Austin suggested that, at least in principle, it might be possible to distinguish between utterances that merely *said* something (constative utterances) and those that *did* something (performative utterances). The defining instances of performative utterances are those whose utterance actually does the thing *described in them.* "I thee wed." "I will my belongings to my daughter Mabel." "I welcome you." In reporting on what had happened in the scenes suggested by these sentences, you probably wouldn't say, "she said she married him," "she wrote that she willed her belongings to Mabel," or "she said she welcomed them." Rather, the more accurate report would be simply "she married him," "she willed her belongings to Mabel," "she welcomed them."

A lot of different projects in philosophy, linguistics, and critical theory since Austin have concentrated on the notion of the performative—often questioning whether it is really possible, even in theory, to divide utterances between the performative and the constative, and calling attention to different senses in which all utterances *do* something *and* at the same time say something.

Your assignment for this week, however, is simpler:

1. Look for more examples of kinds of utterance that clearly belong at the performative pole of Austin's distinction. Marrying, bequeathing, welcoming—what are some other acts that you can perform simply by saying that you perform them? Please work on a list of these; include equivocal cases, and note what you think makes them equivocal.

2. Think about what are the social and discursive preconditions for these various performative acts. (For instance, in some societies you can divorce someone simply by saying, "I divorce you," while in others you can't. What's the difference? If *I* say, "I excommunicate you," you're still not excommunicated, unless you happen to belong to the Church of Sedgwick; but if the pope says it, and you're a Catholic, then it's a different class of utterance.) Some performatives require one or more witnesses; many imply the presence of witnesses. See what generalizations you can make as you think about issues of address, community, and efficacy in performative utterances.

3. *Writing.* From your list, choose a kind of performative that you actually want to and can perform; and perform it. (I anticipate that these will be from one sentence to one page long.)

Note that with this utterance, you should be *actually performing* the specified act. For example, if your performative utterance is "I invite you to a party at my house tonight at eight," then there'd better be a party when we get there!

If you want to explain more about what you have performed, what was interesting or surprising or revealing about the performance, what preconditions it exposed, what relations it established, what effects you expect it to have, and so forth, feel free to add something about that in an appendix.

• Person

This can work with a lot of different readings—if I'm going to use Barthes's A Lover's Discourse *for another assignment, for instance, I'll ask them to look through it with reference to this assignment as well.*

Write a two- to three-page piece in which the assignment of grammatical person changes at least once. (E.g., an "I" turns into a "you" or a "he" or "she" or a "they," and/or vice versa.) Reflect on the differences this change makes: what different things can/cannot be said using a different person? What words or kinds of utterance mean differently? What other effects (and, indeed, causes) can you associate with the change of grammatical person? Can you make connections between this assignment and the one on performative utterances?

Axiom for the week: "I is a heuristic."

• Keywords

Several pages of handouts from: Raymond Williams, *Keywords*; Jan Zita Grover, "AIDS Keywords," in Douglas Crimp, ed., *AIDS: Cultural Analysis, Cultural Activism*; Jean Laplanche and J.-B. Pontalis, *The Language of Psycho-Analysis*; Ambrose Bierce, *The Devil's Dictionary*; Gustave Flaubert, *Dictionary of Received Ideas*.

Write a two- to three-page "Keywords" list for some topic that matters to you.

Like the Jan Zita Grover handout, and the Raymond Williams book on which it is in turn modeled, use various aspects of the definition form as a way of opening up analytical and polemical space. (Think: how can a definition be a performative utterance?)

Specifically, explore the ways the definition form makes use of some of the following elements:

Historical narrative (Where does the term come from? How has it been used? What has changed in its usage, and why?)

Ethnographic description (Who uses the term? To whom is it meant to be intelligible or unintelligible? What audiences or communities are created or shaped or assumed or interpellated by its usage, and why?)

Differentiation (What terms are similar to this one, and how is it different? What are the analytical or other bases of such discriminations?)

Prescription (Why/how/by whom should it/should it not be used?)

You may want to make use of the OED (Oxford English Dictionary) in doing this assignment. Then again, you may not.

• Truth Effects: "In Short, We Have Been Telling Ourselves Some Lies."

This is an assignment I use only with graduate classes.

> Leo Bersani, "Is the Rectum a Grave?" in Douglas Crimp, ed., *AIDS: Cultural Analysis, Cultural Activism.*
>
> Jan Brown, "Sex, Lies, and Penetration," in Joan Nestle, ed., *The Persistent Desire: A Femme-Butch Reader.*

Note that both essays—each in its own discursive context—are structured around the rhetoric, "In short, we have been telling ourselves some lies." Think about this rhetoric and how it works. Is it powerful for you? Does it generate a strong truth-effect? How? What positions and relations does it create? How does it interpellate readers? Writers? What kinds of authority does it assume or create? What energies does it tap into? How does it seem to be working in the context of ongoing political projects (of identity politics? of sexual politics specifically?)? What are other rhetorics that work similarly to this one? Are there forms of rhetoric that work completely differently? What is its relation to readers who do not identify with the "we"?

Your assignment: Write a two- to three-page essay in which you say, "In short, we have been telling ourselves some lies." (This will obviously require you to give some thought, first of all, to a "we" with which you identify powerfully enough to need to make such assertions.)

The next four assignments all come under a rubric of "pluralizing voices."

• Quotation

Read the first two-thirds or so of Neil Bartlett, *Who Was That Man? A Present for Mr. Oscar Wilde.* Pay attention to a lot of things about it—it's a wonderful model of experimental critical writing in many different ways. Pay special attention, though, to the different ways he uses quotations. He doesn't seem to see them simply as "evidence" for a thesis put forth in his own prose—at some points, his book almost reminds me of the German critic Walter Benjamin's fantasy that the perfect book would consist *exclusively* of quotations.

Now write something of one to three pages that finds SOME way of foregrounding the issue of quotation: a fabric of quotations, a *catalogue raisonné* of quotations, an essay that "incorporates" quotation(s) in some especially revealing or productive or offbeat way. (Do remember that the rest of the class is not necessarily in a position to check the accuracy of your quotations.) Use the exercise as an excuse for generating and exploring—at least in your own mind—a range of metaphors for the process of quotation and for the relations reflected or produced by quotation.

• The Obituary Imperative

> Simon Watney, *Policing Desire.*
> Sandra Butler and Barbara Rosenblum, *Cancer in Two Voices.*

Write a three- to five-page piece that pays some attention to, or makes some use of, the issues of representation and address that attach to the processes of loss and mourning.

Think about why/how the obituary impulse in each piece is attached to a form that pluralizes voices. Think also about how such obituary issues and impulses may already be part of such everyday practices as historical or textual scholarship; sexuality and genderedness; activism; urban, domestic, and landscape space; advertising and the media, etc. What do such usages do, and what could they?

• Prose/Poetry Version 1

Read as much as you can (at least half) of Cherríe Moraga, *Loving in the War Years.*

Among the many exciting things to remark in it, be responsive to the ways Moraga moves back and forth between poetry and prose writing. What use does she make of each form? (Don't forget to think about the relation of the poetry/prose shifts to the Spanish/English shifts.) Does she have more than one way of using each form? What features of each form are enabling to her, and how? What does the unexpected *conjunction* of the forms allow her to do that she might not have been able to do using just one or the other? What are the effects on you, as a reader, of moving back and forth between the forms? Does the difference or doubling of forms change the book's reader-relations: does it allow Moraga to appeal to, or create, a different community of readers with different expectations, different relations to her and/or to each other? If so, what and how? How would you relate that to the issues of plural and intersecting identities that form so much of the subject of the book?

Assignment: Write one to three pages of your own that mix poetry and prose in a way that both illuminates what you want to talk about and lets you explore the difference of the possibilities of two different forms—and the highly charged moments of switching back and forth.

For the purpose of this assignment, our working definition of "poetry" will be a very simple one: *Poetry is writing in which the author makes a deliberate decision about where the lines will end.* Poetry is not necessarily more "personal," more emotional, more metaphoric, more rhythmically regular, more patterned in sound, denser, and so forth than prose—prose can have all those attributes, and poetry need not necessarily have any of them. What poetry has that prose does not have is line breaks. Think about the differences that this one differential can make in the processes of writing and reading. For instance: poetry breaks up a page, visually, in a way prose does not. Another, even more important difference: in poetry, the unit of the line will be in *some* relation to the normal English unit of the sentence; but it is up to you to decide *what* relation. You can make a line essentially equivalent to a sentence. You can make a line equivalent to a grammatical unit that makes sense as part of a sentence (e.g., the subject of a sentence in one line, the predicate in the next line). You can have line breaks that cut up the sentence in completely unexpected or even apparently random ways. You can have two sentences in one line. You can have lines without having sentences at all—or you can use the line structure to "deconstruct" what a sentence is, in some ways. And you can move from one of these strategies to another. Various ways of using rhyme, or regular or irregular rhythms, will have a big impact on how readers experience the unit of the line, as well, if you want to experiment with these factors—but you may well choose not to at this point.

• Prose/Poetry Version 2

I begin this assignment by handing out the following text (or at least, a topically relevant version of it, depending on what readings/lectures I want to alert students to) to the part of the class that's sitting on the left half of the room:

Read, if you haven't, Cherríe Moraga's *Loving in the War Years,* and James Merrill's "Prose of Departure." Pay some attention to what differentiates the prose from the verse in these (and similar) contexts: can it be only the ragged or straight right margin? Is it a way of hearing the syllables? Is the address different, the expectation of just who might be listening, and how? What happens to the temporality? What happens to the space of utterance? What's it like to move from one to the other? What are some uses to make of the difference? "In short"—the usual two to three pages, please, incorporating both kinds of right margin.

Oh, and please mark your calendars and tell everyone else about Koestenbaum's reading from *Rhapsodies of a Repeat Offender,* etc., on the seventeenth, at eight. I'm sure you know him as one of the leading critics and most fabulous gay male poets around, for chutzpah and sheer splendor (plus, he's a charmer). BE THERE or be straight.

Students on the right half of the room, meanwhile, are receiving the following text:

> Read, if you haven't, Cherríe Moraga's *Loving*
> *in the War Years,* and James Merrill's "Prose of Departure."
> Pay some attention to what differentiates
> the prose from the verse in these (and similar) contexts:
> can it be only the ragged or straight right margin?
> Is it a way of hearing the syllables?
> Is the address different, the expectation
> of just who might be listening, and how?
> What happens to the temporality?
> What happens to the space of utterance?
> What's it like to move from one to the other?
> What are some uses to make of the difference?
> "In short"—the usual two to three pages, please,
> incorporating both kinds of right margin.
>
> Oh, and please mark your calendars and tell
> everyone else about Koestenbaum's reading
> from *Rhapsodies of a Repeat Offender,*
> etc., on the seventeenth, at eight.
> I'm sure you know him as one of the leading
> critics and most fabulous gay male
> poets around, for chutzpah and sheer splendor
> (plus, he's a charmer). *BE THERE or be straight.*

I begin the discussion of poetry/prose by having someone on the left (prose) side read the assignment, then someone on the right (verse) side—it's eventually clear that the assignments differ; then there's discussion of differences between how verse and prose are processed by readers—differences that make it almost impossible to recognize verse, however jogtrot, when it's written as prose. This turns into a discussion of how meter works, and I ask students to organize their writing this time around issues of rhythm, syllabics, and meter. (In the undergraduate class, I often precede this assignment with one that asks students who have never done so to write something in a deliberately singsong meter, invoking children's verse; more experienced students write something in blank verse.)

• Biographies of Voices

   Wayne Koestenbaum, *The Queen's Throat.*

Use this book as a springboard for thinking about voice—physical voice as well as written voice. Breath, vibration, voice production, embodied and disembodied voices, falsetto and basso; the gaps between voice registers; voices inward and outward; vocal mimicry, voice socialization, vocal inhibition, stuttering, asthma, slobbering, squeaking; a voice changing; wings of song; bad singing; voice in the dark; "He do the police in different voices." Write two to three pages on a topic somewhere in the vicinity of "Where does a voice come from?"

• Situated Biography (A Two-Week Exercise)

For all its brevity, this is actually a wonderful assignment.

   Neil Bartlett, *Who Was That Man? A Present for Mr. Oscar Wilde.*

Using Bartlett as an example, write a three- to five-page biographical study that makes some interesting use of the fact that it is being written *by* somebody, as well as *about* somebody.

• Modularity

   Marilyn Hacker, *Love, Death, and the Changing of the Seasons.*
   James Merrill, "Prose of Departure," from *The Inner Room.*

In the readings, focus on the effects involved when more or less discrete units of the same form (sonnet, haiku) keep happening again and again.

(Clearly, there is a range, between and indeed within the two texts, in how detachable the poem-units are from the overall structure.)

Now write something that plays with the concept of modularity—of more-or-less detachable and/or formally interchangeable units. (This may, but does not have to, involve poetry or verse forms.)

• Collaborative Archaeology (A Two-Week Assignment)

This works well for undergraduates; graduate students can get a more sophisticated version of this assignment.

Look at Wayne Koestenbaum's book *The Queen's Throat,* especially chapters 1 and (in particular) 3. Note the variety of approaches to excavating a single topic, opera—and specifically, note the "scrapbook" form, the short sections with frequent new beginnings, and the movements back and forth between personal history and a larger, social history.

With your group, settle on a topic that has some autobiographical resonance for each of you: a children's book or fairy tale, "school lunch," a person or a television character or genre from your earlier years, animals, the concept of "teacher's pet," or—you get the idea. Don't choose a topic that will disguise the differences among your experiences, but one that will let you explore such differences. Think about good ways of structuring a short but multivoiced, multiperspective, multihistory *archaeology* of this topic. Like Koestenbaum's, your archaeology should draw from both personal experience and historical record. (Yes, you can use pictures, etc.) No particular page limit, but the various sections will need to be brief, so think about how to make them as vividly evocative as possible—including evocations of different private and public spaces, different personalities, different bodies experienced from the outside and the inside. Then, work individually and collectively on the pieces of this archaeology. The final product can be written and/or delivered aloud in class.

• Performative Utterance Revisited

This builds on our very first assignment in this class: to come up with an effective speech act, a performative utterance by which something may actually be changed. Instead of doing it on an individual basis, however, this assignment asks you to work with your small group to plan and perform something that will count as a performative utterance on a more public scale. Please think about the following questions:

What do you think needs to change?

What *representational* acts could effect change?

What are the relations of *address* involved in these acts? (I.e., who is speaking, and to whom?)

Who is *interpreting* these acts, and how? How much control, and what kinds of control, do you have over this interpretive process?

What is the relation of these acts to preexisting forms and conventions of utterance?

What is the relation of these acts to preexisting media of public representation and advertising?

Document your public speech act, describe the process of its development, and evaluate it, in some form to be determined by yourselves (individually or collectively). Be prepared to report on it at the final class meeting/potluck dinner.

SEVEN

This Black Body in Question

Amanda Denise Kemp

Originally performed in November 1994 and January 1995, This Black Body in Question: Contradictions in Black Identities in Johannesburg *is a one-woman show that might also be performed by an ensemble. Developed in response to my experiences as a graduate student living and conducting research in Johannesburg, South Africa, the piece uses performance both as a way of knowing and as a way of showing. It can be understood, on the one hand, as a critical record of "fieldwork"; on the other, it is a performative analysis of the contradictions of this "field" itself, analyzing not only the contradictions that shape the context through which "field research" is produced, but the contradictions through which the field, in turn, produces the researcher.*

In staging it, I chose to avoid natural realism and employed a hyperrepresentational style. For example, the Scholar begins by saying, "Backstage, the Scholar" and then her lines. During performances, I lectured almost all of the Scholar's lines from a podium, whereas the Player's voices were acted out. The Poet's words were always accompanied with movement, typically from the Katherine Dunham Technique.

(Backstage)

Scholar: I am prepared to lecture. We don't need your micro-conflicts *cum* anecdotes acted out. I would simply like to read my lecture and entertain thoughtfully conceived questions. Or perhaps an e-mail or two.

Player: You're not getting out of this, Scholar. You go, we go. Somebody's got to tell the truth.

Scholar: Truth? Be serious. No one makes a Truth claim anymore.

Poet: I am a Sister Outsider here. Inside Blackness and outside African-ness simultaneously. My secret is my secret.

Scholar: Would you please stop stretching and gyrating? Now James Clifford and Dwight Conquergood have already shown, quite convincingly, that identity is performed, processual, dynamic, and unfinished. Why do you insist on exposing me, this Body, to scrutiny? Is it not what I say rather than who I am that is most salient?

Player: Now who's clutching for straws? You only saw what this Body could see, what people let this Body see.

Poet: I am Sister Outsider here. Inside Blackness, outside African-ness simultaneously. If I say nothing I will belong.

Player: If I hadn't insisted on performing, would you ever have given these small incidents any further thought? Representing them here in the U.S., in the university, before a panel of your peers?

Scholar: Exactly, how can we possibly represent the accumulated experiences of fourteen months in twenty minutes? This is a flawed project, destined to falter.

Player: This project has forced us all to consider how this Black Body negotiated space in South Africa, a differently racialized and color-conscious country.

Scholar: Well, we could say a lot more if I lectured for, say, twenty-five minutes. Then the Poet could do a poem. That would be a nice combination.

Poet: I am a Sister Outsider here. Inside Blackness and outside African-ness simultaneously. My secret is my secret. If I say nothing, I will belong.

Scholar: I don't want to stretch. Will you stop doing that?

Player: If you just lecture, this Black Body would disappear in theories of identity performance.
Onstage!

(Onstage)
The Poet

> I am a Sister Outsider
> here inside
> Blackness and outside African-ness
> simultaneously.
> If only I can avoid speaking
> my secret is my secret.
> I harbor it tightly to my chest.
> Lips pursed.
> Resolute in my silence.
> If I say nothing,
> I will belong.

The Player

Outsider: No. No way. I'm not going back.

Sister: We just need a little . . .

Outsider: No. We've done that before. There's already a beginning.

Sister: We don't have a beginning.

Outsider: Well, that's just the point. Beginnings are false. Con-
structs!

Sister: You're just scared to go back.

Outsider: Yes, I'm scared to go back. And, if you were me, you'd be scared
too.

Sister: But I am you.

Outsider: No, you're not. You're some . . . thing else. I go back. I get hurt.
And you, where will you be?

Sister: I'll be there.

Outsider: Why do you want to go back? Wouldn't you rather hang out
with me in another ten years when my shit is together?

Sister: What exactly is you running to, girl? You think home is out there
ahead of you?

Outsider: Yes! In Africa. My new beginning as an African.

Sister: African American.

Outsider: No. African period. As in Cleopatra, Nefertiti, Nzingha, Mandela . . .

Sister: No, African American as in Ida B. Wells. Billie Holiday, Sarah Vaughn, Yo Mama.

Outsider: I'm ignoring you.

Sister: Yo Mama.

Outsider: You're just trying to get me back there and . . .

Sister: How do you know she's not sitting in the audience right now?

Outsider: Stop!

Sister: Where?

The Scholar

Let us begin by titling this afternoon's presentation "Contradictions in Black Identities in Johannesburg: This Black Body in Question." Now that we have a suitable frame, let us proceed. Amanda Denise Kemp, social security number 8460852, U.S. national, recorded as negro (little *n*) at birth arrived in Johannesburg, South Africa, on the direct flight from New York at 4:30 P.M. local time.

The Beginning. Let us not delay and arrive at the beginning. On June 9, 1993, the Black Body in Question arrived at the beginning of a year-and-a-quarter stay in South Africa. Footnote: Of course, this is not the beginning of African American travel and exchange with South Africans. As early as the mid-eighteenth century African American sailors had landed at Cape Town. Moreover, the African Methodist Episcopal Church began its mission work in South Africa at the request of Black South Africans toward the end of the nineteenth century. The Virginia Jubilee singers began touring the country as early as 1890. However, by the end of World War I, South African officials generally kept a tight rein on visiting "American negroes." Even Ralph Bunche, a distinguished academic with all the right credentials—including a letter from Melville Herskovits—had difficulty getting permission to enter the country. Bunche ultimately had to promise not to speak, that is, avoid public speeches, and stick to science as his grant from the Social Science Research Council indicated.

The Beginning. The beginning is actually a journey, is it not? One has to choose where to start. Where? Is it a location, a flow, a time, a space? Paul Gilroy recommends that we shift from understanding space based on notions of fixity and place to understanding a space that is really flow.

Today's presentation re-presents a flow, the problematic space of Blackness from here to there. The methodology is quite simply this Black Body in Question. This Body's meaning in South Africa and the meaning it tried to grasp and project through language, silence, and rage. Blackness as a space and Blackness moving through space.

The Player

(Jan Smuts Airport, June 9, 1993)

Voice Over: Ladies and gentlemen, SAA flight #181 from New York has just arrived. *Dames and . . .* (*in Afrikaans*)

Outsider: I should have known there would be trouble when my arrival at Jan Smuts deeply stirred two Afrikaaner ladies. They had seen the sign "Welcome Amanda Kemp" and expected their heroine.

Sister: Imagine their surprise when an African American, darker than most South Africans with nappy hair and West African jewelry, appeared. Smiling widely.

Outsider: "I'm Amanda."

The Scholar

The Black Body in Question, Amanda Denise Kemp, passport number 861451964, U.S. national, recorded as negro (little *n*) at birth destabilizes social categories as soon as she arrives. "How did you get your name?" Apparently, Amanda Kemp is a common Afrikaans name, both Amanda and Kemp. On a number of occasions, she is asked which language she prefers: English or Afrikaans—this is by telephone, of course. When she indicates she is African American, invariably the response is, "Where did you get your name?" What's in a name? Quite simply, history.

Aspirations are embedded in a name. James Ngugi resurrected N'gūgī wa Thiong'o in a journey toward decolonization. Similarly, many Black South Africans have rejected their "Christian" names. One consultant told me that he had to "work hard to get rid of that name." Recently Ngugi recommended to an audience of African Americans at a Black literature conference to consider changing their names in order to give some indication of their Africanity.

But the very question of how/where did you get your name is a question of origins. Where does Amanda Kemp come from? It is amazing, but in South Africa the small detail of the Atlantic slave trade or slave raiding in the interior and trading at nearby Delgoa Bay is a blur. Thus, claiming and creating "African" names is a way to re-member that history prior to the sixteenth and seventeenth centuries respectively, for Black people on both sides of the Atlantic. Simultaneously, claiming Amanda Kemp as an African American name invades and destabilizes whiteness. In fact, in South Africa the name Amanda Kemp attached to the Black Body in Question went to the heart of Afrikaanerdom. "Are your parents from South Africa? Have you traced your roots?" In other words, "Are you one of our niggers?" as one consultant translated.

The Black Body in Question, Amanda Denise Kemp, American national, born negro with a little *n*, passport number Z7045196, was stopped at the airport.

"Where are you from?"

"New York."

"Are you South African?"

"No."

My passport clearly states that I was born in Mississippi and am a national of the U.S. However, something's not quite right. No matter. I'm used to it. Something was not quite right about me in a Korean grocery in New York. Something was not quite right about an African American riding a bike at night on Northwestern's campus. I'm used to being an alien, a transgressor of expectations and spaces.

Back to the beginning.

The Player

(Hotel suite, Braamfontein Protea Hotel, June 9, 1993)
Porter: What is your mother tongue?
Outsider: Embarrassed, I say, "English."
Porter: NO!
Sister: The porter laughs at our misunderstanding.
Porter: What language do you speak at home with your family?
Outsider: Should I say Black English? I read a book about the distinctions between standard American English and Black English.

Sister: You've already paused too long.

Outsider: "English," I say a little sadly, and offer the coins. "English."

Sister: The porter exits. I told you.

Outsider: Don't start. (*She is unpacking*)

Sister: Do you speak your mother's English?

Outsider: I don't know. Probably not. I'm always speaking the wrong language.

The Scholar

The porter's name was Russell. Soon after, the Body in Question resolves to learn Zulu. At the first class all participants are assigned Zulu names.

In South Africa, language often collapses into ethnic groupings. The Zulus speak Zulu. The Xhosa speak Xhosa. The Pedi speak Pedi. The English speak English. The Afrikaaners speak Afrikaans. Colonialism attempted to cement differences among Africans into fixed, stable categories. However, Africans are clearly multilingual. Moreover, so-called tribal identities were often consciously formed alliances between various clans to protect themselves from attack by stronger forces. Here I am thinking of the Zulus and Sothos, in particular. Thus, these groupings are historically conditioned and not absolute givens.

Nonetheless, language is a social marker. African languages indicate Blackness. Afrikaans and English indicate whiteness. Here I must also add that Afrikaans also marks off Colored. The soup thickens. As soon as one categorizes one must start listing exceptions. (*Cough, cough*)

Let us return to the Black Body in Question as a source of knowledge. The Black Body in Question needed an African language to assure herself of a home category in South Africa. Learning Zulu was my attempt to "pass," to be a part of Blackness. You see while this Body be's Black, without a "mother tongue" it is what Afro-American literature critics will know as the tragic mulatto. That is, too white for the Blacks and too Black for the whites. The Body in Question quickly perceives that three centuries and two score years of colonialism aside, Blackness is a performance.

Ralph Ellison's *Invisible Man* begins with a sermon on the fluidity of Blackness:

"Brothers and sisters, my text this morning is the 'Black of Blackness' " And a congregation of voices answered: "That blackness is most black, brother, most black . . ."
"In the beginning . . ."
"At the very start," they cried.
"There was blackness . . ."
"Preach it . . ."
"and the sun . . ."
"The sun, Lawd . . ."
"was bloody red . . ."
"Red . . ."
"Now black is . . ." the preacher shouted.
"Bloody . . ."
"I said black is . . ."
"Preach it brother . . ."
". . . an' black ain't . . ." (9–10)

Ellison points out that temporal, slippery coast of Blackness that is and at the same time ain't. It is invented. And the codes of it vary from context to context.

So "passing." The Body in Question attempted to pass into Blackness by learning Zulu and shutting up. She is very effective at greetings: "Sawobona. Yebo. Kunjani? Ngikona wena unjani?" She smiles and nods. And nods and smiles until the would-be conversationalist looks at her oddly. Yes, a nod is not an appropriate response to "How long did it take to plait your hair?" She must confess.

The Poet

> *Ngibuya phesheya Amelika.*
> I come from America
> *Angazi okuningi ogwamanje*
> I don't know very much yet.
> *(This is repeated faster and faster until the English falls away and all that is left is . . .)*
> *Ngibuya phesheya Amelika*

The Player

(Book fair at the Market Theatre Precinct, October 1993)

Guard: The security guard eyes me with hostility. A Black woman alone in the Market Precinct, looking at books. Who does she think she is?

Outsider: I consider my strategy: to completely ignore or to go for defusing that pain. "Sawobona, buti." He grabs my arm and speaks. I look at him, shaking my head. "I don't understand."

Guard: "What language do you speak?"

Outsider: "English," I say, pulling loose and moving to the *feminist* book table.

Guard: He follows, stands too close behind me. "You are Black like me. You must speak an African language."

Outsider: I feel the slightly drunken antagonism in his voice. Yes. Black like him. Shall I say, "Listen, most Black people in the world don't speak Zulu or Pedi or Xhosa. We speak French, Spanish, Portuguese. Millions and millions of us lost our languages." Or I could say, "Fuck off." Not happy with either of these, I choose to move to the next table.

Guard: He follows. Now she's really bait. "Where do you stay? I want to come visit you."

Outsider: I try joking. Laughing loudly, I say, "My husband wouldn't like that!"

Guard: "I'm not scared of your husband. I've got a gun." He grabs her by the waist and pulls her close. "I like your accent."

Outsider: "Get the fuck off me, motherfucker!" The two whites at the cashier stare in shock. Should they interfere? Is it a Black thing? Taking advantage of his surprise, I break loose, running to my rent-a-wreck. "This place is schizophrenic. That motherfucker hated me and loved me at the same time because of my fucking accent. Fuck English. That's right, I'm not saying another word in English. I wish I coulda cursed him out in Zulu. I am your sister, motherfucker, your sister!"

The Scholar

English, like a BMW, is aspirational in South Africa. It is not the home language of the huge majority of the population; nor is it in fact the home language of the majority of the white population. Afrikaans is the home language of the majority of whites. Nonetheless, English is the most empowered language in South Africa. One can trace this to the preeminence of English speakers in business, international trade, the desire for acceptance into the international community, as well as the identification of Afrikaans with apartheid. English literacy initiatives predominate among adults and children. The National Education Policy Initiative report *Language* noted that "parents, learners, and some teachers often seem to believe that English has an almost magical power: 'If you know English well, desired things will follow.' The belief may be well predicated on its truer obverse: 'Not knowing English will keep many desirable things out of your reach' " (18).

The Player

(Zulu class number 10)
Outsider: Ngithanda ukwazi kabanzi ngomsantsi Africa.
Sister: Clumsy, lazy tongue. Practice those clicks.
Outsider: Xhosa, cha, Ngqawana.
Sister: Even children speak better than you. You'll never speak it right. You can't even hear the difference. *Ngithanda ukwazi kabanzi ngomsantsi Africa.* Smooth. Try again.
Outsider: No.
Sister: Try again.
Outsider: I can't try again.
Sister: Here you are in somebody else's country and don't have the decency to speak one of their languages. You want everybody to speak English?
Outsider: I don't just speak English. I speak Spanish.
Sister: Imperialist bastards, capitalist dogs, guns to Rhodesia, assassination of Lumumba, isolation of Cuba. Who gave them the right to rule the world? That's what it is, isn't it? You and the whole goddamned United States want the rest of the world to meet you on your terms. Read, write, think, make love in your goddamned terms. Fuck English.
Outsider: Fuck you.
Sister: Fuck you.
Outsider: Fuck you.

Sister: Fuck you.

Outsider: FUCK YOU.

Sister: Just cut the bullshit, Nefertiti.

Outsider: You cut the bullshit. You're supposed to be guiding me, not driving me crazy.

Sister: WRONG. I'm the voice of truth in the crowded dank space you call a mind. And till you're ready to deal with the truth, not this half-hearted, let me go back to Africa to belong bullshit, you are crazy.

Outsider: So you want the truth. I'm an Outsider here and an Outsider there. You want a little more? I don't understand people here even when they speak English. I keep correcting their accents in my mind. I don't know why they can't be direct. These people are too damned polite. And another thing. What's up with this men and women staying in different rooms at a party or on different sides of the same room? Why are African women sneaking cigarettes in bathrooms? And who am I to criticize anything? Who am I?

Sister: Why should anything be any less complicated because you're in Africa?

Outsider: I just wanna be a sister, that's all.

The Scholar

This Black Body in Question, Amanda Denise Kemp, American national, born negro (with a little *n*), passport number 861445196, did not fit into the existing categories. The Black Body in Question destabilized the salient categories in South Africa because they conflate race, nationality, and culture. Thus, this racially Black Body should have been African and a competent practitioner of African culture as indicated by local language facility. There was something disconsonant about American-accented English and Black skin because English is associated with progress, development, affluence, intelligence, and civilization, and Black, especially this dark Black Body in Question, is primitive, poor, illiterate, backward, slow, and stupid. Generally speaking, each racial grouping accommodated my presence in different ways: Afrikaaners tried to place me as one of "their niggers" because of my name. There are Coloreds darker than me. English-speaking whites declared me American, presuming that I had nothing in common with local Blacks and was completely outside their world. Africans demanded that I "get down" and speak one of "our languages."

The problem with Afrikaaner and African responses is that they don't appreciate Blackness as distinct from national boundaries and culture. Blackness is not African-ness. The problem with the English response is that it presumes no connection between Africans and me because I'm from a different nation, a first world nation at that. However, as Gilroy argues, Africans in the diaspora have to be understood both in terms of their current national contexts and within international circulations.

> An intricate web of cultural and political connections binds blacks here to blacks elsewhere. At the same time, they [Blacks in Britain] are linked into the social relations of this country [Britain]. Both dimensions have to be examined and the contradictions and continuities which exist between them must be brought out. (156)

> Analysis of black politics must, therefore, if it is to be adequate, move beyond the field of inquiry designated by concepts which deny the possibility of common themes, motives and practices with diaspora history. . . . To put it another way, national units are not the most appropriate basis for studying this history for the African diaspora's consciousness of itself has been defined in and against constricting national boundaries. (158)

South African liberation struggles have become part of the imagery and fuel of emancipatory struggles throughout the Black world. One need only look at the paraphernalia accompanying Mandela's visit to the U.S. in 1990. One very popular T-shirt bore the script, "Malcolm, Martin, Mandela and ME." I am suggesting there is a Black world, a space in which there are conversations, dialogues, adaptations, disputes, and conflicts across national and continental divides, where Blackness is constituted. The consumption of kente cloth or Mano Dibango or Salif Keita in Salvador, Bahia; Harlem, New York; or Kingston, Jamaica, is the constituting of Blackness. Blackness is a transnational space possible only because of global capital, attendant technology, and transnational discourses such as race and white supremacy. In other words, Whoopi Goldberg may be American, but she is indisputably Black and South Africans are using her to constitute Blackness.

The Black Body in Question spent the first six months of her stay trying to pass because the local categories did not accommodate her. However, about midway through her stay, she settled into a web of social relationships with individuals who allowed for the space of Blackness alongside Africans. These tended to be Africans who had lived outside South Africa for a considerable amount of time or those who consciously consumed and invented transnational Blackness. Africans from other parts of the continent, Black Britons, and other African Americans rounded out this social network. She lived in a flow, where her English changed slowly to include expressions, inflections, and pronunciations of local peoples. I conclude with Ellison's sermon.

> "Now Black is . . ." the preacher shouted.
> "Bloody . . ."
> "I said black is . . ."
> "Preach it brother . . ."
> ". . . an black ain't . . ."
> "Red, Lawd, red: He said it's red!"
> "Amen . . ."
> "Black will git you."
> "Yes it will."
> ". . . an black won't . . ."
> "Naw it won't!"
> "It do . . ."
> "It do, Lawd . . ."
> ". . . an' it don't."
> "Hallelujah . . ."
> ". . . It'll put you, glory, glory, oh my Lawd, in the WHALE'S BELLY."
> "Preach it, dear brother . . ."
> ". . . an' make you tempt . . ."
> "Good God a-mighty!"
> "Old Aunt Nelly!"
> "Black will make you . . ."
> "Black is . . ."
> ". . . or black will un-make you." (13)

WORKS CITED

Special thanks to the "Performing the African Diaspora" seminar, Catherine Cole, Douglas Anthony, and Amakhosikazi Productions.
Ellison, Ralph. *The Invisible Man*. New York: Signet/New American Library, 1947.

Gilroy, Paul. *'There Ain't No Black in the Union Jack': The Cultural Politics of Race and Nation.* Chicago: University of Chicago Press, 1987.

Kemp, Amanda. *Sister Outsider: Journal Notes of an African American in South Africa.* Performed at the Johannesburg Arts Alive Festival, September 17, 1994.

National Education Policy Initiative (South Africa). *Language.* London: Oxford University Press, 1992.

Fig. 8.1. Mady Schutzman, *Hysterical Excess*. Reproduced by permission of Mady Schutzman.

EIGHT

A Fool's Discourse: The

Buffoonery Syndrome

Mady Schutzman

HYSTERICAL EXCESS

My body is sprawled out on a chaise longue. I wear a white suit shirt and brightly patterned tie overlaid with a skintight laced corset. Puffy black pantaloons extend from untucked shirttails to just beyond the knees, where they blend smoothly, elegantly, into black hose and high heels. I appear fashionably smart. My face is painted thickly with rouge, lipstick, and mascara. Occasionally, I try unsuccessfully to lift myself from the divan. My performance of feigned indifference alternates with outbursts of panic.

After a century of neurasthenia, fainting, and "the vapors," it is widely known that the predominant "new" female malady in the late nineteenth century was hysteria. But perhaps less well known is that Jean Martin Charcot, the French neurologist who defined hysteria and charted its "phases" in photographic tableaux, named the second phase of hysteria "the phase of clownism," or the buffoonery syndrome.[1] It was characterized by a series of protracted movements and grand gestures that closely resemble the gestures of heightened exhilaration displayed in today's popular fashion advertising. A woman so delighted by her hose is literally lifted off her feet into an impossible posture of glee; another dons her polka dots and blows her tuba in the streets in tribute to her newfound soft drink. Irrepressible joy and ecstatic uprisings erupt constantly over new fragrances. Women perform sheer energy, broadcasting the infinite potential to be preposterous and making a bizarre and yet enticing show of the violation of the female image. In corporeal expletives and exclamations, the hysteric (of both medical science and contemporary advertising) embodies the gender disorders of the social body and simultaneously screams her distress. Her excessive visual presence both disguises and disclaims her assigned absence within the social sphere. Put yet another way, in her overstated assumption of the mask of femininity, she indicts the very power politics that her body economy suffers. She plays the clown.

While much has been written about hysteria and feminism,[2] I am interested here in understanding the appeal of its theatrical visualization. Why and how did hysteria—as a visual spectacle—become a way to both critique cultural definitions of femininity and advertise the clownish masquerade of identity itself? In particular, how does buffoonery, or a fool's discourse, provide an analytic for reviewing the radical potential of spectacular hyperfemininity?

Avner the Eccentric steps onto the Palace stage of Hollywood's renowned Magic Castle. He and I perform a series of vignettes: (1) Effortlessly, Avner throws himself into a perfectly balanced handstand. Then, slowly, he raises one hand from the ground, bending at the elbow. He gently leans into the elbow, miming firm support beneath. He remains absolutely poised. But when he looks down and notices that his elbow is leaning only on thin air, he panics, he collapses, suddenly prey to the illusion of his own making. The interdependence between control and magic is heightened. (2) With exceptional zest, I kick and kick the one who has double-crossed me. I grow frantic in my failure to effect his downfall, to make him confess, to get him to treat me better. I kick harder and harder until the effort of my inane vehemence results in complete exhaustion and a terrible pain in my foot. The relation between rage and self-torment is aggravated. (3) Avner rubs a smudge on his nose, then off his nose onto his suspenders, from suspenders to shirt, to trousers, shoes, stage curtain, tablecloth, traveling across every article on the stage until it returns to his suspenders, which he then uses to rub his nose. The causal relation between process and end is humiliated. (4) With my right hand I attempt to grab my memory, which is situated atop a huge book that my left hand raises higher and higher, the memory remaining always just out of reach of the desire that grasps for it.

Charcot's female patients performed their hysterical attacks for the medical community of Paris in Charcot's hospital amphitheatre. Charcot had, in essence, created the "living pathological museum" (Charcot's term). His "leading ladies," whom Sarah Bernhardt studied and mimicked in preparation for her tragic melodramas, were praised for being sublime comediennes. While the broad visual ploys of the hysteric were perceived, even cherished, at that time as evidence of her innate disorder, the same swollen language signifies how both hysteric and clown magnify and slander our concept of the ordinary. For instance, both exercise a curious belabored gait that comments on the meaning of ground, of support: astasia-abasia (the "hysterical gait") is a walk in which the patient appears to be *trying* to fall. She performs it only when she knows she is being observed; her deliberate performance of instability is as much a commentary on her condition as it is the condition itself. The clown's gait is characterized by an oscillation from side to side, or back to forward, as if he is never quite balanced over his feet. He stands for detachment and for a desire to be present in all places at once.

In both the hysteric's and the clown's acts, "standing firmly on one's own feet" is recoded as a questionable, if not undesirable, habit. To stand firmly would be to acquiesce to a stature stipulated by a social gaze that is both overdetermined and hostile. To falter is to take another ideological position or "standing," one that is hopeful in its deliberate unsteadiness. It performs the very thing it speaks, which is that hysteric and fool are either appointed as someone else's spectacle or charged to make a spectacle of themselves. The performance of instability and disorder implies both an immersion into and a critique of the spectacle of ambivalence to which they are socially mandated.

MEMORY

I am plagued by an image of myself from another time. A portrait of myself drawn twenty-five years ago by Celoius, an African American recluse artist and astrologer living on Magnolia Ridge four miles off the continental divide in the Colorado Rockies. It is a picture of a solemn, ethereal, androgynous, cross-legged being adorned from head to toe in traditional clown regalia. It struck me as grotesque back then in 1970; all I saw was an outlandish fool in ill-fitting and splashy costume, a misfit, a joke. I took it as a frightening reflection of my concurrent and self-imposed status as a cultural outlaw in the repellent late Nixon era. Did my hip activism render me such a flagrant, repellent oaf? Were my attempts at transgression reducible to a simplistic spectacle of inappropriateness? I quickly rejected this unromantic clod, this lump of absurdity that would only provide others with amusement and detached contempt. But in spite of my evident shame, the image suggested something dignified, discerning. I cherished it, albeit in some unspeakable place, for it invoked a self that was part of me but did not belong to me. A character who shamelessly crossed purposes with the hero. I liked it. And so with great ambivalence I laminated the image on a half inch board and kept it.

Fig. 8.2. Mady Schutzman, *Memory*. Reproduced by permission of Mady Schutzman.

The very nature of spectacle makes "a spectacle of inappropriateness" oxymoronic. Spectacle itself is an act of self-mockery, a replacing of subjectivity with something so grand, so oversignified, as to suggest hypersubjectivity. In its grandiosity it escapes the indignity of sliding signification; it pronounces itself full, meaningful unto itself. But at the same time, it demonstrates its power—if not panic—to arrest that slide, aware that beneath its apparent plethora lies evidence of its deficiency. A spectacle of inappropriateness is always an appropriate spectacle; it captures the very paradox of spectacle making. It is almost sacred, as whores often are, and holy fools.

Celoius wanders like a nomad through my memory, an anomaly in tie-dyed shirt, bell-bottom jeans, and sandals. He carries a hard wooden stool, which he occasionally sets down and then sits upon. He sits quietly and smiles. Occasionally, he laughs uproariously at one of the lines I recite. This is very disconcerting.

I grew up in a family of frustrated Borscht-belt stand-up comics. Consequently, I suffer a joke-phobia; I am stuck in my inability to deal with jokes meaningfully. Should someone innocently but publicly declare, "Wanna hear a joke?" I freeze before a word is uttered, terrified that I will miss the seemingly obvious moment of recognition and laughter, that I won't get it, that someone will undoubtedly turn to me and ask me to explain the joke's essence, that I will be disgraced by my ignorance and naïveté. In my phobia, I am the potential brunt of every joke I hear.

Outside my phobia, what captivates me in the face of a joke is that something nonsensical is brought to my attention but yet never fully disclosed. There is always that bit of sense one cannot get at. That is masked. The word "mask" comes from the Arabic word *maskharat,* meaning clown or buffoon. And the word "buffoon" means "to puff." The fool represents the elusive puffery or mask that disguises what we call sense in such a way as to make us distrust it. That is, through the fool we awaken to the sense of having been taken, once again. The fool's non-sense reveals common sense to be just another spectacle that has been determined without us, that speaks for us, just as the body speaks the hysteric. This awakening situates us far off the stage upon which we normally play, it stretches us outside the actions of our lives with the tendency not to focus, but to dissolve circumstance, to make circumstance irrelevant.

I am lured by the invitation to be abundant where usually I am not—to multiply into an expanse where self-consciousness is a lie, a myth. The *becoming* of a fool implies the abandonment of any consciousness of *being* one. The paradox cautions me: in order to be liberated from the powers that speak for me, I must become all they bid me to be. I become the joke that torments me; I am the phobia incarnate. I assume the only body I have; I embrace the absurd spectacle I am primed to resist. And in foolish abandon—in becoming the mask itself—I get a glimpse of what lurks behind it. Vaguely, and with terror, I sense a knowledge that humbles the seeming wisdom of self-consciousness.

ANIMAL ACTS AND BALANCING ACTS

Images of female clownery are often combined with animals in advertisements. Women and animals are represented as cohabitants of similar symbolic space—a kind of amorous disciplinary laboratory in obedience, tricks, and often bizarre balancing acts. A woman balances a shoe on her head while kissing a chimpanzee. Another woman dressed in a leopard print bathing suit tidies the leopard-motif upholstery and curtains that adorn her home. Women and animals are seemingly trapped in a place of endless misrecognition where they cannot gain access to symbolic space or to a re-cognition that proffers verification in a discourse of power. Women of ads remain quite literally hypnotized by the mirror, and subject, like animals, to subjugation—a "trained act."

The live performances of hypnotized hysterics at the end of the nineteenth century featured displays of unseemly if not grotesque conduct, indicating the malleable and humorous nature of the patients. Interestingly, they often involved the assumption of animal behavior. Discussing one of these scenes, Showalter describes female puppets exhibiting the imaginations of their medical puppeteers:

> Some of them smelt with delight a bottle of ammonia when told it was rose water, others would eat a piece of charcoal when presented to them as chocolate. Another would crawl on all fours on the floor, barking furiously when told she was a dog, flap her arms as if trying to fly when turned into a pigeon, lift her skirts with a shriek of terror when a glove was thrown at her feet with a suggestion of being a snake.[3]

Avner the Eccentric, like his hysterical cousin of one hundred years ago, prances around on a broomstick-horse, shoves a huge plateful of folded white napkins into his already engorged mouth, uses a peacock feather to metamorphose into a bird, then a seal doing tricks, then a donkey. Like a rhinoceros, he squirts water out of his mouth in wide arcs across the audience. I find I am observing a

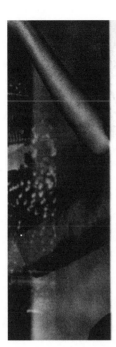

Fig. 8.3. Mady Schutzman, *Animal Arts and Balancing Acts.* Reproduced by permission of Mady Schutzman.

domesticated creature that doesn't experience any embarrassment for the animal-istic proclivities of his play. Avner exhibits an incapacity to act in accordance with social conventions, and so he experiences no guilt or shame. Those of us observing all agree through our laughter that his childishness is delightful, any offense to be taken is no more than that of witnessing an overexcited puppy unwittingly wetting the floor. I think of the actor playing Avner with a certain envy. I come to take a visceral pleasure, perhaps even a critical fancy, in his witless power to violate bounds of many kinds.

Deleuze and Guattari's concept of masochism infers the process of "be-coming-animal."[4] A deal is made wherein one's submission and contrac-tual subjugation release one from the constraints of the law; lawless ecstasy results from the performance of one's humiliation. An even more radical potential may be discovered in the possibilities of subversion during a so-called command performance. Within such a performance abides a kind of "play" that cannot satisfy the romance of resistance; being authorized by the very powers that one desires to denounce, revolutionary expectations give way to something less insolent, more complex, something freed from the burdens of purposefulness. In being resigned (re-signed), this "play" of subjugation becomes "sheer play"; it vibrates with gratuitous and full-bodied immersion in the humiliation. In the abdication of hope (but not of vitality) comes a riotous show of inappropriateness. As feminists we should not ignore the lure of indifference, of de-criticalized subjectivity, as a stance for insubordinate action.

PRECARIOUSNESS

I am suspicious of the angry woman. I am weary of the discourse of female pretense as power when delivered in progressively verbose waves of new feminisms. I'm bored with futile attempts to redeem vapid, anti-committal, postmodern ambiguity and obscurity from its entertaining but safe epistemological theories. Instead, I let precariousness and speculation riddle my body. I fly through the air in impossible postures, hang precipitously over empty space from my knees, then from my teeth. I dubiously brace myself within unstable assemblages of bodies. I walk the spiked pickets of a white picket fence. Perhaps I've surrendered myself to the empty superlatives of popular entertainment, but my own fleshy and exhilarated presence is undeniable. I disappear into the spectacle of power, power as excess, I stop resisting the spectacle of inappropriateness to which I am assigned, I indulge the dignity of inappropriateness, and in this disappearance I am shamelessly full. In embodying spectacle I assume presence, and this presence, even if marked lacking, adds subjectivity to that which is thought to be without it. I give subjectivity to the very spectacle that erases me. I am a radical femme, a female hysteric, a clown. I am acquiring my own untenable gait and I am enjoying it. This is possible only if I ignore the necessity of being a substantial person. Only if I dare for once to move before exhaustively consulting theory, method, and context. Only if I remain silent and overcome the premature urge to give positive expression to the unutterable. At least for this brief moment, the inevitable glut of analysis and self-indulgence is postponed. And I realize pleasure.

But finally, I feel ridiculous and I can't sustain the effort. I fear that my abandon to spectacle will betray me, appear as complicity with the very power structure I despise. Presence for the feminist critic is a dance with phobia.

Fig. 8.4. Mady Schutzman, *Precariousness*. Reproduced by permission of Mady Schutzman.

Fig. 8.5. Mady Schutzman, *Double*. Reproduced by permission of Mady Schutzman.

1st clown: I wish I were two puppies.
2nd clown: Why?
1st clown: So I could play together.

In my mind I carry an image of myself with whom I speak. It resembles the clown's bauble capped with an emblematic replica of himself. My interior bauble never reflects me accurately, so we often pass time in verbal battle. I give the bauble voice, whomever I chose, usually someone who pretends to be the epitome of authority and righteousness. It tries to make a fool of me, like the ventriloquist makes a fool of his dummy. Occasionally I use the bauble to beat on others and to play unexpected tricks, some quite aggressive and obscene. In this way I get my revenge, I make a fool of the bauble. But if I forget my bauble I run the risk of forgetting myself as a contrived composite of disproportions and incongruities, of well-managed ideals and fantasies. I run the risk of assuming that my identity is my own and slipping hopelessly into the turmoil of deluded self-propriety.

I enter from the audience and sit beside myself onstage. I disagree with everything I say. I do the opposite of everything I do. When I win a fight, I mourn my losses; when I lose, I celebrate the victory. This mating dance is never ending and insuperable. I depend on it.

In buffoonery the divided self is performed in a very blatant way in the realm of gender identification. This is illustrated in an entree by the English clown Billy Hayden. Yakking from the back of a donkey, Billy bemoans his ambivalent gender status: "I, too, was once a pretty young lady. A witch came by with an ugly little boy. She took me, the pretty little girl, out of the perambulator, and she put in my place the ugly little boy, and ever since then I've been an ugly little boy."[5] The clown enacts his longing to be the female he was once by dressing in women's clothing. Similarly, in the Marx Brothers' film *A Night at the Opera,* Harpo is caught wearing the clown costume of a pompous opera singer. Outraged, the opera singer orders Harpo to take it off. From beneath the clown outfit emerges the uniform of a naval officer, and from beneath that a woman's dress. The naval attire is supposedly Harpo's masquerade, but the woman beneath it is "real"—the unlayering goes no further. While her portrayal is as much a masquerade as that of the officer, she stands in as a fantasy (or memory) of woman anchored in the male imaginary, whether Harpo (the imaginer) is a "real" man or not.

If Billy and Harpo have anything going for them as far as yielding a cultural critique, it would be their refusal to perform the social roles designated to men. They abdicate heroism, authority, even language, and embrace the indeterminate. They declare with their very physical presence, "I don't know what I am, but I am not that (the stereotypical male)." In this way they mimic, and appropriate politically, the female hysteric "wh[o] become[s] phobic precisely through the law of her exclusion, the interdiction which defines her difference (You must not be *that*)."[6]

Another way the clown expresses his gender confusion is epitomized in the fool's story in *The Magic Flute*. Papageno is in desperate search of his female alter ego. When he finds a woman, he finds a double of himself, Papagena; he enters the encounter between man and woman, but at the same time circumvents it because aside from the difference of sex, she has no identity other than his. We see this relationship played over and over in the popular clown gag in which a clown dances with a large rag-doll woman whose feet are attached to his. The only life in her is what ripples through her from his movements. The notion of a manifestly female clown seems oxymoronic. We have apparently only male clowns seeking their lost female souls. The search for a lost femininity is really a search for that presence before the mirror stage, before the imaginary, before we were lost to ideality and image.[7] Women are portrayed as anarchic in a complex nostalgia for dis-integration that still cannot escape the demands of spectacle. Meanwhile, a hierarchical structure of gender is reproduced in which subjectivity and desire remain a function of masculinity.

Where do we find the gender confusion of the clown manifesting in a female body? In the female iconography of advertisements. Repeatedly, she affixes the raiments of typically male roles—she layers herself in his various social skins. Unlike Harpo and Billy, however, she frequently preserves her gender markings by visibly revealing her feminine undergarments (or entire lack thereof) beneath or over his suit. We see an assumption of male attire in hysterics as well: Augustine was sent to Charcot's hospital in 1875 because she said she did not know who she was when she looked into a mirror. After achieving the status of one of Charcot's most dramatically adept hysterics, she succeeded in escaping the hospital disguised as a man.

But there is another far more frequent form of gender transmutation that the mediated woman enacts. Paralleling Papageno's search for a female alter ego, the mediated woman also splits into self and male alter ego, but not by finding a male counterpart. Instead, she masquerades in garish hyperfeminized attire. She blatantly inscribes onto her body that which defines her culturally as feminine; she assumes the "drag" of her erotic fetishization. She absorbs the male imaginary into her appearance, blurring, rather than doubling, her self. Through this blurring, she visually performs an act of clownery. That is, she reveals that her identity is not her own; she embodies the male imaginary—the authoritative "nonfool," or bauble—that does not reflect her accurately. And like the clown, she makes a fool of the nonfool; she makes a fool of the male imaginary.

I am trying to find critical insight in the representation of the female body as hysteric and fool. I go to a production of *King Lear*. The fool and Cordelia never appear onstage at the same time. I am convinced that their roles are being played by the same actor. I never have to choose between the two, I am Cordelia, I am the fool, always at the same time. I am onstage and offstage always at once. I am seen and not seen simultaneously. In the final moments of Lear's madness and life, Cordelia and the fool merge in the king's imagination, and in their becoming one he realizes, as we have known all along, that they signify the only thing that should have mattered.

BIG TOP

The typical European circus of the nineteenth century was a one ring circus in which each act had the full attention of the audience. The European clown was a speaking clown; he captivated the attention of everyone in the bigtop. It was not until the latter part of the nineteenth century, when the American circus became three-ring entertainment, that the talking clown grew silent, incapable of being heard against the din of competing acts. He thus resorted to visual humor and broad sight gags to address his audience. It was at the same time that an epidemic of hysteria spread throughout Europe and the United States.

The circus tent may be seen as a parallel development to the grand industrial workspace, each a kind of monument to the insurgence of mass culture. And yet the circus, like carnival, seems to stand outside culture, a reminder of the maniacal by-products of cultural progress. The silent clown was its spokesperson, performing a metacultural text of inversions and improprieties within a world of increasingly robotic commands. He fails over and over within the dehumanizing climate of rapid-growth mass production. He refuses repetitive mechanicalness, he can't pull it off, can't manage the simplest of hand-eye coordinations as dictated by the laws of labor, efficiency, or discipline. He epitomizes not work but play, imprecision, waste, bedlam, clutter, and disassemblage. The clown as metasemioti-

Fig. 8.6. Mady Schutzman, *Big Top*. Reproduced by permission of Mady Schutzman.

cian is a product of modernity shrewdly using humor to wreak havoc on the site of modernity. He professionally counterfeits stupidity, he willfully appears a fool who has no capacity to exercise his will. This is his power, and in this way the circus clown ties capitalism to personal history.

The Doctor speaks convincingly. He articulates precisely the buried meaning of my show; he dissects and re-erects it in impressive discursive prose. I am overjoyed to be understood.

That is, the clown, in his masterful refusal of mastery, resembles capitalism's exploitation of its own subversion. The clown is his very own privatized and derealized spectacle, yielding to and yet always rebounding from the threat of annihilation. His "personal history as spectacle" inherently eludes the apocalyptic fate that inevitably razes those who embrace fully and narcissistically the orgy of mastery, or individualism; he *is* the apocalypse, or its infinite deferral. Similarly, capitalism is a simultaneous economy of privatization and derealization; it too remains spectacularly immune to revolution. Capitalism *is* the revolution, a dynamic of internal contradiction that therefore can never fall into a Marxist apocalypse. Capitalism—like the clown—is not *victim* to its contradictions, it *is* its contradictions!

I write down everything the Doctor says, occasionally throwing my head back in spasms of rapture and awe. I plagiarize, I use his terms, his idioms. I read them aloud as if they were my own. But as they fill my body, I confess that I do not always follow their drift. I do not necessarily trust their drift. The trap door is suddenly open beneath my feet, and looking down, I experience vertigo and nausea. I drift, it seems, into invalidity.

Within advertising, the grotesque language of the buffoonish female ties capitalism to hysteria. Here too the impossibilities and inversions abound. Women live inside barrels and bottles. They eat expensive jewelry and ingest toxic perfumes. They imitate coffee cups and waffle irons. They become cash registers, vacuum cleaners, and alarm clocks in spectacular and mocking gadget dances. They are product impersonators and commodity fetishes par excellence.

What is evident is that the clown in the circus, the female body in advertising, and the hysteric within the arena of medical science are mediums for commerce between the apparent and the hidden. The commodity *hides* the process of its production, the mediated female body *hides* the process of its production as hysterical, the clown's body *hides* its awareness of being produced at all. What is perhaps not as evident is how visual wit, exclamatory subtleties, and silent spectacles (and not simply spectacles of silence, not simply "pathological" symptoms of repression requiring a cure) manage to stage a viable critique. How are culture and gender shaped through laughter, jokes, and nonsense? How do simplicity and innocence comment on the complex and the corrupt? How does silence undo dominant narratives? How does image critique ideology?

I am still trying to find critical insight from the advertising of the female image as either hysteric or clown. I hesitate, thinking I will be taken for advocating some reactionary theory of the crude, the old trope of primitive impropriety combating the sophisticated and ambivalent structures of global politics. But what I see in these dramatically silent advertising images is something not at all crude or simple. The clown and hysteric, as culturally configured outcasts, visually reassemble thought so as to challenge its image of coherence, of order, of seamlessness. And in so doing they expose how bereft of vitality and meaning much of our thought is.

I begin to stutter as I speak, incapable of completing full thoughts. Phrases from different sentences commingle and upset the narrative. As words and meanings become more and more garbled, I engage my whole body in the struggle to reclaim sense and order.

The mass proliferation of images in contemporary culture has cast our semiotic universe into civil war. It is not only a war between word and imagery, within which scholars of popular culture perhaps most profoundly struggle. There is also a war between images themselves. More and more, appearances are everything. Their illogical juxtapositions make news, and subsequently provoke thought. My critical faculties sharpen as I become visually adept (not literate), as I skillfully splatter myself like paint onto the canvas of what I want to critique, as I cast my incongruous, conflicted parts into circulation as if I were not afflicted with the dictates of sanity. My critical faculties ebb when I hold these incongruous elements so close as to belabor their connections reasonably, when I speak only when I have made sense of them. It is in the face of this kind of positivist intelligence that my body rants, that the fool speaks, perhaps more wisely than we think.

I put my arm around Avner, who is standing onstage looking profoundly dejected.

He can't seem to sweep away the pool of light that he is standing in. I point up to the stage lights, hoping that I might relieve his frustration with an illuminating ray of common sense. He sees no connection between the glaring bulb above and the stain on the floor. The crowd laughs uproariously. I realize I have become his straight man, the agent of a reasonable world in which Avner has no voice. Avner remains unaware of a need for social identity, he seems disinterested in the articulate, sophisticated, rational other half I offer. He looks at me as if looking into a mirror, responding not with a sudden recognition of his self-lack, but rather with an amused self-sufficiency. He sees me as being part of himself, not as the other. The discrepancies between us don't upset him. They upset me. The hysterical diaspora slaps me in the face and I, playing the delegate of civility, rudely, but fortunately, awaken (again) to my own partiality.

NOTES

1. See D. M. Bourneville and P. Regnard, *Iconographie Photographique de la Salpêtrière,* Vol. 1 (Paris, 1877).

2. See Joan Copjec, "Flavit et Dissipati Sunt," *October* 18 (fall 1981): 22–40; Monique David-Ménard, *Hysteria from Freud to Lacan: Body and Language in Psychoanalysis,* trans. Catherine Porter (Ithaca: Cornell University Press, 1989); Elin Diamond, "Realism and Hysteria: Toward a Feminist Mimesis," *Discourse* 13.1 (fall–winter 1990–91): 59–92; Ludmilla Jordanova, *Sexual Visions: Images of Gender in Science and Medicine between the Eighteenth and Twentieth Centuries* (Madison: University of Wisconsin Press, 1989); Felicia McCarren, "The 'Symptomatic Act' Circa 1900: Hysteria, Hypnosis, Electricity, Dance," *Critical Inquiry* 21.4 (1995): 748; Elaine Showalter, *The Female Malady: Women, Madness and English Culture, 1830–1980* (New York: Pantheon, 1985); Caroll Smith-Rosenberg, "The Hysterical Woman: Sex Roles and Role Conflict in 19th Century America," *Social Research* 39.4 (spring 1972): 652–78.

3. Showalter, *The Female Malady,* 148.

4. Gilles Deleuze and Félix Guattari, "Becoming-Intense, Becoming-Animal, Becoming Imperceptible . . . ," in *A Thousand Plateaus: Capitalism and Schizophrenia,* trans. Brian Massumi (Minneapolis: University of Minnesota Press, 1987), 232–309. See also Gilles Deleuze, *Masochism: An Interpretation of Coldness and Cruelty,* trans. Jean McNeil (New York: Braziller, 1971).

5. William Willeford, *The Fool and His Scepter: A Study in Clowns and Jesters and Their Audiences* (Evanston, IL: Northwestern University Press, 1969), 180.

6. Peter Stallybrass and Allon White, "Bourgeois Hysteria and the Carnivalesque," in *The Politics and Poetics of Transgression* (Ithaca: Cornell University Press, 1986), 183.

7. For an in-depth understanding of the mirror stage, see Jacques Lacan, *Ecrits: A Selection,* trans. Alan Sheridan (New York: Norton, 1977); Anthony Wilden, "Lacan and the Discourse of the Other," in *The Language of the Self: The Function of Language in Psychoanalysis* (Baltimore: Johns Hopkins University Press, 1968), 159–311. For feminist interpretations, see Judith Butler, "Imitation and Gender Insubordination," in *Inside/Out: Lesbian Theories, Gay Theories,* ed. Diana Fuss (New York: Routledge, 1991), 13–31; Peggy Phelan, *Unmarked: The Politics of Performance* (London: Routledge, 1993); and Juliet Mitchell and Jacqueline Rose, *Feminine Sexuality: Jacques Lacan and the école freudienne,* trans. Jacqueline Rose (New York: Norton, 1985).

NINE

Spare Parts

Theresa M. Senft

That all our knowledge begins with experience
there can be no doubt.
                                    —Immanuel Kant

Like Willy Loman, my mother was worth more dead than alive. Death of a
Secretary. Propped up in bed at the Roswell Cancer Clinic, her head circled
in white gauze, she slowly explained to my brothers and me that nothing—not even death—would ever come between her and her children.
This was after the first brain surgery, when she still spoke in full sentences.
She had considered the investment options available to a struggling civil
servant from Buffalo, she told us. Then she decided to buy not one but
several large life insurance policies. She had wanted to surprise us with
the money, but my mother was always lousy at surprises. We used to have
to hide her birthday presents with the neighbors. Instead, she instructed
her children how to spend the cash we were to receive from her dead
body.

I recall my mother telling my brothers and me that we should buy
health insurance, because she couldn't live with the guilt that we had
somehow inherited her cancer. I don't remember much else of what she
said. In an attempt to save her life, the doctors installed a shunt in my
mother's brain. A shunt is a kind of straw that acts as a bridge for cerebral
spinal fluid. Only after the brain shunt treatment was under way did the
doctors admit that surgery, infection, and steroids have been known to
provoke "trauma" in the thinking patient. But not to worry, they told us.
There was medicine for that. Back then, while my mother held court
discussing what her death would mean, I considered it my job to collect
empirical details about her faltering life: evidence of fever, slurred speech,

leaking bandages. I know she wanted each of us to buy ourselves "a little something." I told her I wanted to buy a computer, a big new one. She was enthusiastic. "Get a lot of memory," she said to me, "because you will find you need it."

Do you know how Immanuel Kant's mother died? She was taking care of her best friend, who was ill. To persuade her friend to take medicine, Kant's mother first poured it into her spoon and drank it herself. She forgot, however, to clean the spoon off first. Kant's mother caught her friend's fatal disease, dying soon after. I've always been jealous of the way Kant made meaning out of a world that killed his mother. Sometimes I think that philosophy, and certainly what we call "life," is little more than making meaning from memories. Although Kant began his *Critique of Pure Reason* with the statement "all knowledge starts with experience" (1933: 41), he sure didn't think it ended there. Four hundred pages later, in the same document, Kant would write, "If appearances are things in themselves, then freedom cannot be saved" (466). For Kant, the thing that separated human life from animal existence was freedom. Ben-Ami Scharfstein summed it up this way:

> If there was no freedom, the world in which Kant's mother died helping a friend . . . could be ultimately the real world, and . . . no more than brute, intolerable facts. This possibility was made the more intolerable by Kant's knowledge that his parents' dignity, which he cherished as his inheritance from them, depended on their freedom to act as they thought morally right. (223)[1]

Kant inherited his parents' dignity, and used this inheritance to become a philosopher, thereby justifying his mother's sacrifice. I wish I had bought my computer for reasons as noble as those. Not that my mother would have minded the turn my life has taken. She liked technology, especially computers. She used them all day to process other people's words. The only time I remember my mother being technophobic was the morning she woke up in a sweat, announcing that she was not dying of brain cancer, but rather from the machines running her body. Dr. West, her neurosurgeon, thought she was referring to the IV lines that turned her skin purple each day, but she said no, she meant it all: the radiation, the IVs, the part-time ventilator, and the endless MRIs. They were killing her, she explained. Then she said the words: turn them off. No one listened to her, though. How could they? She was wrong.

"Between health and insanity lies hypochondria," Kant once wrote, and he should know. He himself once went as far as to suggest that his headaches were due to a special kind of electricity in the cloud systems—one that was also responsible for causing a cat epidemic in Vienna. Not wishing to join the ranks of the ill or the hypochondriac, I often ignore my own health. This morning I fell in my shower. The cause was a blinding pain at the base of my spine, running all the way down my leg. "Pinched sciatic nerve," my doctor tells me. "Rest, avoid stress, and stop sitting for hours at the damn computer." He realizes that this is about as useful as telling me not to think. Rationalizing that I will only check my mail, I decide sitting for a few minutes at the computer can't be all *that* bad. Besides, I am on deadline for Prodigy. Terrified that America Online now has the lion's share of new Internet users, Prodigy, the Internet provider once owned by Sears and IBM, is eager to carve a new image of itself. To do this, Prodigy executives have begun courting Net writers they view as "hip." Since this is the first time in my life someone has thought of me as on the cutting edge of anything, I don't want to dissuade them.

I was confused when Prodigy first approached me to pitch them stories about online life. I politely explained that I am really a Net enthusiast with an academic background in feminist theory. I'm not hip; I don't begin pieces with the word "dude." Nonetheless, the folks at Prodigy have always been polite and kind; they bought one story and then another from me, and finally they asked whether I had any ideas for an online column about life on the Internet. I think I know what it is they want to see, so I go for the complete sellout, telling them I will write something called "Baud Behavior." They like the title, and now want me to justify it. I scribble the following blurb on my pad:

> Baud Behavior takes its title seriously: baud refers to the speed at which data travels. Likewise, we'll take for granted that the Net is a series of rapidly changing social spaces requiring skill and finesse to navigate. More than anything, we'll discuss slipping in and out of online situations with grace, wonder, and a sense of humor. In short, rather than concentrating on being a good student of the Internet, we'll be the ones smoking in the bathrooms of cyberspace, asking you to skip school and join us.

I have no idea what any of this means, really, but I have about twenty minutes left on my deadline to e-mail it to Prodigy. I press the red button on the power strip that starts up my beautiful Power Macintosh, courtesy of the power of my mother's death. The fan whirs, and a scratching noise gives way to the soft, off-key chime of the hard drive booting up. I like to think about my computer this way, as the sum of its component parts: the CPU, the case, the RAM, the screen. Kant would have called this cataloguing the *phenomena:* the stuff we can see and touch. He far preferred the *noumena,* that which can't be sensed, but nonetheless exists, like gravity. I find phenomena comforting, myself. They make me feel more in control, reminding me of time spent cataloguing my mother's various parts for the doctors. I press my monitor's "on" button.

My eyes spill over a white surface, desktop, piece of paper, television light, operating lamp. The sunshine of my mother's nightmares. Kant had a thing about the color white. He used it to demonstrate noumena, teaching that there are some things people understand a priori, in other words, prior to understanding and analysis.[2] When a certain wavelength of light hits your retina, he argued, you see what is generally agreed upon as "white," regardless of who you are. Unless of course, you are blind. Remembering that Goethe once described reading Kant as "walking into a well-lighted room" (in Behler ix), I retreat into a light of my own as my monitor slowly floods with the stuff. I hate white. It reminds me of home and empty snow fields.

I am grateful that the white screen has now been replaced by a "desktop." I take my right hand (the one I have been advised against using) and click my mouse. Clicking brings icons to the screen, symbolic images of the computer's brain, kind of like medieval renderings of Christ as God's kid. Kant would have been a Macintosh user; I'm sure of it. All that pointing, clicking, and rearrangement—so many desktop symbols relating to pure concept residing in the central processing unit of the machine. In his later life Kant, convinced that an ordered world was the only one that could sustain him, became what we would today describe as an "obsessive compulsive." Legend has it that he used to organize his guests around the dinner table and forbid them to speak out of sequence. Kant's father was a watchmaker, but he didn't talk about the man much. I feel the same way about my father.

Click goes the mouse, and I change the brain of my computer and click my modem icon. I have an inexpensive modem; some knock-off called a Magnum 14.4. The one I want is called Platinum Global Village, 38.6 baud. I try to imagine this—a modem that would contain in its hardware a silvery-platinum village, one made up of the whole damn globe. I have baud envy. Click goes my mouse again; I have dialed a telephone number. Modem screams, modem hisses, modem yells. Modem fails. Modem disconnects. Anyone who believes computers and medicine are phallic has tried neither. I dial again, and succeed. Of course I have baud envy, I realize. My computer and my telephone are bridged through my modem, like the shunt that bridges the recalcitrant portions of my mother's brain.

Most of my online friends are not particularly interested in the way I am captivated by the Internet, nor by my desire to continue the project of metaphysics into cyberspace. People rightly credit William Gibson with inventing the term "cyberspace," that word Internet users have come to love to hate, as a quick and dirty way to describe the place bridging computers and the phone lines, bigger than the hardware and software and the humans who type there. But what is cyberspace, and *where* is cyberspace? I know the standard explanation: the Internet is not a place at all, but rather the effect of a series of parallel computing operations, occurring simultaneously all over the world. Still, I struggle with this explanation of the no-place of cyberspace as an embarrassing linguistic necessity. If cyberspace doesn't "exist," then how is that I happen to live there?

Perhaps the fact that I read Gibson's *Neuromancer* ten years later than most of my Net friends has something to do with it. For better or worse, Gibson's conception of cyberspace never required the presence of someone as saccharine as Baud Girl, my generic recipe for teen-girl rebellion served up for the men from Prodigy. This is the advantage of writing, as opposed to living, science fiction, I tell myself. Perhaps corporate Internet providers are ready for a new kind of Gibson girl; maybe they mean it when they urge me to be "edgy" in my writing. But I'm just too cowardly to take the chance of being rejected.

Gibson wrote the book I will never be cool enough to write. Nobody seems to remember that nearly everyone in *Neuromancer* is sick in the beginning of that book, and gets better once they enter cyberspace. First there is the protagonist, Case—a destitute man with neural damage who receives an operation to reenter cyberspace and pull off the ultimate hack. Molly, the text's cyborg razor chick–cum–femme fatale, is the only prosthetic woman I ever heard of who didn't wind up languishing in a hospital bed. Dixie, Case's beloved buddy, comes back from the undead and lives on as a RAM construct, all through the power of the computer. Finally, the entire plot of the book turns on the unstoppable desire of a dying artificial intelligence program named Wintermute to unite with its "brother" program, Neuromancer, in the ultimate love that dare not speak its name.[3] It's not insignificant, either, that in Gibson's cosmology, Wintermute is the AI who "thinks," while Neuromancer is the one who "feels." All this love and rebirth occurs in the Matrix, which Gibson describes thus: "Cyberspace. A consensual hallucination experienced daily by billions of legitimate operators in every nation, by children being taught mathematical concepts, a graphic representation of data being abstracted from every computer in the human system. Unthinkable complexity" (51).

"The feeling of the sublime," writes Kant, "is at once a feeling of displeasure, arising from the inadequacy of the imagination . . . and a simultaneously awakened pleasure" (1993: 214). I like to think that Kant—a man whose greatest contribution to philosophy is his ability to draw meaning from that for which there can be no logical proof—would have been sympathetic to my view of cyberspace as sublime. In his *Critique of Judgement*, Kant points out that what the sublime requires is an active mind, one traveling at a high baud rate, I might add. Kant writes, "the mind feels itself set in motion [by the sublime] . . . this movement may be compared with a vibration, i.e. with a rapidly alternating repulsion and attraction produced by one and the same object" (1993: 215). People tell me that I selfishly and willfully misread Kant. They point out that he was a great fan of Newton, and loved nothing more than order in the world. Today, I'd wager that Kant would have been a lousy physicist, but a great computer scientist. After all, it was Kant who came up with the notion of the mathematical sublime: the feeling of awe and power produced when the mind tries, and fails, to conceptualize inconceivable relations of space or size. I know that sensation.

How many parallel computers form the Net, I wonder? No answer for that. How many users exist in cyberspace? No answer for that either. Kant claims that to understand the full effect of the pyramids, a viewer ought not stand too close, nor too far away. I wonder whether the same holds for the Internet. I can't go to the Matrix, so instead I break up my travels: my online "homes" include bulletin boards like Echo and the Well, academic mailing lists, Usenet groups, and requisite pornography sites on the Web. I have a list of online places I need to visit today—some where I will send e-mail, some to chat, some for sex. When I want to be anonymous, though, I go to the service that promises blandness: America Online. "Welcome!" The weatherman voice of my computer greets me. I still have to mail that pitch to Prodigy, and here I am on AOL, "doing research" and writing a much more prosaic ode to forbidden cyberspatial love than Gibson would ever write.

I point, I click, I travel to a place called the People Connection. I am hunting for boys, cyberboys, they might be old ladies or fat daddies in real life, but today I want crazy horny fourteen-year-old insane boys who will do exactly what I want. I call myself something really sleazy, like Full Cups. I make a room, called "Big Mammaries," in deference to my mother's suggestion about how to equip my computer. I know the responses I will receive. I get the same ones every time I go online:

How big? Describe nipples!

I'll play with your bib [sic] mammaries!

Wanna nurse me, you little bitch?

I play with the boys I want, ignore the boys who bore me, rub and type and rub and type and I really only want to talk about mammaries, boobs, breasts, like my mother's, like the ones on other women. I want to be a lesbian, loving my own make-believe big-busted body while crazy cyber-boys send me hot messages. I laugh hysterically at the fact that the boys in my room "Obey Me!" all applaud after I have an orgasm, that sublime "little death" beyond sex words, one finger on the keyboard, typing yessssssssssssss.

I can't see any bodies here, online. Yet words, seemingly attached to bodies in some way, fly past me on this screen. In n-talk (real-time writing) I watch as the cursor key moves back to correct spelling errors of others, transfixed. In the file libraries, there are back-posts from writers who have died. I can read them. This is not to say that the computer defeats death, any more than the library does. Nevertheless, here, in this place that does not defeat death but is itself deathless, that looks like the television and yet is not, where I am playing a part in a drama somewhere, well perhaps not my body, but, nonetheless "me"—where are the bodies?

Kant might call this state of a "bodiless body" an experience of the *dynamic sublime*. For Kant, there were two ways to think of the sublime: as magnitude (which he associated with mathematics) and as dominion (which he associated with dynamics as described by Newton). However, the sublime describes something more complex than size or quality: the trick of the sublime is that it keeps us in awe of phenomenon while it simultaneously separates and lifts us above that which we contemplate. This is why Kant wrote, for instance, that we consider nature dynamically sublime precisely when it is understood as *might that has no dominion over us* (1993: 217). In order for something to be sublime, the person who contemplates it must have no fear. Fear is the province of superstition, suggests Kant, while sublime religious experiences are linked to something else entirely. For this reason, you can't experience something as sublime if you aren't already hallucinating yourself more powerful than it in some way. For Kant, awe and terror are not the same thing.

The television in her room blares, the sound up too loud, as if brain surgery has rendered her deaf. Dr. West thinks it is good to have the television on, and often asks my mother about it, noting her responses in his chart. "Television helps the patients re-orient to reality after surgery," he says. CNN is on. Suddenly I remember that strange news slogan: "Give us twenty-two minutes; we'll give you the world." According to Jacques Derrida, the mathematical sublime announces itself through narrative. "Does not [the colossal,]" he asks, "already call itself, with a narrative voice, the colossal?" (142). In other words, This is CNN. Yugoslavia is burning. Anonymous raped Bosnian women weep. "War itself," writes Kant, "provided it is conducted with order and a sacred respect for the rights of civilians, has something of the sublime in it." Clearly, Kant and I watch different wars.

"They say he raped them that night," begins the article "Rape in Cyber-space," by *Village Voice* writer Julian Dibbell.[4] It describes a cyber-rape, a wholly textual event that happened on an online system called a MOO (multi-user object oriented system). This MOO divides itself into "rooms" where people chat as different personae. Many people online called Dib-bell's article a hysterical piece of writing that belittled "real rape." They argued that if a person feels raped online, she or he can simply log off or hang up the phone. Sure, cyberspace fosters communities, people agreed, but not "real" communities with real bodies and real rules. Several people suggested that Dibbell "get a life" for even suggesting as much.

In cyber-rape, a textual body (a character) performs onscreen to push the erotic imagination of a real body (the typist at the end of a terminal). For this reason, cyber-rape is closer to rape *fantasy* than it is to "real" rape. Both of these types of rapes, far from being "real," serve rather as perfect examples of the aesthetic sublime—the realm in which the mind fantasies itself body-less, paradoxically by calling up and then destroying its own body. Strangely, in the classical sense, the sublime *itself* works on its spectators as a type of rape fantasy. Look at Derrida's description: "[The sublime] throws you down while elevating you at the same time, since you can take it in view without taking it in your hand, without comprehending it, and since you can see it without seeing it completely. But not without pleasure, with a sublime pleasing-oneself-in-it" (139).

It is precisely the moment when the human mind begins to rape *itself* for pleasure ("mind-fucking") that the space of ethics and government is reached. How does this happen? In his *Critique of Judgement,* Kant's answer is this: when I am experiencing the sublime, I am at my most human, and therefore at my most ethical, humbled and empowered by that which is beyond me. In one of his only snappy lines from the *Critique of Practical Reason,* he writes, "Two things fill the mind with ever new and increasing admiration and awe, the oftener and more steadily they are reflected on: the starry heaven above me and the moral law within me."

Perhaps I am being ridiculous for noticing, at this late date, that Kant leaves out women in his discussion of the starry skies and the moral law, and excludes all but the most noble of savages from the sublime. Maybe I am confabulating when I say that it is mostly women and savages who have been raped in the creation of justice in the modern nation-state. Western nations, white peoples, and men are sublime, argues Kant. You could, I suppose, call me hysterical for pointing out that Julian Dibbell spends only two pages out of twelve describing the actual cyber-rape on which his article is based, and the bulk of his piece describing the "new rules" by which the cyberspace in question redefines itself to make itself more "civilized." This story is as old as *The Oresteia:* the state, in its zeal to please and punish its citizenry, makes a woman's physical assault into the stuff of law.[5] Thus, material rape turns into *rape fantasy*—it has to, because rape as violence hardly contains the sublime dimension necessary to move it into the space of ethics. By moving material rape into rape fantasy, the state effectively ignores and locks out the very female bodies it claims to save, for the sake of the nation.

Within Kant's construction of a moral world, of what use is particularity, more specifically, female particularity? Where does the body go? Please don't misunderstand me—I am not completely sold on the body, a priori. My mother's organs were actively being reprogrammed with steroids, antibiotics, and radiation therapy; her skin was punctured by thick IVs and long incisions from surgery. Where was her "real" body in this? Nevertheless, when the horrific, mundane realities of rape are sublimated into the stuff of law (blood tests, testimonies, DNA tests, Rape Trauma Syndrome), can we say with certainty that we know what "real" rape even is? You wouldn't know it, reading Kant, but for some of us, sublimation has its bad days.

The insurance agents arrive in her room, and speak over my mother, IVs in her arms and white gauze around her head.

"Hey!" yells my mother. "No one has to talk about insurance! I am covered, because I have Agent Orange."

"You have *what?*" I ask.

"Agent Orange. I got it in the war. I flew over southeast Asia, once, and got it."

Okay, Mom, I say. Haldol, the doctors say. Haldol is a drug that will stop the confabulation and the night screams, the ones that happen when she dreams she is blinded by radiation bombs and sunshine.

Like the sublime, my mother's madness was architectonic, if anyone cared to look. Take, for instance, her veteran's story. My mother *was* a veteran civil servant of the Veterans Administration Hospital of Buffalo, where she was a $17,000–a-year secretary for too many years, processing the lives of dying and angry men who stupidly went to Korea and Vietnam to fight race wars, only to find themselves homeless, ostracized, and stripped of the whiteness they had fought so hard to believe in. "Comparing the statesman with the general," writes Kant, "the verdict for aesthetic judgement is for the latter" (1993: 221). But none of this was in her medical chart, and so no one knew what to think of her particular brand of sublimation, the one in which she contracted Agent Orange for America. Judging her madness a brand of genius was out of the question, at the Roswell Clinic.

At a certain time during her suffering, my mother began to ask to see a Catholic priest. She wasn't interested in going to mass, or in speaking with him at all—in fact, whenever he did try to speak with her about her life, she told him that a celibate man could have no clue about her, and to shut up, already. All she wanted, each and every day, was the sacrament of the Eucharist. My mother had never been a particularly religious person, but now she dutifully stuck her tongue out, eyes closed, breathing steady, jumping a little in her wheelchair when the wafer finally touched her tongue. Even after she became convinced that the hospital staff was salting all her food, and the wafer made her choke, hold her throat, and whisper to me in terror and confusion, "salty," she continued to ask for Communion. "How come you want to have Communion these days, Momma?" I asked her, once. She was silent for a minute, and then she said, "I am using the body of Christ for spare parts."

Perhaps my mother and I have all of this God stuff wrong. Maybe our thinking has been warped by too much CNN coverage, too many sequences of nameless raped Bosnian women, women who never speak, women whose faces "give us the world" forced on my insane dying mother and me to prove that we both can successfully engage "reality." Reality often kicks the sublime in the teeth. No one knew this like Kant. Of all people, he knew that logical proofs for the existence of God were facile.

There was no reason he ought to believe in God, and yet he couldn't do otherwise. Likewise, there was no reason to believe his mother ought to have died sacrificing her life for the love of her friend, and yet he couldn't believe otherwise. Faith, he answered his critics, steps in where logic is insufficient. But faith, like cyberspace, only exists as a result of performance.

In another text everyone loves to hate, *Postmodernism; or, The Cultural Logic of Late Capitalism,* Fredric Jameson speaks of a newfangled sublime—a sublime that is not about God but about technology, and specifically about communications technology. Arguing that in postcapitalist society, our sublime "Other" is "no longer Nature at all, but something else which we must now identify," Jameson suggests that our experience of technology as sublime is "a figure for something else"—"Yet technology may well serve as adequate shorthand to designate that enormous properly human and anti-natural power of dead human labor stored up in our machinery—an alienated power which turns back on and against us in unrecognizable forms" (35).

Jameson traces the roots of the technological sublime not to God, but to the source from which First World communications technology flows: the feminized, subaltern economies of the "Third World." Though they sound pompous, his words ring in my ears like newscasts from CNN:

> You don't want to have to think about Third World women every time you pull yourself up to your word processor, or all the other lower-class people with their lower-class lives when you decide to use or consume your other luxury products: it would be like having voices inside your head; indeed it violates the intimate space of your privacy and your extended body. (315)

I must say, I have problems with the argument that the "Third World" exists solely to prop up a metaphysic of digital communications. Nevertheless, when Jameson calls the technological sublime a *hysterical sublime,* I think he may just be on to something. Where modernist writers satisfied themselves as thinking through technology as salvation or destruction, Jameson argues that postmodern thinkers lose that luxury: the technological implant is complete; we are cyborgs; the voices are in our heads. Jameson's warning is important: if you consider the politics implicit in the performance of the sublime for too long, you can go mad, or at least become hysterical. It happened to my mother and me.

Of course Kant would object to Jameson, my mother, and me, arguing that all of us misunderstand the sublime entirely. Kant would say that God and technology don't mesh. Likewise, he argued, although women can themselves be sublime objects, they just can't themselves experience sublimity as subjects. In some ways, a technological sublime, performed within the psychic structures of women, with all its political baggage and internal chatter, would seem too close to madness for Kant. After all, this was the man who once wrote, "To eavesdrop on ourselves when our thoughts occur in our mind unbidden and spontaneously is to overturn the natural order of the cognitive powers. If this is not already a form of mental illness, it leads to it and to the lunatic asylum" (in Scharfstein 223).

I think the word "hysterical" has at least two meanings. One is etiologically linked to disease, or at least, dis-ease; the other definition is the one I hear in my uninvolved father's response to my worries about funding my mother's medical care: Oh, don't be so hysterical. In other words, the condition of my mother. Hysterical: diseased and dismissed. I gave my mother a set of rosary beads near the end of her life. She gave them back to me. "Fuck the Virgin Mary, Theresa," she told me, laughed, and went to sleep.

Oh yes, my mother and I are hysterical. My mother cracked herself up. When Jameson allies the technological hysterical sublime with camp, he cracks me up. Yes, the place I know as "cyberspace" began as ARPANET, as much a part of the military-industrial complex as Eisenhower's army-issue boots. But that genealogy grows more and more campy as I stage my cybersexing, my community building, and my fiction writing there. Tragedy is sublime, said Kant, comedy beautiful. Camp is not of tragedy exactly, nor of comedy in a clearly self-evident way. Which is my mother's need to use Jesus for spare parts, or my faux-lesbian cybersex with mystery straight boys? Tragedy or comedy, or neither?

I think of camp as a politics of space—a performance that marks this space as mine, not yours, never yours. Unless you suspend disbelief, and enter my theatre on my terms. Unless you ally yourself with my pain. Don't misunderstand me: I am not advocating experiencing the technological sublime—or by extension, camp—as a full-time day job. But I do believe it is a useful way to make faith out of performance. It gives me something to believe in, when I have spent a significant portion of my life (and not by choice) disbelieving the activities of other theatres not of my own making: hospitals and battlefields come to mind. You may understand my dual obsessions with my computer and my mother as stupid, pointless, facile, not entertaining, exclusive, histrionic. I understand performance as home. My country.

Using Jesus like an old automobile, for spare parts, and resisting the rape of spaces by sexing cyberspace—these certainly would not be Kantian strategies for getting through life and death. "I hardly believe the fair sex is capable of principles," Kant once wrote (1991: 81). I have no doubt that the campy sublime of my mother and me would smack a little too much of madness and bad free verse—things Kant hated. Nonetheless, Kant's struggle, my mother's, and my own are not all that different. We have all been trying to make meaning out of bodies that slide into memory.

Kant struggled for a long time before he figured out a way to demonstrate the nonexistent existence (what he called supersensible) value of faith. He just couldn't stop thinking about how to connect those two famous phrases, "the starry skies above me" and the "moral law within me." He finally realized in his Third Critique that the way was through a detailed analysis of the dynamics of "awe."

Taking the example of a critic who says, "this rose is beautiful," Kant argued that this phrase actually means "this rose ought to be beautiful for all"—else why regard him a critic? He then demonstrated that the statement "the pyramids are sublime" does not and cannot mean "the pyramids are sublime for me," for reasons that are not dissimilar from why a doctor is not expected to say, "the patient is dead, to me," but rather, "the patient is dead." When the critic (one with taste) speaks, it is as if beauty or sublimity moves through his body and toward the object in question. Once Kant figured this out, he argued that this mechanism is precisely how judgment moves from the particular to the universal. Way before J. L. Austin or performance studies departments, Kant argued that embedded in the linguistic performative "I believe" is the corresponding indictment, "you ought."

Finally, he claimed, he had found his "bridge" between knowledge and morals: aesthetics. Kant then turned his attention to morality, arguing that the categorical imperative is precisely that which evokes an "ought" eluding all reason. The realm of "ought," whether in aesthetics or in morality, is the realm of disinterest. For Kant, a painting of an apple that makes you hungry for apples means you can't judge its value as Art. Likewise, a religious faith based on fear and a hope of salvation is merely superstition. Faith, then, must be disinterested, and acquired through awe, the mind's contemplation outside the sensible realm. Where philosophy had gone wrong, he realized, was in searching for God through science, when faith, like genius, has always been the province of art. For a man who never once mentions Goethe, and thought listening to Mendelssohn was like hearing an "infernal moan," finding aesthetics as the bridge between the concrete and the supersensible must have been a shock indeed.

Kant argued that the universal cannot be reduced to its constituent parts. Although the sublime begins with bodily details, it can't go back there. But my mother's question remains: how do you experience the sublime when your body simply is not consonant with that of a white Western male? The sublime cannot employ the parergon, orders Kant. I use the body of Christ for spare parts, answers my mother. I cannot recall my mother's body outside the frame of her hospital bed, and no matter what Dr. Freud counsels, I find it hard to think of rape fantasy separate from other kinds of rape. This is why mother's advice, gleaned from my memories of her, is the best inheritance I have, better even than her money. It imparts its own categorical imperative.

My mother's last act of moral artistry took the form of a banquet. She said that there would be many people there I needed to meet, and that I would have to wear something wonderful, maybe the black sequined dress from her closet. "You are going to have to buy yourself a slip to wear with that," she laughed, "because it is really tight. You are going to look like one shiny black seal in that dress!" When the insurance people came back, my mother insisted that they, too, be at the party. She would wake up from a nap, and see me sitting, watching her. Taking my hand, she would say, "Okay, that's enough. Go get ready for the party." One time, in frustration, she narrated to me a list of names and phone numbers of people who were going to be at this party. I called the numbers, and every one was right. Many were numbers of people my mother knew in high school. Of course none of them knew about the party. Of course there was no sequined dress at my mother's house for me to wear. I looked.

One day my mother fell asleep. From then on, she woke up only from time to time, to smile, or cry. Except for one afternoon, when my brother walked into her room and saw her sitting upright in bed. "What are you doing, Momma?" he asked. "I am trying to die," she answered. "It is hard."

She was right. Technology did kill her. She died of the multiple operations, not the tumor in her brain. And yet even in death, my mother couldn't catch a break. That most sublime moment was something she had to struggle to achieve, finally demanding that the doctors leave her alone and stop trying to save her, and that my brothers move her to a state-sponsored hospice, where the nurses were concerned more about the living and let dead people die, already.

Rousseau, a great influence on Kant, wrote, "Man is free, and yet is everywhere in chains." Yet it was in choosing to respond to the "ought" in life, Kant argued, that the human subject can elude, at least temporarily, the chains of servitude, illness, death. For Kant, God was a performance of faith—one that (as Julia Kristeva would say much later of the theatre) "cannot take (a) place" (1997). Kant used the sublime to get to God. Loving Kant, but loving my mother more, I use Kant's body of philosophy for my own ends—stripping his notions of performance out, trying to make meaning of my own memories. The place in which I make meaning is cyberspace. I'm no longer embarrassed to say that this process is metaphysical for me. Like Kant, I also know that what I am saying is hysterical, illogical, and unprovable. As far as I am concerned, what cyberspace knows is this: although performing can end, performance cannot. Performance predates the arrival and departure of the bodies living, loving, and dying on its stages.

Neuromancer-esque fantasies of the sublime aside, I can't live in the realm of the metaphysical. A girl's gotta eat. I have deadlines. I have stories to tell. I have a body, with a lot of memory. I have a computer, with a lot of memory. I type, I surf, I sex, and I live some of my time in cyberspace in a state of sublimity and anonymity. Then I cry, I come, I laugh, and I time-waste my body, framed by a chair that lacks proper support. If I can meet this deadline for Baud Behavior, I have to go to a party for one of my computer groups. I am going to meet many of the people I have spoken to only online. None of them will know I have had sex, or confessed, or cried, or laughed with their textual bodies, until I tell them. Perhaps, I tell myself, I can really be anonymous, unlike my mother, whose chart was passed around the hospital twenty times over, or the weeping women in Bosnia who continue to decorate American television screens namelessly. I know now that you first need to *have* an identity in order to have the luxury of forsaking it. For this reason, anonymity and invisibility are hardly identical, regardless of what *Wired* magazine believes.

I wonder how I will feel about meeting everyone. I know I will be disappointed to some degree, the way I was when it was pointed out to me that by all accounts Immanuel Kant was a bitter misogynist who would have despised me for mixing his biography up with his philosophical motivations. Frankly, if all knowledge begins with experience, then I am glad I never met the man. But Kant lives on only in books, my mother lives only on in my memories, and I have to leave the house from time to time, so I consider this party. I wonder how much I will tell them about myself. I wonder how different they will seem, "real." I wonder if I will wind up having sex with any of them later, online. I do know one thing. I am going to wear a sequined dress. One that makes me look like a shiny black seal.

NOTES

Thanks to Jill Lane, Peggy Phelan, Misha Iampolski, and Tom Igoe.

1. The details of Kant's life are drawn from Ben-Ami Scharfstein, *The Philosophers: Their Lives and the Nature of Their Thought.*

2. The translation of *Critique of Judgement* is by James Creed Meredith, from the German Library series. It is available via gopher at gopher://gopher.vt.edu:10010/02/107/2. The translation of *Critique of Pure Reason* is by Norman Smith Kemp. It, too, is downloadable, complete with a search engine that scans the text for any search word: http://www.arts.cuhk.hk/Philosophy/Kant/cpr/search.html/. Finally, for more information on Kant than anyone could possibly need, point your web browser to http://www.hkbu.edu.hk/ppp/Kant.html/.

3. I am grateful to Matt Ehrlich for his observations regarding the homosexual desire of Wintermute and Neuromancer in his essay "Turing, My Love."

4. For Dibbell's article, see ftp://parcftp.xerox.com/pub/MOO/papers/VillageVoice.txt.

5. I first came across this argument in Sue-Ellen Case, ed., *Performing Feminisms: Feminist Critical Theory and Theatre* (Baltimore: John Hopkins University Press, 1990).

WORKS CITED

Behler, Ernst, ed. *Immanuel Kant: Collected Philosophical Writings.* New York: Continuum, 1993.

Case, Sue-Ellen. *Performing Feminisms: Feminist Critical Theory and Theatre.* Baltimore: Johns Hopkins University Press, 1990.

Derrida, Jacques. *Truth in Painting.* Chicago: University of Chicago Press, 1987.

Dibbell, Julian. "A Rape in Cyberspace; Or How an Evil Clown, a Haitian Trickster Spirit, Two Wizards, and a Cast of Dozens Turned a Database into a Society." In *Flame Wars: The Discourse of Cyberculture,* ed. Mark Dery. Durham: Duke University Press, 1994.

Ehrlich, Matthew. "Turing, My Love." *Women & Performance: A Journal of Feminist Theory* 9, no. 1, issue 17 (1997).

Gibson, William. *Neuromancer.* New York: Ace Books, 1984.

Jameson, Fredric. *Postmodernism; or, The Cultural Logic of Late Capitalism.* Durham: Duke University Press, 1992.

Kant, Immanuel. *Critique of Judgement.* Trans. J. C. Meredith. In *Immanuel Kant: Collected Philosophical Writings,* ed. Ernst Behler, 129–238. New York, Continuum, 1993.

———. *Critique of Pure Reason.* Trans. Norman Smith Kemp. London, Macmillan, 1933.

———. *Observations on the Feeling of the Beautiful and Sublime.* Trans. John Goldthwait. Berkeley: University of California Press, 1991.

Kristeva, Julia. "Theatre Does Not Take (a) Place." *Substance,* nos. 18–19 (1997): 131–34.

Scharfstein, Ben-Ami. *The Philosophers: Their Lives and the Nature of Their Thought.* New York: Oxford University Press, 1980.

MOVING THE BODY POLITIC

TEN

AmeRícan Accents

Syncopate the State

Doris Sommer

> Every person who reads this Article has an ac-
> cent. Your accent carries the story of who you
> are. . . . traces of your life and identity are woven
> into your pronunciation, your phrasing, your
> choice of words. . . . Someone who tells you
> they don't like the way you speak is quite likely
> telling you that they don't like you.
> —Mari J. Matsuda

"Hablemos el mismo idioma," one of Gloria Estefan's hit songs of 1993,
came out on a CD called *Mi tierra,* the title of another hit.[1] The tellingly
generic homeland of the title counts on our collective nostalgia, despite
the fact that *mi tierra* may not be *la tuya,* while "Hablemos el mismo
idioma" wants to move the feeling of unity toward a better future. Played
to a salsa mix, it translates as "Let's Speak the Same Language" in the
bilingual booklet for the CD. It's an apparently ecumenical accompaniment to make good on the lyric's call for racial rainbows and musical
fusions *(colores de un arcoiris, acordes de un mismo son).* But after listening to
it, one irritated colleague said, "Universalism isn't what it used to be." And
he is right, because the appeal to get beyond differences is pitched to
decidedly Latin locutors. After the first few lines, the song disinterpellates
some listeners when the "us" turns out to be *"nosotros hispanos."* They are
literally put off, even though Estefan had accounted for differences from
the very first lines of her call to unity. She admitted that differences
constitute her as a subject *(A pesar de las diferencias que me hacen quien soy),*
as she enjoined us to think about how much we have in common *(respi-*

169

ramos el mismo aire, despertamos al mismo sol, nos alumbra la misma luna, necesitamos sentir amor).

But then her rhythm of moving from outside to inside falters. It skips a beat, breaks the movement to freeze it in a *syncope,* a term that Catherine Clément takes from musical notation (and from its medical meaning of "apparent death") to name a political or philosophical interruption of predictability. "The queen of rhythm, *syncope is also* the mother of *dissonance*; it is the source, in short, of a harmonious and productive discord. . . . Attack and haven, collision; a fragment of the beat disappears, and of this disappearance, rhythm is born."[2] The pause between strong beats, between unity and selective solidarity, is a break for reflection. Readers who may feel the sting of exclusion don't necessarily stop to think about it, not if they are too quick on the uptake.

Estefan's pitch for pan-Hispanic solidarity rehearses what Puerto Rican Willie Colón, Panamanian Rubén Blades, and Cuban Celia Cruz have been intoning for years, a "trans-Latino" identity that now characterizes urban centers like "the New Nueva York."[3] Improvising on the themes of sameness and difference, the way that musical mixes make salsa from different national styles, Latinos are also saying that universalism is not what it used to be. They are saying it with relief, because they had fit so badly into milky homogenizations. "Racism as universalism" is one result of the colorless abstraction.[4] But universality has renewed hope, say defenders of the public sphere and pragmatists, if democracies can tune in to discord in order to develop an "interactive" politics. Discord among culturally and economically situated subjects locates gaps as the space of democratic negotiation.[5] Without gaps, negotiation would be unnecessary. And because of them, listening is not easy; it requires patience at the *syncope* of communication in a country where citizens do not always speak the same language.

Even when they do speak English, Mari J. Matsuda argued in the *Yale Law Journal,* the range of culturally inflected accents fissures the language community—happily, she adds, because our accents safeguard American diversity from the meanness of one standard sound. Cultural difference is something for democracy to celebrate, not just tolerate.[6] Theodor Adorno had already appreciated the "negativity" inside communities as boundary markers that resist the subject's "greedy thirst for incorporation" of difference into sameness.[7] If there were no difference, there could be no recognition of one subject by another, but only the identification that reduces real external others into functions of a totalizing self. Yet the very gap that allows for enough autonomy to make mutuality possible also risks misrecognition and violence. The risk is worth taking, because without it we allow the violence of forcing sameness on others. Either they are forced to fit or they are forced out.[8] The necessary risk of breakdown that democracies defend as the negative (autonomous) moment of mutuality surely gives some universalists pause about the possibility of a coherent culture and a cohesive polity.[9] But pause is not a bad thing, if it gives time for one to listen to another.[10]

Universalism is promising today because it depends on difference, Ernesto Laclau argues a bit provocatively, along with some critical legal scholars.[11] It has survived classical philosophy's dismissal of particularity as deviation, and it has outlived a European Enlightenment that conflated the universal (subject, class, culture) with particular (French) incarnations. Today's universalism is a paradox for the past, because it is grounded in particularist demands. They unmoor any fixed cultural content and keep universalism open to an "always receding horizon."[12] Dissonance, then, isn't noise. It is a function of the *syncope,* of the "performative contradiction" that can sing "Hablemos el mismo idioma" (a universal theme in a particularist key) and risk liberal improvisation between the "apparent deaths" of the polity. Democracy works in unscored counterpoint. Precisely because citizens cannot presume to feel, think, or perform alike, their ear for otherness makes justice possible.[13] That is why political philosophy and ethics, from Benjamin and Arendt to Bakhtin and Levinas, caution against empathy, which plays treacherously in a subject-centered key that overwhelms unfamiliar voices to repeat sounds of the self.[14]

Pauses and residues from translation, even the limits of comprehension (which still means grasping, owning), are more promising for democracy than we have assumed. Consider, for example, Homi Bhabha's concept of time-lag: it names the temporal gaps between an already existing center and peripheries that cannot (or will not) catch up. Bhabha does some urgent work of underlining the asymmetries and complicating the notion of empty or homogeneous modern time.[15] But time-lag can describe a particular asymmetry: not the inequalities that he decries against the drone of easy multiculturalism,[16] but the rhythmic variations in speech, even when we speak the same language. Time-lag can name a musical notation, a deferred stress, or a delayed apprehension of meaning, the skipped beat in conversation that also marks the rhythm of a joke; time-lag can be the signature of one language through the medium of another. Skewed rhythms and dissonant notes are not noise, but signs of liberal improvisation. We share a polity, after all; differences coexist in time as well as through time. Blockage comes from rushing to fill in the gaps, from not appreciating syncopated sounds.

Signs of difference and of contingent translations are everywhere, unless we continue to ignore them. The gesture that first made me pause was Rigoberta Menchú's peculiar stops and starts at the secrets of her 1983 testimony. Why proclaim her own silence instead of being silent, I wondered, as if declaring secrets mattered more than the ethnographic data? With all those secrets, no amount of information could let intimacy flow. Maybe that was her purpose, I began to think: to engage us *and* to interrupt our universalizing habit of identifying with the writer, sometimes to the point of replacing her. A formidable lesson. Still illiterate, the young woman who spoke a newly learned, halting Spanish managed to turn an ethnographic interrogation into a platform for her own irreplaceable leadership. The stunning move made me think of other books that interrupt universalizing mastery. Among them were slave narratives commissioned by abolitionists, the Inca Garcilaso's chronicles, Toni Morrison's *Beloved,* Elena Poniatowska's novelized *testimonio,* stories about blacks told by self-consciously incompetent whites, even the accommodationist memoir of Richard Rodriguez, in his refusals of intimacy with readers. The examples that drew me back and brought me up short are almost arbitrary. Anyone can think of others. The point is that some ethnically marked writing refuses to keep universalizing time. It halts, syncopates, and demands cautious engagements.

Nineteen ninety-five was an auspicious year for tuning in to the counterpoints of Our Americas.[17] It commemorated José Martí, author of many works, including the Cuban War of Independence and the essay "Our America" (1891). What "Our" means in Martí's celebration of indigenous and African strains in New World Hispanism is a problem, for two reasons. First, the possessive pronoun neutralizes internal differences and claims ownership in monocultural ways that now seem unproductive. Martí's nineteenth-century nationalism needed to focus on victory by squinting at Cuba, compressing its complexity into a thin but homogeneous *cubanidad.* The other problem is that the discriminating pronoun "Our" is so shifty, so available for competing positionalities. In a New World where commercial, cultural, and political border crossings define so many lives, boundary words like here and there, mine and yours, now and then are hardly stable signposts. They are, as always, shifters. Merely to translate the possessive claim to "Nuestra América" as "Our America" is to hear it deformed by the treachery of displacement.[18]

Strategists will know that mobility is not only a cause for worry; it is also an opportunity to gain ground. Perhaps Nuestra América has a future history here, up North. Translation, of course, literally means switching ground, as Puerto Ricans, for example, know very well. Following particular guides is an important precaution, if we hope to avoid the muddle of mistaking "Hispanics" for a homogeneous group. The very rhythm of efforts at solidarity is a cue to the divisions among constituencies usually identified by national origin.[19] Puerto Rico can be the strong case of a nation that maneuvers along the fault line of grammatical shifters, in the space between here and there, now and then, Our America and theirs. An entire population stays on the move, or potentially so, so much so that Luis Rafael Sánchez makes a hysterical joke about Puerto Rican national identity being grounded in the *guagua aérea* (air bus) shuttling across the Atlantic puddle.[20]

Literally a nation of Luftmenschen, half is provisionally on the Caribbean island, and half on and around that other mad-hatter island, which has become a homeland that Tato Laviera calls *AmeRíca.*[21] His genius is to skip a beat, to unravel a seamless label by reading the English sign for America with an eye for Spanish. In Spanish this country looks like "América," because without a written accent on the *e* to give the word an irregular stress, a default, unwritten stress falls on the *i*. Laviera's hypercorrection displaces the logic of diacritical marks from one language to another and performs a time-lag of translation. The alleged omission of an accent mark is an opportunity to read the country in syncopation as AmeRíca, a time-lagged sound whose sign reforms the country's look too. With a foreign stroke if you read it in English (just as superfluous for Spanish), and with an intrusive capital *R* that fissures and then fuses a conventional name into a convincing compound, the orthographic encroachments push both standard languages slightly out of bounds. The result is a practically providential metaphor: AmeRíca transforms what for English or Spanish is just a word into a *mot juste* in Spanglish. Doubly marked mainland Ricans become the most representative citizens we've got.

Independentists resent the doubling, and they resist being taken for endless rides in the *guagua aérea*. They were interrupting America's empire even before the 1917 U.S. decision to confer, or to force, citizenship on Puerto Rico. At that time, José de Diego published a protest simply and unequivocally titled "No." "Crisp, solid, decisive as a hammer blow, this is the virile word that should inflame our lips and save our honor in these sad days of anachronistic imperialism."[22] The alternative "sí" and the cacophonic "yes" in English seem useless. You see, from Spanish to English the words of affirmation do not match up, and the asymmetry opens up a space, a trench like the one we might notice between NAFTA (North American Free Trade Agreement)—sounding so explosive in European languages—and its Mexican counterpart, TLC *(Tratado de Libre Comercio)*—so misleadingly friendly in American English. When a Spanish speaker hears that English "yes," does s/he wonder at the insistent sibilant *s* at the end, where it might have stayed discreetly underpronounced in Spanish, wonder if the word might be a hiss of disapproval or the sound of a serpent stalking its prey? And is it possible that an English listener might hear in a Spanish "sí" not a simple endorsement but an invitation to look at something unsettling? "No," by contrast, is as smooth and hard, as virile as a bullet, not vulnerable to ventriloquism or the jet-lag of endless translations.

Is it really safe, though? The very coherence and traveler-friendly symmetry of the word are betrayals. The problem with "no" is precisely that it translates so effortlessly between its linguistic past and present. The word that refuses intimacy with empire produces that intimacy. "No" is a weapon of self-defense that turns into a deconstructive trap, a roar of resistance that can sound like the moan of irresistible seduction. "No" treacherously adds a supplement: the message of translatability, the essence of a supple and pragmatic war of positions that keeps universalism and particularism in contrapuntal improvisation. It refuses intimacy and therefore names it as a goal; it offers satisfaction, but undercuts it. The rhythm engages a shared language but speaks with particular patterns of stress.

To consider what American or AmeRícan may mean, is first to hear where the accent falls. Does it name exceptionalism, in a paradoxically repeatable project from one American country to another, like early versions of American Studies and like José Vasconcelos's *La raza cósmica* (1925), which named Mexico's synthetic mission to the world? Or is AmeRícan *La raza cómica,* as my Puerto Rican friend Rubén Ríos Avila suggests when missions are madness?[23] Translation produces excess, as in the possessive pronoun that shifts belonging from Nuestra América to Ours, and even the simplest *no* of uncompromising refusal can get stuck in the slime of translation's surplus. But for English and Spanish speakers to avoid translation is, of course, simply to imagine a cultural emptiness on the other side of one Imperial language, to mistake, for example, New York (Nous York, in an Air Canada advertisement) as unusably foreign. Ambiguous and staccato translation is not only a limit of understanding; it is also an asymmetry that cures squinting by winking AmeRícan counterpoints.

Asymmetries keep alive what ethicist Emmanuel Levinas calls the Saying, that is, the mystery and transcendence of social intercourse; they don't allow language to kill the desired other by getting his meaning right. The ambivalence, for example, of hoping to speak the same (Latino) language and issuing a bilingual booklet suspends the copula between the speaker and her identity, so that American cannot yet "be" any essentialized, definitive, or dead thing. It remains a range of staggered be-longings, desired, virtual, but wisely and prophylactically unconsummated connections; they safeguard Saying Our America, in all its rhythmic accents, shifty attributions, and impossible refusals.

NOTES

1. "Hablemos el mismo idioma" is song number 10 on Estefan's very successful CD *Mi tierra*; music and lyrics by Gloria Estefan and Emilio Estefan, Jr.; copyright 1993 by Foreign Imported Productions and Publications, Inc.

2. Catherine Clément, *Syncope: The Philosophy of Rapture,* trans. Sally O'Driscoll and Deirdre M. Mahoney, Introduction by Verena Conley (Minneapolis: University of Minnesota Press, 1994), 4, x.

3. For an excellent review of the sociological literature, see Juan Flores, "Pan-Latino/Trans-Latino: Puerto Ricans in the 'New Nueva York,' " *Centro* (Journal of the Center for Puerto Rican Studies) 8, nos. 1–2 (1996): 171–86.

4. Etienne Balibar, "Racism as Universalism," in *Masses, Classes, and Ideas,* trans. James Swenson (New York: Routledge, 1994), 191–204.

5. See Seyla Benhabib, *Situating the Self: Gender, Community and Postmodernism in Contemporary Ethics* (New York: Routledge, 1992), 3, 5. See also Richard Rorty, *Objectivity, Relativism, and Truth* (New York: Cambridge University Press, 1991), particularly his defense of Dewey as clearing the ground for liberal democracy.

6. Mari J. Matsuda, "Voices of America: Accent, Antidiscrimination Law, and a Jurisprudence for the Last Reconstruction," *Yale Law Journal* 100, no. 5 (March 1991): 1329–1407. She celebrates cultural difference beyond the tolerance that liberals like Rorty defend. I am grateful to Professor Susan Keller for this reference.

7. T. W. Adorno, *Negative Dialektic* (Frankfurt: Surkamp, 1966), 172. The greedy subject is Freud's formulation. See Diana Fuss, *Identity Papers* (New York: Routledge, 1996).

8. Jessica Benjamin, "The Shadow of the Other (Subject): Intersubjectivity and Feminist Theory," *Constellations* 1, no. 2 (1994): 231–54, 245. Her entire discussion is most useful; I am grateful to Kerry Riddich for the reference.

9. See, for example, Naomi Schor, *Bad Objects: Essays Popular and Unpopular* (Durham: Duke University Press, 1995), xiv.

10. Emmanuel Levinas, *Totality and Infinity* (Pittsburgh: Duquense University Press, 1969), 57–58: "The real must not only be determined in its historical objectivity, but also from interior intentions, from the secrecy that interrupts the continuity of historical time. Only starting from this secrecy is the pluralism of society possible."

Jean-François Lyotard, "The Other's Rights," in *On Human Rights: The Oxford Amnesty Lectures, 1993,* ed. Stephen Shute and Susan Hurley (New York: Harper-Collins, 1993), 136–47, 142. "How to share dialogue with *you,* requires a moment of silence. 'Aristotle said: The master speaks and the pupil listens. For that moment, the status of *I* is forbidden to me . . .' The suspension of interlocution imposes a silence and that silence is good. It does not undermine the right to speak. It teaches the value of that right."

11. See Neil Gotanda, "A Critique of 'Our Constitution Is Color-Blind,' " *Stanford Law Review* 44, no. 1 (November 1991): 1–68.

12. Ernesto Laclau, "Universalism, Particularism and the Question of Identity," in *The Identity in Question,* ed. John Rajchman (New York: Routledge, 1995), 93–108, 107.

13. This is a commonplace of political philosophy, one that Mari Matsuda develops for the practice of law in note 6 above. See John Rawls, "Justice as Fairness: Political Not Metaphysical," *Philosophy and Public Affairs* 14 (1985): 223–51. "[L]iberalism as a political doctrine supposes that there are many conflicting and incommensurable conceptions of the good, each compatible with the full rationality of human persons" (248). Robert Dahl, *Dilemmas of Pluralist Democracy: Autonomy versus Control* (New Haven: Yale University Press, 1982); Milton Fisk, "Introduction: The Problem of Justice," in *Key Concepts in Critical Theory: Justice* (Atlantic Highlands, NJ: Humanities Press, 1993), 1–8. "There has to be at least a conflict based on an actual lack of homogeneity for what is distinctive about justice to become relevant" (1). See also Benhabib, 2.

14. Walter Benjamin, *Illuminations,* ed. and intro. Hannah Arendt, trans. Harry Zohn (New York: Schocken, 1969). In thesis 7 of "Theses on the Philosophy of History," 253–64, 256. Hannah Arendt, *On Revolution* (New York: Viking, 1963), see chap. 2, "The Social Question," 69–90. M. M. Bakhtin, *Art and Answerability: Early Philosophical Essays,* ed. Michael Holquist and Vadim Liapunov (Austin: University of Texas Press, 1990), 64, 81, 88; and Emmanuel Levinas throughout *Totality and Infinity* and *Otherwise Than Being* (Boston: M. Nijhoff, 1981). For a proceduralist critique of grounding politics in positive feeling, see, for example, Dahl, esp. Chap. 7, "Changing Civic Orientations," 138–64, 147: "To love a member of one's family or a friend is not at all like 'loving' abstract 'others'

whom one does not know, never expects to know, and may not even want to know."

15. He attributes this notion of time to Walter Benjamin (although we should say that Benjamin named the bourgeois temporal tidiness in order to blast it apart with the interruptions of *Jetztzeit*). See Homi Bhabha, *The Location of Culture* (New York: Routledge, 1994), 95. But he will give Benjamin credit for the critique in "Translator Translated: W. J. T. Mitchell talks with Homi Bhabha," *Artform* 7 (March 1995): 80–119, 110.

16. Homi Bhabha, "Race Time and the Revision of Modernity," *Oxford Literary Review* 1–2: 193–219, 204–5.

17. The reference is to Fernando Ortiz, *Contrapunteo cubano del tabaco y azúcar* (originally Havana, 1941). Since then, the metaphor of counterpoint has been standard in discussions of cultural conflict and conflictual creativity in Latin America.

18. Waldo Frank titled his book about the entire hemisphere *Our America* (New York: Boni and Liveright, 1919). Translated in references as *Nuestra América,* it was, for example, an inspiration and model for José Carlos Mariátegui, the major theorist of a particularized, Peruvian Marxism. "En Waldo Frank, como en todo gran intérprete de la historia, la intuición y el método colaboran. . . . Una-muno modificaría probablemente su juicio sobre el marxismo si estudiase el espíritu—no la letra—marxista en escritores como el autor de *Nuestra América.* . . . Diré de que modo Waldo Frank es para mí un hermano mayor." *El Alma matinal y otras estaciones del hombre de hoy* (Lima: Amauta, 1972), 197, 192. Mariátegui's piece is from 1929.

19. In "Do 'Latinos' Exist?" *Contemporary Sociology* 23, no. 3 (May 1994): 354–56, Jorge I. Domínguez reports this observation from two books under review: Rodolfo O. de la Garza et al., *Latino Voices: Mexican, Puerto Rican, and Cuban Perspectives on American Politics* (Boulder: Westview Press, 1992); and Rodney E. Hero, *Latinos and the U.S. Political System: Two-Tiered Pluralism* (Philadelphia: Temple University Press, 1992). "Very large majorities of Mexicans, Puerto Ricans, and Cubans identify themselves by their national origins, not as 'Latinos' or Hispanics." Domínguez, 354.

20. Luis Rafael Sánchez, "La Guagua Aérea: The Air Bus," trans. Diana Vélez, *Village Voice,* Jan. 24, 1984.

21. Tato Laviera, *AmeRícan* (Houston: Arte Público Press, 1985).

22. José de Diego, "No," in Iris Zavala and Rafael Rodríguez, *Intellectual Roots of Independence* (New York: Monthly Review Press, 1980), 131–33, 131.

23. Rubén Ríos Avila, "La Raza Cómica: Identidad y cuerpo en Pedreira y Palés," *La Torre,* nos. 27–28 (July–December 1993): 559–76.

ELEVEN

Border Watching

Diana Taylor

It all started on my day at the forum. "Authority and Authoritarianism" was a panel presented in Buenos Aires in 1990 to question the ideological and institutional structures still in place in Argentina following the Dirty War, and their effect on artists. In her presentation, Laura Yusem, a well-known director who did Griselda Gambaro's *Antígona furiosa* among other important plays, was arguing that an artist could be conscious of authoritarian paradigms and undo them. She cited her staging of Eduardo Pavlovsky's play *Paso de dos* as an illustration of this dismantling. I had recently sat through this particular production, in which a military torturer from the Dirty War stripped, beat, raped, and finally killed his beautiful female victim/lover—all to the rhythm of a haunting tango. I suggested that the eroticized representation of violence against women might inadvertently reproduce, rather than dismantle, the military's authoritarian discourse. The junta leaders had belabored the trope of Argentina as a bleeding feminine body, infiltrated and violated by her enemy others. In fact, Argentina has a history of mutually enabling performances that link the creation of the *ser nacional* to the elimination of the feminine—beginning with the sixteenth-century descriptions of nature as a "disloyal and fearless" Señora who hates and kills men.[1] Someone from the audience called me a fascist for trying to restrict or censor what could or could not be shown. Yusem pointed out that I wasn't Argentinean, I hadn't lived in Argentina during the Dirty War, I hadn't experienced torture and therefore knew nothing about it and should keep quiet. She dismissed me as a "Yanqui feminist."

Standing in the auditorium in front of two hundred people, I suddenly felt trapped in the spectacle of nation building and dangerous border crossings. I was the observer who had suddenly become the object of scrutiny. I had, unwittingly to be sure, become part of the drama of identity and identification. The fact that my "identity" and alliances as a Canadian/Mexican woman living and working in the United States were not easily reducible to "Yankee" was beside the point. There I was, suddenly "American," from a prestigious academic institution, speaking against authoritarianism but weighing in with a different kind of authority. The positioning itself had a history, reaffirming the old hierarchies and tensions between the "First" and the "Third" Worlders, one that I was powerless at that moment to challenge or complicate. As the foreigner, I marked the outside, highlighting the boundary between "them" (Argentineans) and the not-one-of-them (the other *against* whom nationality is always implicitly set up). And though I marked the border, I was by no means out of the picture. I wasn't standing on some geographical or moral terra firma outside the scenario; I was right there, playing to and into this web of looks.

But, I would have said if I'd had the presence of mind, dialogues and alliances are constantly being established between people with significant "differences" to achieve similar ends. Now that we're talking about the Dirty War, we have only to think of the military, economic, and ideological ties between the Argentine junta and the Reagan administration. *And don't forget,* I might have insisted, that national identity is not the only basis for identification and mutual recognition—as the abductions and disappearances of Argentineans by Argentineans made clear. Women, for example, can align across national boundaries to demand that women's rights be treated as internationally recognized human rights. *And furthermore,* the theatre expert in me could have added, isn't there more than a little irony in a director telling an audience member that she can't understand the show because she hadn't lived through the experience? The whole point of theatre is that one doesn't have to go mad to identify with Lear and blind to empathize with Oedipus.

But, as Brecht would have put it, "this is what she was thinking, but could not say." In part, it was because (I admit it) I was stunned. But I also vaguely perceived that the explosive confrontation was also about something else. My remarks, which I had intended as *constative,* in J. L. Austin's definition of it as a "statement" conveying my concern regarding the representation of violence, were heard as performative. My words, which did not in themselves qualify as a "speech act," had nonetheless done something—they had provoked, interfered, intervened. That "Yankee" was not so much about my identity as about my audacity in carrying through an imperialist gesture in a specific historical context—the after-math of the Dirty War—in which many Argentineans were keenly sensi-tive to the whiffs of international condemnation or disdain.

This day at the forum intensified my interest in the politics of looking. As a theatre and performance studies person, I've always known that my passion for looking is an occupational hazard. But now I wondered whether looking always constitutes an intervention. Is an equal, reciprocal exchange possible across borders, between entities that have historically been set up as unequal: "center"/"periphery," "First" World/"Third" World, "developed"/"developing" countries? And if not, what then? We can't *not* look because spectacles work internationally. Everything crosses borders, from people to capital, from markets to armaments to e-mail. Fantasies, too, are exported and imported; staging techniques travel; speech acts echo each other; performances have histories, or as Joseph Roach would put it, genealogies.[2] The neo-Nazis in the United States today who advocate white supremacy belong to the same world as the neo-Nazis in Argentina with their black shirts, and both groups mimic Hitler's performance. The totalitarian spectacle of the Dirty War arose from our shared cultural repertoire. It was yet another repetition, or iteration, an-other example of the twice-behaved behavior that Richard Schechner and Derrida associate with the performative. Through what act of negation, of self-blinding, can we maintain that what happens in another country has nothing to do with us?

We are always looking across borders, whether national, ethnic, or cultural. The issue is not *if*, but *how*, we look. The encounters are staged in various ways—from the surveillance practiced by the *migra* to the "*no se paga por ver*" of the street vendors. We participate in acts as disparate as witnessing, watching, peeping, as well as percepticide or self-blinding. Those acts entail different modes of identification, misidentification, seeing, or disbelieving what we see with our own eyes. Here, I will merely outline a couple of the problems attending the visual, beginning with the seeming non-encounter that results from denial and percepticide.

Martin Jay has recently argued that we have entered into an age of anti-ocularcentrism in which, after one *trompe l'oeil* too many, we question the relationship between the seen and the known. Our distrust of vision has been brought about by the very instruments—the telescope, the micro-scope, the camera—that theoretically were meant to enhance and expand our visual control.[3] Extending this observation from the realm of the epistemic to the political, we might say that part of our resistance to engaging politically (rather than emotionally) with the problems in the world around us is a product of studied disbelief. Viewers, often quite rightly, have come to suspect the way events have been structured as "problems," as "news." Not only do the media traffic in violence, milking catastrophes to excite viewers and hook them to the nightly news,[4] but there's the violence we don't see or, better put, that's not staged as *violence.* Poor children in the United States go without adequate food, education, and health care because white men in silk socks and Italian shoes want to save "us" money.[5] The way that spectacles are framed and transmitted through the mass media threatens the truth value of what we see, turning any and all "real" occurrences into one more exotic commodity on our screen.

But denial stems not merely from the questionable linkage between the seen and the known. We are so thoroughly submerged in the scopic field that at times we find it necessary to disengage from what we see or know to be "true." Devastating images from around the world lead to "compassion fatigue"—how many famished children and train wrecks can we take in without feeling that we have to turn a blind eye for the sake of self-preservation? As waves of undifferentiated violence wash over us, differentiation seems impossible—after a while, it's all the same. We either resist identification—what happened in Argentina is not about me—or we over-identify. Identification, understood in psychoanalytic literature as the "internalization of the other,"[6] functions as an act of metaphoric substitution, supplanting the "you" with the "as-if-it-were-me." All of a sudden, the specificity of the problem vanishes. Watching the blows during *Paso de dos,* I might feel as if I were the torturer's next victim. Instead of reacting politically to end torture or violence against women, for example, we are paralyzed by extension. It's only one more step before we feel that these images tyrannize us and that *we* are their victims. The double mechanism of undifferentiation and overidentification results in percepticide, for the same gesture that denies specificity ("it's all the same after a while") commands our overidentification (it's about us—our money, our security, our national well-being). But this drama is not about me—as such—for I am neither the victim (who is helpless) nor the perpetrator (who is guilty). My role is not to take on one's fear or the other's guilt, but to understand my role as *spectactor* in enabling or disrupting the scenario.

Peeping and watching—to move to another "kind" of looking— more explicitly call attention to the relationship between the see-er and the seen. Rather than the disavowal or cannibalism of percepticide—which supplants the relationship or questions the objective truth value of "the seen"—peeping and watching set up a unidirectional gaze. Both depend on perspectival vision that locates the seen within the scopic field while leaving the viewer safely out of the picture. We see as through the keyhole—the unseen see-er. Those who "just watch" what happened in Argentina risk engaging in Said's orientalism (or what Francis Aparicio has called *tropicalization* in relation to Latin America). Argentina is turned into a spectacle of excess (be it brutality or inflation) that feminizes it. It is "out of control." There's something fishy about the showy, macho, "Latin" virility. The military's performance of masculinity is overstated, if not parodic. The "othering" mechanism situates Argentina as the spectacle of transgression and the "body" of deviance. It serves as a cautionary message: that way disorder, dissolution, and danger lie. Moreover, it invisibly posits the watching "us" as the stable center. This nonreciprocal seeing is part of the colonialist and militarist gesture of appropriation and internalization of the "other" to reinforce the defining "self."

But there is another "kind" of looking—one that for lack of a better word I'll call witnessing—which I've drawn from theatre. This differs radically from the Western scientific ideal of the "objective" observer. Witnesses in Greek tragic drama are actual characters, with their own particular strengths and foibles. They are flesh and blood, there in the scenario, viewing events from their specific and limited perspective. Whether they're present by invitation or because they stumbled onto the wrong set, they participate in what is constituted as somebody else's drama. The position of the witnesses is always multiple. There is the "internal" witness of the play itself who willingly or reluctantly sees and reports the event to the wider community—the other characters, the chorus, and, indirectly, the audience. Audience members are "external" witnesses, that is, external to the script but fundamental to the continuation of the play. Then, as in Gambaro's *Information for Foreigners,* we have all those other witnesses, the ones who read about the events, recounting the plot they've heard but haven't seen to another group of witnesses. The witnesses, those who receive and act on (e.g., transmit) the drama, participate in the meaning-making process. It's the spectators/witnesses' job to challenge the plot, interrupt the action, and reinterpret events. If they don't buy into the drama, no communication is possible. If they withhold their support, the meaning-making enterprise of spectacle is interrupted and perhaps even rendered ineffectual.

Witnessing, then, functions within a different scopic economy than peeping or watching. Gone is the comfort of perspectival vision—the safe vantage point from which the visual field is opened up and organized before the seeing "I" but that leaves the viewer out of the frame. On the contrary, witnessing belongs to the Lacanian field of the "gaze," that register that locates us, and within whose confines we look at each other. The border has suddenly moved—it's no longer a question of the outer looking at the inner—we inhabit the expanded border zone of the "inner." There is no stable footing here—the viewing subject is also the object of the gaze; the outsider is incorporated into the play of looks. We were all looking, looking at each other looking. The same scopic structure that situates the object to be looked at, to paraphrase Lacan, puts "us" into the picture. We are all caught off balance in the spectatorial gaze, suddenly aware that the "object" of our gaze is also a subject who looks back, who challenges and objectifies us. Instead of the power and authority of the unseen see-er looking down from some higher place, reciprocity upsets and destabilizes the authoritarian vantage point. What become immediately visible are the specificities of our position and the ensuing limits to our perspective. We can't see everything; we can't occupy the visual vantage point of those located somewhat differently in the frame. What we see is clearly a function of where we happen to be standing—literally, politically, economically, and metaphorically. Though mutuality can be profoundly disconcerting and uncomfortable—perhaps the terms Yusem and I would have applied to our encounter—it stops us short, obliging us to rethink and look again. This pause, as Doris Sommer has so eloquently argued in her recent work, is not a bad thing if it encourages us to question easy notions of free access and rights of passage.

Witnessing presupposes that looking across borders is always an intervention and that the space of interlocution is always performative. It works within an economy of looks and in a scenario where positions—subject/object, see-er/seen—are constantly in flux, responding to each other. Each staging, as my example of the forum illustrates, makes visible and/or challenges certain relations of power, whether we like it or not. The physical setup of the encounter influences the denouement of events. If Yusem and I had had the same conversation in private, my guess is that the outcome would have been different. As it was, our interface made evident the degree to which we were both trapped in our performative traditions—me, a by now decidedly "First" World feminist who is free to come, critique, and go, and Yusem, authoritarianly defending boundaries that had been negotiated away long ago. Recognizing the performative frame of the encounter allows us to recognize how both of us were caught in the spectacles we critiqued.

This encounter started me thinking about my role in a drama I had preferred not to think of as my own. *Qué vela tengo yo en este entierro,* anyway? It was comforting to think that *no se paga por ver. Pero se paga.* Looking entails a responsibility, a risk, and a danger. However, it is not only the responsibility of receiving, decoding, and acting on a scenario. Of course, there is the heavy duty of the witness to the Holocaust that Dori Laub described in *Testimony,* in which the "listener" participates in the "process and place wherein the cognizance, the 'knowing' of the event is given birth to" and is therefore "party to the creation of knowledge."[7] Witnesses, of course, make witnesses of others, ensuring that the memory of injustice and atrocity is engraved upon, rather than erased from, collective memory. And, no doubt, the process of receiving, processing, and communicating horror is often a painful one. The messenger in *Oedipus Rex* prefaces his description of the catastrophe: "what horrors you will hear, what you will see, / what a heavy weight of sorrow you will shoulder."[8]

But some of the risks and dangers that worry me are less lofty. Though witnessing is not without risks, they're not the same risks facing the main players, or perhaps facing the witness to atrocity, though the temptation to confuse them may be strong. I, a self-conscious and uneasy witness, worry about my intervention. At times, I am surprised by the narcissistic pull toward mis/overidentification that converts "me" into the victim or casts "me" as the critic/hero. But I am neither. Even when I make no claims to the authority conceded to the immediate, lived experience of which I write, I worry. Having admitted that I'm not Argentinean and I haven't been tortured, the diva in me sees an opportunity to stage her own "confession," inserting myself in the recent performance of mea culpa staged by members of the Argentine military. I can own up to the self-indulgent regret that I am not authentic enough to have anything of interest to offer. Maybe I, like the silent spectators I criticize, should keep quiet, act like them. Performances, after all, are contagious. I, like Pavlovsky, like Yusem, am trapped in the others' moves, mimicking the very iteration I critique. Like others who write against violence, I too have wished for more options, better scripts, braver interventions. But witnessing, however singular and limited, is vital. By complicating the picture, it broadens the scope of the possible, expands the audience, and allows for a wider range of responses. Thus, I join my perspective to

others'—internal and external witnesses, historians, researchers, artists—
who have struggled with the problem of documenting and representing
violence. My role in this drama is not to keep quiet but to be a better
spectator. For the drama of uneasy interventions across dangerous borders
implicates us all. And it's against the diminishment of our complex and
interconnected visions that we must struggle.

NOTES

1. "Romance Elegíaco" by Luis de Miranda, qtd. in Cristina Iglesias and Julio
Schvartzman, *Cautivas y misioneros: Mitos blancos de la conquista* (Buenos Aires:
Catálogos Editora, 1897), 20.

2. In Andrew Parker and Eve Kosofsky Sedgwick, eds., *Performance and Performativity* (New York: Routledge, 1995).

3. Martin Jay, "Photo-unrealism: The Contribution of the Camera to the
Crisis of Ocularcentrism," in *Vision and Textuality*, ed. Stephen Melville and Bill
Readings (Durham: Duke University Press, 1995), 344–60.

4. Max Frankel, "The Murder Broadcasting System," *New York Times Magazine*,
Dec. 17, 1995, 46–48.

5. Ruby Duncan, founder of Operation Life, an organization run by poor
women to help poor women in Nevada, described how she attended a meeting
of the Ways and Means Committee that was withdrawing public support for
impoverished families: "so I'm standing here, and around this table was nothing
but white men, silk suits, silk ties, silk socks, shiny black loafers and shoes. And I
said, 'You don't have money for welfare?' " Alexis Jetter, Annelise Orleck, and
Diana Taylor, "Mothers at Risk: The War on Poor Women and Children," in
Populations at Risk in America, ed. Georges Demko and Michael C. Jackson (New
York: Westview Press, 1995), 104.

6. Diana Fuss, *Identification Papers* (New York: Routledge, 1995), 4.

7. Dori Laub, and Shoshana Felman, *Testimony: Crises of Witnessing in Literature, Psychoanalysis, and History* (New York: Routledge, 1992), 57–58.

8. Sophocles, *Oedipus Rex*, ed. R. D. Dawe (Cambridge: Cambridge University
Press, 1982), 1350–55.

TWELVE

Staging Crisis: Twin

Tales in Moving Politics

Randy Martin

A Crisis of Theory or of Politics?

It has become a commonplace to speak of a "crisis" in contemporary politics—a feeling that we cannot respond adequately to the pressing demands of the present. Nor is it hard to be sympathetic to this assessment of our times, given the magnitude of the assault on the conditions for sustaining social life despite an incredible amassing of wealth. A cursory review of recent Marxist/socialist writings finds that a notion of historical rupture or "crisis" is the recurring critical frame in the interpretation of our present social condition. Witness, for example, Arif Dirlik, *After the Revolution: Waking to Global Capitalism* (1994), Carl Boggs, *The Socialist Tradition: From Crisis to Decline* (1995), and Bernd Magnus and Stephen Cullenberg's anthology *Whither Marxism? Global Crises in International Perspective* (1995). Other writings occasioned by the breakup of the Soviet Union have taken this "crisis" as a basis for socialist renewal itself, as for example, the essays collected in Robin Blackburn, *After the Fall: The Failure of Communism and the Future of Socialism* (1991). What Stuart Hall and Martin Jacques have, in turn, called "new times" in their 1990 volume of that title seems to refer as much to current social conditions as to novel forms of political response. Indeed, the seminal works of Stanley Aronowitz in *The Crisis in Historical Materialism* (1981) and Ernesto Laclau and Chantal Mouffe in *Hegemony and Socialist Strategy* (1985)—which argued that radical democracy rather than socialism provides the most appropriate frame for promoting progressive political projects—also posit a notion of fundamental historical rupture as the occasion for their renewed leftist response. While these authors have diverse theoretical dispositions, their works accept and elaborate a narrative of before and after, decline and renewal, as a means to orient themselves in the present.

Rather than thinking of crisis as the special purview of the left, I believe that the notion of crisis itself is one of the features of the political scene out of which—and through which—the left and right are differentiated. The left, often by its own hand, is said to be in crisis; this crisis is attributed to its purported inability to capture the popular imagination or to sufficiently understand its own predicament, or its having lost ground over earlier gains. These problems are synoptically illustrated in the idea of "collapse," a trope of absolute end and beginning that speaks to a desire on the part of the left to be unburdened from its history, and a willingness to overlook the ambiguities between the nominal and phenomenal meanings of the very term "collapse." The extent to which the right shares in this predicament is thus easily overlooked; the right's hasty pronouncements of triumph appear to be free from their own strains of crisis. From this perspective, left and right may be less fixed positions on an objective political spectrum than divergent temptations within a certain episteme. Hence, rather than beginning within the taxonomy of left and right, I aim to explore, by means of certain shared tropes and other social conditions, the terrain they share and out of which they become differentiated.

If the very sense of crisis is a recurrent phenomenon and not simply a feature of the present historical moment, then we need to interrogate the political field itself to understand what generates this condition. I suggest that this revised notion of crisis as both unique and recurrent refers fundamentally to the problem of seeing and doing, imagining and enacting, or better, theory and practice. Perhaps the time has come to let the tensions within these binaries play themselves out in a different key than the tuneful wail of conventional political thinking. As we will see, what sounds at first like the inadequacy of practice to theory can be rehearsed as a far more gratifying relation. This is what I have in mind by thinking politics through performance.

To do so, I will deploy politics and performance heuristically, without elaborating the complexity and diversity of each domain. My intention is to explore a given idea about performance in order to inform how we think about politics. I am interested in the most general understanding of how performance calls attention to itself, how it operates as a social practice that can inform other practices, rather than how it is assessed in its particular aesthetic dimensions. At the same time, this performative imaginary of the political may entail a more restrictive conception of performance itself than has come to be typical of such discussions. If the idea of the performative rests on an act of speech that turns out to underlie any activity of speaking, then its gain against some putatively nonperformative mode of sociality is difficult to discern. But as there can be no generic performance activity, attaching this conception of politics to a fabulation of the theatrical insists on a certain materialization of space, of creative activity, of mutually socializing and disruptive difference that may elude the linguistic metaphor. By way of provisional definition, I take performance to be a temporally and spatially framed theatrical activity, a live encounter that brings together performers and audience. Politics, in turn, can be seen as a deliberate mobilization of human agency in the name of some explicit critical difference in the shape or conduct of human affairs (in shorthand, an intervention in the name of a project).

When performance is treated as a self-reflexive form of public encounter, we have a model of the social in which crisis is made acute but is also survived. Any given performance is organized around the irreducible difference between its status as a presentation that can be staged again and the fact that it can never really be repeated—especially from the vantage of the audience in attendance as an ensemble. Performance harbors a division of labor that formally separates its moments of action and reflection, only to bring the two into contact. While politics oriented toward certain ends is said to be "in" crisis, performance can be said to occur *through* crisis: one sensibility is brought to an end and it becomes possible to dwell on and survive the excessive intensity of experience thereby produced.

The uniqueness of a given performance derives from the combination of forces that gather the various assemblages that will constitute the performance. These forces combine and bring together audience, performers, text, revenues, management, scenic space, costumes, and scenic objects, drawing them out of larger fields—the population of a city, the pool of actors, the moneys spent elsewhere—in which people had otherwise shared no such immediate connection. This process of gathering or mobilization is, for any given performance event, momentary and nonrepeatable. Even if the occasion recurs, what gathers (at) the scene is a determinate particularization of what transpires between performers and public. The interface between performers and public can be restated on another occasion, but even that restatement must be collected all over again by means of myriad pathways that meet on the field of play. While one can reify the performance as an event that exceeds the labor that brings it into being, as Herbert Blau has observed, the stability of the event is elusive, given that what specifically makes any performative moment disperses as soon as the event is consummated. Hence what appears in the course of performance may be recalled or reinscribed elsewhere, but it leaves no trace of the constellation of forces that mobilized its appearance in the first place.

By means of these unstable conditions, performance brackets an internal and external time off from one another so that the performance appears as the negative of both its past and its future. On the one hand, what is taken as external to performance is momentarily laid to rest during that performance; on the other, the momentary combination of forces that make up the performance (the gathering and dispersal of forces that yield the sense of immediate temporal presence) cannot account for itself or its own formation. This arrest of life to make a show of the living is the crisis that brings performance into being and points to its early demise.

The unique internal moments of performance are doubled by a recurrent condition of arrested motion that constitutes crisis in and as performance. If we were to line up a series of performances, we would find in each its uniqueness, but also, in the very recurrence of those particular events, a displacement of what is momentarily taken as the terms of involvement in the present. While the moments never repeat themselves, what does recur is—precisely—this internal movement of combination and displacement. Thus the accomplishment of displacing motion appears as a demand to begin all over again. The model of crisis proposed by performance carries this double aspect: at once a unique moment produced by a combination that negates its own past, and at the same time, the recurring movement of displacement that is an irreducible feature of creative social activity.

But a crisis of theory is generated when one mistakes this movement for stasis, when what is constitutive is taken to be merely momentary. The recurrent labor of theory is lost to the passing of the theorized event or object. These two inextricably bound yet opposed aspects of crisis resonate in much rhetoric about politics: the sense that an era has ended; the feeling of arrested motion; the anxiety not simply over where to go, but how to notice we are getting there. The contradiction between these two internal aspects of crisis is highlighted when we ask, for example, precisely how a movement in history can conclude by any means other than the movement of something different from itself.

The imaginary of performance enacts and survives precisely this kind of contradiction. The performance enacts a sudden loss of (external) referents only to introduce its own (soon to be lost or terminated) universalizations. That these breaches recur suggests that the division between what is internal and external to the performance is less a passing absolute than an artifact of the performance's own passing, the means through which what is mobilized in performance becomes fully vested and divested. Translated to political terms, the example of performance does not teach us that there cannot be accretions of power or institutional accumulations, that all is forgotten and made anew with each crisis. Rather, performance teaches us that the limitations of individual political formations in relation to what they promise are not the limitations of politics per se—a claim that is intimated by so much recent reflection on the contemporary scene.[1]

Fable 1: The Nation in Decline

The question of how one historical moment yields to another underscores the periodizing assumptions that fuel the profusion of the performative in contemporary politics. Rather than purging politics of reference to beginnings and endings (as if one could be cleansed of the temptations to bad faith), we should realize that most "crisis talk" already presupposes conceptual boundaries around what is considered the present. Therefore the burden of any analysis is to place its own fantasy of the present on the table. The bracketing effects of what is taken as here and now are not simply temporal but spatial; we can speak of the United States itself as made up by forces of combination and displacement, provided we do so in reference to its global context.

If a fable be told, we could imagine a radical shift in the way politics inhabits its terrain. Once upon a time, let us say some two decades ago, certain conditions for political identity, namely, a world carved into national containers by the forces of European colonialism, crashed on the rocks of its own success. The nation that inherited the mantle of empire saw itself defeated in a war that had threatened no expansion by an enemy not its equal, while within its hallowed backyard, a culture raged against the purported unanimity of national purpose. This, the empire's last stand (as nation but not as state), did not eliminate the beast, only its burden. Containment, so central to the strategies of cold war anticommunism, turned out to be as much directed inward as outward: the hostility unleashed against movements for abolition, suffrage, and labor was something of a national anthem, always accompanied by foreign fugues and xenophobic cantatas. So long as the national space remained expansive as a site of internal development, the national mythos of inclusion had a material base that could be extended—albeit unevenly and not without new regimes of exclusion—to various populations.

But with anticommunism, the call for extreme and immediate global vigilance achieved symphonic proportions, to the point of rationalizing the sacrifice of national security for future generations. The citizens who were told they had so much to gain by sacrifice wound up *losing* their investment in the nation to the global menace—but not the feared menace of communism, rather, the global menace of hypermobile capital. The United States lost the nation in Vietnam, and the abandonment of developing the former was no less complete than the un-nationly refusal to reparate the latter. One might say that the indelible lesson of Vietnam for the guardians of warfare was that the very division of the nation into "internal" and "external" spheres was no longer adequate as a template for expansive accumulations.

At the same time, the visual administration of countable corpses came to undermine the efficiencies of prosecuting war. The proof that the war was being won painted it as a lost cause, a representational syndrome that has prevailed through the incursion in the Gulf, which sought to correct the problem by means of simultaneous intervention and disengagement. Now similar visual techniques of body count are tied to racialized domestic crime in a gesture to bring the war home; fear of lost bodily security and public place stand in for outrage at witnessing one's own nation run wild on the ground of others. The belief expressed in popular polls that it is crime, not the economy, that accounts for domestic insecurities is itself a symptom of the abandonment of the nation as a frontier for development.

Under these conditions, the machinery for producing identity, previously moored to the nation, now confronts a certain "denationing," a condition in which states as political units are increasingly incommensurate with the economic scale of their operations.[2] For example, transactions in financial instruments such as stocks, bonds, derivatives, and currencies are now conducted in institutions in a global urban network that includes New York, Tokyo, Paris, and Amsterdam. This denationed terrain not only unleashes capital itself from its own prior conditions of reproduction, but it has also revised the very terms for the production of identity. Denationing is in no way inconsistent with an effusion of nationalisms. It only means that the state itself can no longer be the sole arbiter of these mobilizations by any means other than repression. Because the terms of exchange in the social economy have retreated from the universalizing category of citizenship, the conditions of recognition are turned back on the popular multiplicities themselves—here the entire field of social movements—making the arena of identity formation substantially less circumscribed.

This surfeit—this hyperproduction of identity—is the key site of performativity in the present narrative of national decline. The prior exchange of state sovereignty for individual citizen-identity has broken up into multiple and more fully socialized currencies through which identity is traded. The movement of identity, now without fixed geopolitical referent or social unit (the nation-state), has come to be called "new social movements," and what is "new" about them cannot be grasped apart from political economy. These performative mobilizations relate to the further commodification and socialization (in Marx's sense of a mutually interdependent association of producers) of economies of service and consumption, and the extension of the regulatory apparatus, even under the guise of deregulation and privatization. Regulation of bodies along lines of gender, race, age, citizenship have proliferated as much as has state intervention on behalf of transnational trade or federally mandated assignments of risk to workers for their pensions.

The sudden excess of identifications that is forged by the (new) nonfixity of state and capital must now be regulated in relation to the more extensive scale of affiliations. This displacement also has its impact upon the state's representative face—its means of governing as opposed to its areas of operations (which continue to expand coercively into the newly politicized private domain). In effect, the state lost its monopoly on authorizing identity claims; now the state must perform its own self-justification as if it too were a type of mobilization in search of affirmation from some status-granting other. In other words, the larger political economy can only partially be recognized by the state. Politics oriented around the category of identity, unlike the category of citizenship, can ground only certain limiting claims and resources. Some dimension of gender, sexuality, or race remains beyond recognition or redress by the state (and, for that matter, the nation). Such so-called failures or limitations can eclipse whatever social goods the various new mobilizations actually place in motion; in turn those politics of recognition can become the very terms by which the efficacy of the new movements are evaluated.

This movement beyond the parameters of the nation-state could, in conventional public discussion, be interpreted cynically, indicating that political needs can no longer be redressed socially (hence are "in crisis"). Instead, what seems excessive or overwhelming in the proliferation of politics should properly be thought of as mobilizations that *expand* the reach of the social. Here politics appears performance-like because of the surfeit of the political in relation to the standard means of evaluating the social movements. The impasse produced is as much an impatience with these more difficult terms of success as it is a heightened interference with the viability of the various projects associated with the burgeoning reach of the political.

Fable 2: In the Theatre of Theory and Practice

Time for another fable, but this one, still more allegorical, can be told as the tale of theory and practice itself, as we trace the etymological footpath back to Greece. The forebears of what is now known as theory were visitors, as John J. MacAloon recounts, "ambassadors" to the games, positioned to return elsewhere and let the truth be known of what others had done. Within the arena itself, reflection could only distract the players from their own involvement. Now surely, this is a very circumscribed idea of gaming, as it is of theatre, but the notion of a mutual exteriority of theory and practice frequently remains faithful to the divide between knowing and acting, seeing and doing. Theory takes visual hold of action to make of it an object, and practice passes through its action without remarking on itself.

This spectacular image of the relation between theory and practice is critical to the conditions under which any self- critical political tendency may take its identity. On the one hand, the ability to see beyond activity provides the insight to grasp what makes things work and to imagine other valuations of daily enactments. The ability to arrest the present serves to incarcerate the taken-for-grantedness of social life and to project what is lacking there onto a programmatic stage. Yet this latter move also turns theory against its object, and tempts one to interpret practice as the source of some lack—lack of what could or should be—when in reality that lack is no more than an artifact of the theorist's appropriative projection. If the ability to show what is wrong with the world is taken as an act of mere observation, rather than a production in its own right, then the circumstances that make theory possible seem resolvable only if we exclude theory from what it most desires to be part of. This unhinging of theory and practice, which fixes the latter and exiles the former from its own conditions of possibility, treats what is excessive as if it were scarce.

It is not enough in this context to say that theory is, of course, another instance of practice that must treat its own arresting ambitions as necessary for critique but insufficient for its self-evaluation. Theory is not simply one type of practice among others, but also a moment of every practical activity. If we are to embrace the conditions of crisis without succumbing to the anxiety that there will be no further crises (hence no politics), a more intimate imbrication of theory and practice is crucial. Here the imaginary of performance again becomes helpful. Specifically, we can revisit the relations of spectacle from which theory and practice derive, but with greater attention to what makes such performances possible. Instead of focusing on the traffic of ambassadors shuttling between fixed and stable domains, we might attend to the way the gathering of a public actually occasions the performance, which in turn provides the stage that allows acts of reasoning to become realized as ideas.

Further, we might reverse the usual pairings of theory with audience and practice with performance. We can view what transpires onstage as an instance of performative agency, as that which brings into being a self-delimiting idea; we can imagine the irrecuperable movement that constitutes an audience, a movement produced by so many hitherto scattered impulses to attend the promised performance. The gathering that occasions the event is the interiority of practice; it places on display the animating quality that gives any idea of history-making its forward motion. The performance occurs through the mutual displacement and insinuation of these forces, a process that renders the relations of performers and audience, agency and history, the materializable idea and the material body of its reception two moments of a fragile dialectic.

From outside performance, these two moments appear fixed and separable: audiences come and go, but the show must go on. Yet it is the collision of these forces of difference that enables the performance to occur, only to depart without leaving a trace of the terms of exchange that had been established there. Theory recuperates its idea only in the retrospect of an irrecoverable loss. The loss to consciousness of what placed that idea in motion renders thought part of the conditions it critiques. Against the anxieties provoked by notions of crisis as arrested motion and of critical inquiry as placeless, the relation of theory and its practice ventured here can subvert this effacement of critical activity.

In this more expansive view of politics, what was seen as scarce—political prospects—now becomes abundant. Thinking through the perspective of performance, we find that theory arrests its own development: at the moment its agency is realized by its reception, its occasion is momentarily dispersed in the conditions that had first mobilized the public encounter. The sense that theory is missing its audience, in other words, is its founding condition. Theory prepares itself in anticipation for this moment of its own dispersal; it is the prime moment of agency in the exchange and collision of difference. The willingness to bear this loss, to enter again upon the terrain of depletion, presupposes not an absolute deficit of the material, but the very surplus of the social. It presupposes the excess movement of bodies that can never wholly absorb and therefore terminate agency's moments of opportunity. The acceptance of crisis as a condition for theorizing is the very disposition that makes more abundant both theorizing and its politics. And if this is so, the imaginary of performance allows a rethinking of the relation between crisis as the end of a determinant historical moment and crisis as the arresting of what moves in/as the present.

To the current crisis talk, then, the infusion of performance into political theory recasts certain voicings and claims. The ends of eras may not be over; what moves them is already in motion. But rather than banishing theory from politics as suddenly irrelevant to lead the public to the theatres of history, the places of theory abound in the service of what to make of so much motion. Shifted to the side of the excessive, theory no longer need await its agency or its conjuncture. Inside the very politics it so desires, the din may still render orientation difficult, but the expectation of resolution, of a final self-silencing, may extend the moment of engagement upon which theory depends. The willingness to let what the present produces be dispersed is, after all, a way to have crisis without succumbing to it.

NOTES

1. My own thinking on these issues has been developed in collaboration with Michael E. Brown; see our "Rethinking the Crisis of Socialism," and "Left Futures," both published in the journal *Socialism and Democracy,* and a forthcoming book we are preparing together.

2. The term "denationing" is meant to join in a debate over the fate of nation-states and national identity in the complex process of globalization. At times, as Gayatri Spivak has noted, the postnational condition is asserted as if populations were free from the constraints and entitlements of nation-as-exchange in the global order. See Gayatri Chakravorty Spivak and David Plotke, "A Dialogue on Democracy"; Ross Poole, "Nationalism: The Last Rites"; Paul James, "Reconstituting the Nation-State: A Postmodern Republic Takes Place"; and the essays in Paul James, ed., *Critical Politics*. More recently, Saskia Sassen has used the term to denote a particular space, still situated within the nation that undermines its conditions of sovereignty.

WORKS CITED

Aronowitz, Stanley. *The Crisis in Historical Materialism*. New York: Praeger, 1981.

Blackburn, Robin. *After the Fall: The Failure of Communism and the Future of Socialism*. London: Verso, 1991.

Blau, Herbert. *The Audience*. Baltimore: Johns Hopkins University Press, 1990.

Boggs, Carl. *The Socialist Tradition: From Crisis to Decline*. New York: Routledge, 1995.

Brown, Michael E., and Randy Martin. "Rethinking the Crisis of Socialism." *Socialism and Democracy* 14 (1991): 9–56.

———. "Left Futures." *Socialism and Democracy* 18 (1995): 59–89.

Dirlik, Arif. *After the Revolution: Waking to Global Capitalism*. Hanover: Wesleyan University Press, 1994.

Hall, Stuart, and Martin Jacques, eds. *New Times: The Changing Face of Politics in the 1990's*. London: Verso, 1990.

James, Paul. "Reconstituting the Nation-State: A Postmodern Republic Takes Place." *Arena Journal,* no. 4 (1994–95): 69–89.

———, ed. *Critical Politics*. Melbourne: Arena Publications, 1994.

Laclau, Ernesto, and Chantal Mouffe. *Hegemony and Socialist Strategy*. London: Verso, 1985.

MacAloon, John J., "Interval Training." In *Choreographing History*, ed. Susan Foster, 32–53. Bloomington: Indiana University Press, 1995.

Magnus, Bernd, and Stephen Cullenberg, eds. *Whither Marxism? Global Crises in International Perspective*. New York: Routledge, 1995.

Poole, Ross. "Nationalism: The Last Rites." *Arena Journal,* no. 4 (1994–95).

Sassen, Saskia. *Losing Control: Sovereignty in an Age of Globalization*. New York: Columbia University Press, 1996.

Spivak, Gayatri Chakravorty, and David Plotke. "A Dialogue on Democracy." *Socialist Review* 94, no. 3 (1995): 1–22.

THIRTEEN

Bodies outside the
State: Black British
Women Playwrights
and the Limits of
Citizenship

May Joseph

In his account of Black British cultural production and its transatlantic influences in *There Ain't No Black in the Union Jack,* Paul Gilroy outlines the elaborate regimes of production, consumption, and circulation that make Black Britishness a tangible and permeating presence within the British state. What hovers around Gilroy's intricate archive are the unseen economies of Black British women's cultural work, demonstrating yet another dimension of the possibilities, anxieties, and contradictions of cultural citizenship within the modern state. Yvonne Brewster, the grande dame of Black British women's theatre, recounts in an interview by Stella Oni that she was the first Black woman drama student in England, trained at the Royal Academy, emerging as a qualified actress in 1965. In 1982, Brewster became the first Black woman drama officer in the Arts Council.[1] While at first glance this seems an anecdote of minor significance, it assumes for me an opening into the largely unmapped terrain of Black British women's cultural production and its circulation in the public sphere from the 1960s to the 1990s. This essay focuses on Black women's playwriting as an evocative site of citizenship, while situating their emergence within the broader spectrum of media practices.

Prior to the early 1980s, the discourse of identity and the narratives of belonging in Black British cultural production were predominantly male narratives, foregrounding Black male subjectivity. The playwright Mustapha Matura, poet/performers Linton Kweisi Johnson and Benjamin Zephaniah, and playwright/director Jatinder Varma were among the early innovators of Black theatre. Lionel Ngakane, Horace Ove, Menelik Shabazz, and Rasheed Araeen were other media practitioners at this time whose preoccupations often foreground the dilemmas of arrival, class antagonisms, pan-African sympathies, Black identity, and the tensions of masculinity—marking the absence of Black women as subjects with agency.

The thriving Black Arts movement, propelled by the Greater London Council's funding initiated in 1981, generated new spheres for Black British women's cultural contributions. With impetus through the movement, Black women playwrights acquired a new visibility, transforming the gendered rhetoric of belonging in new ways. This reconfiguration of concerns created a proliferation and fracturing of coalitions during the 1980s along the lines of class, gender, ethnicity, and sexuality. The result was the formation of various groups and collectives such as Theatre of Black Women (1982), Talawa Theatre Company (1985), Temba, Umoja, Tara Arts Company (1976), Tamasha Theatre Company (1989), Assati, Black Theatre Co-operative, Carib, Black Mime Theatre (later known as the Women's Troop), Unlock the Chains Collective, Munirah, Double Edge, Roots Theatre, Black Theatre Co-op, the Women's Theatre Workshop, and Theatre Centre, most of which came into existence during the 1980s and 1990s.[2] Yvonne Brewster, Winsome Pinnock, Maureen Blackwood, Stella Dadzie, Hazel Carby, Pratibha Parmar, Amrit Wilson, Ravindher Randhawa, Bernadine Evaristo, and other Black feminists gained increasing public attention. Their work cumulatively destabilized earlier narratives of women as structured absence, filling the invisible histories of Black women as active agents within British struggles for cultural and legal citizenship.[3]

The rest of this essay will explore the ideas of intersectionality and positionality of legal citizenship in the modern state through a reading of Black women's playwriting during Margaret Thatcher's era. By analyzing the plays of Rukhsana Ahmad, Meera Syal, Jacqueline Rudet, and Winsome Pinnock, I outline some of the intertwined themes of cultural and legal citizenship that shape Black women's subjectivities. I argue that the precarious and marginal positions that Black British women occupy as bodies "outside the state" shape the periodization narrative of their recent emergence as citizens within British culture.

Beginning with the dismantling of Britain's empire through the relinquishing of India and its Caribbean possessions and the decolonization of Africa, and concretely located in the arrival of the first sizable contingent of West Indian people to England on the SS *Windrush* in June 1948, Britain's colonial legacy came to a crisis within its own shores.[4] Along with the traumatic change from being a seat of empire until the Second World War to being the vestige of a world power, Britain experienced a new wave of immigration from its former colonies, largely in the form of economic migrants seeking a better means of living, as Winsome Pinnock's play *A Hero's Welcome* (1989) poignantly dramatizes.[5] Drawn from the array of former colonial sites ranging from British Guyana, the Caribbean, Africa, Hong Kong, Malaysia, and South Asia, these semiskilled or unskilled workers catalyzed a shift within dominant "race" discourse in British citizenship. Arriving in Britain by virtue of belonging to the New Commonwealth (as characters in Jacqueline Rudet's *Basin*, Zindika's *Leonora's Dance*, and Bonnie Greer's *Munda Negra* do) or having a British passport from an ex-colony, these new ethnicities emerged for the first time as a threatening mass to be stopped, eradicated, and repatriated. But in the work of Black British women playwrights, the impact of these communities in Britain is dramatized and celebrated.[6]

British immigration laws from the 1960s onwards determined the type of immigrant that was possible; hence much Black British playwriting until the early 1990s involves concerns around forging new kinds of multicultural citizenship. Former British subjects of ex-colonial nations could no longer claim immigration rights to Britain solely on the basis of having the appropriate papers. By the mid-seventies, immigration from Africa and Asia was brought to a grinding halt through a series of legislative moves designed to both racialize and restrict the growing presence of Black communities. These communities of ex-colonial subjects organized around common issues of disenfranchised minorities whose presence in Britain continued to be articulated along the lines of "race" by the state. From now on, the rhetoric of migration becomes racinated in very specific ways and pathologizes Black immigration and expatriation.[7]

For Black women in Britain, the policies of immigration worked doubly to limit their access to legal rights and cultural citizenship. While the first wave of immigration from the West Indies during the 1950s saw high proportions of women who were single and economically active, subsequent waves resulted in the control and restriction of Black women entering Britain in the sixties. Migrancy affected single Black women in very different ways from Black men. In 1968, the British government altered the legal rights of entry for Asians by introducing a voucher system; vouchers were issued only to heads of households, normally men, and for certain categories of dependents. Consequently, Asian women were denied immigrant status unless they had kinship ties to relatives in Britain. This affected women coming to Britain as well as those born in Britain, since they had enormous difficulty proving they were heads of households as widowed, deserted, or divorced women. Furthermore, the gendered immigration legislations such as the 1962 Commonwealth Citizens Act and the 1972 Immigration Act made it difficult for Asian women holding British passports to acquire legal rights of entry within Britain as dependents. This severely restricted the movements and access to education for most women from the immigrant Black communities since now they had to deal with the structures of patriarchy within their own cultures as well as the complexities of struggling for survival within the postcolonial British state.[8] These extensive regulative effects of immigration laws on Black women's lives shape the forms, issues, and themes of Black women's struggles for citizenship, as both Meera Syal's screenplay *My Sister-Wife* and Rukhsana Ahmad's play *Song for a Sanctuary* (1990) demonstrate. The largely private spaces of Black women's urban social life explored in these texts radically disrupt dominant assumptions about access to cultural representation, spectatorship, and citizenship, often raising new questions about representational politics and its micro-economies of invisibility and disempowerment.

While it is beyond the scope of this essay to delineate the specific distinctions of visibility politics within specific mediums such as film, visual culture, and theatre, which have developed independently, it is important to bear in mind that the particular narrative being mapped here is contingent on the interrelatedness of these various art practices. Decentering the notions of "Black" culture into its possible realizations in the Western metropole by challenging the notion of who is "British" and coming to terms with the constantly shifting implication of what it means to be "English" informs much Black art of this period. Instead of fictions of cultural homogeneity, these art practitioners suggest a transforming urban syncretism that is altered and in turn shapes its various immigrant and indigenous presences. The work of the film and video collectives such as Retake, Star, Ceddo, Sankofa, Black Audio, and the Women's Collective is particularly noteworthy. These collectives pushed the boundaries of representation beyond a mere repositioning of Black identity within the British imaginary. They complicated received ideas of the postcolonial citizen along the axes of gender, sexuality, generations, and immigrant histories. These collectives generated work for many artists in different mediums simultaneously.

I want to underscore here the particular economies of race, representation, and necessity that coalesce to make working across mediums a necessity in the early decades of Black representational struggles in Britain. During the 1980s, theatre actresses such as Corinne Skinner Carter of *Passion of Remembrance,* Rita Wolf of *My Beautiful Laundrette, Burning and Illusion,* and *Khush,* and Meera Syal of *Sammy and Rosie Get Laid* and *My Sister-Wife* work in film as well, while playwrights such as Tunde Ikoli, Hanif Kureishi, and more recently Winsome Pinnock and Meera Syal write and direct for film and television while continuing to work in the theatre. Visual artist Sonya Boyce works as a set designer on the film *Dreaming Rivers,* directed by Martina Attile of Sankofa Film and Video Collective, while filmmakers John Akomforah, Isaac Julien, Robert Crusz, Maureen Blackwood, Martina Attile, Gurindher Chadha, and Pratibha Parmar find themselves defining new critical territories as theoreticians and practitioners, blurring the boundaries between mediums. This interlinked terrain provides a mass of work focused on the relationship of Black cultural production to cultural citizenship. Sites like theatre and live art produce independent though interrelated economies of dependence and intervention within Black struggles for British citizenship.

Intersectionality and Individual Rights: Rukhsana Ahmad's Song for a Sanctuary *and Meera Syal's* My Sister-Wife

In her essay " 'Woman's Era,' " Hazel Carby indicates how the texts of Black women from ex-slave Harriet Jacobs to educator Anna Julia Cooper are testaments to the racist practices of the suffrage and temperance movements and are indictments of the ways white women allied themselves not with Black women but with a racist patriarchal order against all Black people. According to Carby, "only by confronting this history of difference can we hope to understand the boundaries that separate white feminists from all women of colour."[9] Feminist, postcolonial, and queer scholarship over the past two decades has complicated the Black and white boundaries that Carby invokes, by opening up the links and crossroads between race, gender, nationality, and sexuality.

Arguing for such an intersection from the context of critical legal theory in "Demarginalizing the Intersection of Race and Sex," Kimberlé Crenshaw points out that the tendency to treat race and gender as mutually exclusive categories of experience and analysis is perpetuated by a single-axis framework that is dominant in antidiscrimination law in the United States and that is also reflected in feminist theory and antiracist politics.[10] According to Crenshaw, such a single-axis analysis distorts the multidimensionality of Black women's experiences and results in their erasure. By using Black women in the United States as the starting point, Crenshaw demonstrates how dominant conceptions of discrimination condition us to think about subordination as disadvantage occurring along a single categorical axis. This limits inquiry to the experiences of otherwise privileged members of the group. In the race discrimination cases that Crenshaw discusses, this tends to be viewed in terms of sex- or class-privileged Blacks; in sex discrimination cases, the focus is on race- and class-privileged women. For Crenshaw, only by considering the problems of intersectionality can one begin to embrace the experiences and concerns of Black women in the United States. While Crenshaw's work is specific to the United States in its cultural moorings, her arguments for intersectionality and dismantling the single-axis framework are crucial to an understanding of the political junctures within which Black peoples—particularly women—in the United States, Europe, and Britain function. Taken together, the works of Crenshaw and Carby point a way toward the dismantling of single-axis frameworks and the problematizing of existing paradigms. Both Crenshaw and Carby argue for the multidimensionality of Black women's experiences and demonstrate the struggle to do so within prefabricated legal and institutional structures. What Crenshaw in the field of legal theory and Carby in literary theory are reconfiguring, a number of Black British women have articulated in their art.

In Rukhsana Ahmad's moving portrayal of a London Women's Refuge home in *Song for a Sanctuary*, for instance, the horrific conditions of immigrant women's lives in Britain slowly unravel through the regulative structures of religion, patriarchy, honor, duty, and community structures that limit the kinds of citizenship to which women like Rajindher have access. Cocooned within the rigidly patriarchal and dogmatic boundaries of embattled religious ideologies, in this case Sikh culture, and its culturally resilient practices of the control of women, Rajindher struggles to understand her dependence on her husband as well as her invisibility as a subject within the state.

Rajindher's complex history of fifteen horrific years of domestic violence, torn between the psychic economies of privacy, secrecy, and pride which relegate such material conditions to the realm of the private, poses the difficult question of subjecthood within the state. For Rajindher, caught between her culture's prohibitive and punitive economy and the state's secular intrusions into her psychic and personal space, citizenship in Britain is continually shaped as a negation of her psychic self, from her arrival to her eventual brutal death, when she is stabbed by her Punjabi husband Pradeep's *kirpaan* or dagger, in the refuge home.[11] Pradeep is a grotesque caricature, grounded in feudal and agrarian notions of ownership and retribution, blind to his violent and abusive outbursts.

Ahmad relentlessly pursues the interstitial realms of women's lives such as the refuge home, where the limits of legal, psychic, and economic citizenship simultaneously impinge on the rights of immigrant women within the state. Rajindher is caught between the British notion of individual rights and her culturally specific realm of experience, where notions of duty and honor supersede if not entirely displace Western notions of individual rights, making it difficult for her to come to terms with her condition, despite her fifteen years in Britain.

As Crenshaw's paradigm of intersectionality reminds us, Rajindher's rights within the British state are interlocked within the heterosexual matrix of the law, since she is a dependent by virtue of being married. In order to be eligible for state support and housing, she has to reconsider her own subjectivity, which is only partly read by the state, because the assumptions of state regulations do not take into account the real-life micro-economies of control such as Sikh notions of duty, honor, virtue, and retribution. As Pradeep says when he stabs Rajindher, "This is not murder, it is a death sentence, her punishment for taking away what was mine. . . . She can't leave me, she's my wife." Pradeep's sense of the righteousness and absoluteness of his act falls completely outside the sphere of a Western notion of rights as he invokes a feudal though culturally coherent notion of ownership and possession, in which the wife is devoid of individual rights by virtue of her marriage.

What Rukhsana Ahmad raises through the portrayal of a British Sikh family's gradual disintegration into incest, violence, child abuse, and eventual death is a crucial aspect of cultural and legal citizenship within the modern state, the tensions between common law and customary practice, which is rarely the subject of discussion in secular states such as Britain and the United States, except as the expression of individual or human rights, as in the volatile debates surrounding clitoridectomy and the practices of infibulation. Customary practice, which often works as regulative economies of women's bodies regardless of its cultural specificity as Sikh, Hindu, Jain, or Muslim, does not translate easily into the legal discourse of secular nations like Britain and the United States, and therefore renders invisible the very complex mechanisms of control through which women from Hindu, Buddhist, Confucian, and Muslim countries must forge psychic and legal access to individual rights.[12]

Like Ahmad's work, Meera Syal's dark screenplay *My Sister-Wife* contends with the irreconcilable and fraught forces of individuality and communality as they explode in South London, within the domestic spaces of a Pakistani Muslim household. What Syal deftly portrays in a series of reversals reminiscent of Genet's play *The Maids* are the competing logics between customary practice such as Islamic law and the law of the state, civil law. With great wit, Syal sketches the tortuous and circumlocutory ways through which immigrants in Britain negotiate between antediluvian feudal traditions of former homelands and the less evident, more contemporary orthodoxies of the secular culture within which they must live as British subjects.

The plot is framed between two poles of immigrant British Muslim women's subjectivities. Farah is the modern, urban professional woman, born in Pakistan, brought up in Britain to cultured, upper-class Pakistani businesspeople. Maryam is a traditional Pakistani bourgeois woman who is in an arranged marriage to Asif Shah, a rich, successful, binational businessman who travels between Britain and Pakistan. With this *ménage à trois*, Syal sets the stage for the psychic struggle between individual rights and customary practice.

What follows is a compelling exploration of the epistemological crevices of competing psychic and sexual economies, with the common denominator being the oppression and interdependence of Black women. Syal's work shreds the illusion that education and modernization can buy middle-class women enough consciousness to opt out of the patriarchal circuits of exchange and subjection. Instead, Syal skillfully lays out the more powerful and intangible psychic economies of cultural insularity, immigrant self-perpetuation, and isolation through which Asif's and Maryam's cultural ambivalence takes root and finally overwhelms Farah's British sense of self and individuality. Syal paints a contemporary picture of interlocking interests of desire and patriarchy, both Muslim and Western (read as secular) through which this particular British Muslim household must determine its fate, and it does, by killing the source of its discontent, Asif.

Like Rukhsana Ahmad's portrayal of the dilemmas of intersectionality, Meera Syal's *My Sister-Wife* raises further questions about the limits of juridical logic. Crenshaw's paradigm of intersectionality becomes particularly useful in this instance, as it enables one to consider the ways the legal, material, and representational practices of the law elide the limits and possibilities through which many disempowered constituencies of immigrant and minority women struggle for representation and rights.

Positionality and the Critique of Bourgeois Feminism: Jacqueline Rudet's Basin *and Winsome Pinnock's* Rock in Water

Black British women's art engages with the possibilities and limits of positionality. The notion of positionality is deeply fraught, as it struggles between the totalizing narrative about the subject and the eternal sliding of the signifier. For emergent forms of citizenship such as Black British women's subjectivity, the dangers of totalizing subjecthood are delayed, as more urgent forms of emergent subjectivity grapple with the very basic forms of British citizenship, such as legal representation, cultural legitimacy, public mobility, and media visibility. Positionality in this case implies locating oneself as a subject already overdetermined by various contingent narratives, and self-consciously engaging in foregrounding those narratives that become crucial in demarcating the boundary one has chosen to occupy, such as Black lesbian, Black Marxist, Asian feminist, and so on.

The term "positionality" becomes important for an understanding of subjectivity, as it is through the realization of a certain series of identifications that one comes into voice. Positionality is crucially linked to the notion of subjectivity, particularly for emergent forms of citizenship; for working-class Black British women who do not write or speak in English, the process of coming into voice is literal. It simply means learning that one has legal rights, learning to use those rights, and learning how to get heard, after which visibility politics becomes possible.[13]

As the embattled site of legal and cultural citizenship, positionality presupposes an understanding of intersectionality. On the one hand, the post-structuralist premise that the fragmentation of the subject into multiple subject positions in postmodernity renders subjectivity a shifting space of sliding signification, and "reality" a simulacra. On the other hand, the deconstructionist position of the post-Marxist Stuart Hall insists on the need for arbitrary closure to necessitate meaning. As Hall says, "All the social movements which have tried to transform society and have required the constitution of new subjectivities, have had to accept the necessarily fictional, but also the fictional necessity, of the arbitrary closure which is not the end, but which makes both politics and identity possible." One can punctuate the eternal sliding of signification with meaning by contextualizing it within history, however arbitrary such a closure might be.[14] But this argument is not gender-neutral. For example, Black women have historically been subsumed under the rubric of "race" via the construction of "the Black community," which typically elides the patriarchal structures of control and oppression within notions of collective subjectivity. In this context the question of "race" functions as a totalizing value that underscores the structural exclusions of certain cultural or racial communities but which cannot account for how constituencies within those communities—such as Black women, lesbians, or gay men—may be affected differently by those structural exclusions.

Locating themselves within what Meenakshi Ponnuswami calls "the Newer Left constituencies of Thatcher's era," Pinnock and Rudet respectively address what Ponnuswami identifies as the failure of British feminist historiography and New Left theatre to account for the emancipatory alternative economies of Britain's Black populations. Ponnuswami points out that the white feminist historiography of Caryl Churchill, Pam Gems, Women's Theatre Group, Monstrous Regiment, Deborah Levy, and Shirley Gee, among others, critiques bourgeois feminism without providing alternative avenues for feminism's more emancipatory intersections. As Ponnuswami rightly observes, the New Left's cursory acknowledgment of feminist practice and its exclusion of race left the constituencies of Black women outside the discourse of even the left.[15]

Elaborating on the elision of their presence in dialogues within the British left, Rudet and Pinnock illuminate how the question of class again subsumed the issues of both race and gender in working-class politics, thereby ignoring or silencing the presence and role of Black women in the formation and politicizing of Black workers as a racinated and delegitimated class. By privileging the logic of intersectionality in their distanciation from British left culture, both playwrights critique the foregrounding of class as the prism through which to view the workings of material and social relations. Instead, they unpack the very tangible ways through which gender and sexuality play out in these processes, and are unaccounted for and ultimately erased within the predictable class agendas of left politics.

Finally, for Black British women articulating the politics of positionality, the question of gender was inextricably linked with Anglo-European feminist movements that invariably excluded Black women and avoided the issues of race and immigration.[16] Both Pinnock's Black communist feminist Claudia Jones in the play *A Rock in Water* (1989) and Rudet's Black lesbian feminist Susan in *Basin* (1985) critique white British bourgeois feminism. They propose alternative economies of identification to those of white British feminism as Claudia Jones's U.S.-Trinidadian past and Susan's Dominican references invoke the transnational relationships with other Black diasporas of the New World.

As representative instances of some of the issues raised by Black women's playwriting in the 1980s, Rudet's and Pinnock's plays merit close attention. They were among the first few Black British women's plays available in print, thanks to the efforts of Yvonne Brewster.[17] They are both situated within the context of the diaspora Black experience of the twentieth century. While *Basin* is structured around the lives of Black lesbian women of Afro-Caribbean descent and their desires and mythologies in postcolonial Britain, *A Rock in Water* foregrounds the struggles of Black women in a transnational framework, struggling for legal and cultural citizenship within the United States and Britain, both instances of modern secular democracies.

Rudet's *Basin* is a linear piece of theatre, realistic in form. It was directed by Paulette Randall, one of the founding members of the Theatre of Black Women, begun in 1982.[18] Exploring a distinctly Afro-Caribbean British women's culture through culturally specific paradigms such as the basin and "zammie," *Basin* raises epistemological questions about alternative economies of meaning in the postcolonial European city. Rudet specifies that the basin symbolizes the one article that all Black women possess, as mothers teach their daughters about cleanliness. For Rudet, "zammie" is a more permeable and fluid term to describe the close friendship between two women that falls outside Western notions of what the boundaries of relationship might be. According to Rudet, " 'zammie' is not 'lesbian' in patois. The word refers more to the universality of friendship between Black women; no matter what nationality, no matter what class, all Black women have very important things in common. They're the last in line; there's no one below them to oppress." Rudet states that "every Black woman is the 'zammie' of every other Black woman. It's almost an obligatory thing."[19] While Rudet's generalizations are reductive and essentialist in their assumptions, her portrayal of the zammie relationship reflects the more nuanced specificities of everyday life in the city for Black women. Rudet's invocation linking zammie love to the basin evokes Audre Lorde's prologue to *Zami*, "When I sit and play in the waters of my bath I love to feel the deep inside parts of me, sliding and folded and tender and deep."[20] Rudet's play emerges as a northern memory of Caribbean women's identity in conversation with its transatlantic counterpart *Zami*, the biomythography narrativized by the North American writer Lorde: "Madivine. Friending. Zami. How Carriacou women love each other is legend in Grenada."[21]

Positionality in *Basin* is located along the axis of sexuality and class as well as cultural specificity. By invoking the icon of the "basin" as an archetype that connects all Black women, *Basin* argues for an imaginary history and mythology that link all diasporic Black women. Here, while the premise of commonality is based on an essentialist construction of race, the rupture occurs across gender and sexuality. The idea of zammie is proposed as an alternative economy of desire, outside the heterosexual matrix of Western bourgeois feminism, while operating within the experience of Britishness. Similarly, the word "basin" proposes a central philosophical tension with English forms of cultural citizenship, by drawing into Western notions of love an expressive system of fragmented epistemological undercurrents from the Caribbean.

The kinship networks of Black women in *Basin* disarticulate British notions of heterosexual nuclear families, thereby critiquing the founding myths of the British state. All three women in the play are Black British. Susan, a lesbian actress, convinces Mona, whose generous personality leaves her materially abused by men and women alike, to cross the boundaries of her own heterosexual assumptions into that of zammie love. This transformation in Mona alienates Michelle, a single mother whose own unbridled and economically desperate heterosexuality is positioned as disempowering and dependent. What emerges is a contradictory space of simultaneously fixed and shifting representations, where "Blackness" is fixed but sexuality's constructions are dismantled, negotiated, or displaced. *Basin* opens out a dynamic field of identification that contentiously plays out the ideological and epistemological contradictions of postcolonial positionality. It reasserts the claim that if it is difficult for Black men to survive within the deeply hostile British society, Black women are multiply bound within the structures of tradition, the colonizer's culture, the British law, the disenfranchised space of the "third world subject," and the political economy of labor.

In contrast to the privatized sphere of Rudet's *Basin*, Winsome Pinnock's play *A Rock in Water* situates itself within the global histories of Black British women and their politicization through international feminisms, radical left politics, the struggles of Black peoples in the Caribbean, the United States, and Africa articulated by Black consciousness, Black power and other independence movements, and the work of Black intellectuals such as June Jordan, Angela Davis, Maya Angelou, C. L. R. James, Alice Walker, Toni Morrison, Mahatma Gandhi, W. E. B. Du Bois, Edward K. Brathwaite, Steve Biko, and others. Privileging the transnational cultural formation of Black British identity through the character of Claudia Jones, the African American political activist and protagonist of *A Rock in Water*, the play links three different histories of Black struggle, in Trinidad, the United States, and Britain in the first half of the twentieth century.

A Rock in Water premiered at the Royal Court Theatre Upstairs, London, on January 12, 1989. Its protagonist, Claudia Jones, is an African American political activist who is credited with having started the Notting Hill carnival in Britain. She was also instrumental in running one of the first Black presses in Britain, the *West Indian Gazette*.[22] The play demonstrates the range and extent to which Black women were actively engaged in political action in both the United States and Britain during the 1940s and 1950s by inserting women from different backgrounds and contexts into a political treatise about the power and surveillance of the democratic state. It juxtaposes the interests of the state and those of human action along the grids of "race," gender, and class in order to complicate any simple notion of political identification. In the play, capitalist, socialist, and communist ideologies intertwine to demonstrate the inextricable interplay of all these influences in the formation of women's subjectivities. By dramatizing the intersections, the play marks out the ways certain social formations generate particular kinds of discursive power in order to keep particular constituencies in power, such as bourgeois capitalist men.

Structured as Brechtian vignettes, the play episodically unravels Claudia Jones's persecution as a Black communist and radical feminist during the 1950s by the U.S. government, and her deportation across the Atlantic. It moves spatially from a street in Brooklyn in 1927 to Trinidad, Harlem,

Manhattan, Ellis Island, Alderson prison in West Virginia, and eventually London. By charting Jones's voluntary and involuntary migrations and eventual exile, Pinnock displaces the assumption that Black women are passive agents outside history, acted on rather than willfully determining the paths of their futures. If Claudia Jones's representation dislodges any notion of Black women's absence from British cultural politics prior to the 1960s, the work of Rukhsana Ahmad, Jacqueline Rudet, and Meera Syal does suggest that the sites of women's cultural interventions were largely privatized and concealed from the public sphere by virtue of their status as third-class citizens with second-class citizenship.

A Rock in Water portrays the contradictions of both intersectionality and positionality, as Jones's own political and geographical contexts keep shifting through the years. Through Jones, Pinnock comments on the transnational connections between citizenship, left politics, and the policing of the state for Black people on either side of the Atlantic. Focusing on the material conditions of domestic and undocumented labor, factory work, and state-legitimated coercions, Pinnock unleashes a scathing critique of bourgeois left society. The repressed labor histories of invisible constituencies are represented in the play by the Black prison officer, the women laborers in the garment factory, the foreman of the garment factory, working-class activists, and Mary, a Black woman from the South whose only chance of work in New York in 1927 is as a domestic. These characters operate metonymically, juxtaposing the complex intersectionality through which relations of disempowerment and privilege, legitimacy and disavowal within the state are produced. To the extent that Black women could gain a hearing, have access to publicity or recourse to independence and economic power to determine their own positions during the first decades of their presence in Britain, they played an important role in the process of identity formation for Black British citizenship. The common experience of disempowerment along with the similar history of colonialism and servitude created alliances across classes, cultures, and languages of various nationalities reinventing themselves as Black British subjects.[23]

Transnational Affiliations, Transatlantic Collaborations, and Epistemological Dilemmas

Much of what I have discussed so far has kept the printed script as the primary commodity of discussion, and this is no accident. The demise of the Greater London Council in 1986, the growing recession, deepening conservatism, and increasing cuts in arts funding have taken their toll on creative ventures on both sides of the Atlantic. However, the resilience and critical mass of emerging minority cultural constituencies have never been greater. Certainly the critical mass of emerging Black women's performance work available in print has increased in small but monumental bounds, largely because of the commitments and imaginative resources of women like Yvonne Brewster, Kathy Perkins, Roberta Uno, Catherine Ugwu, Kadija George, and others. Certainly there are growing new audiences that are hungry for work that reflects their experiences of the world in the struggle for cultural citizenship.

The scripts I have drawn on bear the baggage of Thatcher's Britain's ungenerosity and xenophobia, while simultaneously articulating global affiliations that exceed the narrow spectrum of British citizenship. All four playwrights, Rukhsana Ahmad, Meera Syal, Winsome Pinnock, and Jacqueline Rudet, locate their plays across national boundaries: Punjab and Britain in *A Song for a Sanctuary*; Pakistan and Britain in *My Sister-Wife;* the United States-Trinidad-Britain triangle in *A Rock in Water;* Dominica and Britain in *Basin*. In doing so, they foreground the increasing interdependence of cultural affiliations across ideologies of belonging. Transnational avenues of identification inflect all forms of dialogue in these texts, dismantling older notions of Englishness, nationness, and groundedness, while simultaneously struggling to grasp for coherence in rapidly shifting political and psychic terrains of experience. Considered together, these texts present the contradicting and pleasurable sites of transnational affiliations, caught in the promise of the post-everything while struggling to maintain the points of coherence and convergence through which meaning is forged, legitimated, and made into policy across national and legal boundaries.

NOTES

I am indebted to Meenakshi Ponnuswami, Radhika Subramanium, Jill Lane, Peggy Phelan, and Geoffrey Rogers for reading versions of this chapter and sharing with me their insightful comments. To Peggy Phelan and Jill Lane I owe much thanks for their editorial suggestions and support.

1. Yvonne Brewster, "An Interview with Yvonne Brewster, O.B.E.," interview by Stella Oni, in *Six Plays by Black and Asian Women Writers,* ed. Cheryl Robson (London: Aurora Metro, 1993), 18.

2. Kadija George, introduction to *Six Plays by Black and Asian Women Writers,* ed. Robson.

3. Beverley Bryan, Stella Dadzie, and Suzanne Scafe, *The Heart of the Race: Black Women's Lives in Britain* (London: Virago, 1985).

4. Peter Fryer, *Staying Power: The History of Black People in Britain* (London: Pluto, 1984), 372–86. Also see Errol Lawrence, "Just Plain Commonsense: The 'Roots' of Racism," in *The Empire Strikes Back: Race and Racism in 70's Britain* (London: Hutchinson, 1982), 68–71.

5. Winsome Pinnock, *A Hero's Welcome,* in *Six Plays by Black and Asian Women Writers,* ed. Robson, 44. On a nameless West Indian island in 1947, Stanley, Minda, and Sis fantasize about England, and succumb to the "Come to England," "Come find a job in England," "The motherland needs you" posters pasted all over the island.

6. John Solomos, Bob Findlay, Simon Jones, and Paul Gilroy, "The Organic Crisis of British Capitalism and Race," in *The Empire Strikes Back,* 14–16, 30.

7. Lawrence, "Just Plain Commonsense," 70. Also see Peter Fryer, "The Settlers," in *Staying Power.*

8. Pratibha Parmar, "Gender, Race and Class: Asian Women in Resistance," in *The Empire Strikes Back,* 245–47. See also Amrit Wilson, *Finding a Voice: Asian Women in Britain* (London: Virago, 1984); Shabnam Grewal et al., *Charting the Journey: Writings by Black and Third World Women* (London: Sheba Feminist Publishers, 1988).

9. Hazel Carby, " 'Woman's Era': Rethinking Black Feminist Thoery," in *Reconstructing Womanhood* (Oxford: Oxford University Press, 1987), 6.

10. Kimberlé Crenshaw, "Demarginalizing the Intersection of Race and Sex: A Black Feminist Critique of Antidiscrimination Doctrine, Feminist Theory and Antiracist Politics," *University of Chicago Legal Forum,* 1989, 139–67.

11. Rukhsana Ahmad, *Song for a Sanctuary,* in *Six Plays by Black and Asian Women Writers,* ed. Robson. The *kirpaan* is a curved dagger, sacred to Sikhs.

12. For further elaboration on the distinction between civil law and customary practice, see Mahmood Mamdani, *Citizen and Subject* (Princeton: Princeton University Press, 1996), 109–10, 112–19. As a result of the colonial judicial system of British indirect rule, a bipolar system of justice emerged. Customary law was meted out to natives by chiefs and British commissioners while modern justice was handed out to nonnatives by white magistrates. This dualism in legal theory emerged out of two distinct but related forms of power, the centrally defined modern state and the locally governed native authority. Civil law marked the secularity of the modern state, while customary law and practice were the elaboration of local customs, mores, and tribal authority. Customary law emerges during and after colonialism as the complex and indeterminate collision with

the secular and the modern, as narrativized by British common law. Examples of customary practice include Muslim law in colonial African states like Nigeria, "African Law" in Lesotho, customary law in Tanzania, and customary courts for all "tribesmen" in Botswana.

13. The following collection documents the early consciousness-raising attempts of Black women to acquire cultural and legal rights: Bryan, Dadzie, and Scafe, *The Heart of the Race.*

14. Stuart Hall, "Minimal Selves," in *The Real Me: ICA Document 6,* ed. Lisa Appignanesi (London: Institute of Contemporary Arts, 1987), 45.

15. Meenakshi Ponnuswami, "Feminist History in Contemporary British Theatre," *Women and Performance: A Journal of Feminist Theory* 14–15 (1995): 287–305. In this important essay, Ponnuswami points out the failures of the New Left and British feminist historiography to incorporate the new constituencies of Britain.

16. Pratibha Parmar, "Black Feminism: The Politics of Articulation," in *Identity: Community, Culture, Difference,* ed. Jonathan Rutherford (London: Lawrence and Wishart, 1990), 103–5.

17. Jacqueline Rudet, *Basin,* in *Black Plays,* ed. Yvonne Brewster (London: Methuen, 1987); Winsome Pinnock, *A Rock in Water,* in *Black Plays: Two,* ed. Yvonne Brewster (London: Methuen, 1989).

18. Elaine Aston, *An Introduction to Feminism and Theatre,* (London: Routledge, 1995), 88.

19. Brewster, *Black Plays,* 114.

20. Audre Lorde, *Zami: A New Spelling of My Name* (Trumansburg, NY: Crossing Press, 1982), 7.

21. Ibid., 14.

22. Brewster, *Black Plays: Two,* 46–47.

23. Hazel Carby, "White Woman Listen! Black Feminism and the Boundaries of Sisterhood," in *The Empire Strikes Back.*

PERFORMANCE IN THE FIELD

FOURTEEN

Genre Trouble:

(The) Butler Did It

Jon McKenzie

Nearing the crack of millennia, genre troubles the end(s) of performance. It's been a long time in coming, and its initiation is marked by machinating ends, genres, performances, and troubles. I'm writing now, while there's still time, to affirm once again that the butler did it . . .

The Liminal-Norm

The end(s) of performance come at a time when different genres of performance collide at high speeds across distant fields of research. Just five years ago, Peggy Phelan noted, "To date . . . there has been little attempt to bring together the specific epistemological and political possibilities of performance as it is enacted in what are still known, for better or worse, as 'theater events' and the epistemological and political openings enabled by the 'performative' invoked by contemporary theory" (15). The disciplinary guardrails between event and discourse have been surveyed by Janelle Reinelt and Joseph Roach, who describe "the history of the discipline of theater studies [as] one of fighting for autonomy from English and speech departments, insisting on a kind of separation from other areas of study." They argue for a more interdisciplinary approach focused on the "role of performance in the production of culture in its widest sense" (5). With Reinelt and Roach's anthology *Critical Theory and Performance* and other anthologies by Phelan and Lynda Hart, Elin Diamond, and Andrew Parker and Eve Kosofsky Sedgwick, a wide range of theorists have engaged performance in both its embodied and its discursive senses. Within the field of performance studies, perhaps no theorist has had as wrenching an impact in this respect as Judith Butler, whose *Gender Trouble* (1990) and *Bodies That Matter* (1993) have troubled performance, its genres, and its end(s).

What follows is a close reading of Butler that focuses on the significance of her work for the future of the performance studies field. In particular, I am interested in her citation of two theorists, Victor Turner and Richard Schechner, whose closely related concepts of liminality have become, paradoxically perhaps, something of a norm within the field. That is, performance scholars have come to consistently define their object and their own research, if not exclusively, then *very* inclusively, in terms of liminality—a mode of embodied activity whose spatial, temporal, and symbolic "betweenness" allows for dominant social norms to be suspended, questioned, played with, transformed.

Turner developed his concept of liminality from a reading of Arnold van Gennep's *Rites de Passage* and from his own study of Ndembu rituals. Schechner in turn generalized the concept, displacing it across a wide range of cultural activities, from rituals to theatre and beyond. For two generations of performance scholars, liminality has also been a crucial concept for theorizing the politics of performance: as a mode of embodied activity that transgresses, resists, or challenges social structures, liminality has been theorized both in terms of the political demonstrations of the 1960s and 1970s and the political performance art of the 1980s and 1990s. Yet the concept has not simply been applied to performances; it has also helped *construct* objects of study by guiding the selection of activities to be studied, as well as their formal analysis and political evaluation. Indeed, the liminal rite of passage might function both as the exemplary case study in the field and as a striking emblem of the field itself, of its own initiation. In his introduction to the anthology *Rite, Drama, Festival, Spectacle: Rehearsals toward a Theory of Cultural Performance* (1984), John J. MacAloon suggests as much:

> Dell Hymes has coined the phrase "breakthrough into performance" to describe the passage of human agents into a distinctive "mode of existence and realization." "Breakthrough into performance" equally well configures certain initially independent intellectual developments in the 1950s that have served as a foundation for the now rapidly expanding and coalescing interests in the study of cultural forms exemplified by this volume. (2)

Performance studies has thus put liminality to several ends: to delimit its *field of objects*; to situate its own problematic passage into a field, a discipline, a *paradigm of research*;[1] and to articulate its own interdisciplinary, intercultural *resistance* to the normative forces of institutionalization, forces installing themselves as the field sets up its reading machines in departments and programs across the United States and abroad.

In the beginning of performance studies was limen, and in its end(s) as well. Given the paradoxical norm of liminality, I have come to call this emblematic concept the *liminal-norm.* More generally, the liminal-norm refers to any situation wherein the valorization of transgression itself becomes normative—at which point theorization of such a norm may become subversive. I made up the term "liminal-norm" not long after reading another citation of rites of passage, this one by Michel Foucault. In an interview entitled "Rituals of Exclusion," Foucault discusses how capitalist norms are inscribed pedagogically: "the university is no doubt little different from those systems in so-called primitive societies in which the young men are kept outside the village during their adolescence, undergoing rituals of initiation which separate them and sever all contact between them and real, active society. At the end of the specified time, they can be entirely recuperated or reabsorbed" (*Foucault Live,* 66). In other words, the very same rituals that performance scholars have long cited in theorizing the subversiveness of performance, Foucault cites in terms of the university's normativity.

There's trouble at the limen of performance, and if Judith Butler isn't the only troublemaker, her *Gender Trouble* remains something of a script for coming to or getting at the end(s) of the liminal-norm. I have transcribed her title from English to French and back, reading it again and generating *genre* trouble, for *genre* translates as both gender and genre. I am gambling with the French that deconstructing the performativity of gender has everything to do with subverting not only the genders but also the genres, and indeed, the genealogies, generation(s), gens, and genus of performance. As Jacques Derrida shows in "The Law of Genre" (1980), marking genre involves a generalized citation *and* displacement of borders. The law or clause that genres cannot be mixed only emerges out of the law of the law of genre, the troubling clause that the mark of belonging does not belong, that property rights involve writs of impropriety. This citationality of borders, of limen, opens the gates to what might be called *genredegeneration:* genre of generation, genre degeneration. Derrida is at the gates, writing with this outlaw law of genre:

> The clause or floodgate [*écluse*] of genre declasses what it allows to be classed. It tolls the knell [*glas*] of genealogy or of genericity, which it however also brings forth to the light of day. Putting to death the very thing that it engen-

ders, it cuts a strange figure; a formless form, it remains nearly invisible, it neither sees the day nor brings itself to light. Without it, neither genre nor literature comes to light, but as soon as there is this blinking of the eye, this clause
or this floodgate of genre, at the very moment that a genre or a literature is
broached, at that very moment, degenerescence has begun, the end begins.

The end begins, this is a citation. Maybe a citation. (213)

Maybe the end(s) of performance will have been its initiation, its rites
and writs of passage. By attempting here to resituate the borders of performance studies in relation to its liminal-norm, I am by no means suggesting
that this paradigm only functions normatively. While I am interested
in how the institutionalized study of performance involves normative
processes, this is because I am even more interested in how researchers can
better challenge these very processes. In citing some of the norms that
guide the study of performance, I believe such challenges can become
more diverse and concrete. There's still time, the end is initiating. Come,
we must pick up speed.

What the Butler Did

I'll begin by cutting to the chase and defining what, *for me,* is Butler's most
significant and singular contribution to the performance studies field. Not
without parody, I'll try to distill it down to its essence and bottle it for
distribution in small amounts. Although Butler has become recognized as
a leading practitioner of queer and feminist theory, I would not single out
these dimensions of her work in relation to performance studies. After all,
issues of gender and sexuality have long been theorized in this paradigm.
Nor would I single out her contribution as a critical genealogist or decons-
tructivist; again, such approaches are not so new to performance scholars.
Rather, I would point to what Butler's critical genealogy of gender and
sexuality *creates,* something that troubles the genres traditionally studied
by performance studies. We have seen that both Turner and Schechner
theorize performative genres as liminal, that is, as "in-between" times/
spaces in which social norms are broken apart, turned upside down, and
played with. What Butler creates in the time and space of several articles
and two books is a theory of performativity not only as marginal, transgressive, or resistant, but also as a dominant and punitive form of power,
one that both generates and constrains human subjects. To try to bottle

the essence of what Butler did—and continues to do: *she theorizes both the transgressivity and the normativity of performative genres.* If Turner's centrality lies in his theory of performative liminality, Butler's subversiveness lies in her theory of performative normativity.

Now we're going too fast. We need to brake down a bit and look more closely at the relation between the performance genres theorized by Turner and Schechner and the sense or direction in which Butler takes the performative. In the first section of her article "Performative Acts and Gender Constitution" (1990), she writes that "the acts by which gender is constituted bear similarities to performative acts within theatrical contexts" (272). While Turner and Schechner use theatrical action to theorize liminal and potentially transgressive performances, Butler takes another route, toward an analysis of compulsory heterosexual norms: "as a strategy of survival within compulsory systems, gender is a performance with clearly punitive consequences. Discrete genders are part of what 'humanizes' individuals within contemporary culture: indeed, we regularly punish those who fail to do their gender right" (273). This performance of gender is not expressive; its does not exteriorize an interior substance, identity, or essence; instead, gender emerges from performances that disguise their constitutive role. Butler's concept of gender constitution, which draws on existential phenomenology, challenges its presumption of individual subjectivity. Subjects do not expressively perform their genders; rather, gendered subjectivity is itself constituted through compulsory performances of social norms. Through repeated performances, these norms become sedimented *as* (and not in) gendered bodies. "From a feminist point of view, one might try to reconceive the gendered body as the legacy of sedimented acts rather than a predetermined or foreclosed structure, essence or fact, whether natural, cultural, or linguistic" (274). For Butler, the personal is political because it always already involves socially normative performances.

In order to flesh out her performative reading of gender, Butler turns in the next section to anthropological discourse and—of particular interest here—to Turner's theory of ritual, but with a twist. Reiterating the importance for feminism of a theatrically based theory of social action, she asks,

In what senses, then, is gender an act? As anthropologist Victor Turner suggests in his studies of ritual social drama, social action requires a performance which is *repeated*. This repetition is at once a reenactment and reexperiencing of a set of meanings already socially established; it is the mundane and ritualized form of their legitimation. When this conception of social performance is applied to gender, it is clear that although there are individual bodies that enact these significations by becoming stylized into gendered modes, this "action" is immediately public as well. (277)[2]

Why do I say that Butler turns to Turner—*with a twist?* Because her reading explores gender issues recognized as important but not systematically pursued by him. The twist, however, comes not only in Butler's application of social drama to gender, but also in her reading of Turner's ritual. Ritual for him is sacred, not mundane or profane. Further, Butler writes that Turner's research "suggests . . . that social action requires a performance which is *repeated.*" Butler's emphasis on repetition is most suggestive, for while repetition is certainly implied in any ritual, Turner's theory does not explicitly focus on it. Indeed, Butler reads ritual performance in a manner from which he might turn away: as a compulsory routine. In his essay "Acting in Everyday Life and Everyday Life in Acting," he writes, "Ritual in [Central African] societies is seldom the rigid, obsessional behavior we think of as ritual after Freud" (*From Ritual to Theatre,* 109). Let us also note that Turner opposes ritual to "technological routine." He thus seems to minimalize the repetitive valencies of ritual, and these valencies are what most interest Butler. Rather than simply repeating the familiar reading of liminal ritual as transgressive, she reads Turner's theory of social drama as a theory of normativity. By stressing performative citationality, Butler allows us to see how his theory of ritual may be generalized to understand both transgressive and normative performance.

Shortly after her discussion of Turner, Butler cites Schechner while distilling the differences between theatrical and social acts. She cautiously suggests that "gender performances in non-theatrical contexts are governed by more clearly punitive and regulatory social conventions" than those in theatrical contexts ("Performative Acts," 278). Her citation of Schechner then comes in a passage that could itself be read as a script:

Indeed, the sight of a transvestite onstage can compel pleasure and applause while the sight of the same transvestite on the seat next to us on the bus can compel fear, rage, even violence. . . . On the street or in the bus, the act becomes dangerous, if it does, precisely because there are no theatrical conventions to delimit the purely imaginary character of the act, indeed, on the street or in the bus, there is no presumption that the act is distinct from a reality; the disquieting effect of the act is that there are no conventions that facilitate making this separation. Clearly, there is theatre which attempts to contest or, indeed, break down those conventions that demarcate the imaginary from the real (Richard Schechner brings this out quite clearly in *Between Theater and Anthropology*). (278)

A footnote placed at the citation of Schechner's text directs the reader to "See especially, 'News, Sex, and Performance,' 295–324." To perform the role of scholarly drag, I make this correction: the title is "News, Sex, and Performance Theory." In this essay, Schechner writes that the "world that was securely positional is becoming dizzyingly relational. There will be more 'in-between' performative genres. In-between is becoming the norm" (*Between Theater and Anthropology*, 322). This citation returns us to performance studies' liminal-norm, which Butler can help us rearticulate.

We've seen that Butler twists Turner's theory of ritual into a theory of normative performance. In citing Schechner, she theorizes the transgressive aspects of performance (writing that the transvestite in transit "challenges, at least implicitly, the distinction between appearance and reality" ("Performative Acts," 278). In light of these citations of Turner and Schechner, let me repose the paradox of the liminal-norm this way: liminality can be theorized not only in terms of a time/space of anti-structural play, but also in terms of a time/space of structural normalization. Further, the subjunctive "as if" mood, used by Schechner and others to theorize liminality, might be understood not in opposition to an indicative mood of "it is," but as intimately related to an *imperative* mood, which orders, "it must be." The liminal-norm thus entails a *command performance*.

Butler explains the political stakes of performative citation in *Gender Trouble*

> The subject is not *determined* by the rules through which it is generated because signification is *not a founding act, but rather a regulated process of repetition* that both conceals itself and enforces its rules precisely through substantializing effects. In a sense, all signification takes place within the orbit of the compulsion to repeat; "agency," then, is to be located within the possibility of a variation on that repetition. (145)

Acts become sedimented precisely through the orbit of their historical repetition and desedimented through, shall we say, "exorbitant" variations on such repetitions, variations that nonetheless also involve repetition, citation, rehearsal, and parody. Thus, the "task is not whether to repeat, but how to repeat or, indeed, to repeat and, through a radical proliferation of gender, *to displace* the very gender norms that enable the repetition itself" (148). Such displacement is the trickiest part of deconstruction's "two-step program" (the other step, too often made too quickly, is the reversal of binary terms), and Butler uses drag to theorize how parody can operate to repeat and displace performative gender norms.

> *In imitating gender, drag implicitly reveals the imitative structure of gender itself—as well as its contingency.* Indeed, part of the pleasure, the giddiness of the performance is in the recognition of a radical contingency in the relation between sex and gender in the face of cultural configurations of causal unities that are regularly assumed to be natural and necessary. (137–38)

Contra Fredric Jameson's dismissal of pastiche as a humorless and politically conservative parody that mocks its original, she finds in gender parody a "laughter [that] emerges in the realization that all along the original was derived" (139). However, since normative sedimentation and transgressive desedimentation both involve repetitive performances, Butler explicitly warns that "[p]arody by itself is not subversive, and there must be some way to understand what makes certain kinds of parodic repetition effectively disruptive, truly troubling, and which repetitions become domesticated and recirculated as instruments of cultural hegemony" (139). Drag thus may further sediment gender identities by repeating and reinforcing the orbit of hegemonic significations, while also destabilizing those very significations through exorbitant, hyperbolic repetitions that give rise to political resignifications.

Reciting Oneself Otherwise

Between the publication of *Gender Trouble* and *Bodies That Matter,* Butler offered some corrections to her readers, corrections that entail a certain rewriting of the relation between performance and performativity. The performance theory of *Gender Trouble* itself is first reread in her article "Critically Queer" (1993). Here Butler returns to the question of gender performativity and drag, now stressing the *discursivity* of performatives. "Performative acts are forms of authoritative speech: most performatives, for instance, are statements which, in the uttering, also perform a certain action and exercise a binding power. . . . The power of discourse to produce what it names is linked with the question of performativity. The performative is thus one domain in which power acts *as* discourse" (17). In the second section, "Gender Performativity and Drag," she turns to the effects of her own discourse, namely, the theory of subversive gender parody posed in *Gender Trouble*. Butler asks rhetorically, "If gender is a mimetic effect, is it therefore a choice or a dispensable artifice? If not, how did this reading of *Gender Trouble* emerge?" (21). She offers two reasons for this reading while also suggesting there may be others. First, she says that she herself cited "drag as an example of performativity (taken then, by some, to be *exemplary,* that is, *the* example of performativity)" (21). Second, with the "growing queer movement . . . the publicization of theatrical agency has become quite central" (21). If I may offer a third and closely related reason for the misreading of Butler's theory of performativity: given the numerous critical theories that articulate performance as transgressive and/or resistant cultural practices of marginalized subjects, many readers may have too quickly passed over Butler's stress on performativity as both normative and punitive and instead installed her work within more conventional, that is, radical, readings of performance. Another passage suggests that she may have sensed this third reason: "Performativity is a matter of reiterating or repeating the norms by which one is constituted: it is not a radical fabrication of a gendered self" (22).

The reading Butler gives in "Critically Queer" involves a certain breakup, or at least braking down, of the close alliance between theatrical performance and performativity that she forged in *Gender Trouble*. If there she sought to theorize performativity via performance, in this later essay she also emphasizes performativity *contra* performance. To reiterate her corrective reading of performativity, she now clearly distinguishes it from performance and does so in a paragraph *entirely* italicized.

> *In no sense can it be concluded that the part of gender that is performed is therefore the "truth" of gender; performance as bounded "act" is distinguished from performativity insofar as the latter consists in a reiteration of norms which precede, constrain, and exceed the performer and in that sense cannot be taken as the fabrication of the performer's "will" or "choice," further, what is "performed" works to conceal, if not to disavow, what remains opaque, unconscious, un-performable. The reduction of performativity to performance would be a mistake.* (24)

This passage calls for comment. Butler is obviously not referring to the ritualized performance she reads in Turner, wherein performance always already entails a citational process. Instead, she refers to performance as an act in the here-and-now, that is, as a presence, one bounded in the will of the performer. She has, in effect, resignified performance, from providing similarities with performativity to concealing and disavowing "what remains opaque, unconscious, unperformable." This resignification of performance, in turn, involves a resignification of "performative": opening her essay by citing Sedgwick's reading of J. L. Austin, Butler makes it clear that she now wishes to distinguish embodied performances from discursive performatives, to transfer performance from theatrical to discursive contexts.

To follow Butler's rereading of performance and performative, let's ourselves make a transfer to *Bodies That Matter: On the Discursive Limits of "Sex"* (1993).[3] In the introduction, Butler again clarifies her emphasis on the discursive and its relation to the body:

> To claim that discourse is formative is not to claim that it originates, causes, or exhaustively composes that which it concedes; rather, it is to claim that there is no reference to a pure body which is not at the same time a further formation of that body. In this sense, the linguistic capacity to refer to sexed bodies is not denied, but the very meaning of referentiality is altered. In philosophical terms, the constative claim is always to some degree performative. (10–11)

(This last phrase echoes something suggested above: that is, the indicative mood always harbors an imperative.) Butler then distinguishes performativity and theatricality in this way:

> Performativity is thus not a singular "act," for it is always a reiteration of a norm or set of norms, and to the extent that it acquires an act-like status in the present, it conceals or dissimulates the conventions of which it is a repetition. Moreover, *this act is not primarily theatrical*; indeed, its apparent theatricality is produced to the extent that its historicity remains dissimulated (and, conversely, its theatricality gains a certain inevitability given the impossibility of a full disclosure of its historicity). (12–13, my emphasis)

The attempt to constatively refer to a pre-discursive sexed-body or, more generally, to a pure materiality presupposes a present act that would escape the citation of social norms. Such an act is produced only by a certain inevitable theatricality or dissimulation, a certain performance, namely, the concealing of performativity.

Recapping Butler's troubling of liminal norms: by theorizing performance as both normative and transgressive, she challenges the genres studied by performance studies. In "Performative Acts and Gender Constitution" and *Gender Trouble,* she uses theories of anthropological and theatrical performance, specifically, Turner's theory of ritual, to construct a theory of performativity as the citation of social gender norms. In "Critically Queer" and in *Bodies That Matter,* however, Butler resignifies both performativity and performance: performativity now refers to a *discursive* compulsion to repeat norms of gender, sexuality, and race, while performance refers to an *embodied* theatricality that conceals its citational aspect under a dissimulating presence. Thus, in addition to stressing performance as both normative and transgressive, Butler also stresses both the discursive and the embodied dimensions of performativity. She even warns that the *"reduction of performativity to performance would be a mistake."*

However, in these later writings, Butler also contributes to what I have elsewhere outlined as a general theory of performance.[4] After clarifying the distinction between discursive performativity and embodied performance, she then suggests their convergence. "It may seem . . . that there is a difference between the embodying or performing of gender norms and the performative use of discourse. Are these two different senses of 'performativity,' or do they converge as modes of citationality in which the compulsory character of certain social imperatives becomes subject to a more promising deregulation?" (231). Here Butler's use of the term "performance," while it retains the sense of embodiment, also restores the repetition she found suggested in Turner's theory of social drama.

In the end(s) of performance coming out of Butler's twisted readings, the concepts developed by Turner and Schechner to theorize the transgressivity of rites of passage may paradoxically become crucial to understanding normative performance. Schechner's concept of performance as the restoration of behavior, for instance, has much affinity to Butler's own concept of performativity as the "reenactment" and "reexperiencing" of socially established meanings. Although she does not explicitly cite his essay "The Restoration of Behavior," this passage from "Performative Acts and Gender Constitution" suggests that Butler has read more than one essay from *Between Theater and Anthropology:*

> [the] act that one does, the act that one performs, is, in a sense, an act that has been going on before one arrived on the scene. Hence, gender is an act which has been rehearsed, much as a script survives the particular actors who make use of it, but which requires individual actors in order to be actualized and reproduced as reality once again. (277)

To do our own twist with Schechner: gender is a normative ensemble of restored behaviors and discourses, a mundane yet punitive regime of *performances* and *performatives,* a sedimented stratum of performance always already repeated for the *n*th time.

How to *know* the difference between these citational performances? Butler raises this question as she closes *Bodies That Matter.* "Performativity," she writes, "describes this relation of being implicated in that which one opposes, this turning of power against itself to produce alternative modalities of power, to establish a kind of political contestation that is not a 'pure' opposition, a 'transcendence' of contemporary relations of power, but a difficult labor of forging a future from resources inevitably impure" (241). This implication, this turning of power against itself, forces a strange figure upon us here, one that turns itself inside and out, over and over: not a torus nor a mobius strip, but that fabulous Klein bottle whose neck turns back against its body and, twisting in on itself, opens back up outside. Could this become known as some queer parody of "woman-as-vessel"?

> How will we know the difference between the power we promote and the power we oppose? Is it, one might rejoin, a matter of "knowing?" For one is, as it were, in power even as one opposes it, formed by it as one reworks it, and it is this simultaneity that is at once the condition of our partiality, the measure of our political unknowingness, and also the condition of action itself. The incalculable effects of action are as much a part of their subversive promise as those that we plan in advance. (241)

Indeed, this last passage can also be read in relation to the incalculable Kleinsian twists of Butler's own work, specifically, the "misreadings" that *Gender Trouble* produced. Despite its subversive promise of theorizing a normative performativity, *Gender Trouble* was paradoxically normalized by those who read it as only theorizing a subversive performativity. And in light of Butler's rereading of herself, this normalization underlines perhaps the most subversive promise of *Bodies That Matter,* one relating to the paradox of what I've called the liminal-norm. What Butler did in rereading herself, in reciting herself otherwise, was to suggest that theories of subversive performance genres can be normative, and theories of normative performance genres subversive. What the incalculable effects of this may be, well, that must be uncorked at other times and places.

Before coming to our uncertain end or stop, I want to make one last pass at what Butler did—and does—with performance, this time reading her concepts of signification and resignification. In the version of "Critically Queer" published in *Bodies That Matter,* she takes up the term "queer" by citing another theatrical source, this time asking, "how is it that a term that signaled degradation has been turned—'refunctioned' in the Brechtian sense—to signify a new and affirmative set of meanings?" (223). She then proceeds to analyze how the homophobic term "queer" has entered a process of collective contestation and resignification, one that, however, remains open to becoming stabilized in another proper usage, another signification. In doing so, Butler affirms her hand in the resignification of "queer" by shifting suddenly from its substantive to its verbal form (a shift that might be bottled as another essence of her performance):

> If the term "queer" is to be a site of collective contestation, the point of departure for a set of historical reflections and futural imagings, it will have to remain that which it is, in the present, never fully owned, but always and only redeployed, *twisted, queered* from a prior usage and in the direction of urgent and expanding political purposes. (228, my emphasis)

Analyzing "queer," Butler not only theorizes how this term has been refunctioned, she also theorizes resignification as a queering or twisting of discourse, something she herself performs textually.

Shifting now to the term "performance," you can perhaps already sense my direction: within performance studies, Butler has in effect challenged the sedimented signification of "performative" as referring primarily to oppositional cultural practices and sought to queer the term so that it also refers to normative practices and discourses. One might protest that such queering amounts to a misuse of language. "Surely, Butler's performative refers to something else!" "It's linguistic rather than embodied!" "It means normativity as much as subversion!" "Couldn't she use another term!?" Rather than attempting to justify her use of this term by again citing *Gender Trouble*'s alliance of theatrical performance and discursive performativity, I shall entertain the thought that it *is* a misuse, and that this misuse is itself a tactic of resignification, of queering.

Butler theorizes the political dimension of such misuse in "Arguing with the Real," another chapter of *Bodies That Matter,* which engages the discursive performativity of naming. Summarizing Sual Kripke and Slavoj Zizek's theories of referentiality, she writes, "It is Kripke's position to argue that the name fixes the referent, and Zizek's to say that the name promises a referent that can never arrive, foreclosed as the unattainable real" (217). Butler instead argues that the referent is neither fixed nor foreclosed, but produced through the differentiation of proper and improper usage. However, "the instability of that distinguishing border between the proper and the catachrestic calls into question the ostensive function of the proper name" (217). If the referent emerges in the unstable limen of proper and catachrestic usage, then Butler's resignification involves a strategic use of catachresis, which Merriam-Webster defines as "the misuse of words: as a: the use of the wrong word for the context b: the use of a forced figure of speech, esp. one that involves or seems to involve strong paradox." Thus, while she commends Zizek's work on the politics of the sign because it connects the question of the unsymbolizable to minoritarian social groups, Butler seeks to theorize referentiality not in terms of negation, lack, and a universalized Real, but instead through an affirmation of the historic and symbolic possibilities uncorked by a politics of catachrestic naming.

> Here it seems that what is called "the referent" depends essentially on those catachrestic acts of speech that either fail to refer or refer in the wrong way. It is in this sense that political signifiers that fail to describe, fail to refer, indicate less the "loss" of the object—a position that nevertheless secures the referent even if as a lost referent—than the loss of the loss, to rework that Hegelian formulation. If referentiality is itself the effect of a policing of the linguistic constraints on proper usage, then the possibility of referentiality is contested by the catachrestic use of speech that insists on using proper names improperly, that expands or defiles the very domain of the proper. (217–18)

Catachresis troubles property rights and is crucial to the futural imagings that Butler calls for, the affirmative resignification of "queer," as well as "women," "race," "class," and, as I will really end up arguing, the "genus" of "performance."

Machinic End(s)

The future of the field is catachrestic, if not catastrophic. We're rehearsing its end(s) here and now, reciting its paradoxical liminal-norm in a twisted naming, a *catachristening* of performance. By helping introduce questions of discursivity and normativity into performance studies, Butler's performativity of gender troubles the genre of performance, its conceptualization as embodied liminality. As cited earlier, Derrida's "Law of Genre" situates the deconstruction of gender in a matrix composed of related concepts: genre, generation(s), gens, and genus. Troubling one troubles them all. Let's end this script by entertaining another thought: generalized citationality challenges a certain genus of performance, its naming as a liminal passage of *human* agents.

Both Butler's theory of discursive performatives and Schechner's theory of embodied performances focus on human performativity. However, through their emphasis on the fundamental citationality or rehearsal process of discourses and practices, they raise the possibility of performatives and performances being mechanically and/or electronically cited, stored, played back, and transformed. Schechner himself addresses the impact twentieth-century technologies have had on performance traditions. "Almost everything we do these days is not only done but kept on film, tape, and disc. We have strong ways of getting, keeping, transmitting and recalling behavior. . . . We live in a time when traditions can die in life, be preserved archivally as behaviors, and later restored" (*Between Theater and Anthropology,* 78). Machines, however, can also be said to perform in their own right: in a wide variety of scientific fields, performance concepts function to evaluate existing technologies, to guide the design of new technologies, and even to market technologies to consumers. In the fields of engineering and computer science, especially, performance has emerged as a concept used to evaluate and design machinery, communication networks, and computer systems. Further, a highly specialized branch of technological performance research has been institutionalized in industrial, military, scientific, and commercial sites, as can be seen in this partial list of "high performance computing centers" found on the Internet:

Army High Performance Computing Research Center
High Performance Computing at NRaD (Naval Research and Development)
Maui High Performance Computing Center
Mississippi State Distributed and High Performance Scientific Computing
NASA High Performance Computing and Communications Program
National Consortium for High Performance Computing
NOAA High Performance Computing and Communications
University of Illinois at Urbana-Champagne Center for Reliable and High Performance Computing
University of Texas at San Antonio High Performance Computing and Software Lab

These centers indicate that even if the concept of technological performance has not yet received critical reflection, the research that invented and continues to deploy it has become institutionalized across the United

States. Although additional investigation would have to test this hypothesis, a comprehensive study would, I suspect, show that a second paradigm of performance research, what I call "techno-performance," has developed since the 1950s, right alongside performance studies.[5]

And what of discursive performatives—how might emerging technologies interface with their border-crossing citationality? In their introduction to *Performativity and Performance* (1995), Andrew Parker and Eve Kosofsky Sedgwick cite "another range of usages" of the term "performativity," one associated with Jean-François Lyotard's *Postmodern Condition* (1984), which, they write, uses the term "to mean an extreme of something like *efficiency*—postmodern representation as a form of capitalist efficiency" (2). In a brief footnote, Lyotard connects efficient and discursive performativity: "The two meanings are not far apart. Austin's performative realizes the optimal performance" (*The Postmodern Condition,* 88n). More important for us, *Lyotard names the postmodern legitimation of knowledge and social bonds "performativity" and also defines this power as the "hegemony of computers."* Capitalist efficiency, for Lyotard, means technical efficiency, the calculation of "input/output matrices" (xxiv). In some sense, performativity *is* the postmodern condition: not simply a form of representation, it names a specific historical stratum of power/knowledge, and its lessons for the future are electronic.[6] In a section entitled "Education and Its Legitimation through Performativity," Lyotard writes, "To the extent that learning is translatable into computer language and the traditional teacher is replaceable by memory banks, didactics can be entrusted to machines linking traditional memory banks (libraries, etc.) and computer data banks to intelligent terminals placed at the students' disposal" (50).

I'm outta here. It's coming, the end(s) of strictly human performatives. You can sight it for yourself at <www.cs.umbc.edu/kse>, where you'll read of the Knowledge Sharing Effort, sponsored by the Department of Defense's Advanced Research Projects Agency. This alliance of research institutions, initially called ARPA,[7] developed a computer network in 1969 called the ARPANET, which would later become the Internet. Today, as part of the Knowledge Sharing Effort, the Department of Computer Science and Electrical Engineering of the University of Maryland Baltimore County is generating KQML—Knowledge Query and Manipulation Language—a high-level communication language for artificial intelligent agents. I just pulled this performative citation off the site:

> KQML is a language and protocol for exchanging information and knowledge. KQML can be used as a language for an application program to interact

with an intelligent system or for two or more intelligent systems to share knowledge in support of cooperative problem solving. It focuses on an extensible set of performatives, which defines the permissible operations that agents may attempt on each other's knowledge and goal stores. The performatives comprise a substrate on which to develop higher-level models of inter-agent interaction such as contract nets and negotiation.

Informative performatives, database performatives, query performatives, effector performatives, generator performatives, capability-definition performatives, notification performatives, networking performatives, facilitation performatives: in this language game of a future already upon us, these performatives pass not primarily between humans and humans, nor even between humans and machines, but between machines and machines.

I end here, writing only that, in light of all these electronic performance sites, a certain *genre machinic* is already online, troubling the future of the field and pointing toward a performativity programmed by other agencies. It's coming, the end(s).

NOTES

1. MacAloon, whose text anthologizes the 1978 Burg Wartenstein Symposium, writes that "the study of cultural performance is in, as yet, a 'preparadigmatic' stage" (1). Schechner, for his part, writes in 1989 that the "performance studies paradigm came to the fore in the mid-'50s." "PAJ Distorts the Broad Spectrum," 7.

2. Another version of this passage appears in *Gender Trouble*. There the reference to Turner is downshifted from the text to a footnote.

3. *Bodies That Matter* also includes a revised version of "Critically Queer." I read from this version below.

4. See McKenzie, "Laurie Anderson for Dummies." I outline this general theory much more extensively in *Perform—or Else: Performance, Technology, and the Lecture Machine*, forthcoming from Wesleyan University Press. The reading proposed here of Butler is situated there in relation to Austin and Derrida.

5. Among the factors that have contributed to the emergence of techno-performance are (1) the extension of the American military-industrial complex beyond World War II and into the academy, giving rise to what Stuart Leslie has called the military-industrial-academic complex. The effects of this "MIA" complex reach far beyond departments of engineering and physics and incorporate themselves in psychology and sociology; (2) the political climate of Sputnik and the space race, the Viet Nam War, Star Wars—in short, the Cold War

atmospherics that socially legitimated the MIA complex in the United States; (3) the increasing application of concepts drawn from cybernetics or general systems theory to develop and evaluate all sorts of technologies, not just those developed by the military; and (4) the emergence of a veritable "meta-technology," the electronic computer, which is not only designed and evaluated in terms of performance, but also widely used in the design and evaluation of other techno-logical performances.

6. The normative dimensions of Lyotard's theory of performativity have been largely missed by theorists who cite *The Postmodern Condition* in relation to experimental performance. The reason for this odd pattern of citation is related, I suspect, to what produced the initial reading of Butler's performative: the liminal-norm of performance studies.

7. The agency is still often referred to as ARPA, though its official name is now DARPA, the Defense Advanced Research Project Agency.

WORKS CITED

Butler, Judith. *Bodies That Matter: On the Discursive Limits of "Sex."* New York: Routledge, 1993.

———. "Critically Queer." *Gay and Lesbian Quarterly* 1 (1993): 17–32.

———. *Gender Trouble: Feminism and the Subversion of Identity.* New York: Routledge, 1990.

———. "Performative Acts and Gender Constitution: An Essay in Phenomenol-ogy and Feminist Theory." In *Performing Feminisms: Feminist Critical Theory and Theatre,* ed. Sue-Ellen Case. Baltimore: Johns Hopkins University Press, 1990.

Derrida, Jacques. "The Law of Genre." Trans. Avital Ronell. *Glyph* 7 (1980): 202–29.

Diamond, Elin, ed. *Performance and Cultural Politics.* London: Routledge, 1996.

Foucault, Michel. *Foucault Live (Interviews, 1966–84).* Trans. John Johnston. Ed. Sylvère Lotringer. New York: Semiotext(e), 1989.

Leslie, Stuart W. *The Cold War and American Science: The Military-Industrial-Aca-demic Complex at MIT and Stanford.* New York: Columbia University Press, 1993.

Lyotard, Jean-François. *The Postmodern Condition: A Report on Knowledge.* Trans. Geoff Bennington and Brian Massumi. Minneapolis: University of Minnesota Press, 1984.

MacAloon, John J., ed. *Rite, Drama, Festival, Spectacle: Rehearsals toward a Theory of Cultural Performance.* Philadelphia: Institute for the Study of Human Issues, 1984.

McKenzie, Jon. "Laurie Anderson for Dummies." *Drama Review* 41, no. 2 (1997): 2.

Parker, Andrew, and Eve Kosofsky Sedgwick, eds. *Performativity and Performance.* New York: Routledge, 1995.

Phelan, Peggy. "Reciting the Citations of Others; or, A Second Introduction." In *Acting Out: Feminist Performances,* ed. Lynda Hart and Peggy Phelan. Ann Arbor: University of Michigan Press, 1993.

Reinelt, Janelle G., and Joseph Roach, eds. *Critical Theory and Performance.* Ann Arbor: University of Michigan Press, 1993.

Schechner, Richard. *Between Theater and Anthropology.* Philadelphia: University of Pennsylvania Press, 1985.

——. "PAJ Distorts the Broad Spectrum." *Drama Review* 33, 2 (1989): 4–9.

Turner, Victor. *From Ritual to Theatre: The Human Seriousness of Play.* New York: PAJ Publications, 1982.

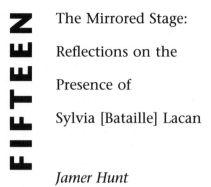

The Mirrored Stage: Reflections on the Presence of Sylvia [Bataille] Lacan

Jamer Hunt

Targeting absence, I set off to Paris to look for a woman who had been married to Georges Bataille and to Jacques Lacan. Despite her movie stardom in the 1930s, Sylvia Lacan herself, like the fact of her relationships, was almost entirely unknown within the American academic context.

The Real has its lures, that is unquestionable. Anthropology, my discipline, has staked its claim in the territory of the Real, and only recently has it even budged from that position. Face-to-face fieldwork and the written ethnography are its conventional methods for finding, isolating, and ultimately displaying its capture—an other's knowledge. Reflecting back, I might describe my search for Sylvia Lacan as an ethnographer's attempt to decide between two models of the world. The first is made up of identity as simple presence and reality as that which is empirically verifiable and knowable. The second (and in my case prevailing) model envisions the world as a constituted network of competing discourses; the Real is then not something "out there" but a problematized field of agonistic practices in which being is always provisional and performed. Weaned as I was on the "end of the Real," I saw my trip to Paris as a chance to either ignore its fulsome mass or learn to reengage with its vicissitudes. Texts, for all their polysemy, are manageable, their intimidation rhetorical. It was the potential dynamics of face-to-face encounters that challenged my illusions of theoretical control. Having conceptualized Sylvia Bataille as a rhetorical figure of absence, I needed to test the integrity of anthropological empiricism. If I was a "naïf in Paris," as my hesitant voice too frequently admits, it was a naïveté in the face of this dilemma.

How then can I account for my encounter with Sylvia Lacan? There was, on the one hand, the white-hot, unrepresentable presence of Madame Lacan, and on the other hand, the uncanny sense that what she was telling me I had read before. She shifted between being herself, performing her self, and performing her biography. All this time I was playing the seducer: trying to draw information out of her, I was working at unpeeling the layers of performance that kept me distant from her "truth." Cannily, she kept disappearing behind the smoke screen of professed reticence. Presence and absence, self-effacement and self-presence, she kept fading as I kept grasping.

As I recollect that meeting, and as I rewrite it, I sometimes see what I was missing and miss what I was seeing. At times it is nothing but the ineffaceable impression of Sylvia Lacan; other times, I see nothing but shadows and mirrors. It is as if, as Peggy Phelan writes, "[p]erformance's being, like the ontology of subjectivity . . . becomes itself through disappearance."[1] Perhaps it is at the moment of undecidability that one's theoretical architecture realizes its weakest point and collapses on itself. Or, to phrase it differently, Sylvia Bataille had been an actress; should that not have told me something? I, too, in seeking her out, had tried on various guises: naïf, scholar, cosmopolite, bumbler, and sleuth. She, I should have realized, would be playing herself. I had fallen for a false choice: misrecognizing performance as the ornament of the being, I confused two mutually supporting actualities. The Sylvia Lacan that I met was neither more nor less real than the discursive traces that I had discovered about her or the theoretical architecture that I had constructed around her. It was she, in fact, who implied as much. Rehearsing and retelling her life history, she denied me the certitude of a straight path out of my dilemma. In fact, her uncanny self-presentation staged the limits of my categorical preconceptions.

*   *   *

[A]nxiety occurs not when the object-cause of desire is lacking; it is not the lack of the object that gives rise to anxiety but, on the contrary, the danger of our getting too close to the object and thus losing the lack itself.

—Slavoj Zizek, *Looking Awry*

8 April 1993

CONTACT! After I had given up the ghost on the possibility of ever contacting Madame Lacan, she answered the phone on the first ring. Having effectively given up hope that Madame Lacan would ever respond to my letter of introduction and inquiry that I had sent to her on 29 March 1993, and quickly running out of time, I did what for me was the unthinkable— I picked up the phone and called her unannounced. Working under the assumption that her phone number was the one listed in the phone book under "Bataille, Georges 3 rue de Lille" (her ex-husband, who had not lived there for half a century), I tried calling on several occasions. Given the months, or even years, of buildup that led to actually making voice contact, it was not surprising, then, that I suffered from a more than modest amount of symptomatic anxiety. I was, literally, sick to my stomach from the tension.

When I tried to explain myself she was totally combative and ornery. When I stammered that I wanted to hear the stories of the "role of women in Surrealism," she retorted that it was all men, and I continued to stammer that it was women that interested me, women. She had absolutely no clue who I was, didn't seem to have received my letter, and generally seemed to have awfully strong opinions about my search. I was in a total blur, having not expected any response, and having assumed that she would have some idea of who I was. Finally, after saying, "Listen . . ." three or four times, she blurted out, "You are here in Paris for how much longer? Listen, call me again on the twentieth of April and I will give you an appointment." Click.

She was about as far from being refined and reserved as one could imagine. Lively, contentious, and opinionated come more immediately to mind. And will she remember me when I call on the twentieth, and will she care to give me an appointment? The whole conversation, quite appropriately, started out with a confusion over identity, since she had no idea who I was and I didn't even suspect that it was she. It took two or three exchanges before the identities were even sorted out. I became decidedly less sure of the project than I was before the call, since it was much easier to deal with nothing than to deal with a gap in language and the general and overall confusion that stems from my linguistic handicap and a hard-of-hearing older woman. But contact was made! A very poor connection, sparks flew, but contact nonetheless.

This is not to suggest that the course of events progressed any more smoothly in the subsequent few weeks. I quickly dashed off another letter, nearly identical to the first, just to remind her who exactly I was, what I was doing, and when I would call her again. But more significantly, during the twelve days that separated my first conversation with her and my next call, I was struck by a strange feeling that I could not dispel. It was as if in finally personally contacting her I had somehow pierced the bubble, the aura, that surrounded her. My goal now achievable, my object within range, the spell was broken.

10 April 1993

For some reason I have a very bad feeling about what transpired or what will transpire with Sylvia Lacan on Thursday. I don't know if it is because I feel somehow duplicitous, or that I am bothering someone who clearly does not wish to be, or something else. I can't quite put my finger on it, but it is as if now that I have made contact with her, something is finished, the desire is filled. All the excitement is gone, all the energy, the mystery, the charm, the thrill, the fear, the anxiety (I am sure that that will return with no problem). It is as if in finally making her present I have finished something. Lack filled, not satisfying. Of course I had really filled no lack. I had only made the possibility real and imminent. All the possible scenarios (which included my never finding her) were immediately foreclosed. All that was left was to make the phone call and set up the appointment.

20 April 1993

The day of reckoning turned out to be the strangest of all. After I finally got up the nerve to call her, the same thing happened all over again: "C'est qui à l'appareil?" she squawked [a phrase that I would become tragically familiar with, it translates literally and somewhat antiquatedly as "Who is it at the apparatus?" and more colloquially as "Who is there?"]. As I explained myself all over again, there finally seemed to be a moment of recognition, and then just as quickly she stated, "I cannot see you this week, call back next week." "OK, good-bye." The first thing that came to my mind was the stupid confusion over my unpronounceable last name [in French "Hunt" sounds simply like a breathy grunt], and the apparent lack of recognition on her part. I couldn't tell whether she was blithely dismissing me, whether she knew who I was or not, or whether she was simply too busy. I was despondent over the fact that still nothing had been resolved; that I should have to wait another week just to have her defer me again seems ludicrous but unavoidable.

Her second deferral had really shaken me. With no real sense of whether she had any intention of seeing me or was simply being somewhat polite in evasion, I did not know how to read her response. I was due to fly back to the United States in two weeks and I was quickly abandoning any hope of ever meeting her. It was early in the day still, so I put off any decision about leaving for the next day, since I was in no frame of mind to make any sound judgments. I decided that, for diversion, I would make a brief tour of some of Paris's many cinema memorabilia shops in the hope of finding some Sylvia Bataille publicity materials or photo stills. As Paris offers several dozen of these shops, I picked a handful and set off. I had especially been hoping to find the original poster from *Une Partie de campagne,* or at least a reproduction, since it would assuredly have a picture of Sylvia Bataille on it. I was told, however, that it had never been reprinted in facsimile form and the original was, of course, quite rare. Finding nothing of much use in the first few shops, I was ready to abandon this venture as well, chalking up the entire day to bad fortune.

I had two shops left on my list, so I decided to go to the one closest by metro and then to quit for the day. Strangely, and I have never since been able to explain this, the train did not stop at the station of my choice but proceeded on with no announcement. Fortunately, the final shop was two stops further along, so I determined I'd visit that one instead. As I entered, the shop owner was on the phone, so I looked around. The store was very small, with little of immediate interest, and I was about to leave, but, not wanting to appear rude, I waited for the owner to finish his conversation.

Really simply for politeness' sake, and some nagging sense of duty, I asked whether he might have the poster from *Une Partie de campagne.* He smiled and pointed directly above him to a rather modest but handsome poster that had not a photo of Sylvia Bataille but a hand-drawn illustration from the film. After a few questions about it, I asked how much it cost. Again he smiled and responded in English (apparently having divined my accent), "One thousand dollars." I laughed, and joked in response that, sadly, I had but nine hundred dollars with me at the moment. This having broken the ice a bit, he explained the reasons for its high price (proudly admitting that he had sold his previous copy several years before to Martin Scorsese). This copy, he added, had arrived just three days before.

I asked him whether he had any memorabilia pertaining to Sylvia

Bataille, to which he answered that he had had some in the past, but no longer. He then asked why I was interested in her particularly, to which I gave a brief summary of my research. Had I interviewed her yet? he inquired. Detailing the tortuous path by which she had managed to keep me at bay, I admitted that no, I had not, that I had spoken with her only this morning, that she had rebuffed me again, and that I was planning on leaving the country shortly in any case. It was then that the single largest bombshell dropped: he was a good friend of hers. He would call her right away to set up an appointment.

Electrified by this possibility (and yet somewhat horrified that she might be feeling harassed by this American who had bothered her only several hours before), I watched as he called home to get the number for her and then placed the call. Numbed, I witnessed unfolding the lightning bolt of chance that would crack open this sealed door. When he got through to her, I heard a rather familiar problem present itself: "Sylvia? Sylvia, it's Jean-Louis . . . Jean-Louis . . . it's Jean-Louis C. Sylvia, it's Jean-Louis C. Yes, how are you today, surviving the heat in your apartment?" I could not hear, but could certainly imagine the repeated "C'est qui à l'appareil?" that followed his multiple attempts at recognition. They had a nice conversation, during which he mentioned that an American gentleman was here in his store and wanted to see her, and could she possibly do him the favor of seeing this young man? After a good deal of catching up, he got off the phone and told me that I only had to call her the following Saturday at ten in the morning, when I could set up an appointment to see her. Literally hours away from deciding to leave Paris with nothing positive to show for my efforts, I stumbled into an opportunity that could only be described as miraculous. I do not know whether it is more Lacanian or Zen, but in any case, there is some truth to the adage that the less one seeks the object of desire, the closer one comes to obtaining it.

Due to call her on Saturday for an appointment that day, as I presumed, I hurriedly composed a list of questions to ask her; with nothing guaranteed, I reasoned that this might be my only chance to see her, so I wracked my brain for every possible question I might want to ask and then for every possible variation on those same questions. I did not have much time left in Paris, so I had to evaluate my options after our first meeting for the possibility of further interviews. Given the capricious nature of the process to this point, I was not about to save any questions for "next time."

24 April 1993

Day of reckoning, take three. I was told to call her at 10 A.M. After four hours of sleep, my stomach queasy since yesterday morning, I manically wrote out my interview questions, finished precisely at ten, called, and no one was there. Tried two more times, no one. Is she avoiding me, did she forget, has she taken ill, is she dead? My physiological reaction to all this is so intense that at times I thought it might be impossible to go through with it, and now what? I don't even dare eat much, and will probably end up in some catatonic state foaming at the mouth or fainting if I ever do get to 3 rue de Lille. The deferral continues.

Later That Day

Finally, I got through to her. We had quite a normal conversation, and I see her at 2:30 on Monday. More delays, of course, but at least it is set. She seemed much more talkative, admitted that she had a hearing problem, and wanted to warn me that she really didn't occupy herself much with the women Surrealists. I think that she will be quite nice, in fact, and more could come of this than I had hoped a few days ago. At least now I can eat—stomach calmed.

A strange sense of calm spread over me in the two days I had left until the meeting. Perhaps the most palliative balm was the fact of our having a quite pleasant conversation on the phone. By finally humanizing this "object" that had attained mythic proportions during my search for her, I deflated the anxiety of the encounter with what Lacan would call the Real; perhaps it was now into the realm of the Symbolic, where the codes and rules of more routine interactions are played out. She had assured me repeatedly in our conversation that she had absolutely nothing to say or contribute about the relationship between women and Surrealism (the general aim of my interest as I had explained it to her), despite my recipro-cal protestation to the contrary.

Her one warning was to be on time, as she did not hear very well and her helper could only stay until 2:30 to answer the doorbell when I rang. Giving myself a few extra minutes in which to find some flowers to bring to her, I headed off on the metro to her neighborhood. As anyone who has spent much time in Paris knows, there are flower stores everywhere in the city; it is one of its charms. I, however, could not find one in the vicinity of her apartment, and I started to wander impatiently and more urgently as the time approached 2:30 P.M. By the time I finally located some, it was already 2:30, I was blocks from her address, and I was going to be late. Jogging, with flowers in hand, an uncomfortable suit coat on, and drops of perspiration beading on my forehead, I arrived, rang the doorbell, was buzzed up to the apartment, flew up the spiral staircase that led to her floor, and knocked on the handsome door.

Not expecting Madame Lacan herself to answer the door (not knowing what to expect, in truth), I was surprised to see a thin, elderly woman greet me. It had all happened so fast. The moment had arrived. The very first words she spoke to me were "Vous êtes fou! [You are crazy]." And so she whisked me into the apartment, gave the flowers to her companion to take care of, and escorted me into her living room.

What I will undoubtedly most remember from that afternoon is the frequency with which I found myself laughing heartily out loud. Not even out of nervousness, as I might have expected, but instead out of the sheer pleasure of our conversation and the sparkling, mischievous, and playful sense of humor that Sylvia Lacan possessed. But the generosity with which she received me into her apartment that afternoon was matched only by the reticence with which she admitted to any role of her own in the artistic and cultural milieus that she had been a part of. Her self-effacement was extraordinary and almost impenetrable; I was simply unable to convince her that the life she had led could be of interest to anyone, and she even went so far as to apologize on a half dozen occasions for having so little to respond to the questions I posed. If my desire was to make her role and contributions more visible and legible, hers seemed to be to efface herself entirely from the picture, to write herself out of the text.

She was eighty-four years old, her memory was extremely sharp, and, as might be expected, she was most animated while recollecting her film career. Still rail thin (as she had been in the pictures), she was very simply attired in pants and a sweater. We talked in the living room, a room that boasted several remarkable paintings on the wall, a scattered array of sculptures, a plush, elegant couch, the chair I was sitting in, and a large television set. Madame Lacan smoked several cigarettes during the interview, politely offering one to me as well (though I had never smoked before in my life, I was so caught up in the moment that I almost accepted one). Her apartment was richly appointed in discreet, handsome furniture, and had I had the occasion, I would certainly have profited from a closer look around. Instead, I was absorbed in the interview. Then, just as quickly, Madame Lacan whisked me out of the apartment, owing to a medical appointment for which she was already late. She had only recently had a cataract operation (which accounted for her reluctance to meet with me previously, as she later informed me), and needed to return to the doctor for some follow-up tests. Explaining that her recent operation had been quite traumatic, she admitted that she was not in her best form. She even went so far as to express that she was ashamed not to have more engrossing material for me. Also, a certain amount of her reluctance might simply be explained by a kind of propriety that someone of her social standing adheres to. In other words, she did not want to appear too "easy," to divulge great quantities of information at the first question I posed to her. We set up a time for two days later when we could meet again, and as she escorted me out the door, I realized the true privilege that was mine.

Despite being ill at ease with my ability to elicit information from her during our time together, I left with a sense of a relationship started. I began to realize that the whole affair had been a game of sorts: while I exhorted her on to tell me more, marveling at her fascinating life, she "reluctantly" parceled out anecdotes and details, denying her own significance while increasingly revealing more. The long list of questions I had brought I had never taken out of my bag. A combination of novice nerves and a sense that I might not ever get another chance caused me to jump rapid-fire from one question to the next; I rarely allowed the discomfort of silence to provoke her into telling more than she might otherwise. Had I learned much that I did not already know? Not really. In fact, many of her recollections echoed those that I had read in the few interviews that she had granted. What did emerge was the keen sense of a person, the intangible qualities that defy two-dimensional representation: wicked humor, cagey intelligence, a sparkle in her eye, radiant charisma.

She called me Tuesday night before our next meeting. She needed to go to the doctor again for more tests. She was worried about more tests, and was of no mind to entertain visitors. I reluctantly acquiesced and offered to see her a few days thereafter. To that she responded that one could only guess at how she might feel, so I should call her later in the week. I was now faced with the problem of leaving on the following Saturday. She seemed to be in good health generally, other than her eyes, so I could only hope that I would be able to see her again in the fall when I was intending to return. She might even be in better spirits and no longer suffering the aftereffects of the surgery.

Hoping to see her just one more time before I left in order to cement, in some sense, our rapport, I called her on Friday morning. As she answered in her now familiar voice I introduced myself in the usual fashion: "Hello, this is Mr. Hunt, may I speak with Madame Lacan?" To this, she replied, in a phrase I was all too familiar with, "C'est qui à l'appareil?" Speaking a bit more forcefully, I repeated, "It is Monsieur Hhhunnt," silently swearing at the misfortune of name in French. "Madame Lacan n'est pas là [Mme. Lacan isn't (t)here]," she answered. Click.

I was bewildered. While I had become mildly accustomed to her various forms of rejection throughout this process, this was different. Had it really been she on the phone? Did I mistake her for someone else? The answer to both was categorically "no." What of our relationship? What of our newly fashioned rapport? She had never hesitated to tell me before when medical complications prevented our meeting, so had it been her health she could simply have admitted as much. This simple sentence—Madame Lacan n'est pas là—had turned my world upside down. I was incapable of determining its significance, short of fitting it into paranoid delusions and conspiracy theories. That it perfectly summed up the original premise of my undertaking was humor that, while not lost to me at that moment, hardly seemed amusing.

With this all too strange (and yet somehow predictable) turn of events, I was left to pack up and go home. I took its pregnant symbolism as a sign that things had come to an end. It was simply a most fitting note to end on.

Had it not been for the sensible advice of those around me, I would have left it at that. I was dissuaded from leaving without at least calling one more time. So, Saturday morning, only a few hours before my departure, I rang her one more time. She answered, as usual, immediately recognized me, and then asked whether I might be inclined to visit her that afternoon. I had no choice but to politely decline, cursing my bad timing. I asked whether she would be willing to continue our conversation again in the fall upon my return. She answered affirmatively, though she suggested that I wait until after August. I thanked her again for the opportunity to finally meet her in person. As I bade her farewell, she did the same, reminding me, in charmingly broken English, to "have a good trip."

The weight of the Real had not come crashing in on me, suffocating me, as I had expected. Instead, it had bedazzled me. One never really fills a lack, satisfies a desire, or meets the Real, that was clear. But what did

happen was that Sylvia Lacan had exploded my expectations. More brilliant than any version of her that I could conjure up in my head or on
paper, her vivid presence only amplified the staggering dimensions of her
absence.

NOTE

1. Peggy Phelan, *Unmarked: The Politics of Performance* (New York: Routledge,
1993), 146.

SIXTEEN

Virtual Criticism and the Dance of Death

Marcia B. Siegel

In the most ironic moment of Robert Redford's mordant movie *Quiz Show*, Charles Van Doren is making a last desperate effort to preserve his self-respect after being forced to admit he's won a lot of money cheating on television. Up to now he's gone along with the game, receiving the answers to questions he might have known unprompted, on the premise that even a rehearsed genius on the quiz show *Twenty One* would boost the image of the intelligentsia. The producer, Dan Enright, is disabusing him of the public's credulity—everyone knows it isn't really Gary Cooper falling off a horse, the magician doesn't saw the lady in half, it's just entertainment. Van Doren rears up in indignation: "But I am a *college professor!*" Behind him, someone pokes a head in the door and says to Enright, "They need the professor in makeup." Not just real life, but real idealism, had become show biz.

In 1959 I didn't have a television set. I was that kind of intellectual. Neither did Van Doren's famous intellectual father, Mark, till Charlie bought him one with his winnings. But like everyone else, I knew all about the quiz show scandals, and I was so incensed at what I considered Van Doren's betrayal that I wrote a righteous editorial about it for the small-town paper where I was working as a suburban reporter. I believed then that the mind was not something you could fake or sell in a good cause. Nearly forty years later, it's hard to imagine the outrage the quiz show scandals stirred up. Today there's nothing unsavory—or at least unusual—about consuming news as entertainment, viewing programmed personalities as spectacle, or treating the winner in a rigged game as if he were a hero.

Time and technology have eroded the demarcations between art, fiction, entertainment, real life, politics, and merchandising. These seemingly disparate categories have always had affinities. At least as long ago as the mid-nineteenth century, there were touristic reenactments of historical events, carnivalesque displays of medical experiments and tribal villages. The invention of photography made it possible to represent intimate, shocking, or vulgar scenes from everyday life in artful ways. Movies, then television, increased the possibilities for photorealism. From the start, motion pictures were public entertainments that not only borrowed from the vaudeville stage but replicated everyday life and captured live news events. As cultural historian David Nasaw points out, producers quickly learned to simulate what they couldn't film on site.[1] At the same time, art as a process grew harder to define, and also harder to justify, since some of the things art satisfies—our curiosity, our desire for entertainment and fantasy— became so much more easily and cheaply available in the media. The quiz show scandals were another marker in this continuing realignment of the borderlines between private and public life, reality and fiction.

In 1959 on television, heroes were supposed to last forever. Prewar codes of conduct still ruled the media. You couldn't say the word "damn" on television, let alone show a dead body or a baby being born. You couldn't televise lawyers wrangling through a murder trial, or teenage girls accusing their boyfriends of being unfaithful, or citizens running for their lives as wars broke out in their streets. Now we get instant moralizing and ever novel tragedies. All of it can be fabricated and often is. Promising limitless disclosure, media culture hides its motives—we seem to see everything, but half the tale is behind the screen.

Arlene Croce's condemnation of choreographer Bill T. Jones was based on some anachronistic vision of a purer, calmer world.[2] Croce, longtime dance critic of the *New Yorker,* stirred up a furor by refusing to see Jones's AIDS-related work *Still/Here,* and then blasting the piece anyhow in an indignant attack on what she labeled "victim art." One of the things that Croce most objected to, although she didn't see it and it wasn't in the piece, was the presence of "raw human suffering," of "sick people" whom she thinks Jones "worked into his act."

In case any reader doesn't yet know, *Still/Here* is a two-act dance work exploring illness and endurance, with a visual score made from edited videotapes. To gather information for the piece, Jones ran a series of "survival workshops" for terminally ill people all over the country, and videographer Gretchen Bender taped them with their full knowledge that the footage would be used in a performance piece. The tone of the piece, far from being gloomy or unspeakable, evokes a sort of 1970s positivism, an almost poignant faith that supportive friends and self-awareness can help even those who are imperiled to live bravely. No one in the dance is visibly ill, deformed, or otherwise in a condition to disturb the squeamish. The piece is not realistic in that way. There's nothing radical about the use of documentary footage in a performance piece either, and with the exception of some visceral looking micro-edited sequences, even the media images in *Still/Here* are mainly talking heads. Actually, it isn't their health that bothers Croce at all, but the idea that Jones asks us to pay attention to death and dying. In Croce's nasty inference, Jones "thinks that victimhood in and of itself is sufficient to the creation of an art spectacle," and the audience she refuses to join is *"forced* [her italics] to feel sorry for [them] because of the way they present themselves."

The aversion Croce feels toward "victim art" is extremely puzzling to me. I'm sure she does have compassion for sick people, and if she objects to hearing their stories sentimentalized, she has a right to say so. But this isn't exactly what *Still/Here* serves up. Jones and his collaborators, principally designer Gretchen Bender and composers Kenneth Frazelle and Vernon Reid, have put the original workshop "victims" through a gamut of art processes. The images are blown up, cropped, collaged, and otherwise edited. They are projected on movable screens so they become larger or smaller during the piece. The subjects are further translated by the compositional process. Their words become chants and arias sung by Odetta. Their gestures are copied and then set into extended motion by the dancers. Jones has always constructed his dance out of material appropriated from the culture at large. Only here, he makes his choreographic sources known to the audience. Far from the photojournalistic confession-mongers Croce must have been expecting, the original "victims" are depersonalized and distanced, larger than life. They're as flat as icons on a billboard.

No one living in the twilight of the twentieth century is exempt from the blandishments of the disenfranchised, the bombed-out, starving, marginalized masses. Mail arrives daily soliciting funds on their behalf. Politicians use them as a bargaining chip in their budgetary board games. Their pleasing images enter our living rooms; they have become as banal as the deodorant commercials that bring them to us. The accessibility and the immediacy, quick disappearance, and replacement of images have taken away the power they have to shock us. If there is such a thing as victim art, I think its *purpose* is to shock us, to arrest our complaisance about human catastrophe. One of Croce's greatest misconceptions about *Still/ Here* is its supposed shock value. In fact, with the technics of a rock show, the heart-rending courage of its informants, the transformation of their testimony into virtuosic dancing and charismatic sound, the piece is more appealing than offensive. Otherwise it couldn't have toured the country's biggest theatres and opera houses, or been screened for a national audience on Alive TV.

Television can flatten the world into one endless, boring spectacle. If we don't get a stimulus within thirty seconds, we switch to another channel. We haven't the time or the skill to examine these casually received images for authenticity. We can't always tell—most of us have given up trying to tell—the spontaneous from the reenacted from the rehearsed; the plain from the cosmeticized from the digitally enhanced; the fuzzy, confusing, unfocused real event from the attention-capturing, skillfully choreographed feature with an appropriate mood-inducing sound track. Was Joan Rivers more sympathetic, more real, more funny—or less?— when she played herself in a docudrama about her husband's suicide? Was O. J. Simpson acting when he tried on the "bloody glove"? Was the MTV battle for another famous glove between Hammer and Michael Jackson real or fabricated? Is Michael Jackson a pied piper or a pedophile?

Perhaps it isn't important. These are entertainers; we find their stories and their personas diverting, dispensable but not necessarily to be taken as true. Arlene Croce wouldn't consider them offensive; she wouldn't consider them art. But then, what about the hundreds of less easily categorized moments that make up our daily intake of art and information? The disaster films combining newsreels of exploding dirigibles with actors playing the doomed passengers in reenactment shots that have been skillfully doctored to match the faded quality of the documentary scenes. The parades staged by commercial parade producers to sanctify political events and/or dramatize chauvinistic feelings.[3] The dances that tell the stories of people's lives in more or less literal interpolation with more or less abstract dancing.[4] The new ballets and changes to old ballets in which, toward the end of his life, George Balanchine reflected on dying, parting, and martyrdom.[5]

Bill T. Jones's packaging of autobiography, idealism, spectacle, hard news, and exploitation went just too far along this continuum for Croce's sensibility. She could neither look at it nor sanction its claim to respectability. Although her piece testifies to her dismay and confusion with the changing status of art in this country, she wants to keep "art," meaning high art, separate from what she calls, in varying tones of contempt, "post-neo-Dada," "utilitarian art," "anti-art," "Warholism," "some wholly other sphere of action than dance theatre," and Jones's "messianic traveling medicine show."

Her insistence on distinguishing the "real" unfortunates in *Still/Here* (which is not art) from "artistic" representations of victims veered even more off course when she contrived in the same article to praise David Gordon, another brainy, charismatic choreographer who "deals with sickness and dying in cathartic terms." Just why Gordon's performance piece *The Family Business* is OK, why he and not Jones has "escaped being trapped by the logic of sixties permissiveness" Croce does not explain.

Perhaps "art" is no longer a meaningful term; perhaps we should suspend the category for a while and see where the present transition is leading. Trying to protect art's old, presumably unpolluted identity, I think, only isolates it further, restricts it to a diminishing sector of the population. What we used to know as art, before the counterculture changed everything, may have been demoted, but it isn't thrown out of the game just because some formerly non-art players become legitimized. And claiming that anything at all can be art is as foolish as casting anything that isn't into Croce's critical purgatory.

Croce seems to have felt some sympathy for Jones at the beginning, perhaps because he didn't make overtly black dances. After the death of his partner, Arnie Zane, from AIDS in 1988, she would have us believe, he sold out to political interests, "the campaigns of the multiculturalists, the moral guardians, and the minority groups." Croce believes that these groups have no business making art, that they don't satisfy the mysterious fixed criteria of fastidious taste. The mere idea of Bill T. Jones, an out, HIV-positive African American who's danced brilliantly along the art-life boundaries for years, offends her because she thinks he flouts the beleaguered aesthetics of Western high art. Maybe she's simply elevating her personal preferences to the level of critical norms, but she doesn't acknowledge that this bias, or this kind of standard-making, amounts to ideology. We readers were left with the implications of racism, homophobia, and political reaction that her critics quickly seized on.

The issues of "victim art" and critical responsibility were discussed for months, in conversations, classrooms, and the media. The *New Yorker* printed four pages of responses, many of them apparently solicited from Croce's neocon allies. Other publications jumped in. Croce's pre-*New Yorker* career, writing in conservative journals, was carefully traced by Lynn

Garafola in the *Nation*.[6] In June, at the end of a national tour of *Still/Here* in Pittsburgh, the Dance Critics Association annual conference devoted several sessions to the controversy, including a Town Hall speakout and a keynote by Jones. Croce declined to attend, but sent a statement maintaining the same position, which she claimed no one understands. In fact, she not only elaborated on her definition of "victim art" but assured the conference attendees that she wouldn't have changed her opinion that *Still/Here* is "neophilistinism" even if she *had* sat through the dance. She actually seemed to think she was presenting her colleagues with a purely aesthetic and unbiased critical interpretation. But Croce's critical neutrality was compromised long before she proudly submitted this latest refusal to see what she was judging.

The quiz show scandals were one of many precursors of that massive reevaluation known as the counterculture. Among the questions artists were asking then was, What is the relation between life and art? In many ways they tried to transpose one reality onto the other. Dancers asked us to look at them walking, standing, sitting, falling. Could that be art? They showed us films of the atrocities in Vietnam. Could that be art? They drove motorcycles, climbed trees, threw paint at each other. Protest, regression, revision. But art? Arlene Croce hated every minute of this and emerged with relief in the 1970s, with a few enduring paradigms of dancing—Merce Cunningham, Twyla Tharp—to fortify the classical stronghold.

In 1980 she finished off what was left of the counterculture's experiments with a new polemic cloaked as critical analysis, "Slowly Then the History of Them Comes Out," the title borrowed, unfortunately without a sign of irony on Croce's part, from Gertrude Stein.[7] Presenting a loopy version of the facts in a tone of absolute certitude, she arranged the lineage of downtown dance—most of which she had avoided reviewing—so that everything up to that time derived from either the trance-inducing "mysterians," led by composer Philip Glass, or the "Mercists," who took their cue from Merce Cunningham and really danced. With her usual icy sarcasm she attacked all the then-current mysterian artists who employed repetition and avoided virtuosity. (Her category embraced Lucinda Childs, Meredith Monk, Kenneth King, Laura Dean, and Robert Wilson.) She called this work "T'ai Chi stuck in a groove," "compulsive and lethargic," "head dance." In comparison with "Discussing the Undiscussable," this article seems quite mild, but it elicited a stream of angry rebuttals and corrections from the avant garde. Unmoved, Croce reprinted the piece word for word in her next volume of collected reviews, with a long note of self-justification intended to cut the absent protesters down to size.[8]

By 1990 the culture was going elsewhere. Ballet and modern dance were thoroughly shaken up by the counterculture, and hurting for leadership as a wave of premature deaths swept across the active ranks of choreographers, at the same time that a senior generation was ending. New ideas about dance and performance were seeping into the gaps. Croce lashed out at the dangers of multiculturalism and its misguided promoters in the university. She attacked "the political advocacy of other than Western (or non-'Eurocentric') forms of dance," "divisive notions of culture popular in the universities."[9] Instead, she offered the thematic eclecticism of then-emerging formalist choreographer Mark Morris as a model that should satisfy our cravings for the exotic without requiring us to abandon Western classical notions of dance and art.

Multiculturalism, like postmodernism and victim art, constitutes a terrible threat to Croce's aesthetics, and also to her power (she would say her autonomy) as a critic. Croce is the leading voice for a school of dance criticism that dates back to the early twentieth century. When the first explosions of modernism hit the European stage via Serge Diaghilev's Ballets Russes, Russian expatriate André Levinson maintained that "classical dance is a world of countless possibilities."[10] It would absorb or rise above the savage and discordant attractions of modernism, had already converted everything worthwhile the ancient Greeks had to offer, and need not respond unduly to faddish attempts at reform.[11] Levinson and his followers, chiefly Lincoln Kirstein and Croce, were guarding not only a style, but an ideal that envisions dancing as a transcendent form of art, to be practiced only by the most intensively trained and rigorously selected initiates. As Levinson asserted in 1925, "the constant transfiguration . . . of the classic dancer from the ordinary to the ideal is the result of a disinterested will for perfection, an unquenchable thirst to surpass himself. Thus it is that an exalted aim transforms his mechanical efforts into an aesthetic phenomenon."[12] Until 1983 George Balanchine was this aesthetic's greatest exemplar.

Truth and Beauty are concepts defined by culture; our perception of them in art depends on how we've been trained to grasp them, by parents, religion, school, television, critics. The art of classical ballet was cultivated by, about, and for the ruling classes of Europe. That it now occupies high-art status in American culture doesn't mean it's any more transcendent or beautiful than the dance of Native Americans, Yoruban orishas, Korean shamans, or Voudon priestesses, than Balinese legong, Indian Odissi, Javanese bedoyo. I don't say it is invalid, that it hasn't produced wonderful dancing and choreography I've learned to love. But it is a political as well as a theatrical imagining of a particular kind, one that encompasses only one segment of the world most of us know or would like to know.

For the zealots of classical ballet, Balanchine's death was a shattering loss. Not only was there no choreographer alive comparable to him, no repertory to match what he created for the New York City Ballet, there was no real line of succession to preserve the craft he conquered. Ballet itself, both here and abroad, was already embracing alien forms and signs to attract new audiences—elements of popular culture, expressionistic movement, sexual violence, trendy music and narrative—and taking less care to transform them than Balanchine had.

Croce's response to this state of affairs was to review less and less frequently. You could feel a distaste for the diversifying dance world in her withdrawal. Nothing going on was of interest to her, was worthy of her discriminating attention. In "Discussing the Undiscussable," she finally let the real demons out. She could barely tolerate slipping standards, but what she couldn't confront at all was a world overtaken by the Other. Those very aliens and exotics who scared Levinson and infuriated Kirstein before her now threatened to imprint their unacceptable bodies, their earthly miseries, and their lower-class origins onto the holy name of art.

Critics of the Levinson/Kirstein/Croce persuasion like to think they are saving us by preaching how uplifting their dance is, as opposed to the gross indulgences and primitive emotings of everything else. They believe they've been appointed to tell us what good art is—and how harmful bad art is. The public takes Croce seriously because she is serious and passionate, and a gifted, convincing writer. It's often not even the opinion she wields but the deadly quotable catchwords ("victim art"), the sarcasm ("I understand that there is dancing going on during the talking"), and dismissal ("Jones's personal story does not concern me") that make her sound so confident, so right. Hers is the voice of intellectual authority, of reassurance, and, in the face of ephemeral, unnameable happenings like dance, it has a curious hold on the public's attention.

"Discussing the Undiscussable" in part is Croce's desperate defense of power, both the establishment's and her own. The essay seems to be about art but is really about authority. Bill T. Jones incurred her displeasure years ago, after she used the novel term "fever swamps" to put down some work of his. He playfully, perhaps maliciously, named a dance *Fever Swamp*. This action transgressed the limits of the critic/artist relationship. When artists make audible gestures, it seems, they're out of Croce's game. They can't make any justifiable comeback to a critic; their only motive would be self-interest. In other words, "performers can tolerate only as much criticism as can be converted to the uses of publicity."[13]

While bashing Jones and the "victim artists," Croce portrays herself as exploited, intimidated, aggrieved, and thwarted in the exercise of her critical responsibility. A victim, in fact, or nearly so, saved only by her resolute decision. "In not reviewing 'Still/Here,' I'm sparing myself and my readers a bad time, and yet I don't see that I really have much choice." She admits that her antipathy for 1960s dance was rooted in its disdain for criticism, its "self-awarded privileges," its intention "to relieve critics of their primary task of evaluation," and ultimately its instigation of a national policy to fund art that was beyond her power to suppress.

What Croce calls the "arts bureaucracy" began in the 1960s with the creation of the National Endowment for the Arts, the state arts councils, and other local funding agencies. For the first time this country officially recognized a responsibility to support its artists. At the beginning this was all right, she thinks, because it separated "art and art appreciation" from "community outreach." In other words, minority artists and others who did not try to make it into Croce's approved category could be considered for funding outside it. She didn't have to think of them as artists. Croce served on the NEA dance panel in the late 1970s, when she thinks it had not yet succumbed to "utilitarian art." Gradually a reversion to the "proletarian" spirit of the 1960s destroyed our ability to tell good art from non-art, and poisoned criticism itself by giving critics permission to "describe" dance without evaluating it.

According to Croce, a critic's most important skill or talent, her most serious responsibility, is to be a judge. Croce now provides us with the most extreme evidence of where this can lead. Her "judgment" in this case is not only absolute but insulting, cruel, dismissive. Besides the epithets I've already quoted, she refuses to dignify Bill T. Jones with the title of choreographer or even dancer. She calls what she thinks he does "a barely domesticated form of street theatre," "paranoid accusation," "intolerably voyeuristic," and so on. What he does belongs in the cultural ghetto of community art, which is unprofessional, unaesthetic, and definitely undeserving of either financial or critical support.

The National Endowment is ultimately to blame for fostering the type of work Jones does. It not only set the tone for public and private support of what Croce calls "the ethos of community outreach," but also somehow exposed us to other dangerous symptoms of society's current ills. "Jones and Mapplethorpe, parallel self-declared cases of pathology in art, have effectively disarmed criticism." The blood, the revelations of mortality, the appeals for justice or for sympathy must go. Not by being looked at and rejected, but by being cut off from funding before they can harm us. The NEA was crumbling nicely under the legislative sledgehammer without Croce's condemnation, but her contribution lends a bit of class to the thuggish way Congress has discredited the arts in the process of defunding them. Before long, individual artists and community projects will get nothing from the NEA, though the unimpeachable major institutions will continue to reap the majority of whatever funds it ekes out of Congress. But I'm not sure even this drastic retrenchment would keep projects like *Still/Here* off the boards, since it's a perfect example of a mainstream spectacle with a contemporary theme.

One thing Arlene Croce and I would agree on: the machinery of promotion and manipulation has become extremely efficient in recent years. It is hard to judge, or even sit calmly in the theatre and look at what's on the stage, when you have previously been subjected to outrageous hype, sympathy-eliciting personal disclosures, inside information about what went into the dance. Dancers are canonized by powerful publicity campaigns before they get onstage. Critics in many instances are forced by their publications to take part in this process by writing the advance stories that will sell the tickets. Previewing is replacing reviewing in publication after publication. As one editor told me, "We'd rather tell people what to see than tell them what they missed." All critics are expected to be lackeys for the profession, flacks rather than commentators, conveyors of what we're told the artist wants to convey instead of what we see in the work for ourselves. Often if we're not needed as ticket-sellers, or might be too independent in our responses, we don't get complimentary seats.[14]

Bill T. Jones excels at manipulating his audience and his critics. I've known him a long time, and from the first he struck me as a master at flattering and challenging us, keeping us on the edge between pleasure and antagonism. In his early solos he'd brazenly display his gorgeous body, do some outrageous turn from a minstrel show with a seductive smile on his face, then, while we were still enjoying it, snarl some retaliatory joke or whisper a humiliating experience he remembered. He could sing with a velvet voice, he could dance, he could do acrobatics that looked like love scenes with his white lover-partner, Arnie Zane, he could pull one-liners out of the day's news or quote from a book. You didn't know if he was making it up or spilling his guts. When he modeled $2,000 outfits in the *New York Times Magazine,* I didn't know whether to be offended (this is a starving artist?) or thrilled (this is a starving artist!).[15]

And in most of these talking dances he'd slip in a remark about the critics who were present. A couple of years ago, he generously agreed to appear at New York University for almost no money. The studio was jammed with students. He did two solos and showed a video he was making. In the middle of one dance he remarked that he hadn't performed it in a while, and was nervous about doing it because I was there. Was he really flustered? Heads turned in my direction. The students were impressed; I was pleased and embarrassed. He went right on. You can't dislike a performer who does that. He knows it perfectly well. *Still/Here* is born of a very savvy talent, a talent that sells itself as a sex symbol, an angel, an embattled victim, whatever it takes to get our attention. All of them are his true self.

Since Arnie Zane's death, Jones has staged his polymorphous personality on a bigger and bigger scale. He's cultivated himself as a symbol of intersecting social dilemmas, a "poster boy for the Zeitgeist," as he was pictured by Henry Louis Gates, Jr., in a reverential *New Yorker* profile.[16] Not only does Jones own up to an identity facing multiple challenges, he is extremely skilled at seizing and mastering the instruments with which to make those challenges visible.

He has published an autobiography, cast in the same outrageously confessional but not really introspective tone as his solo dances.[17] He writes lovingly of Zane and the development of their partnership, yet says little about Zane's own work. *Secret Pastures* (1985), the collaborative theatre piece on which Zane's brainy, witty imagination left its imprint, is barely mentioned, but his account of Zane's illness, decline, and death is graphic and devastating. The dances he made afterward obsessed about dying and dependency. "Tell me what to do, baby. I'm coming apart. You've always been the one telling me what to do."[18] Devoted, seemingly self-effaced, he intones, "Everything I did for myself would be in the name of what we had been."[19] This kind of tribute, which runs through the book, reads rather badly now, since Jones has so spectacularly played the survivor.

Jones's own health is in jeopardy too. But he celebrates his body with a defiant pleasure. At one point in his book, he ironically lists all the debilities of aging that he won't have to face. His literary gestures are part of the bigger performance through which he hopes to wake up a public he thinks is insufficiently sensitive to the plight of the dying, the marginalized, the powerless.

Just after the book was published, he touched off another scandal with a casual remark about Jews supposedly controlling the media. This took place during a long public interview with dance critic Deborah Jowitt on a

"Conversations" series at the 92nd Street YM-YWHA. He was "on" that night, role-playing as always in public; reading sections from his book; swatting at his detractors; jumping up to show bits of dancing, singing, preaching; telling stories about purposely outrageous things he'd done. Smooth as snake oil and staunch as a crusader, he objected to Croce's picturing him as some kind of revivalist/patent-medicine salesman. He launched into one of his monologues, demanding to be understood as a "historical person at a time when a great cultural discourse is shifting."[20] His "people controlling the media are Jewish" remark was only one of many preposterous and contradictory things he said, and no one in the large audience there, in that hub of the city's Jewish culture, raised a word in disagreement. They accepted Jones as a professional provocateur and Jowitt as a nonpartisan facilitator. Nevertheless, both Jones and Jowitt heard from the Anti-Defamation League after sensationalized accounts of the evening had been published. Jones says now he feels his remarks were spontaneous and ill-considered. Yet he and Jowitt both had to make their obeisances to the guardians of correct speech, and a year later Jones offered the Y a solo concert in atonement. "I feel like I made a mistake, but I don't want to do *mea culpa* the rest of my life," he told me.[21]

The most serious victimization artists suffer from today is economic. Their mania for publicity seems to them a way to survive the funding squeeze, and maybe to toy with the discouraging odds on mortality. What's scary is not that art resembles life any more than it ever has, but that it resembles the mass fictions of television and advertising. Dancing has always had the potential for selling the body, and the display of the body is a perfect sales pitch for dance performance. In 1996 Jones was featured, both as a subject and a principal salesman, in another kind of show that seemed to cycle the art/commerce process up to a new level of visibility. His naked form, identified in minuscule type, started appearing in magazines and newspapers to herald an upcoming exhibit of work by fashion photographer Herb Ritts at the Museum of Fine Arts in Boston. Underwritten by Donna Karan, the show turned out to be an extravaganza of fashion and fame, perhaps intended to establish a measure of seriousness for the trendy Ritts. Controversial and popular, the show was held over two weeks, giving it a four-month run at the MFA.

After six rooms hung with famous faces and torsos being quirky for the camera (Madonna in a pair of Mickey Mouse ears, Richard Gere as bozo with truck tires), Jones had the last space all to himself. In the big, dark chamber, two walls featured his image—one a single blow-up, the other an eight-panel montage. Naked, he poses with strategic primness, his form arranged for immortalization. Maybe Ritts was trying to portray him as latter day Greek statuary, his arty attitudes suggesting imprisonment, subjection, pleading, introspection, aspiration, anything but dancing.

Jones, who admires Ritts's work, didn't expect to be featured in such a dramatic way, but he says he thinks Ritts is retailing the iconography of an era, and he doesn't mind being along as a major player. He wasn't prepared, he says, to be an item in the merchandise mart the viewer finds on leaving the last gallery. I counted eighteen different Ritts tokens on sale, from the exhibition catalogue (a $75 paperback) to magnets, note cubes, and shower curtains, all decorated with images from the show.

The more Bill T. Jones stages himself, the more famous he gets. While *Still/Here* was still touring the country, he sold out Alice Tully Hall in July 1995 for three performances of *Degga*, with Toni Morrison and Max Roach. Here, with two high-powered collaborators, the roughness and the forthright genius of Jones were more apparent than in the artful, almost mellow *Still/Here*. With Roach drumming intensely and Morrison reading excerpts from her writings, he danced a long solo in which every move seemed to refer to something provocative in his history: slavery, minstrelsy, disease, androgyny, a life lashed with anger but devoted to entertaining people. Throughout the piece, wearing as little as possible, he subverted even the obvious black-body-beautiful image by behaving more like some stereotypical sexy female, say, Vanessa Williams, than any standard male hunk. If Jones is theatricalizing his HIV identity, it's surely not to portray himself as a victim. Rather, he's making dances all over the place, experimenting in different formats, role-playing across a daring spectrum, and taking responsibility for it. Whatever you may think of his aesthetics, he gives as skilled and persuasive a performance as his virtual critic.

NOTES

1. Nasaw describes how, during the Spanish-American War, the Vitagraph Company "manufactured its own battle scenes on its rooftop studio with cutout pictures of battleships floating in one inch of water ringed by cigarette smoke." *Going Out: The Rise and Fall of Public Amusements* (Basic Books, 1993), 150.

2. Arlene Croce, "Discussing the Undiscussable," *New Yorker,* 26 December 1994, 54–60. All quotes by Arlene Croce not otherwise cited are taken from this article.

3. See Mark Sussman, "Celebrating the New World Order: Festival and War in New York," *TDR: The Journal of Performance Studies* 39, 2 (summer 1995): 147–75.

4. David Rousseve, Blondell Cummings, and Jawole Willa Jo Zollar are currently prominent choreographers who use their personal histories in their dance. Trisha Brown told personal anecdotes in *Accumulation with Water Motor,* and several of Jerome Robbins's dances may refer to his own life and times. These are just some obvious examples. There are countless others.

5. See the heartbreaking farewell scene in *Divertimento from Le Baiser de la Fée,* added in 1974 to the 1972 staging; Ravel's macabre *Gaspard de la Nuit* (1975); the funeral march section of *Emeralds* (added in 1976 to the 1967 work); *Davidsbündlertänze* (1980) on the tortured life of Robert Schumann and perhaps any creative artist; the last movement, *Adagio Lamentoso,* of Tchaikovsky's *Pathétique Symphony* (1981).

6. Lynn Garafola, "Black Dance: Revelations," *Nation,* 17 April 1995, 536–39.

7. Arlene Croce, "Slowly Then the History of Them Comes Out," *New Yorker,* 30 June 1980, 92–95.

8. Arlene Croce, *Going to the Dance* (Knopf, 1982), 285–93.

9. Arlene Croce, "Multicultural Theater," *New Yorker,* 23 July 1990, 84–87.

10. André Levinson, "The New Ballet versus the Old," in *Ballet Old and New,* trans. Susan Cook Summer (1918; Dance Horizons, 1982), 81.

11. Two collections of Levinson's extensive and influential writings have been published in English: *Ballet Old and New,* and *André Levinson on Dance,* ed. Joan Acocella and Lynn Garafola (Wesleyan University Press, 1991).

12. André Levinson, "The Spirit of the Classic Dance," in *André Levinson on Dance,* 48.

13. Croce, *Going to the Dance,* 291.

14. In Pittsburgh, the presenters of *Still/Here,* the Pittsburgh Dance Council, refused to give me a press ticket. In fact, they allotted no complimentary seats to the organization of critics whose meeting in their city was prompted by this performance. Finally they granted me a house seat way over on the side of the elephantine, nearly sold-out Benadum Center, in return for my promise to mention them in this article. At the start of the tour, I was given the usual press courtesy of two tickets from Brooklyn Academy of Music.

15. Hal Rubenstein, photographs by Lois Greenfield, "Turn Me Loose," in "Men's Fashions of the Times," *New York Times Magazine,* part 2, 28 March 1993, 33–37.

16. Henry Louis Gates, Jr., "The Body Politic," *New Yorker,* 28 November 1994, 114.

17. Bill T. Jones with Peggy Gillespie, *Last Night on Earth* (Pantheon, 1995).

18. Jones and Gillespie, 176.

19. Jones and Gillespie, 185.

20. Transcript of Bill T. Jones in conversation with Deborah Jowitt, 92nd Street YM-YWHA, 9 November 1995.

21. Jones's conversation with the author, 6 January 1997, the day after his solo concert at the Y.

SEVENTEEN

The Bed Took up Most of the Room

Jane Blocker

Kenneth Patchen was born in 1911 in Ohio, where his view of life was shaped by his immersion in the culture of coal mining and steel production. His child-hood was spent during the First World War, and at the start of the Depression he attended college for brief periods until he was forced to quit school and began traveling around the country without finishing his degree. He published his first book, Before the Brave, *in 1936, and although he received a Guggenheim Fellowship that year, the prevailing conditions of his life were poverty and struggle. In 1937 he suffered an injury to his back that was misdiagnosed as arthritis, thus beginning a history of pain, immobility, and ineffectual and inappropriate treatments. For the next thirty-five years he endured surgeries and therapies, performed his poetry with jazz ensembles, protested the war and the arms race, was periodically confined to his bed, and produced over forty books of poetry and prose. He died in 1972 of a heart attack, a result of nearly three decades of immobility.*

Bed

In 1946 two reporters interviewed Kenneth Patchen in his bedroom, where he was trying to recover from an agonizing back injury. Their detailed description of the poet is literally framed by the bed:

> The bed was massive and so was the man. He wore a faded gray sweatshirt with washed-out blue cuffs and pocket. The shirt was tucked into the waist-

band of black woolen trousers that were frayed at the cuffs. Patchen wore blue, maroon and tan Argyle socks, but no shoes. His body seemed muscular and powerful; his face was delicate and sensitive. His skin was white and his eyes were a deep blue-gray. The bed took up most of the room.[1]

The reporters' perception of the bed's enormity derives not only from its physical dimensions but also from its gigantic metaphoric dimensions within a postwar mythology of illness and cure. By the time the reporters interviewed Patchen, a significant amount of writing about him had already established the bed as the symbolic site wherein pervasive cultural disease was made visible. In this site, the poet, more sensitive to the threat of nuclear destruction, social unrest, and economic injustice than the average person, performs *our* illness as much as he recovers from his own.[2] Patchen was said to express the symptoms of that illness in his poetry, which is described as angry, hysterical, and feverish. In the writing about (and sometimes by) Patchen, he is figured as "diseased" rather than injured, and disease, in turn, is made the analogue for the debilitating illogic of modern life.

In reviewing Patchen's 1941 antiwar novel *The Journal of Albion Moonlight,* for example, William Carlos Williams explains, "For what we're after is a cure. That at its best is what the book's about. A man terribly bitten and seeking a cure, a cure for the bedeviled spirit of his day."[3] In a similar use of the metaphor, Patchen remarked, "I used to get pneumonia regularly every year. Even now, injustice and cruelty upset me to the point of becoming really sick."[4] In each example, Patchen seems to suffer, not from a back injury, but from a mythological "environmental illness"; his body reacts violently to the allergens of contemporary social and political life.

The two interviewers, Holly Beye and William McCleery, simply expand the metaphor by providing a "scene" for this illness and its cure, a stage on which it is performed. In short, they situate Patchen rhetorically in the politicized site of the bed. What better backdrop could there be for a poet whose emotion, Henry Miller tells us, "tears loose in clots"?[5] Just as the bed threatens to overtake Patchen's room in the reporter's description, so it grows animistically to fill the discursive space in which he is housed. Miller, for example, describes him as a "sick giant" lying on "a huge bed in a doll's house."[6] Thus in thinking about his poetry and paintings one finds oneself tripping over the bed, negotiating its corners, squeezed up against walls. Displayed upon it, Patchen is a contradictory figure: sick and giant,

Fig. 17.1. Photograph of Kenneth Patchen by Arthur Rothstein, *Look,* June 12, 1951, 112. Reprinted by permission.

massive and ordinary, muscular and wounded, powerful and delicate. The bed is the source of these contradictions, a stage for the performance of disability and cure, power and powerlessness, joy and loss, the body and its radical disappearance.

A photograph appearing in *Look* magazine in 1951 (fig. 17.1) makes evident the bed's ability to stage Patchen in a contradictory role.[7] The photograph shows him in bed wearing striped pajamas and covered with a mountainous blanket. He is uncharacteristically bearded, making him the "sick giant," a real-life Paul Bunyan. By the side of the bed there is a small table on which rests a glass of water. His wife, Miriam, bending in from the right border of the picture, appears to be handing him a bottle of medicine. Two canes slant against the head of the bed as though portending both recovery and permanent disability. The photograph shows how the bed sets the stage for an ambivalent performance; as in the reporters' description, the bed provides a visual frame for the poet so that his body is made an image. The text accompanying the photograph gives important clues about how to interpret that image: "Reading their poetry at a New York rally for Patchen, the seven gave an audience preoccupied with war an impressive reminder of the importance of the creative artist in a free world. They likewise compellingly reaffirmed their faith in the dignity of the individual."[8] The magazine uses the photograph of Patchen to represent the "creative artist in a free world." With his physical affliction he embodies the disability of the poet caught between politics and creativity, between his power as a symbol of freedom and his vulnerability in a world threatened by communism. The ambivalence of the photograph is an index of its visual potency; it elicits sympathy for the poet's frailty while making assurances of his strength. The article's subtitle ("Creative artists of America, England and France start drive to establish a fund for the medical treatment of the American poet Kenneth Patchen") casts the poets as allies in the war for the "dignity of the individual" and Patchen as the embattled country for whom their efforts are mobilized.

I want to emphasize that it is the bed itself that makes this kind of contradiction possible. The bed's inherent qualities make it unique for its ability to represent both strength and vulnerability: (1) it makes the body visible but, more precisely, makes it a powerful image or spectacle; (2) it disciplines the body, makes it coherent, and inscribes it in narratives of birth, illness, dreams, sexuality, and death; (3) it is a means of representing the body as a problem to be solved, and therefore indicates a fundamental belief in transformation and intervention; (4) it is an asylum, that is, a secure refuge but also a place out-of-bounds, one that is ostensibly exempted from (but more often the direct object of) social strictures; (5) because of its horizontal regime, it is consonant with the grave and therefore stages a rehearsal of death; (6) it is, finally and contradictorily, a utopia, not-a-place.

This essay concerns the work Patchen produced in his bed, a series of paintings that he called "picture-poems," which, like the *Look* photograph, stage an ambivalent performance but one that Patchen himself directed. It seeks first of all to show an analogous relationship between the bed on which Patchen lay and the paper on which he painted. Second, it attempts to establish this relationship as performative; and finally, it considers how these paintings, by virtue of their performativity, work to disable their viewers.

The analogy that compares bed to paper (or canvas) makes creation into performance because in these terms creation is no longer just making something, but living in it with one's body. The creative product, as a result, cannot remain a stable, whole, unique, transcendent object, but becomes a performative artifact that invokes space, movement, and absence. Because this artifact is produced on the bed's terms, it bears the imprint of human contact, the stains of bodily secretions, and the odor of illness and death.

One of the most significant examples of this analogy occurs in Isak Dinesen's story "The Blank Page," in which the linen sheets lain on by princesses on their wedding nights are framed and hung in a gallery dedicated to the loss of virginity. Dinesen uses the page/canvas/bed as a metaphor for narrative; each of the blood-stained sheets tells its own story of sexuality and patriarchy. Even, or perhaps especially, the one sheet left blank is a story that brings the unyielding body of the storyteller into being.

The other obvious example of this analogy is Robert Rauschenberg's painting *Bed,* in which he has tacked a quilt (instead of canvas) across stretcher bars and affixed a pillow at the top. On the canvas/bed, Rauschenberg paints in the vivid colors and frantic strokes of the abstract expressionist, but his painting cannot be read as the pure, disembodied expression of identity or psychic existence normally associated with that movement. Rather, it locates "action painting" in the mortal body, which, as in Dinesen's story, is called into being by the work of art.[9]

A more recent example may be drawn from the work of Felix Gonzales-Torres, who turned his photograph of a bed into billboards around Manhattan. The image depicts a now vacant bed, its white pillows bearing the imprint of its former occupants. The chillingly beautiful monochromatic photograph is imbued with death. It metaphorically shows the photographic page to be an index of loss; the shadow fixed on paper is, like the indentation in the pillow, made with the body. Similarly, Patchen's picture-poems reveal the bed/paper metaphor. Like Dinesen's sheets, Rauschenberg's quilt, and González-Torres's pillows, Patchen's paintings bear the trace of his body.

Bed/Podium

It is obvious to anyone who has read Patchen's antiwar poetry that had he written the text for the *Look* article it would not have contained the jingoistic rhetoric of patriotism. In Patchen's picture-poems he does indeed stage contradiction, but his differs markedly from that of the magazine blurb. His script casts the artist as the angry but feverish symbol of social responsibility rather than as the mighty but threatened symbol of democratic freedom. In these works the bed is a site of both power and marginalization where the artist's role is to protest. "Out of that protest," Patchen explains to his interviewers, "will come whatever validity there is in art. It's not just going on record against something—that's journalism. It must be more than an intellectual thing; it must affect the artist's whole being." [10] Protest is therefore not something one writes *about*, but something experienced in one's body, rather like illness. Beye and McCleery report that, when asked what the artist should protest against, Patchen responded, "The artist must protest against evil. He must point at the specific evil in society and write against it." As he said this, according to the two reporters, he "banged his fist on the hard surface of the bed for emphasis." [11] This description makes clear the bed's potential to stage contradiction. On one hand, Patchen seems angry, powerful, committed to political ideals; he strikes out at the world from his bed/podium. On the other hand, that power is limited by the bed; the blow he strikes is only to the mattress on which he is confined.

Patchen's paintings are the analogue of this conflicted site. Each one is the podium for his angry protest; each one is a bed absorbing his blows and betraying his real infirmity. A representative example of these works reveals an impassioned, extemporaneous style (fig. 17.2). The text, which is written in a careless scrawl, surrounds a pen-and-ink drawing of a lionesque creature with a cockeyed stare:

How Do You Mourn These Dead? Who Are Still Alive / Forgive us O little children & all other guiltless helpless creatures For we know what we do! Any evil is good, provided it is our evil! Under These Christ-Masks, You Prepare The Murder of the World / In the name of Mankind, of Truth, of Sanity, of Life Itself, I denounce you!—as I denounce your "enemies"—Down with you! Down with all of you! Madmen! Liars! Murderers!

The shrill tone of this invective, its threats and sarcasm stand in stark contrast to the childlike handwriting, the strange animal creature, and the carelessness of the lettering. The ideas expressed are well suited to the public rhetorician whose rising tone carries the sweeping indictment of his audience; the appearance of the writing and drawing is, however, more helpless and pleading. It trembles with infirmity. Patchen's fist pounds emphatically on his podium while his hand falls in exhaustion on his bed.

Fig. 17.2. Kenneth Patchen, *How Do You Mourn These Dead . . .* , c. 1968. Picture-poem, 45.2 x 27 cm. Kenneth Patchen Archive, Special Collections, University Library, University of California, Santa Cruz. Reproduced by permission.

If, as I am attempting to suggest, his paintings are analogous to the bed in which he painted, Patchen's views on the role of the artist mark that relationship as performative. It is not a matter of the paintings simply representing the struggle of the artist, but of the struggle marking the paintings indexically and bringing the artist into being. In his poetry and paintings he reveals a picture of the artist who is, on one hand, uniquely gifted to the task of social critique, and is, on the other, weakened and sickened by that task. One poem, inspired by his childhood in Ohio, depicts the poet's struggle:

The Orange Bears

The orange bears with soft friendly eyes
Who played with me when I was ten,
Christ, before I left home they'd had
Their paws smashed in the rolls, their backs
Seared by hot slag, their soft trusting
Bellies kicked in, their tongues ripped
Out, and I went down through the woods
To the smelly crick with Whitman
In the Haldeman-Julius edition,
And I just sat there worrying my thumbnail
Into the cover—What did he know about
Orange bears with their coats all stunk up with soft coal
And the National Guard coming over
From Wheeling to stand in front of the millgates
With drawn bayonets jeering at the strikers?

I remember you could put daisies
On the windowsill at night and in
The morning they'd be so covered with soot
You couldn't tell what they were anymore.

A hell of a fat chance my orange bears had!

(Kenneth Patchen, *Collected Poems of Kenneth Patchen*. Copyright 1954, 1957 by New Directions. Reprinted by permission of New Directions.)

The poem describes the ubiquity of black coal dust in the air, the back-breaking labor of the steel mill, and the inevitability of despair in a life in which one's body is simply fuel for the blast furnace of industrial capitalism. An obvious cultural critique, it combines innocence (as represented by the bears), despair (as represented by the brutality of the mills), and their relationship to an art that seems a sadly irrelevant romanticization of working-class American life (as represented by Whitman's poetry). In a self-reflexive gesture, Patchen uses Whitman to represent the poet whose art remains, in the face of real tragedy, a purified, unsoiled object untainted by coal dust, hot slag, or the smell of a creek polluted by industrial waste. In this sense his poetry is disabled, that is, deprived, by virtue of its own conventions, of its intended force.

One of Patchen's contributions to American poetry was his systematic attack on such conventions. His work was hopelessly out of step with American New Criticism, whose tenets were widely adopted from the 1930s to the 1950s.[12] This literary formalism, espoused by I. A. Richards, held that poems possess an internal unity having nothing to do with the writer, social or economic forces, or historical specificity. From the New Critic's point of view, Patchen's writing was seen as too emotional, too political, too deeply related to his own life. James Dickey, for example, said that Patchen had "produced a genuinely impassible mountain of tiresome, obvious, self-important, sprawling, sentimental, witless, preachy, tasteless, useless poems and books."[13] The romantic quality of Patchen's writing, its emotion, inelegant phrasing, obvious puns, melodrama, and invective helped earn him that reputation.

Jean Untermeyer's 1947 review sharply censures his writing and what she describes as Patchen's "crudeness," unformed "taste," and "lack of vocabulary": "When Kenneth Patchen tries to be tough he succeeds only in being gauche. The animal ferocity akin to toughness does not suit him. And these poems reveal qualities in Mr. Patchen that make us wish he would turn from his Darwinian to his divine inheritance."[14] This pithy critique produces a vivid image of Patchen that progresses from a lower-class malcontent caught outside his proper social station, to a primitive beast whom we are supposed to imagine is Darwin's missing link. In this description Patchen becomes a gorilla at a tea party, a crude, ill-mannered, ungroomed, and awkward figure who has entered the field of poetry quite by mistake.

In response to the elitism of the literary world, Patchen wrote a scathing review of his own in a poem (published in 1949) whose main literary image is, interestingly enough, a bed. The poem is a remarkable thesis on performativity and artistic production:

> *Portrait of the Artist as an Interior Decorator*
>
> Aaa, haa, it is a pity that you were put to the trouble
> of being born.

You're such a nerveless little whelp.
It's a damn shame you had to be bothered.

Painting, music, poetry, etc., etc., are really quite boring
unless, of course,
you can tinker them nicely spitless, gutless, and quite
quite unsoiled
with your delicately tapering fingers with their fine, dry
hairs.
(—And eating, sleeping, sleeping with etc., etc.)

Go to it
pretty-pinkie away at it
at your 'beautifully' beautiful, 'artfully' artful
something or other—which, for the sake of accuracy,
I'll call a bed (NOW DON'T BE FRIGHTENED), a precisely
fashioned, precisely daubed and plumed and caparisoned
bed . . . where nobody, but absolutely nobody, would ever have
the bad taste to take a woman
or himself to get an honest night's sleep
or to beat out an illness or a drunk
or to die.

You're such a clever, lifeless little phony,
with precisely *the* correct manner for doing everything
that's useless, worthless, and quite quite safely dead.
I can guess what it is that bores you.
It's a damn shame you have to be bothered with breathing.

Patchen's poem is a melodrama staged in and around the bed for a working-class audience. It begins with the hero's dramatic discovery of the cowering villain who has been hiding in the plain view of everyone. "Aaa, haa," the hero's voice rises as though the villain were caught in some act of treachery and was being led by the ear, quivering, to center stage where his crimes will be made a spectacle. The hero's voice grows soft with elaborate sympathy, his eyes well with artificial tears for his nemesis: "it is a pity that you were put to the trouble of being born." Under the weight of such bitter tenderness the villain shrinks; he is costumed in his own victimization. He is vaguely European and effeminate with "tapering fingers" and "pretty pinkies." He is a phony aspiring to aristocracy through practiced gestures of cultivation that fool no one.

With cloying affection the hero catalogues the villain's puny crimes, of which the most egregious are cowardice, lifelessness, and decoration. Then, in the ultimate insult, both his crimes and his tragic boredom are anticlimactically shown to be unworthy even of scolding. The hero turns him loose and mockingly encourages him to continue his villainy because it does not so much threaten as entertain. "Go to it," the hero says, goading the villain to pursue acts of banal inconsequence, "pretty-pinkie away at it at your 'beautifully' beautiful, 'artfully' artful something or other—which, for the sake of accuracy I'll call a bed." The bed is the villain's enterprise, which the hero points to with mock terror and cutting derision.

He exposes to his audience the real identity of his enemy, humiliates and deconstructs his villainy and exposes it as effeminacy. This bed, he tells them, like crime, is not legitimate work; it symbolizes the occupation of dabblers, "tinkerers," those of the leisure class. With its "daubs" and "plumes" it is more of artifice than art, more of transitory and excessive fashion than clothing. The villain is engaged in dandyism, in making what is useful useless by spectacularizing it. His practiced hands make over the bed from a performative object into a purified image. With this transition it becomes an empty place devoid of humanness where no one is allowed to sleep, recover from illness, have sex, be born, or die. The hero speaks in an aside to his audience; this man's bed, he tells them with a snicker, is "unsoiled." Finally, the hero makes his triumph complete, not by vanquishing his opponent, but simply by suggesting that he is not worthy of murder. The villain is awarded a much harsher punishment—to live on in the state of lifeless immortality that he has created for himself. With this poem Patchen engages in performance theory. He mocks the kind of temperance and manners that critics like Untermeyer consider the hallmarks of good poetry.[15] These critics promote a kind of poetry that (if it can be put in terms of the bed) is like a bed that is no longer used, but that is merely looked at. Patchen, conversely, dramatizes the dangers of the bed's visibility, the loss that occurs when it is made into an image. The bed Patchen derides is a spectacle, a metaphor for beautiful language, respect for tradition, and poetic skill. In his view, when real experience—real illness, sex, death, sleep—is transformed into an image, made visible in this way, it is made useless. Poetry, he warns, if composed according to the standards of taste and tradition, can normalize, prettify, and dilute the very aspects of life it is its duty to express. As a result, the bed, which was once the tragic stage for real experience, becomes a useless picture in which no one can actually sleep or recover. By engaging in this battle, Patchen abjures the bed-for-show and imagines himself in the soiled bed of performance.

Soiled Beds

To create his picture-poems, Patchen lay in bed with his knees propped up supporting a wooden board to which drawings in progress were tacked. Miriam would lift his knees to support the board, bring it to him, and take it away when he finished. For pigments and materials he used whatever he could get his hands on—things nobody else wanted. The paintings began when a friend from Stanford University brought him fine laid papers that had been used to store botanical specimens and that were going to be thrown out. As a result, the picture-poems are small—their dimensions less than eleven by seventeen inches—and they are made with materials and methods that could be managed in a position somewhere between sitting and lying down.

The crudeness and fragility of their creation seem intimately related to the desperate handwriting that scrawls across them, and in turn to the injured body feverishly writing. James Schevill makes this connection when he writes that

> Patchen's distinctive handwriting adds to the effect of his work. A round, rolling scrawl, it is a kind of American anticalligraphy . . . voicing its humorous desire to wander around in words and encounter laughing mysteries. It is the handwriting of a man who has endured a lifetime of pain, who has transformed that pain into a singular joy.[16]

The handwriting, the messages it inscribes, the collaged bits of paper, the drawn and painted decorations and borders of these works all seem to tremble with pain, delirium, joy, and confinement. As Miriam Patchen explained, "physically torturous for him since he cannot sit, lie on his back, or move more than slightly without incurring monstrous pain, painting little words on paper gives him air from the cramped bedroom, everything else, including the page, closes in."[17]

It is difficult to describe accurately or completely the appearance, construction, and emotional effect of these works. They are not made well. They seem at times carelessly constructed with whatever was close to hand: fine Chinese laid papers, construction paper, card stock, pen and ink, watercolors, Easter egg dyes, tempera, acrylic, gesso, Magic Marker, crayon. They usually start with a sheet of laid paper on which Patchen pasted fantastic hybrid creatures cut out of construction paper, or torn pieces of paper glued in layers, which he then made into creatures by painting on eyes, legs, or feathers. Then he fitted the text into the spaces around these images. Although it might seem totally improvised, the text, which grows smaller and larger, squeezes into cramped corners and between drawings, is almost always written over a carefully marked penciled rule. Sometimes Patchen wrote the text on a separate sheet of paper, cut it out in a square or rectangle, and collaged it to the bottom sheet. Often this seems not to be necessitated by design but by the need to cover over some mistake in drawing or dissatisfying poetic phrase. All of this contributes to a sense that the works were made under extreme privation—hand-me-down materials manipulated by an artist who pays dearly in pain for the time, the strength, and the agility to bring anything like skill to bear on the project.

One work on which I want to focus is no easier to describe than any of the others (fig. 17.3). Even attempting to transcribe the written text scrawled across the picture is an impossible task because it imposes an ordered reading on words whose very purpose is to defy linear narrative:

> Alas, I remember most what never happened—I am not a silver-bearded king nor yet am I any man's slave / my fist against all enemies of life / The light fills this room on the table a tiny bell, water glass, papers covered with writing—The Human Winter—I Wonder What Ever Became of Human Beings / a tiny bell a water glass pens ink paints / THE EVIL GROWS / Dear god the world it's still here—They're trying but / LETTERS FOR MIRIAM / I remember running through the summer fields when I was, oh say, twelve—and as I ran I'd put new words to the tunes of the poems which my grandfather said for me—he was an Irishman raised in Scotland—I never said "my" words to him / my fist against them / Darkness outside the window of this room—yes, "my" words. I've many now that are not for saying / O light upon this table / The tunes are from life the anger the anguish this room the staring of these walls O dear & patient hands shaped to my care O beautiful eyes filled with tears for me / AH, NO SILVER-BEARDED KING NOR YET A SLAVE*DEAR GOD*THE TINY BELL THE*WATER GLASS* LIGHT IN THE DARKNESS / This room, this battlefield

"This room, this battlefield." It's not a title. Although it is the largest of the written fragments in this picture-poem, and is the only one written in white paint on dark paper (rather than black ink on buff-colored paper), it

Fig. 17.3. Kenneth Patchen, *This Room, This Battlefield* . . . , c. 1968. Picture-poem, 45.2 x 26.6 cm. Kenneth Patchen Archive, Special Collections, University Library, University of California, Santa Cruz. Reproduced by permission.

reads more as a setting, as an establishing shot in a filmic narrative. Like a bank of trees painted in receding perspective, it creates a fictional scene in which the rest of the composition is arrayed; the little bird characters exist in this impossible setting, and the text surrounding them seems to be spoken from this stage. At the same time, these words establish a scene for the picture's own creation. The caption marks the work as diaristic, contingent, epistolary, and unfinished. "This room" can be taken to refer both to the cramped space in which Patchen constructed the work and to the cramped space of the work itself. The painting has been made in and sent forth from a bed in a room that is oppressive, enclosed, safe, and embattled. At the same time, the painting is itself stale, airless, cramped, and passionate.

The text that issues from this picture is not a story. There is no beginning. You can't read it from left to right, top to bottom. There is no end. You can arrange the fragments as you like. It is not finished but seems to have been designed that way—as a fragment that is built up and scraped down, pasted on, and cut away. Like the words scrawled on it, the collage is built up of fragments that encode the time of its own making, the accrual of materials added on in layers: paper then pencil, then watercolor over that. Ink covers the pencil, then tempera paint covers the ink. Cut pieces of card stock, torn pieces of construction paper are pasted on and painted over: the tempera is chalky, the inks shiny, the watercolors fading. A quill pen has been used to scratch the surface, to unearth what has been buried and to leave it there unreadable—a useless archaeology. There is no pictorial logic, no focus, no composition.

This work is a performance where different voices speak simultaneously; one catches fragments of those words that momentarily have been given more emphasis. The words speak in the first person like a monologue, but then words are jammed into sentences that previously seemed unwilling to make space for them. Words are scratched out, painted twice for emphasis, written in capitals, thin and quiet, thick and loud. To read it one must turn it in one's hands, follow the letters in circles, sometimes read backwards, enter the dialogue, come up short. The words swirl around, growing fat and ungainly, then they get squeezed into awkward spaces between bits of collaged drawings: a desperate mass of captions, aphorisms, titles, prose descriptions, epistolary fragments, prayers, and one dedication.

The words circle around a collaged pen-and-ink painting of two bird-like creatures facing each other in profile. They are the fanciful characters who seem engaged in dialogue but whose eyes, like those of well trained actors, turn toward their audience even as their bodies are face to face in conversation. Above them and to the right Patchen has pasted a crudely cut oval shape. He has painted it with ink and tempera in concentric circles, which close in on a gaping hole ruthlessly cut out of the center like an eyelid opening on a cyclopean eye. It watches us, implicates us in the dialogue. It serves as the omnipotent eye of some god. Beneath the central image of fanciful birds in dialogue Patchen has glued a rectangle of dark blue construction paper on which is written in white tempera, as though it were just the beginning of a longer but as yet unfinished sentence, "This room, this battlefield." Patchen has signed it as though it were a painting, and dedicated it to his wife, Miriam, as though it were a book.

In reading this work one is pulled along on its continually changing rhythms, driven in circles by the multiple voices speaking in differing accents, pitches, and tones. One voice threatens. "My fist against all enemies of life." Another warns and prays. "The evil grows Dear god." Yet another describes the plight of the invalid speaker. "Darkness outside the window of this room. . . . O light upon this table / The tunes are from life the anger, the anguish this room the staring of these walls O dear & patient hands shaped to my care O beautiful eyes filled with tears for me." These phrases place the text emphatically in the present, imbuing the image with an immediacy that can only be described as performative. Other phrases place the text in the past by reminiscing about a lost childhood. "I remember running through the summer fields when I was oh say, twelve." Such phrases mark the passage of time, the mortality of the speaker, his disappearance on the page.

The performative relationship between this picture-poem and the bed is carefully built into the chaotic prose and the naive imagery. First, the painting produces space: we enter the work as we would a cluttered room where the darkness and foreboding of the exterior world press threateningly against the windows. We imagine the sound of the "tiny bell" ringing to summon aid to the bedside. It is a bed marked by long habitation, surrounded by pens and brushes, a water glass, sheets of paper, and unfinished manuscripts; it is not simply for sleeping but for living in. It is an ambiguous space that is both simple room and violent battlefield. Second, the painting produces time: it is caught somewhere between the present and the past, presence and absence, life and death. In that tremulous moment the bed floats adrift between the urgency of the ringing bell and the nostalgia of childhood memory. Third, the painting is dialogic: it is produced through conflicting voices that implicate the viewer. Finally, the painting brings the artist into being, performing him, producing him as a conflicted character on the bed/stage. Neither a "silver-bearded king nor yet . . . any man's slave," the artist can claim neither absolute power nor absolute abjection.

Disability

Patchen's picture-poems embody a contradictory state of being that I would call disability. On a physical level, Patchen's excruciating back pain clearly dis-ables him from writing, and the poems vividly reveal that state of dependency, exhaustion, and frustration. On a philosophical level, he is disabled by the conflict between art and protest, as though he had been wounded in a land war over literary priorities. He occupies the contested border between two oppositional forces—between his desire for poetry to promote justice, and the censure of the New Critic. On the level of performativity, however, his picture-poems may be said not only to reveal *his* disability, but actively to disable. I want to conclude by moving beyond Patchen's own relationship to these works and think for a moment about how, for their viewers, the paintings generally match the disabling experience of performance.

Disability is a contradictory state of being that, like the bed, can script empowerment along with struggle.[18] Its etymological roots link it to performativity in a way that Patchen's work illustrates. To the extent that "ability" relates to "habere" or "that which may be easily held," "*dis*ability" signifies that which escapes one's grasp. At a certain level this is the very definition of performance: it offers itself to be held, to tangibility, but simultaneously asserts its own disappearance. In other words, a rather common way of thinking about performance is that it is both more "real" than other kinds of representations and more intangible.

I feel myself pricked by this very kind of disability in another picture-poem in which a relatively large profile drawing represents the "silver-bearded king" mentioned in the other painting. He is accompanied by a towering bird whose two enormous circular eyes sparkle with daubs of vibrant color (fig. 17.4). This work is less jumbled than the last one I described; the words are written, for the most part, horizontally from left to right. The text reads,

IT IS OUTSIDE US AS WE ARE WITHIN IT Ecstasy!—"Thinking" is always outside in the light—THE LIGHT IS ALIVE! At its touch the "mind" dances! The

Fig. 17.4. Kenneth Patchen, *It Is outside Us . . .* , c. 1968. Picture-poem, 45.2 x 27 cm. Kenneth Patchen Archive, Special Collections, University Library, University of California, Santa Cruz. Reproduced by permission.

Flowing Animal Light Is All! The Sleeping-Awakeness-Joy Joying! The Being-Present Self—But words make mistakes Then The Light moves away THE LIGHT IS THE ####

The exuberance of this poem, its thrilling progression carried along on exclamation points, ends up in confusion. The writing runs aground on obscure scratchings that obliterate whatever text now lies beneath. This dark patch of opaque inks powerfully wounds and disables me.

The text only momentarily takes hold of the thing it tries to describe, something as ineffable as ecstasy, as intangible as light, as fleeting as thought. It describes a border crossing where thought traverses the limits of the body and moves "outside in the light." While reading, I am suspended in "sleeping-awakeness," stopped for a fleeting moment in contemplation of the "being-present self." Here I confront the "real" aspect of performance, its ability to produce the now, to speak always in the present progressive, to assert its own contingency. The text holds me in that present real for only a brief moment like a feather held aloft on a breath. That moment is too soon lost, however. Something goes wrong, "words make mistakes," and I am faced with the void, reminded that I am reading, that the poet's back aches. The spell is broken; my grasp on the present is undone and it slips into the past. The painting makes me a witness to disappearance, that dark side of performance. Like this awkward and somber bird, I stare with wide sparkling eyes as I myself am first called into being by the painting and then ushered into oblivion.

NOTES

The author wishes to gratefully acknowledge the generous assistance of Miriam Patchen and Rita Bottoms, Head of Special Collections at the University of California at Santa Cruz, in the preparation of this essay.

1. Holly Beye and William McCleery, "The Most Mysterious People in the Village," in *Kenneth Patchen: A Collection of Essays,* ed. Richard Morgan (New York: AMS Press, 1977), 46.

2. In this context Henry Miller writes, "Setting himself apart from the world, as poet, as man of vision, Patchen nevertheless identifies himself with the world in the malady which has become universal." Quoted in Larry Smith, *Kenneth Patchen* (Boston: Twayne, 1978), 43.

3. William Carlos Williams, "A Counsel of Madness: A Review of *The Journal of Albion Moonlight,*" in Morgan, 4.

4. Quoted in Beye and McCleery, 47.

5. Henry Miller, "Patchen: Man of Anger and Light," in Morgan, 34.

6. Ibid.

7. The purpose of the article was to publicize the efforts of poets W. H. Auden, e. e. cummings, Archibald MacLeish, Marianne Moore, and William Carlos Williams to organize others in the arts to raise funds for Patchen's medical treatment. Clearly this photograph was used by *Look* to elicit sympathy in its readers. Ironically, the surgery that it made possible was botched, leaving Patchen in greater pain and confining him more permanently to his bed.

8. "Poets Gather to Help a Poet," *Look,* June 12, 1951, 112.

9. For an interesting discussion on Rauschenberg and the implications of the bed, see Helen Molesworth, "Before *Bed,*" *October* 63 (winter 1993): 69–82.

10. Beye and McCleery, 48.

11. Ibid.

12. Smith, 36.

13. Quoted in Jonathan Williams, "Out of Sight, Out of Conscience," in Morgan, 59.

14. Jean Untermeyer, "The Problem of Patchen," *Saturday Review of Literature,* March 22, 1947, 16.

15. Another critic, Iain Fletcher, later wrote a scathing critique of Patchen's work, in which he stated, "Mr. Patchen is a poet of respectable talent; but vulgar achievement," in "Stopping the Rot-II," *Nine* 2, no. 1 (January 1950): 50.

16. James Schevill, "Kenneth Patchen: The Search for Wonder and Joy," in Morgan, 103.

17. Miriam Patchen, in *Kenneth Patchen: Painter of Poems* (Washington, D.C.: Corcoran Gallery of Art, 1969), 6.

18. I do not in any way want to romanticize real physical disability, although I think that even that may be used powerfully at certain times. Rather, my focus is on disabling effects of politics, the struggle to write, and performance.

MAKING NEW BODIES

EIGHTEEN

Orlan's Performative

Transformations

of Subjectivity

Tanya Augsburg

Je provoque donc j'existe.
　　　　—Orlan

Toward a Theory of Feminist Medical Subjectivity

The political struggle for women to become recognized as autonomous subjects has been complicated by the growing theoretical realization that "subjectification entails subjection."[1] This conceptual conundrum, notes Susan Hekman, was already explicit in Simone de Beauvoir's well-known thesis, "one is not born but becomes a woman." Hekman interprets de Beauvoir's work *The Second Sex* as an attempt to " 'open up' the category of the subject."[2] Women have been traditionally excluded from philosophical discussions of subjectivity because they have been "made" or constituted as inferior, irrational beings. According to Hekman, de Beauvoir's solution to women's subjection was for women to constitute themselves by embracing modernist male (i.e., constituting) subjectivity.[3]

De Beauvoir's work, Hekman implies, points in the direction of the poststructuralist "decentering" of the subject, which Michel Foucault described as "the calling into question of the theory of the subject."[4] Throughout his career Foucault consistently challenged the notion of a universal static subject, although Foucault's theorization of the subject did change along with his thinking about power. To be brief, in his early "archaeologies" of knowledge Foucault demonstrated how subjects are constituted by institutions; in his late genealogies of power, essays, and interviews Foucault became increasingly interested in theorizing the intricate ways subjects develop their own identities.

This tension between Foucault's conceptions of constituted and constituting selves has special relevance for any theory of feminist medical subjectivity. All potential medical subjects must now first give their informed consent, a very recent phenomenon, which, arguably, is not informed consent at all but rather ambivalent compliance.[5] Biology, medicine, gynecology, obstetrics, psychiatry, psychoanalysis, and more recently, cosmetic surgery: the imbrication of these sciences and disciplines continues to constitute women as inferior beings dependent on doctors. Women's informed consent is phantasmagoric at best since they have had the additional burden of having their bodies, bodily processes, and emotions not only medicalized but pathologized. To put it differently, the difficulties in theorizing women as medical subjects, let alone as feminist medical subjects, are to be found in the extent to which women have been constituted by modern science and medicine.[6]

Given its emphasis on the body, contemporary performance/body art appears to be well suited for "staging" new possibilities of feminist medical subjectivity. As Philip Auslander has argued, "the body in some postmodern performance can be understood, . . . as a body that exposes the ideological discourses producing it, through performance that insists on the body's status as a historical and cultural construct and that asserts the body's materiality."[7] Unlike modernist performance artists, who were interested in performance as a means of transcending the body's material limitations, postmodernist performance artists foreground the impossibility of such transcendence by critiquing the means of representing the body. Since the body in performance is, as Auslander points out, "always both a vehicle for representation and, simply, itself," deconstructing its representation inevitably entails demystifying or deconstructing performance to some degree.[8] In other words, the exposure of how the body is constructed seems to involve the simultaneous exposure of the shortcomings of the performing body.[9] For example, "post-porn" performance artist Annie Sprinkle appropriates the medical gaze when she campily invites spectators to inspect her cervix with the aid of a speculum.[10] Paradoxically, she succeeds in desexualizing the obscene pornographic body only by medicalizing it.

To engage in a visceral critique of the discourses and institutions that "create" the ideal female medical body by one's own volition, as the French artist Orlan does, seems to entail making a spectacle not only of medicine and of beauty culture but also of oneself—in other words, to make visible the tensions between one's social restraints and one's personal choices. The diversity and multiplicity of Orlan's art challenge us to reformulate existing theories of the subject.[11] Hence, the references to numerous philosophers and theorists in this essay reflect the hazards of trying to situate Orlan's work within twentieth-century theoretical frameworks. Because Orlan's art is constantly changing, no single theory of the subject will suffice.[12] Nonetheless, Orlan's medical performances provide us with a timely occasion to consider what possibilities exist for a theory of feminist medical subjectivity.

Surgical Intervention as a Technique of Gender

Orlan has recounted the circumstances surrounding her first surgical performance on numerous occasions; one could say that it has become part of her ever growing mythology. The story goes something as follows: during a 1978 performance symposium in which she was scheduled to speak, Orlan suddenly became ill. Instead of focusing completely on her physical pain and discomfort, Orlan reflected on the possibilities her medical crisis offered. As she was being rushed to a hospital, Orlan asked that a camera crew accompany her to the emergency room and document what was to be emergency surgery for an extrauterine pregnancy. Orlan had the idea that a videotape of the event could be shown to fill the gap in the symposium program created by her unexpected absence. In an attempt to approximate the immediacy and urgency of her surgical performance as much as possible, Orlan requested that an unorthodox but extremely efficient courier service—a medical ambulance—deliver the videotape back to the symposium.[13]

Orlan's impromptu performance was nevertheless a fully self-conscious one. Because she insisted on having only local anesthesia, Orlan could observe the surgery being performed on her body. Her video performance consisted of Orlan's recognition of being seen in the act of observing the female self, since the camera recorded Orlan witnessing her own body cut up and exposed, as well as her viewing the excision of a nonviable fetus from her own reproductive system.

Since 1990 Orlan has had multiple elective cosmetic surgeries as part of a multimedia conceptual project series entitled *The Reincarnation of Saint Orlan,* in which she frames the actual surgeries as performance. Orlan's unusual ability to distance herself through acts of radical self-conscious- ness and self-observation such as the one just described has led many observers, critics, and even health professionals to question not only the credibility of her art but also her sanity. Thus the question, "Is it Art?" for many of her commentators becomes a sort of preliminary meditation for a more central concern: "Is she mad?"[14]

To ask such questions, as Foucault asserts in his controversial conclu- sion to *Madness and Civilization,* is unavoidable in the twentieth century, given our current conceptions of madness as mental illness as well as mode of unknowing.[15] But to foreground the connections between art and madness without considering what the artwork has to say is to foreclose the possibility of arriving at an understanding of the work. For example, Orlan's elective cosmetic surgeries, although frequently described as such, cannot simply be reduced to extreme acts of self-mutilation in the guise of art.[16] Orlan's multimedia surgical theatre is meant to be *transformative* as well as risky; by undergoing a planned series of cosmetic surgeries, Orlan is self-consciously exploring a means of identity transformation that is cur- rently glamorized in our mediatized society without much reflection.

Orlan's surgical performances, which are here understood as processes of transformation, thus align her more closely to feminist body artists such as Sue Maddon and Eleanor Antin, who, as Lisa Tickner has pointed out in her pioneering essay, "The Body Politic: Female Sexuality and Women Artists since 1970," have documented the effects of "change" on the fe- male body. According to Tickner, Maddon envisioned "cleansing" and "removal rituals," such as cleaning one's face and shaving one's legs and armpits, which, in Maddon's words, "wipe away women's identity." Tick- ner also describes how Antin documented a ten-pound weight loss over thirty-six days with 144 photographs of her naked body in a piece called *Carving: An Intentional Sculpture.* Given Tickner's descriptions of what she calls "transformations and processes,"[17] the visible effects documented by feminist body artists appear to be not so much the result of "change" than what Foucault called "techniques of the self," that is, the specific "operations" that constitute an individual's sense of self.[18] Feminist body artists have placed particular attention on those techniques that constitute a sense of oneself as a gendered being, or, as the popular song goes, that make one "feel like a woman." Orlan, like Maddon and Antin before her, undergoes a particular beauty ritual—cosmetic surgery—in order to expose and question those techniques of gender that simultaneously construct and discipline "beauty-conscious" female identity.

The Technoself and the Female Material Body

Orlan's use of technology in performance as a technique of the gendered self tends to be "on the cutting edge" as well as exhaustive. Orlan showcases her reliance on technology since she recognizes that it is not merely a technique of the self, but an integral part of the self in the so-called Age of Information. While medical technology makes possible Orlan's gender transformation, communications technology makes possible the disclosure of such transformation. For instance, her November 1993 surgical performance *Omnipresence* illustrates how we increasingly rely on the "technological gaze."[19] Although the performance was "live" since it unfolded in "real time," its "liveness" was not immediate but mediatized. Its spectators viewed the performance through the lens of various mediums of communications technology outside the operating room.[20] The telecast live event utilized satellite broadcasting, video phones, and faxes, all of which enabled Orlan to communicate with others from fourteen galleries around the world during her surgery. As an instance of communication art, *Omnipresence* underscores how communication has become mediated by technology.

Orlan furthermore relies on technology to record and preserve the performance event (to the extent that performance can be "preserved").[21] Orlan's own video of the surgical event reveals the tremendous efforts of the media technicians to record the surgical event just as it documents the medical personnel expediting and/or performing the surgery. But despite her interest in the production and reproduction of images for the medical construction of the technobody, Orlan does not completely lose sight of the enduring materiality of the biological body, precisely because it is the fate of her body that is in question. Hence Orlan supplements her technological documentation of the surgical event by making art objects out of the performance's material by-products; her postoperative gallery installations include, in addition to videos, photographs, and computer images, the exhibition of the blood-splattered surgical gowns and the display of relics containing preserved body tissue and fat.

Orlan's dual emphasis on technology and the body's materiality has certainly demystified some of the most prevalent if not "sacred" cultural myths surrounding cosmetic surgery, which, by its very name "cosmetic" or "aesthetic" surgery, implies beautification as its ultimate purpose and goal. Orlan goes against the grain of conventional cultural practice with her refusal to enhance her appearance according to the current supermodel ideals of beauty. Instead, Orlan has gradually deformed herself in the process of carving onto her body an ideal composite autoportrait by surgically appropriating various renowned facial features from the history of Western art. Auslander interprets her self-conscious "uglification" as follows: "that Orlan's unconventional physiognomy is the result not of defiance of her culture's standards, but rather, of an effort to conform to canonical models of beauty is an irony not to be overlooked."[22] Indeed, Orlan's appearance attests to the prevalent futility of both the fragmentation and the fetishization of body parts in medicine and in art.

Another irony to be considered with respect to Orlan's appearance is that her cosmetic surgeries have not succeeded in reconstructing exact replications. As Anne Balsamo points out in her critique of imaging techniques used to project postoperative appearances, it is impossible to predict how the body's soft tissue will heal in response to surgery. Balsamo emphasizes this last point: "How those incised tissues heal is a very idiosyncratic matter—a matter of the irreducible distinction of the material body."[23] Even though Orlan has summoned the skills of top plastic surgeons, the surgeries have left Orlan with a lopsided smile and bumpy temples, which, as Auslander has put it, look "distinctly unnatural in appearance."[24] But that is exactly Orlan's point: ideal representations of women have little if anything to do with nature, yet they have been naturalized to the point of becoming normative, if not regulative, for our culture.[25]

Women are being increasingly pressured to look more attractive or younger; while men feel this pressure too, women who do not comply are increasingly made to feel inadequate *as women* since they have failed to live up to gender ideals that masquerade as gender norms.[26] (In contrast, men are still generally regarded as more "manly" if they do not undergo plastic surgery, although this view too is beginning to change.) In other words, while feminine "natural beauty" has become increasingly pathologized, elective cosmetic surgery, as Kathryn Pauly Morgan has observed, has been naturalized.[27] Orlan has dismantled the effects of such naturalization through techniques of Brechtian estrangement. In her U.S. gallery installations in New York, San Francisco, and Atlanta following her November 1993 surgeries, she juxtaposed a series of forty-one photographs with a matching series of computer images. The photographs documented the daily change in her appearance from before her surgery to her postoperative transformation, while the composite computer visualizations displayed a seemingly infinite amount of virtual possibilities for her face. The wild dream of synthesizing art and body that the computer images represent is effectively shattered by their juxtaposition with the documentary photographs foregrounding the body's grotesque responses to surgery.

For all her efforts of exposing plastic surgery as a lengthy, laborious, imprecise, and imperfect process rather than a quick and easy end result, Orlan has been pronounced a hysteric, a narcissist, a fetishist, a scalpel slave (or polysurgical addict), and even a sufferer of Body Dysmorphic Disorder, a recent psychiatric nomination to describe extreme obsessions with body parts and faciality.[28] Art critics who diagnose artists raise questions concerning the limits of cultural authority, questions that are relevant for discussions on contemporary art criticism. However, I will leave such questions aside to examine more in-depth how Orlan negotiates between her public roles as artist, educator, and feminist and her more private ones as participant in psychoanalysis, member of contemporary Western culture, and woman through a cursory survey of a career that spans over twenty years. Since Orlan's art, like much twentieth-century performance art, intentionally blurs the distinction between life and art, the categories "public" and "private" tend to get conflated in discussions of her work. But even as Orlan insists that her art is her life, all that we know of Orlan's life is what she tells us, or in other words, what she has already selected as relevant to our understanding and—dare I say it—our critical "appreciation" of her art.

By "critical appreciation" I do not mean that I am condoning her body practices. Rather, a critical appreciation here entails, I believe, a recognition of Orlan's feminist deconstructive strategies aimed at salient critique of Western representations of the female body. Orlan's medical performances alone, as some have already noted, radically exemplify the critical reaction to the age of technologized beauty. The works of Orlan, scholar Kathryn Pauly Morgan, and cyberpunk novelist William Gibson represent a moment circa 1990 when intentional ugliness was conceived as an effective means of social resistance. The difference between Orlan and both Morgan and Gibson is distinct, however: while Morgan and Gibson were extreme in their respective visions of a future when individuals would intentionally deform themselves, Orlan took advantage of her present.[29]

Considered as a whole, Orlan's career can be interpreted as a critical exploration of feminine images, during which she has reclaimed and recontextualized religious Christian iconography of powerful or phallic women while experimenting with or disregarding altogether certain enduring secular images of women, particularly that of the female invalid. Orlan's construction of a feminist medical self who refuses to acknowledge publicly her pain is a form of gender theatricalism or metaperformance, since it simultaneously cites and rejects traditional and contemporary performances of the mad/sick woman.[30] On the one hand, Orlan enacts polysurgical addiction by having multiple surgeries; on the other hand, Orlan never complains of being or feeling ill. Nor does she present herself as being emotionally out of control, as Karen Finley frequently does.[31] Orlan's curious predicament of having been "diagnosed" by the psychoanalytical theory she has studied and literally incorporated illustrates the dilemma faced by the late twentieth-century self-conscious and self-critical feminist artist who seeks entry into the public sphere: her theatricalism with regard to her gender is subject to misinterpretation, as it can be regarded (and thereby easily dismissed) as pathological by medical discourse.

Early Influences

Prior to Barbara Rose's February 1993 *Art in America* article entitled "Is It Art? On Orlan's Transgressive Acts," Orlan was virtually unknown in the United States, and she is still best known for the work produced since 1990. Her previous work remains obscure, since the trajectory of her career has not been either systematically or sufficiently documented, not even by Orlan herself. With this in mind, we can better understand Orlan's plethora of surgical artifacts and paraphernalia: she is clearly attempting to overcompensate for the dearth of documentation of her previous work.

"Orlan" is the name the artist gave herself as a twofold gesture of self-creation and self-autonomy. If we are to take Orlan's own statements about her life and work seriously, we need first to consider her art in relation to her autobiography. Orlan's art takes root in her reaction against the prevailing images of femininity with which she grew up. Born in St. Etienne, France, on 30 May 1947, Orlan's strained relationships with her mother and older sister, both chronically ill, drew her to a strong identification with her father, who worked as an electrician for a local theatre. Orlan claims that she was a timid child with a hard shell, yet she nevertheless rebelled against the conventional models of femininity both her mother and sister offered her. As Orlan told Gladys Fabre, she hates the kind of femininity that her mother, and mothers in general, impose on their daughters.[32]

In an interview with Maurice Mallet for *VST,* a French psychoanalytical journal that dedicated an entire issue to Orlan's "case," Orlan described her mother, her sister, and their relationships in terms of illness, both mental and physical:

> The search for dust, that's all. Chronic mental crises, screams and chronic hysteria. She was a housewife, married, two children, normal. . . . We were always very distant. I used to assert myself when she used to telephone asking how it was going, only as she was hanging up. . . . It was necessary for me to tell her, "I'm sick," for her to become interested in me. My sister always followed her example. She was always sick and is still *always* sick. When I call her, the only thing she talks about is her illness.[33]

Orlan's description of her mother is reminiscent of de Beauvoir's attack on idle housewives in *The Second Sex*; indeed, it can be viewed as the succeeding generation's rebellion against its predecessors. Orlan's mother belonged to a generation of women who believed they were fighting a war against invasive germs in the home. The "search for dust" was a battle to control the rest of the family's health even if one's own health remained uncertain.[34] As Orlan herself admits, her mother was "normal." For Orlan, that was her mother's problem. Orlan's turn away from her domestic mother and sister thus can be interpreted in Lacanian parlance as a rejection of the maternal signifier. Dissatisfied and disappointed with its limited and limiting possibilities of signification, Orlan turned to the history of art for its canon of ideal images of femininity.[35]

After attending l'École Nationale de Beaux Arts in Dijon, Orlan began to perform in the streets of St. Etienne during the late sixties. Through her gallerist Ben Vautier she met numerous Fluxus artists.[36] Although she is not included in recent histories of the movement, Orlan was a participant in at least one official Fluxus concert in 1976 and numerous Fluxus-inspired performance events.[37] Indeed, Orlan's claim in her 1994 "Intervention" that she was opposed to the prevailing attitudes in much of the art produced in the eighties is effectively a way of saying that she has remained loyal to Fluxus's underlying principle of anti-commercialism.[38]

From Self-Revelation to Self-Transformation

In 1971 Orlan baptized herself Saint Orlan. While several of her commentators have discussed the possible significance of the masculine name "Orlan," with its allusions to Virginia Woolf's transsexual character Orlando, other connections between "Saint Orlan" and literary characters/personas have yet to be explored.[39] With this name Orlan invites comparison with another twentieth-century French artist who took up a saintly identity: Jean Genet. In *Saint Genet*, Jean-Paul Sartre considers Genet as a radically self-conscious artist who actively creates his identity by affirming the negative accusations against him during his youth; thus, Genet's crucial moment of identity occurred, according to Sartre, when he said, "Yes, I will be a thief!" Sartre traces the possible links between Genet's multiple identities as thief, social outcast, homosexual, and artist with those of a saint and a martyr. In Sartre's view, what the saint and the thief have in common is that they both only consume.[40] The saint produces nothing other than pure spectacle through acts of humiliation and martyrdom. From Sartre's Western Marxist perspective, we can link Orlan's decision in 1971 to baptize herself Saint Orlan to the spirit of Fluxus, as an antibourgeois gesture of extravagant consumerism for its own sake.

Unlike Sartre, however, Foucault discerns an important utility in saintly religious displays. In a late essay, "Technologies of the Self," Foucault considers the early Christian renunciation of the self, which involved theatrical displays of self-destruction, that is, martyrdom, as a principal means of disclosing the self. Foucault's discussion of the various ways the self was "known" in antiquity figures prominently in his genealogy of the modern self in which the individual sense of self is constituted through acts of verbalization (i.e., through confession).[41]

Foucault's insight leads us back to Orlan. By assuming a religious identity, Orlan seems to have returned to the premodern Christian theatrical technique of self-discovery. Saint Orlan was interested in acts of self-revelation throughout the seventies; thus she engaged in performances that questioned the relations between prevalent female social roles (woman as saint, whore, madonna) and the institutions that instrumentally determined them (the history of art, the museum, the art gallery, the market, the tradition of religious iconography, and the Catholic Church).

More specifically, Orlan questioned her own self-determined role as artist through performances that problematized traditional means of producing representations of women in art. Evidently, the female body for Orlan is unintelligible without the mediation and materiality of representation. She underscored this idea by engaging in performances that involved her wearing dresses of silk-screened photographs depicting actual-size images of her own nude body. During one performance at the Louvre, as part of a collective performance organized by Jean Dupuy on 16 October 1978, Orlan revealed her dress underneath her black coat and skirt only to rip open the geometric pubic triangle, displaying her pubic hair underneath. Once revealed, Orlan pulled out her preshorn and reglued pubic hair to uncover her shaved genital area. With an already dipped paintbrush, Orlan covered up her nakedness, first, by painting her pubis black, and then by holding a white artist palette before her "painting" as if it were a fig leaf.[42]

Highlighting her self-conscious appropriation of the romantic and modernist conceptions of the virile male artist who uses his paintbrush as a metaphorical penis, Orlan next inserted her paintbrush through the hole of the palette before slowly turning her back to the audience, pausing momentarily to display the profile of her "erect" paintbrush.[43] With this extremely condensed performance, Orlan seems to be acting out what Lynda Nead interprets as the structure of penis-as-paintbrush metaphor: "the canvas is the empty but receptive surface; empty of meaning—naked—until it is inscribed and given meaning by the artist."[44]

Alternatively, Orlan restaged the scene of castration by displaying her lack of a penis only to follow the display with a compensatory, showy simulation of the phallus.[45] For a brief instant Orlan unveiled what could be called "an impossible figure of totality," in which she presented herself as both being and having the phallus.[46] As Silvia Eiblmayr notes, "fantasies of totality . . . always refer to the problem of sexual difference," which is why, according to Eiblmayr, they always seem to carry "the seed of their own destruction" in some material sign of rupture such as the surgical suture. For example, Eiblmayr views Orlan's bulges on her temples as her self-recognition that the explicit fantasy of her *Omnipresence* is indeed impossible.[47] In the earlier Louvre performance, however, rupture is not limited to the material. The fleeting transience of the figurative image also marks performance as impossible fantasy, which is why Orlan's performative presentation of a fantasy of artistic fulfillment could last but a moment and only through self-recognition of her own complicity in the act of penetration.

While the piece is detailed by Orlan herself in the appendix of Dupuy's anthology *Collective Consciousness*, its implications for feminist performance theory have yet to be considered, which is why it is included here. Orlan's public display of her pubis situates her with other feminist artists who were engaged in "vaginal iconology" during the seventies.[48] But one does not get the sense from the description of this performance that Orlan was celebrating her vagina as the source of feminine essence. Rather, Orlan's self-recognition of her own complicity in the patriarchal, phallic order that both produces and reproduces oppressive images of women will become a central motif in her subsequent work.

In another performance piece executed during the 1970s, *Baiser de l'artiste*, Orlan again acknowledges her own complicity, this time in the market demands that pressure the artist to sell "herself" as a commodity in order to gain recognition as an artist. During a Parisian art festival in 1977, Orlan situated herself as a marginal presence outside the festival by the entrance gates to the Palais Royale. Orlan invited spectators to her "pedestal of myths, those of the madonna, the whore, the artist." Her installation consisted of a platform bearing, among other things, a bouquet of white lilies and two life-size photographs of herself. One photo was of Saint Orlan in her baroque costume with breasts exposed, the other was of Orlan's torso that was converted to a kissing slot machine. Orlan urged the spectator to insert five francs in the slot between the breasts of the vending machine and to watch the coin roll down to the transparent crotch/cavity. As soon as the coin reached its final destination, a metal grid "box" of sorts hanging below the torso, Orlan would jump up from her pedestal and offer the spectator a kiss.[49]

After this performance, which by all accounts caused a media scandal,[50] Orlan abandoned the image of the prostitute. According to Fabre, the public reaction indicated that Orlan's performance was interpreted too literally.[51] In other words, Orlan discarded the image of the prostitute because once in the public sphere she no longer had control of her representation, which seemed to overshadow completely the other figures represented, those of the madonna and the saint. Thus the tension created by her ambiguously doubled "dialectical image" of the virgin prostitute/ saintly artist was reduced to a univocal image of woman as commodification of sex.[52]

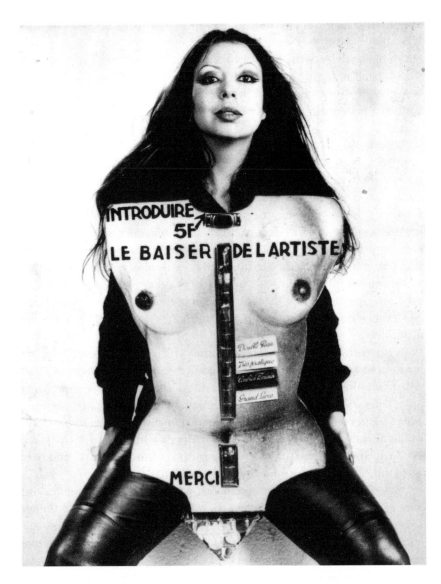

Fig. 18.1. Orlan, *The Kiss of the Artist*. Grand Palais, Paris, 1977; by permission of Orlan and SIPA Press.

While Orlan rid herself of the prostitute figure through trial and error, the eventual decision to remove it from her repertoire of feminine archetypes points to her realization that the image lacked recuperative power overall. The figure of the prostitute, while often beguiling, is one that typically lacks any real sense of control or agency. As Linda Singer points out in her analysis of the male client's attraction to the prostitute, "Power is associated not with not having to sell oneself, but rather in being so vested with excess that one can use it to elicit what one wants from another on demand. When one pays the piper, one can also call the tune."[53]

Little wonder, then, that Orlan would prefer to represent the artist's complicity as an act of necessary martyrdom than as an act of prostitution. To be a martyr is to be a living saint: it involves self-sacrifice and loss of social status; one undergoes humiliation, pain, even death for the sake of a higher purpose. Martyrdom as a self-conscious loss of self is nevertheless the result of free choice—even if that act of choice stems from a sense of obligation or duty. Artists can be viewed as secular martyrs to the extent that they must defer to their institutional sponsors as well as to the critics who compare their works with the works of other artists for the sake of their art. In other words, artists must comply with constant surveillance and evaluation before they can be "officially" recognized as artists by institutions.

In her performance series *Measurements,* Orlan turned the table on art institutions by using her body as a measurement device to measure *them.* Orlan measured churches, convents, and museums; she also "measured up" the legacy of other artists with her own by measuring streets bearing artist's names (e.g., rue Victor Hugo). Draped in a white "trousseau," Orlan would lie down, mark off the length of her body with a piece of chalk, get up, lie down at the mark, and then repeat the entire action over and over again until the act of measurement was completed.

As performances, these measurements, which were slow in tempo and long in duration, have been compared to Christ's Passion.[54] Orlan underscored and transformed the sense of Christ-like self-sacrifice by calling her outfit a trousseau, thus linking her artistic sacrifice more closely with bridal sexual sacrifice.[55] After completing her measurement, Orlan would remove her sullied trousseau and clean it publicly in a tub of water. Her purification ritual is thus an attempt to introject ritual and religiosity back into contemporary, secularized art. But in order to be purified, one must be purified of something. Accordingly, Orlan would complete her measurements by pouring the dirty bathwater into bottles so that it could be later displayed as part of gallery installations. Preserving the liquid, Bernard Ceysson has insisted, was not an attempt to glorify the material.[56] Unwilling to give up or disregard that which is usually cast off and forgotten, Orlan presented a public abject self that does not respect society's exclusionary boundaries.

The Public Abject Self

In *The Powers of Horror,* Julia Kristeva emphasizes the importance of separation as exclusion: Kristeva thus reworks anthropologist Mary Douglas's concepts of the body's surface as a boundary that guarantees one's sense of a "pure" self by excluding all that is indeterminate or, to invoke Douglas's terminology, polluted. Kristeva takes Douglas's analysis one step further by connecting Douglas's notion of pollution with Bataille's notion of abjection.[57] As Nead points out, "Kristeva describes abjection in terms of ambiguity and uncertainty."[58] That which is uncertain is neither subject nor object; it is that which can be expelled from the body: fluids, excretions, tears, vomit, menstrual blood, and so forth. The abject's significance is that it is defined in relation to the self; excluded to the margins, it nevertheless remains a constant threat as it is what makes the constitution of the subject possible. The self then has but a precarious existence, since it must be constantly, inexhaustibly posited as a defense against the threat of disorder and bodily dissolution. Both Douglas and Kristeva stress the significance of expulsion for social formation; a society constitutes itself in terms of what it excludes as unclean (taboo) or uncontrollable (which, for Kristeva, accounts for women's secondary status).[59]

Drawing from Freud, Lacan, Douglas, and Kristeva, Judith Butler politicizes abjection as a strategy of social power. That which is degraded to abjection in society is hence cast out. Individuals who are designated as abject are thus both marginalized from society and stripped of subjectivity:

> The "abject" designates here precisely those "unlivable" and "uninhabitable" zones of social life which are nevertheless densely populated by those who do not enjoy the status of subject, but whose living under the sign of the "unlivable" is required to circumscribe the domain of the subject. . . . In this sense then the subject is constituted through the force of exclusion and abjection, one which produces a constitutive outside to the subject, an abjected outside which is, after all "inside" as its own founding repudiation.[60]

From Butler's perspective, then, *Measurements* could be interpreted as the struggle to elevate the political status of the abject female artist. Orlan traverses the boundaries between society and the excluded through acts of complicity in order to be recognized, even if that recognition results only in the recognition of the other. By foregrounding her own "saintly" abjection, Orlan explores its subversive possibilities. Like Jean Genet before her, Orlan seems to exalt in her own cast-outness through acts that affirm it.

The Ecstasy of Saint Orlan

In 1980 Orlan carved a resin prototype sculpture of Saint Orlan, a composite figure of the artist, Bernini's Saint Teresa, and baroque images of the nursing Madonna. With one arm pointing upwards and the other downwards, the sculpture depicts a figurative contradiction, a body pulled in two directions at once, as if in convulsion. The sculpture would become the centerpiece of an excessively *fausse* if not kitschy baroque chapel, a 1980 installation called *Made in France*.[61] Numerous similar installations would follow, as would a heterogeneous multitude of photographs, videos, and films featuring the artist as Saint Orlan. She would mimic the gestures inscribed onto the sculpture in *tableaux vivants* that alluded to baroque religious paintings, with one significant difference. Instead of depicting the grandeur of heaven and earth, Orlan's *tableaux vivants* would foreground detritus. Bubble wrap, cinder blocks, garbage bags, and broken fountains: Orlan replaced the natural world with excremental culture. Orlan theatricalized her 1984 photo series, *Saint Orlan and the Elders,* by situating it within Artaud's Theatre of Cruelty; Orlan even underscored the Artaudian reference by casting patients from the Charles-Foix Hôpital of Ivry, an asylum where Artaud spent some time, as the "elders" who "adore" "the Saint."[62]

Orlan would spend much of the 1980s embodying ideal images through performance in order to accentuate the body's own figurality. For Orlan the body is a figure *par excellence*; thus Orlan chose to utilize her body as its own medium for self-representation. In a sense, as Bernard Ceysson suggests, Orlan has become her own Pygmalion-machine, since she gives life to her own self-representations by means of performance.[63] Orlan would supplement images of Saint Orlan dressed as Saint Teresa with those of white and black leatherette-clad virgins. The black virgin became especially significant as a pragmatic solution to Orlan's earlier problem

Fig. 18.2. Orlan, *Baroque Madonna no. 10.* Photo by Anne Garde; by permission of Orlan and SIPA Press.

with the prostitute figure; Orlan could rely on the black virgin, a figure of mourning, knowing, and independence, as a contrast and foil to the "too pure" images of the white virgin, the madonna, and saint. With one breast always exposed, Orlan emphasizes the amazonian, phallic quality of these images. Moreover, Orlan underscores baroque iconography's ecstatic sensibility in her presentation of images of self-totality and self-satisfaction; she, like Bernini, highlights the ambiguity between sexual *jouissance* and religious ecstasy for a theatrical effect.

Art critic Craig Owens has posited in his discussion of Cindy Sherman's photography that postmodernist art is categorized by a sense of what he calls "impossible complicity": it is only through complicity that postmodern art can execute its deconstructive strategies.[64] As we have already seen, Orlan staged gestures of impossible complicity at the start of her career, and the recognition of complicity continues to be a central concern in her work. On the one hand, the repetition over time and the redundancy of the images have congealed the artist's identity as a female saint; on the other hand, Orlan's strategies of repetition and redundancy have illustrated acute anxieties concerning identity and the compulsion to posit one's identity inexhaustibly because it is so precarious. For Orlan, identity is theatrical, larger than life, but always fleeting and unstable. Orlan's fictive saint furthermore points to the fictive nature of identity: identity has to be actively pursued, constructed, created; one has to create one's identity through repetitive self-representations before identity can become self-identity. The excessive, baroque quality of her acts of self-creation point to the fact that we are not always in control of our own representations of identity. "Representation," Peggy Phelan tells us, paraphrasing Jacques Derrida, follows two laws: "it always conveys more than it intends, and it is never totalizing. The 'excess' meaning conveyed by representation creates a supplement that makes multiple and resistant readings possible. Despite this excess, representation produces ruptures and gaps; it fails to reproduce the real exactly."[65]

Fatty Displays

Orlan's first four cosmetic surgeries all took place in 1990.[66] Her early surgical performances involved primarily liposuction performed by the inventor of the procedure. Orlan had her ankles, knees, hips, backside, waist, and neck reduced and reshaped. Although it does not appear that she has had her body remolded according to the history of art, the liposuction has served her well in the production of relics, which she both exhibits and sells. By confronting us repeatedly with her own fat, Orlan presents us with an abject substance that, for our weight-conscious culture, evokes not only repulsion but real terror, especially for women.[67] Using her own fat as an artistic medium, Orlan goes a step beyond Joseph Beuys, who often employed lard and margarine as sculptural mediums. An important difference exists between Orlan's use of fat and Beuys's, however. Although Beuys was interested in experimenting with abject materials in his art, fat for him was not abject at all but life-giving, since it literally saved his life. Beuys's biography is not unknown: when he was found almost frozen to death by Tatars during World War II after he miraculously survived his plane being shot down, he was wrapped in fat and felt.[68] Subsequently, fat and felt would become important materials to signify life-giving warmth in a cold, destroyed world in Beuys's art. For Orlan, however, her own body fat serves as a synecdoche of the artist becoming literally a work of art.

The Baudelairean Impulse

Orlan repeatedly claims that she has gone further than any other artist by becoming a work of art. What could that possibly mean other than that Orlan considers herself, as Barbara Rose has suggested, to be both art subject and object?[69] The artist's dream to become both the subject and object of art is hardly new, as it was already expressed by Charles Baudelaire in both his art criticism and his poetry. The history of performance art is full of examples of artists attempting to blur the subject/object distinction because in a real sense performance is categorized by the blurring of the distinction itself. The difference between Orlan and her predecessors, then, is to be found in the direct manner she returns to the Baudelairean dream.

In his study of the poet, entitled simply *Baudelaire*, Sartre argues that Baudelaire's "drama" was the theatre of reflection: "The problem was to recover *himself* and—as sight is a form of appropriation—to see *himself.* . . . Because he did not succeed in his attempt to see *himself,* Baudelaire made up his mind that . . . he would explore himself as the knife explores the wound. . . . Thus the tortures which he inflicted on himself simulated possession."[70]

Sartre ties the impulse to be both subject and object to a heightened sense of consciousness. Baudelaire's poetry expresses this impulse through the metaphorical desire to be both the knife and the wound, which Sartre connects with the impossible desire to possess oneself completely.

As Mary Kelly has argued, this desire for self-possession became an important concern for performance artists working in the sixties and seventies.[71] If Orlan has succeeded in going further than any other artist in making Baudelaire's dream a concrete reality, she has done so by literalizing his metaphors. Allowing the surgeon's scalpel to stand in for her reflective consciousness so that the wounds it creates on her body can serve as sites of self-reflection, Orlan nevertheless repossesses her own body by deciding exactly how it will be reconstructed. Of course, she cannot do so without the discourses of the institutions that construct the female body: medicine, science, and art. Thus Orlan's *Reincarnation* project necessitates the acknowledgment of her complicity in, and dependence on, these institutions in order to stage the resistance she enacts. Orlan's technique of the feminist medical self foregrounds the following two processes: first and foremost, problematizing the subject/object relation by using her own body to produce art, and second, documenting her struggle to become an active participant in the medical process.

Staging the Medical Subject

Most individuals subject themselves quite readily, even when they undergo elective cosmetic surgery, to the rules and regulations of medical authority. Most patients when they have surgery do not have control of the *mise-en-scène* even if they have decided on the surgery's location. But then again, most patients are not concerned with the aesthetics of their surroundings beyond those that indicate the latest technology and safety standards. Think about it: how many of us would even think of asking a surgeon to paint the walls of the operating room a different color, as Orlan has? In all likelihood we wouldn't dare to inquire because we have internalized the norms of medicine. Although surgical patients are indeed medical subjects, they usually become literal objects in the operating room as they themselves do not consciously witness the bloody acts of surgery. General anesthesia suppresses their consciousness to a coma-like state, to prevent pain surely, but also to prevent the psychological trauma of seeing one's own body operated on. Thus the patient enters a liminal state, in which one is hardly alive but not dead either. Under general anesthesia one becomes the embodiment of passivity, completely dependent on doctors for maintaining and continuing one's own precarious existence.

Orlan resists complete passivity during her operations, first, by transforming the medical milieu into a bloody, slimy, ghastly, yet also celebratory carnivalesque scene reminiscent of Gargantua's birth in the writings of Rabelais. Although Orlan does submit to the risks of surgery and willingly gives her informed consent rather than compliance, her plastic surgeons must reciprocally consent to her unusual demands, not only of body transformation, but of surgical protocol. Surgeon, attendants, and observers—save for the notable exception of television anchorwoman Connie Chung in the New York performance—wear futuristic designer surgical gowns, as does Orlan; in doing so, they both defamiliarize and desanctify conventional views concerning cosmetic surgery. Orlan's very public parody of plastic surgery as covert event, as a secret yet highly valued cultural performance, is an ironic slap in the face for us all, since our culture currently glamorizes plastic surgery as well as those celebrities who undergo it to the extent that for many individuals it has become a necessity not only for self-esteem but also for employment and "personal happiness"—whatever that means. Paradoxically, admitting to having had such surgery is pretty much taboo. Consequently, the patient's postsurgery disavowal or silence has become an integral part of our accepted cultural performance practice of cosmetic surgery.

What is truly transgressive about Orlan's surgical performances is the extent to which Orlan disrupts the surgical ritual. She declines to enter any liminal state. Instead, Orlan remains fully conscious throughout her surgery, reading French philosophical and psychoanalytical texts and holding estranging props such as a devil's pitchfork whenever possible, staring at the camera when she cannot.[72] I wish to emphasize this last point. Orlan may allow her body to be cut, stretched, and resculpted, but her persistent gaze signals not only her resistance to becoming the completely docile body that medicine requires but also her insistence on being recognized at all times as *more than just a body*. Her art demands of her audience that we witness her self-awareness not only of her surgery but of *us* looking at her. In other words, Orlan not only returns the viewer's gaze, but expects—if not demands—that her recognition of us be in turn recognized by each individual.

Orlan depends on her audience to complete her art,[73] depends on us to recognize the individual patient named Orlan undergoing the surgery rather than merely to be mesmerized or revolted by the exposure of the living tissues that make up her body. In effect, she challenges us by highlighting the body's grotesque abjection in surgery and in recovery while preventing us from reducing the complexity of her performance to the visceral spectacle. To put it bluntly, Orlan's art does a lot more that just gross all of us out: she provokes us to become more self-reflexive in our roles as spectators. Orlan is quite explicit in this provocation when, immediately preceding her surgeries, she reads as a performative speech act a passage from Michel Serres in which Serres divides the theatrical audience into two possible spectator positions: general audience members (who "will have left the auditorium, tired out by ineffectual theatrical effects, irritated by the turn from comedy to tragedy, having come to laugh and deceived at having been made to think") and "knowledgeable specialists" or scholars.

As Butler has pointed out, performative speech acts are forms of authoritative speech.[74] By citing Serres, Orlan appropriates his intellectual authority in the act of differentiating audience members. While Orlan's quotation of Serres is condescending to those spectators who are unwilling to watch her performances in their entirety, it also mocks those scholarly types who try to catch up with Orlan and/or to become experts on her art by virtue of their learning or authority. By reading/performing the text as a metaperformance, Orlan is acknowledging her anticipation of the audience's difficulty, inability, and even failure to understand/appreciate her performances.

The Politics of Pain as Gender Theatricalism

Whenever Orlan appears in public to discuss her work, she is inevitably bombarded by questions concerning pain and suffering. If pain and suffering remain tricky issues for artists who foreground performance, they become doubly so for one whose performances necessitate medical intervention. Although female and male "masochistic" performers alike[75] have undergone "hardship" or "ordeal" art in order to develop an aesthetics of pain that, in Phelan's judgment, rehearses the experience of death,[76] such performances, when performed by women, have succeeded primarily in reinforcing traditional, stereotypical associations between women, pain, pleasure, masochism, and illness.[77] Not surprisingly, performers who display pain and suffering are frequently perceived as masochists who enjoy their pain and suffering because they want to remain weak and incapacitated.

Such clichés are absolutely unacceptable for Orlan. She refuses to acknowledge either her postoperative pain or her suffering; she admits only to the psychic pain caused by her initial decision to carry out her conceptual project. Apparently, thoughts for Orlan are painful in ways that bodily experiences are not. To admit to physical pain then would be to confess vulnerability, which in turn could be used against the artist to dismiss her work as the work of a madwoman. While the typical question asked by spectators, "Do you feel pain?" is more benign than the critic's question, "Is she mad?" both types of questions aim at discrediting Orlan's ability to think for herself, to be rational, and to make decisions about her own body. In effect, such interrogations disallow Orlan the full extent of her subjectivity. Because she perceives the insidious intent behind such seemingly innocent questions, Orlan resists further diagnosis with disconcerting refusals, silences, and displays of self-control.

Orlan's refusal to acknowledge pain is a feminist strategy: she remains silent about her emotional and physical discomfort because she absolutely refuses to be associated with the figure of the sick/mentally ill woman. Instead, she presents a feminist medical self who actively consents to compliance, who makes demands on her doctors, and who both participates in and resists the medical process as much as any medical patient can. In so doing, Orlan resists female passivity and objectification by empowering the traditional image of the female patient. In the process of reconstructing her literal image, Orlan reconfigures a mythical one as well.

Silence is also a technique of self for Orlan that is perhaps borrowed from Foucault, since he infamously avoided "the confessional moment."[78] She does not delve much into her subjective experiences: no great secrets are confessed, not much talk about her emotions, absolutely no disclosure whatsoever about her erotic life. As we have seen with her earlier performance series, *Measurements,* Orlan chooses to reveal her self performatively rather than through confession. Thus she does not talk about her experiences as much as she demonstrates through performance how they constitute her sense of self.

Orlan resists the diagnosis of mental illness most effectively by portraying herself as superrational, calm, quiet, even stoic. The effort to control her emotions so absolutely is a burden for her, but she does not complain in public. One can only see the weariness in her eyes afterwards. In this sense Orlan's public persona of the nineties is the converse to the ecstatic Orlan of the eighties. If Orlan seems pathologically detached from her experiences, it could be as she claims: she insists that she is just as curious as we are concerning how her physical change will affect her—not only on the surface of her body but in terms of her sense of self-identity.[79]

Orlan as a Feminist Medical Subject before the Law

Orlan has been inconsistent about how many surgeries she will have, claiming that she will have as many as she deems will be necessary. What she has been consistent about is how *The Reincarnation of Saint Orlan* will be completed: Orlan will ask an advertising agency to change her name and then will go to court to have her name changed legally. For an artist who seeks as much autonomy over her work as Orlan has, her plan to end her project by asking another entity to rename her appears self-contradictory, yet the act is not as passive as it may initially appear. By allowing an advertising agency to rename her, Orlan is proposing to resolve the subject/object problem rather parodically by foregrounding herself not as her own possession/property but rather as a market product to be promoted for consumption—an ironic commentary on the "selling out" of artists.[80]

Before we begin to dream up ad campaign slogans for Orlan, we should keep in mind that our parents usually bestow us with our legal names shortly after birth. The birth certificate that records the child's name and parentage is the legal entry into society, not the biological/medical event. The example of birth illustrates how the medical subject is inconceivable without its inscriptions/encodings by the law. If, as Auslander has aptly put it, Orlan's medical performances end where her legal ones begin, it is because Orlan recognizes that the status of the medical subject in society can be permanently altered only by legal means.[81] Thus acts of medical compliance and/or complicity are to be understood as obeying the law. It does not follow that acts of resistance are instances of breaking the law, for as Hobbes has taught us, where there is no specific law, there can be no specified crime ("Where no civil law is, there is no crime").[82] The elusive nature of Orlan's resistance is precisely the locus of its power.

NOTES

1. Susan Hekman, "Reconstituting the Subject: Feminism, Modernism, and Postmodernism," *Hypathia* 6, no. 2 (summer 1991): 45. See also R. J. Goldstein,

preface to *Remarks on Marx: Conversations with Duccio Trombadori,* by Michel Foucault, trans. R. James Goldstein and James Cascaito (New York: Semiotext(e), 1991), 9.

2. Hekman, "Reconstituting the Subject," 46.

3. Ibid.; Sonia Kruks, "Gender and Subjectivity: Simone de Beauvoir and Contemporary Feminism," *Signs* 18, no. 1 (fall 1992): 96.

4. Foucault, *Remarks on Marx,* 58.

5. As Linda Singer notes, "one is not free to give one's own consent," since "one will not be admitted to the hospital without it." Linda Singer, "Hospitalization and AIDS," in *Erotic Welfare: Sexual Theory in the Age of the Epidemic,* ed. Judith Butler and Maureen MacGrogan (New York: Routledge, 1993), 103. See also Ruth R. Faden and Tom L. Beauchamp in collaboration with Nancy M. P. King, *A History and Theory of Informed Consent* (New York: Oxford University Press, 1986).

6. Kathryn Pauly Morgan has deemed the medicalization of women "the double-pathologizing of women's bodies." "Women and the Knife: Cosmetic Surgery and the Colonization of Women's Bodies," *Hypathia* 6, no. 3 (fall 1991): 39. Also see Emily Martin, *The Woman in the Body: A Cultural Analysis of Reproduction* (Boston: Beacon Press, 1992); Carol Tavris, *The Mismeasure of Woman* (New York: Simon and Schuster, 1992).

7. Philip Auslander, "Vito Acconci and the Politics of the Body in Postmodern Performance," in *After the Future: Postmodern Times and Places,* ed. Gary Shapiro (Albany: SUNY Press, 1990), 188.

8. Ibid., 186.

9. I am indebted to Philip Auslander for discussing with me the implications of his argument.

10. On Sprinkle's utilization of speculums, see Elinor Fuchs, "Staging the Obscene Body," *Drama Review,* 33, no. 1 (spring 1989): 33–58; Annie Sprinkle, interview with Andrea Juno, in *Angry Women,* ed. Andrea Juno and V. Vale (San Francisco: Re/Search Publications, 1991), 34.

11. See Kaja Silverman, *The Subject of Semiotics* (New York: Oxford University Press, 1983).

12. Arguably, Orlan's art raises the question of whether ascribing to any single theory of subjectivity is feasible or even desirable. Judith Butler argues that "the term 'construction' belongs at the grammatical site of the subject, for construction is neither a subject nor its act, but a process of reiteration by which both 'subjects' and 'acts' come to appear at all. There is no power that acts, but only a reiterated acting that is power in its persistence and instability." *Bodies That Matter: On the Discursive Limits of "Sex"* (New York: Routledge, 1993), 9.

13. Various versions of the tale exist. Orlan offers a summary in "Intervention," published in this volume. For other versions, see Jim McClellan, "The

Extensions of Woman," *Life,* 17 April 1994, 40; Michelle Hirshhorn, "Orlan: Artist in the Post-Humanist Age of Mechanical Reproduction" (M.A. thesis, University of Manchester, 1994), 12.

14. Barbara Rose has foregrounded this question in "Is It Art? Orlan and the Transgressive Act," *Art in America,* February 1993, 82–87+. Also see Margalit Fox, "A Portrait in Skin and Bones," *New York Times,* 21 November 1993, sect. 9, 8:1; Kurt Hollander, "Mental Illness and Body Art," *Poliester* 3, no. 9 (summer 1994): 20–29.

15. Michel Foucault, *Madness and Civilization: A History of Insanity in the Age of Reason,* trans. Richard Howard (New York: Vintage Books, 1965).

16. See, for example, Laura Cottingham, "Orlan: Sandra Gering Gallery, New York," *Frieze* 14 (January–February 1994): 60. Auslander contests such a reductive reading, but sees "a penchant for self-mutilation" in Orlan's work. See Philip Auslander, "Orlan's Theatre of Operations," *Theatre Forum* 7 (summer–fall 1995): 26.

17. Lisa Tickner, "The Body Politic: Female Sexuality and Women Artists since 1970," *Art History* 1, no. 2 (June 1978): 236–71.

18. Michel Foucault, "Technologies of the Self," in *Technologies of the Self,* ed. Luther H. Martin, Huck Gutman, and Patrick H. Hutton (Amherst: University of Massachusetts Press, 1988), 18.

19. Anne Balsamo, "On the Cutting Edge: Cosmetic Surgery and the Technological Production of the Gendered Body," *Camera Obscura* 28: 209.

20. For a discussion of "liveness" in mediatized culture, see Philip Auslander, "Live Performance in a Mediatized Culture," *Essays in Theatre* 11, no. 1 (November 1992): 33–39.

21. For a compelling argument that critiques the attempts to preserve and reproduce performance, see Peggy Phelan, *Unmarked: The Politics of Performance* (London: Routledge, 1993).

22. Auslander, "Orlan's Theatre of Operations," 25–31.

23. Balsamo, "On the Cutting Edge," 225.

24. Auslander, "Orlan's Theatre of Operations," 25–31.

25. On the "normalization of elective cosmetic surgery," see Morgan, "Women and the Knife," 28.

26. For an excellent explanation of how gender ideals are normalized, see Judith Butler, *Gender Trouble* (London: Routledge, 1990), 134–49; idem, "Imitation and Gender Insubordination," in *Inside/Out: Lesbian Theories, Gay Theories,* ed. Diana Fuss (London: Routledge, 1991), 13–32.

27. Morgan, "Women and the Knife," 28–31. Also see Balsamo, "On the Cutting Edge," 216–21.

28. See, for example, Hollander, "Mental Illness," 27 and *passim*; he equates Orlan's art with expressions of Body Dysmorphic Disorder (BDD).

29. Morgan proposed a revalorization of "the domain of the 'ugly,' " envisioning, among other things, the sewing and carving of wrinkles onto the body as well as the advertising and selling of freeze-dried fat cells. See Morgan, "Women and the Knife," 45–46.

In *Neuromancer,* the prototypical cyberpunk novel, William Gibson described anarchist terrorists in the following manner:

The Panther Moderns differ from other terrorists precisely in their degree of self-consciousness. . . . The one who showed up . . . was a soft-voiced boy called Angelo. His face was a simple graft grown on collagen and shark-cartilage polysaccarides, smooth and hideous. It was one of the nastiest pieces of elective surgery Case had ever seen. (William Gibson, *Neuromancer* [New York: Ace Books, 1984], 58–59)

30. For a discussion of how the performativity of gender can cite existing sex norms and gender prescriptions, see Butler, *Bodies That Matter,* 12–14. Gladys C. Fabre anticipates Butler in her essay on Orlan when she writes, "Orlan's iconographical research . . . discloses (at the same time as she discloses herself) a whole series of citations and references that she found through a serious reflection of the history of art." See Fabre, "Femme sur les barricades, Orlan brandit le laser time," in *Orlan Skai et Ski and Video,* exhibition catalogue (Paris: Galerie J. and J. Donguy, 1984), n.p. Translation mine.

31. See Maria T. Pramaggiore, "Resisting/Performing/ Femininity: Words, Flesh, and Feminism in Karen Finley's *The Constant State of Desire,*" *Theatre Journal* 44, no. 3 (October 1992): 269–90.

32. Fabre, "Femme sur les barricades."

33. Orlan, "Signalement d'Orlan," interview by Maurice Mallet, *VST* 23–24 (September–December 1991): 14. Translation mine.

34. See Diana Price Herndl, *Invalid Women: Figuring Feminine Illness in American Fiction and Culture, 1840–1940* (Chapel Hill: University of North Carolina Press, 1993), 153–65.

35. Fabre makes a similar point when she writes, "Rejecting her mother and her model of identification, Orlan will attempt to become her own master. Her art is best defined thus as a work of identity and not a work on identity that was acquired and remains to be discovered." See Fabre, "Femme sur les barricades."

36. Rose, "Is It Art?" 86.

37. See, for example, Janet Jenkins, ed., *In the Spirit of Fluxus,* exhibition catalogue (Minneapolis: Walker Art Center, 1993). In her ever growing résumé, Orlan lists performing an action during a 1975 Fluxus concert in Nice.

38. Orlan, "Intervention."

39. Eugénie Lemoine-Luccioni, *La Robe: Essai psychoanalytique sur le vêtement* (Paris: Edition de Seuil, 1984), 140; Fabre, "Femme sur les barricades."

40. Jean-Paul Sartre, *Saint Genet: Actor and Martyr,* trans. Bernard Frechtman (New York: Pantheon, 1963), 195.

41. Foucault, "Technologies of the Self," 42–49.

42. Orlan, "Orlan," in *Collective Consciousness: Art Performance in the Seventies,* ed. Jean Dupuy (New York: PAJ, 1980), 202–3.

43. See Carol Duncan, "Virility and Domination in Early Twentieth-Century Vanguard Painting" (1973), reptd. in *Twentieth-Century Art Theory: Urbanism, Politics and Mass Culture,* ed. Richard Hertz and Norman M. Klein (Englewood Cliffs, N.J.: Prentice Hall, 1990), 216–34. See also Rozsika Parker and Griselda Pollock, "God's Little Artist," in *Old Mistresses: Women, Art and Ideology* (New York: Pantheon, 1981), 82–113.

44. Lynda Nead, *The Female Nude: Art, Obscenity and Sexuality* (London: Routledge, 1992), 56.

45. For a discussion on the phallus as simulacrum, see Jean-Joseph Goux, "The Phallus: Masculine Identity and 'The Exchange of Women,' " trans. Maria Amuschastegui et al., in "The Phallus Issue," special issue of *Differences* 4, no. 1 (spring 1992): 40–75.

46. See Parveen Adams, "Waving the Phallus," 76–83, and Kaja Silverman, "The Lacanian Phallus," 84–115, both in *Differences* 4, no. 1 (spring 1992).

47. Silvia Eiblmayr, "Suture: Fantasies of Totality," 3–16, and Parveen Adams, "This Is My Body," 48–56, both in *Position en Zumich Kamerabilden,* ed. Silvia Eiblmayr, exhibition catalogue (Kiel: Museum of Kiel, 1994).

48. The term is Barbara Rose's. See "Vaginal Iconology," *New York Magazine,* February 1974, 59. On art that exemplifies Barbara Rose's term, see Tickner, "The Body Politic," 241–43.

49. Rose, "Is It Art?" 85–86.

50. Ibid.; Fabre, "Femme sur les barricades"; Arnaud Labelle-Rojoux, *L'Acte pour l'art* (Paris: Les Editeurs Evidant, 1988), 304.

51. See Fabre, "Femme sur les barricades," third page of unnumbered text.

52. The term "dialectical image" is Walter Benjamin's; Susan Buck-Morss notes that its conception is "overdetermined in Benjamin's thought." *The Dialectics of Seeing: Walter Benjamin and the Arcades Project* (Cambridge: MIT Press, 1989), 67.

53. Singer, "Hospitalization and AIDS," 48–49.

54. Bernard Ceysson, "Orlan: Ultime chef-d'oeuvre," in *Les 20 ans de pub et de cine de Sainte Orlan,* exhibition catalogue (Caen, France: Contemporary Center of Art of Lower Normandy, 1990), 13.

55. Orlan stressed the symbolic significance of the trousseau during one of our conversations in August 1994.

56. Ceysson, "Chef-d'oeuvre," 13.

57. Julia Kristeva, *Pouvoirs d'horreur: Essai sur l'abjection* (Paris: Editions du Seuil, 1980), 79–82. I am indebted to Griselda Pollock and Michelle Hirshhorn for stressing the importance of Kristeva's notion of abjection in relation to Orlan's work.

58. Nead, *The Female Nude,* 32.

59. Kristeva, *Pouvoirs d'horreur,* 85–86, 92–94.

60. Butler, *Bodies That Matter,* 3.

61. For a relatively detailed description of *Made in France,* see Fabre. "Femme sur les barricades."

62. For a discussion of Orlan's debt to Artaud, see Hirshhorn, "Orlan: Artist," 17–19.

63. Ceysson, "Chef-d'oeuvre," 6.

64. Craig Owens, "The Allegorical Impulse: Toward a Theory of Postmodernism, Part 2," reptd. in Craig Owens, *Beyond Recognition: Representation, Power, and Culture,* ed. Scott Bryson, Barbara Kruger, Lynne Tillman, and Jane Weinstock (Berkeley: University of California Press, 1992), 85.

65. Phelan, *Unmarked,* 2.

66. Elizabeth Couturier, "Happenings au Bloc Operatoire," *Paris Match,* January 1991, 8.

67. Upon being presented with a relic by Orlan herself, Madonna commented publicly, "It looks like caviar," which speaks volumes about Madonna's economic situation and her body politics. Madonna's conquest of her own body fat by rigorous self-discipline and athletic training has undoubtedly contributed to her cultural influence and economic success. See the segment on Orlan shown on Connie Chung's *Eye to Eye,* televised November 1993. On Madonna's body politics, see Susan Bordo, *Unbearable Weight: Feminism, Western Culture, and the Body* (Berkeley: University of California Press, 1993), 265–75.

Kim Cherkin proposes that for women with eating disorders, fat represents that part of the self one rejects. See *The Hungry Self: Women, Eating, and Identity* (New York: Harper Perennial, 1985).

68. Beuys is quoted telling the story in Caroline Tisdall, *Joseph Beuys* (London: Phaidon, 1979), 16–17. See also John F. Moffitt, *Occultism in Avant-Garde Art: The Case of Joseph Beuys* (Ann Arbor: UMI Research Press, 1988).

69. Rose, "Is It Art?" 125.

70. Jean-Paul Sartre, *Baudelaire,* trans. Martin Turnell (New York: New Directions, 1950), 25–27.

71. Mary Kelly claims that through performance, artists present subjectivity as an effect of self-possession; see "Re-Viewing Modernist Criticism," *Screen* 22, no. 3 (fall 1987): 52.

72. See, for example, Orlan's *A Mouth for Grapes,* photograph mounted on

aluminum, 20 by 31 1/2 inches, from the fourth operation/performance, *The Mouth of Europa and Figure of Venus,* photo by Joel Nichols. Reproduced in Rose, "Is It Art?" 86.

73. For a scathing condemnation of such theatricality, see Michael Fried, "Art and Objecthood," *Artforum,* June 1967, reptd. in *Minimal Art,* ed. Gregory Battock (London: Studio Vista, 1969), 143–46.

74. Butler, *Bodies That Matter,* 225. See also J. L. Austin, *How to Do Things with Words,* 2d ed. (Cambridge: Harvard University Press, 1985); Eve Kosofsky Sedgwick, *Tendencies* (Durham: Duke University Press, 1993), 11.

75. See Kathy O'Dell, "The Performance Artist as Masochistic Woman," *Arts Magazine* 62, no. 10 (June 1988): 89–91.

76. Phelan, *Unmarked,* 152.

77. Judith Barry and Sandy Flitterman-Lewis, "Textual Strategies: The Politics of Art-Making," *LIT: Feminist Arts Journal* (1981–82).

78. Butler, *Gender Trouble,* 101. Also see Michel Foucault, "The Minimalist Self," in *Politics, Philosophy, Culture: Interviews and Other Writings, 1977–1984,* ed. Lawrence D. Kritzman (New York: Routledge, 1988), 3–16.

79. See Philip Auslander, "The Surgical Self: Body Alteration and Identity" (conference paper delivered at the First Annual Performance Studies Conference, New York University, New York, 25 March 1995).

80. Kelly sees such parody as characteristic of performance art: "By putting himself in circulation, the performance artist parodied the commercial exchange and distribution of the artistic personality in the form of a commodity." "Re-Viewing Modernist Criticism," 53.

81. See Auslander, "The Surgical Self."

82. Thomas Hobbes, *Leviathan,* ed. Michael Oakeshott, intro. Richard S. Peters (New York: Collier Books, 1962), 217.

NINETEEN

Intervention

Orlan

In French, "intervention" also means "operation."

Few images force us to close our eyes:
Death, suffering, the opening of the body, certain aspects of pornography (for certain people) or for others, birth.

Here the eyes become black holes in which the image is absorbed willingly or by force. These images plunge in and strike directly where it hurts, without passing through the habitual filters, as if the eyes no longer had any connection with the brain.

When you watch my performances, I suggest that you do what you probably do when you watch the news on television. It is a question of not letting yourself be taken in by the images and of continuing to reflect about what is behind these images.

In my performances, in addition to the medical personnel and my team, there is a sign language interpreter for the deaf and hearing-impaired. This person is there to remind us that we are all, at certain moments, deaf and hearing-impaired.

Her presence in the operating theatre brings into play a language of the body.

My surgical performances began on May 30, 1990, in Newcastle, England. It was the logical development of my preceding work, but in a much more radical form.

This performance has two titles:
The first, *The Reincarnation of Saint Orlan,* alludes to the character that was gradually created by appropriating the religious images of madonnas, virgins, saints.

The second title, *Image—New Images,* winks at Hindu gods and goddesses who change appearances to carry out new deeds and exploits (for me it is about shifting referents, passing from Judeo-Christian religious iconography to Greek mythology), something that I do after all my operations. On the other hand, this title alludes to the said new images—i.e., new technologies—because I make myself into a new image in order to produce new images.

We could say that this performance is a command performance. In fact, English curators, having seen one of my performances at the Centre Georges Pompidou, during a demonstration over the Fluxus movement and Happenings in June 1989, came to see me to invite me to participate in their festival, to do a piece on the theme "Art and Life in the Nineties."

With this opportunity, I found the means to say loudly and clearly all that I thought was negative about artistic production in the eighties.

I therefore decided to do an anti-performance, as counterpoint to what was taking place in the panorama of contemporary art.

During these years, the majority of artists (I'm not saying all) had become completely adapted to the society and hyperadapted to the laws of the market.

Often my students at the École Nationale in Dijon asked me for recipes on how to sell and how to get into certain galleries in certain circles.

I was at the other end of the spectrum from this attitude.

My work emerged during the seventies (I should specify that I was twenty-three—I was born May 30, 1947—and that my first street performances were done in 1965, when I was eighteen), when art was engaged with the social, the political, the ideological, a period when artists were very invested intellectually, conceptually, and sometimes physically in their work.

During this time, I had already used surgery at a performance symposium that I organized in Lyon for five years. I had to be operated on urgently: my body was a sick body that suddenly needed attention. I decided to make the most of this new adventure by turning the situation on itself, by considering life an aesthetically recuperable phenomenon: I had photography and video brought into the operating room, and the videos and photographs were shown as if it had been a planned performance.

Being operated on is not frivolous; the experience was very intense: I was certain that one day, somehow, I would work again with surgery.

I wanted to take up again these tropes and ingredients of my work to elaborate a performance without being false to myself, a performance in continuity with previous steps and approaches.

A performance facing the future, using up-to-date techniques. One of my favorite mottoes is "Remember the Future."

I wanted to make a performance radical for myself and beyond myself . . .

It was upon reading a text by Eugénie Lemoine Luccioni, a Lacanian psychoanalyst, that the idea of putting this into action came to me (a passage from reading to the carrying out of the act).

At the beginning of all my performance-operations, I read this excerpt from her book, *La Robe:*

> Skin is deceiving. . . . In life, one only has one's skin. . . . There is a bad exchange in human relations because one never is what one has. . . . I have the skin of an angel but I am a jackal . . . the skin of a crocodile but I am a poodle, the skin of a black person but I am white, the skin of a woman, but I am a man; I never have the skin of what I am. There is no exception to the rule because I am never what I have.

Reading this text, I thought that in our time we have begun to have the means of closing this gap, that, with the help of surgery, it was becoming

Fig. 19.1. Orlan, *Operation Réussie*, 8 December 1991. Paris. Photo by Alain Doumé; by permission of Orlan and SIPA Press.

possible to match up the internal image to the external image.

I say that I am doing a woman-to-woman transexualism by way of allusion to transexuals: a man who feels himself to be a woman wants others to see him as a woman.

We could summarize this by saying that it is a problem of communication.

One can consider my work as classical self-portraiture even if initially it is conceived with the aid of computers. But what can one say when it comes to permanently inscribing this work in the flesh? I will speak of a "Carnal Art," in part to differentiate myself from Body Art, to which nevertheless it belongs.

Carnal Art is a work of autoportraiture in the classical sense, but with the technological means of its time. It oscillates between disfiguration and refiguration. It inscribes itself in the flesh because our era begins to lend itself to this possibility. The body is becoming a "modified ready-made" because it is no longer that ideal ready-made waiting to be signed.

Unlike Body Art, from which it distinguishes itself, Carnal Art does not desire pain, does not seek pain as a source of purification, and does not perceive pain as Redemption. Carnal Art is not interested in the final plastic results, but in the surgical operation-performance and the modified body, as venue for public debate.

For me it is about pushing art and life to their extremes.

My work and its ideas, incarnated in my flesh, interrogate the status of the body in our society and its evolution in future generations via new technologies and upcoming genetic manipulations.

My body has become a site of public debate that poses crucial questions for our time.

At the inception of this performance, I constructed my self-portrait by mixing and hybridizing, with the help of a computer, representations of goddesses of Greek mythology—chosen not because of the canons of beauty that they are supposed to represent (seen from afar), but for their histories.

Briefly:

- Diana was chosen because she is insubordinate to the gods and men; because she is active, even aggressive, because she leads a group.
- Mona Lisa, a beacon character in the history of art, was chosen as a reference point because she is not beautiful according to present standards of beauty, because there is some "man" under this woman. We now know it to be the self-portrait of Leonardo Da Vinci that hides under that of La Gioconda (which brings us back to an identity problem).
- Psyche because she is the antipode of Diana, invoking all that is fragile and vulnerable in us.

- Venus for embodying carnal beauty, just as Psyche embodies the beauty of the soul.
- Europa because she is swept away by adventure and looks toward the horizon.

After mixing my own image with these images, I reworked the whole as any painter does, until the final portrait emerged and it was possible to stop and sign it.

I do not want to resemble Botticelli's Venus.

I do not want to resemble the Europa of Gustave Moreau—who is not my favorite painter. I chose the Europa of this painter because she figures in an unfinished painting, just like so many of his paintings!

I do not want to resemble Gérard's Psyche.

I don't want to resemble Diana of the Fontainebleau School.

I don't want to resemble Mona Lisa, although this continues to be said in certain newspapers and on television programs despite what I have said on numerous occasions!

(The media fallout, from which I cannot escape, be it televisual or written press, makes claims the meaning of which will be felt in ten years. I propose that the resulting media images in galleries and museums form an integral part of my work since, whatever their reductive tendencies may be, they allow me to see my impact on a public I'm addressing, a public that isn't necessarily part of the micro-milieu of art.)

These representations of feminine personages have served me as fabric of inspiration and are there deep underneath in a symbolic manner, and in this way their images can resurface in works that I produce, with regard to their histories.

With this computer-generated work, I then went to see the surgeons, asking them to bring me as close as possible to this image.

At first finding a surgeon was a difficult thing. After many rejections, I found one, a cautious one who proceeded to go ahead a step at a time, which allowed me to understand where I was going and what it was possible to make happen in an operating room,[1] what the limits were, what my limits were, how I would react, how my body would react; and thus to learn better how to orchestrate the entirety of these operations.

Each operation was like a rite of passage.

As a plastic artist I wanted to intervene in the surgical aesthetic, which is cold and stereotyped, and to confront it with others: the decor is transformed, the surgical team and my team wear clothing conceived by established fashion designers, by myself, or by young, up-and-coming stylists (Paco Rabanne, Franck Sorbier, Miyaké, Lan Vu).

Each operation has its own style. This ranges from the carnivalesque (which is not for me a pejorative word; the word *carnival* originally means *carne vaut*) to the high-tech, passing through the baroque, and so forth.

For I think there are as many pressures on women's bodies as there are on the body—on the physicality—of works of art.

Our era hates the flesh; and works of art cannot enter certain networks and certain galleries except according to preestablished molds. Among others, the parodic style, the grotesque, and the ironic are irritating, judged to be in bad taste and often scorned.

I recite the texts as long as possible during the operation, even when they are operating on my face, which gave during the last operations the impression of an autopsied corpse that continues to speak, as if detached from its body.

Each performance-operation is built on a philosophical, psychoanalytical, or literary text (Eugénie Lemoine Luccioni, Michel Serres, Sanskrit Hindu texts, Alphonse Allais, Antonin Artaud, Elisabeth Betuel, Fiebig, Raphael Cuir, Julia Kristeva).

The operating room becomes my studio, from which I am conscious of producing images, making a film, a video, photos, drawings with my blood, relics with my body fat and my flesh, kinds of *sudaria* and other objects that will later be exhibited; these works attempt to varying degrees to be autonomous. I try to inscribe again in substance the same ideas that presided in the elaboration of the performances—from which they issue— so that the quality of this materiality reveals the essence of these ideas. In the plastic work, it is less a question of equaling the transition to action and the violence of the act, as it is a bringing to light of the elements of construction of a thought, which affords itself the freedom of transgression of the taboo act. That is to say, like any artist, to take off from a position, from a social project and/or an artistic problematic, and to have to find and put to work a plastic solution.

I'm on my ninth performance-operation.

The first six were performed in Europe with two French surgeons, Dr. Kamel Chérif Zahar, Dr. Bernard Cornette de Saint-Cyr, and a Belgian surgeon, Dr. Pierre Quin.

The seventh operation (the most important one) and the eighth and ninth were performed by Dr. Marjorie Cramer, a feminist plastic surgeon in New York.

The seventh performance-operation, which took place on November 21, 1993, was based on the concept of Omnipresence.

It was broadcast live by satellite from the Sandra Gering Gallery in New York, to the Centre Georges Pompidou in Paris, the McLuhan Center in Toronto, the Multi-Media Center in Banff, and a dozen other sites with which we were in contact by means of interactive transmission (see figure 19.2).

Spectators could thus participate in the operation from several countries around the world and, in addition, ask questions, to which I responded live when the operating procedure permitted.

The performance was about, among other things, desacralizing the surgical act and making a private act transparent, public.

By the same token, in the gallery, the photographic installation rested on two ideas: to show what normally is held secret and to establish a comparison between the self-portrait made by the computing machine and the self-portrait made by the body-machine.

In order to do this, I placed forty-one metal diptychs in the gallery, corresponding to forty days of exhibition,[2] plus one for the final image: on the bottom half of each diptych was a photo of a computer screen showing a face made with the help of morphing software. I exposed the "space between," in other words, an image of the exact, unretouched space con-

Fig. 19.2. Orlan, *Omniprésence,* 21 November 1993. New York, *Surgical Performance, no. 7.* Photo by Vladimir Sichov; by permission of Orlan and SIPA Press.

ceived as the intersection of my face and the portrait of my reference personages. On the top half of each diptych, each day we affixed with magnets the *image du jour,* therefore that of a face first of all bandaged, then multicolored: from blue to yellow, passing through red, and sufficiently swollen. Each metal plate was dated.

On the last day, the installation was complete, and by dint of that the exhibition was over.

During the last three operations, the largest implants possible for my anatomy were put in, and two more (normally used to enhance the cheeks) were inserted at each temple to create two bumps.

The next operation will probably take place in Japan, to construct a very large nose, the largest nose technically possible (in relation to my anatomy) and ethically acceptable for a surgeon of this country. This nose must start at the forehead in the manner of Mayan sculpture.

This operation will only take place in three or four years, as time is needed to find the technical and financial infrastructures and to develop the project as a whole.

But also, I take this time because the greatest risk I run is that this radical, very shocking performance could eclipse all the plastic work that comes out of it. Furthermore, my present objective is to produce and to show the works that have come out of the preceding operations, making known the processes of construction of this performance and taking up with the largest possible public the questions they raise.

My work is not against cosmetic surgery, but against the standards of beauty, against the dictates of a dominant ideology that impress themselves more and more on feminine flesh . . . and masculine flesh.

Cosmetic surgery is one of the sites in which man's power over the body of woman can inscribe itself most strongly.

I would not have been able to obtain from the male surgeons what I obtained from my female surgeon; the former wanted, I think, to keep me "cute."

Feminists reproach me for promoting cosmetic surgery. In fact, although I am a feminist, I am not against cosmetic surgery, and I can explain this: in the past we had a life expectancy of forty to fifty years. Today, it has jumped to seventy or eighty (and is constantly going up).

We all have a feeling of strangeness in front of a mirror; this often becomes more acute as we age. For some people this becomes unbearable, and the use of cosmetic surgery is very positive in this case.

Obviously, cosmetic surgery ought not to become compulsory! Here again, social pressure must not prevail over individual desires.

Cosmetic or not, surgery is not natural, but taking antibiotics in order not to die of infection is not any more natural! It is a phenomenon of our century, one of many possibilities, a choice.

I am the first artist to use surgery as medium and to alter the purpose of cosmetic surgery: to look better, to look young.

"I is an other" *["Je est un autre"]*. I am at the forefront of confrontation.

Like the Australian artist Stelarc, I think that the body is obsolete. It no longer is adequate for the current situation. We mutate at the rate of cockroaches, but we are cockroaches whose memories are in computers, who pilot planes and drive cars that we have conceived, although our bodies are not conceived for these speeds.

We are at the threshold of a world for which we are neither mentally nor physically ready.

Psychoanalysis and religion agree in saying, "One must not attack the body," "One must accept oneself." These are primitive, ancestral, anachronistic concepts. We think that the sky will fall on our heads if we touch the body!

Nevertheless, many people have had organ grafts, hip replacements, and a good number of crash victims' faces have been reconstructed. And how many more straightened or bobbed noses are out there enjoying the air without physical or psychological problems?

Are we still convinced that we must bend ourselves to the decisions of Nature, this lottery of genes distributed by chance?

My work is a struggle against the innate, the inexorable, the programmed, Nature, DNA (which is our direct rival as artists of representation), and God!

My work is blasphemous.

It is an endeavor to move the bars of the cage, a radical and uncomfortable endeavor! It is only an endeavor.

I based one of my operations on a text by Antonin Artaud, who dreamed of a body without organs. This text mentions the names of poets of his time. Then it enumerates how many times these poets must have defecated, urinated, how many hours were needed to sleep, to eat, to wash, and concludes that this is totally disproportionate to the fifty or so pages of magical production (as he calls the creative act).

A few words about pain. I try to make this work as unmasochistic as possible, but there is a price to pay: the anesthetic shots are not pleasant. (I prefer to drink a good wine with friends rather than to be operated on!) Nevertheless, everyone is familiar with this. It's like at the dentist: you make a face for a few seconds. And as I have not paid my tribute to Nature in experiencing the pains of childbirth, I consider myself happy. After the operations, it is more or less uncomfortable, more or less painful. I therefore take analgesics.

As my friend the French artist Ben Vautier would say, "Art is a dirty job, but somebody's got to do it."

In fact, it is really my audience who hurts when they watch me and the images of my surgeries on video.

I compare myself to a high-level athlete. There is the training, the moment of the performance, where one must go beyond one's limits—which is not done without effort (or pain)—and then there is the recuperation.

Like a sportsman who makes a solitary crossing of the Atlantic, we often do crazy things without necessarily being crazy.

"I have given my body to Art." After my death it will therefore not be given to science but to a museum and, mummified, will form the centerpiece of an interactive video installation.

When the operations are finished, I will solicit an advertising agency to come up with an artist's name and logo; next I will retain a lawyer to petition the Republic to accept my new identity and my new face. It is a performance that inscribes itself into the social fabric, that challenges the law, that moves toward a total change of identity. (Should this prove impossible, in any event, the attempt and the pleading of the case by the attorney will form part of the work.)

I will conclude with two excerpts of a text by Michel Serres, which served as a framework in the construction of the sixth surgical operation. The first excerpt of this text was used in making a series of relics.

The idea of these series is to produce the most reliquaries possible, all presented in the same manner, always with the same text but each time translated into another language, until the body is depleted; each time in a different language until there is no more flesh to put in the center of the reliquary.

> The current tattooed monster, ambidextrous, hermaphroditic and cross-bred, what can it make us see, now, under its skin? Yes, blood and flesh. Science speaks of organs, functions, of cells and molecules, only to admit at last that it's high time we stopped speaking of life in laboratories; but science never mentions the flesh, which, quite rightly, signifies the conflation, here and now, in a specific site of the body, of muscles and blood, skin and hair, bones, nerves and diverse functions, that inextricably binds that which pertinent knowledge analyzes.

The second part of this text was not used for the reliquaries but was read during the operation and on video:

> Now already for a while many spectators will have left the auditorium, tired out by ineffectual theatrical effects, irritated at the turn from comedy to tragedy, having come to laugh and deceived at having been made to think; there will be some even—knowledgeable specialists no doubt—who will have understood on their own terms, that each portion of their knowledge resembles the coat of the Harlequin, since each one works at the intersection of many other sciences and at the interference point of almost all of them. Thus their academy—its encyclopedic institution—formally rejoins the comedy of art.

Carnal Art loves the baroque and parody, the grotesque and free-form because Carnal Art is opposed to social pressures that exert themselves as much on the human body as on the body of artworks. Carnal Art is anti-formalist and anti-conformist.

ORLAN 1995. Translated by Tanya Augsburg and Michel A. Moos.

TRANSLATORS' NOTES

1. We translate *"ce que l'on pouvait arriver à faire bouger"* as "what it was possible to make happen," yet the sense has more to do with disruptive, innovative, and subversive acts that form the statements of Orlan's work.

2. The word *"exposition"* in French can refer in this instance to the duration of the gallery exhibition as well as to the development, in a photographic sense (i.e., it is being documented photographically), of the temporal, physical transformation that takes place in the forty days following the operation—a kind of exposure.

TWENTY

Of Mice, Bugs, and Women

Deb Margolin

(Sound of insect buzzing.)
(Enters.)

Hello! Exterminator! Exterminator!

I got it! I got it! *(Pulls out fly swatter, looks for insect, swats. Sound of buzzing off)*

Hello, exterminator! Tell me about your problem! And yes, I'm still the exterminator! Still on the job! You know, people think because it's exterminator that I no longer have the job, but I'm still on the job! Exterminator! See it's Latin! EX is Latin! Anybody here take Latin? Anybody! Anybody! See, ex is Latin for out! It means out! Like EX-IT means you go OUT of IT! Or like EX LAX means it gets the shit OUT! Or like EXTERMINATOR! OUT of people like me, they make a TERMINATOR! Exterminator! Now! Tell me about your problem!

Now! A woman I service on the East Side got them big thick roaches! Waterbugs! You know she actually tried to kill them by stamping on them, covering 'em up with oaktag! She'd herd 'em all up, put oaktag cardboard over 'em, and jump! Took two hours a shot! Now! Tell me about your problem! You know, bugs! I'm a bugs man and a mouse man! Bugs and mice are different! Okay! What's the difference between a bug and a mouse? Right! A mouse is bigger but there's another difference! Bugs and mice! What is it? What is it? It's . . . *motivation! Motivation!* Because a bug just tries to survive, but a mouse is burdened with an actual *will to live!*

Will to live! Separates the bugs from the mice! Will to live! See, a bug . . . all right, now what is a bug? Okay, it's an insect . . . maybe it has wings or whatever, but it's no falcon! And you, senator, are no Jack Kennedy! HaHa! That was very good when he said that! HaHa! Whereas a mouse has no wings, but flight is its middle name! It flees! It flees! Silently! See, what's the most devastating thing about a mousetrap? Anybody! Anybody! It's the *noise* it makes! Because it's attention! Mice don't want no attention! Bugs don't mind! I saw a mouse once, brown. Lived at the apartment of one of my clients. Lived there so long it was listed in the phone book! Tried everything. Tried everything with this mouse. One day, mouse left. My client was going to work, fumbling with her keys. The mouse ran out of her house and under the door into her neighbor's house. Moved out all at once, just like that. Gal called me up the next day, said she missed the mouse! Said she didn't have no closure with the mouse! Made me come back and look for it! Crazy gal! Crazy gal!

And now the bugs won't move when they've got it good! Now! Tell me about your problem. Now, bugs swarm around the dead! Mice don't swarm around the dead! Saw a frog once, dead! Dead, it looked like a bearskin rug! Dead before it had a chance, flattened by a guy walking to the swimpool! It looked like a fossil! Fossils are funny! Okay, what is a fossil? Anybody! Anybody! Fossil's an impression! You know, not the creature itself, but the impression it makes on a soft surface! Impressions of the dead last for years! Centuries! Impressions of the dead! Anybody! Impressions of the dead! So there's this dead frog, you know, and it's like Tavern on the Green for the flies! Now, this young frog's mother did not intend for her baby to lie squashed under flies like the buffet table at a bar mitzvah. But you take a mouse! A mouse won't do that! Mouse won't do that! Mouse won't get all gussied up to come out and eat barbecue from the dead! Why? Because it's publicity, you see! Publicity! A mouse don't want no publicity! Like a criminal, or a celebrity on vacation! Mouse is private! Quiet! Good neighbor, you see!

Saddest mouse I ever seen in Port Authority! They beep me, tell me Port Authority! I go over there, second floor up the escalator, there's a mouse in the candy corn! Ploughing with its feet in the candy corn, it can't even eat 'cause it can't walk, can't walk 'cause it can't get no traction, like a treadmill! Treadmill of death in the candy corn! Couldn't breathe too good in there either! Flailing its legs, wagging its tail, trying to move, scared. I get

Fig. 20.1. "The Exterminator." Photograph by Donna McAdams. Reprinted by permission.

it out for them, they re-open the store, don't clean up or nothin', little kid comes in, what does he want, he wants candy corn, mother buys him candy corn, he's eating it. I show him the mouse, he falls in love with it. Had little orange crumbs on it. Killed it with the spray gun.

Tell me about your problem! See! I know a lady got porcupines! Porcupines, they eat houses! Lady's got porcupines lunching on her house, see! She buys a gun, right? She puts on a hat, lies down on the ground near the floorboards, starts shooting! But she shot a mouse! Because the porcupine's too smart for that! The porcupines, they loaded their guts with wood, laid down, waited it out, like at McDonalds! Kid hid in the dishwasher till it was all over, see! Twenty-three people dead, kid hid in the dishwasher! Kid hid in the dishwasher! Wouldn't come out! Didn't know it was over, wouldn't come out! Wouldn't come out till the cops drug him out!

It's against company policy! See, I'm not allowed to kill anything myself, see! With my own hands, see! It's against company policy, see! I just create an atmosphere, see, where they just drop dead! Or an environment. But I don't do it myself, see! I'm an operative! And I got a radio, see! A radio! Someone got bugs, they can reach me! Call the front office, they send me right out! To the exact place and everything!

One lady calls me up for a bee! Christ I got stories! She calls me up for a bee! See, she's sitting there in a bathing suit with a cup of coffee, and there's a bee caught between the screen and the blinds! Buzzing deep! She's aging! I see her, a young woman! This is the best moment of her life, see, she's been swimming, she's got coffee, she's strong, see, but she's listening to this bee! She's at the top of the V! See, your life is an upside-down V! Everyone's is! You reach the top of the V at, let's say, twenty-nine! And you perch up there in a little outfit with a cup of coffee, see! And you know that's the best it's gonna get! See! And how long it goes on like that depends on how long you can sit with your ass perched on a spike that sharp! Anybody! Anybody!

So she's listening to the bee! See, it was gonna die anyway! The buzz was low! See, when the buzz is high it's got a will to live! Well, not a will to live, but it's trying to survive! It's conserving energy, which is a bee's form of hope, see! But when the buzz is low, it's weak and angry! And that's a bad combination, weak and angry! Can't conserve! Can't conserve! It's death in a matter of minutes, see! So here was this beautiful gal! And her life was at its best moment! See, I could tell! I could tell! Swimming! Coffee! Summer! Bathing suit! Enough money to call a man to kill a bee! Listening to a bee trying to die at four o'clock in the afternoon in the summer! So I said, tell me about your problem! And while she was telling me, the bee died. I'm like a psychiatrist or something! That's what they do!

One guy's got ants! He lays on the window sill cause he got nowhere else to sleep! And red ants ate him alive, so he calls me.

See, psychologically she knew! She knew! She knew she was at the top of the V, she was balanced at the top, and the bee was on the way down! That's what was upsetting her! They were heading in opposite directions, and she couldn't take it! See that's I-ronny! See, when something is sitting over here, and the other thing's going in the opposite direction, it's I-ronical! Got to have a stomach for it! Like doctors, military men! They got a stomach for it! She got no stomach for it!

See, then you got lightning bugs! They're nice, right, everyone likes 'em, right? Little kids and so forth, right? But they're not all they're cracked up to be! Okay, what is a lightning bug? Anybody! Little flashes of light all night! What mosquitoes do with sound they do with light! They whine with light! Meaio, Meaio!

(Sound of insect buzzing.)

The Novelist

Planes and flies. All night long, I've got these planes and flies. They've got us right on the flight pattern here. So I'm sorry about the flies, the planes I can't do anything about. Well I can't do anything about the flies either, but people don't know that, my friends all: spray this! Spray that! I'm not going to spray these things, who knows? Who knows what they have in them? I heard about this ultrasonic device that sends out a high-pitched sound above the spectrum of human perception, and this sound suppos-edly gets rid of both bugs and rodents. They all just line up at the front door of your home with their things in a little scarf tied to a stick, and try to emigrate to a better life as quickly as possible, that's the impression they try to give you they're selling it in one of these catalogs. So you buy one, you think it's okay, you plug it in, and your mice and bugs leave; your house looks great, you're throwing dinner parties left and right, and the next thing you know you're jumping out the window! And you say to yourself: now why am I doing this? And it's from listening for three months to the shrieking of this machine you didn't even think you heard!

You know they have us right on the flight pattern here. I'm not even going to go to the airport anymore, I'll just take my luggage and go up to the roof, they can pick me up there, it's right on the way. All night, those planes. It's like having your ear to a huge stomach in the throes of a terrible hunger. They sound like pangs to me, these planes. No wonder I can't sleep. Plus alcohol. I always think if I have a glass or two of wine it'll help me sleep, but it never does. Oh. I fall asleep . . . but then I wake up like a dog on a leash on a sidewalk in the summer whose master jerked him to attention. I've got sweat in a circle around my lips.

Anyway, that's just the way I write. It's just that way, always has been. I'm having a fuck of a time.

Writing's so hard, it's amazing I get anything done. Terribly hard. Terribly hard to get anything done. I wake up, and out the curtains through the window I see the mountain, and that draws me outside onto the porch, and then I smoke a cigarette, and after I smoke I get hungry, so I come inside and eat; then after I eat of course I need to go back out and have a cigarette, then after I smoke a cigarette I feel like lying down, and once I'm lying down I go back to sleep again. And this palindromic series of events follows me in cycles many times throughout the day; it's terribly hard to get anything done at all.

You know, thirty-four years ago I sat down and I wrote the first industrial novel since the postindustrial era, and it was *terribly* hard. And I thought it was hard because it was my first novel, but every novel has come equally hard, and hard in the same way.

See, I'm not an intellectual really, I'm just a good listener. I don't sleep well. I get up at night and I hear people talking; sometimes it's my neighbors, sometimes it's voices in my head. And I listen and I write down what I hear, that's all; plots invent themselves out of voices. And I insist on politeness from my characters. I want to get to know them. I don't like it when real or imaginary people tell me their whole life story when I don't even know them. It's false intimacy, I hate it. I once moved into a building and said hello to a good-looking young lawyer type who lived in the apartment below me. Next day we happened to get on the same subway car and he ended up telling me about his sixteen-year-old daughter, you know he's divorced of course, and how he took her with him on a Club Med vacation, and how she happened to walk in on him screwing a girl about her own age. Now did I need to hear that? Did I? Now every time I think about the American Bar Association I think of statutory rape at the Club Med.

Same with my characters. I need to listen to them, chat with them for months before I'm ready for stories like that. I had one gal who wouldn't wait. Young college student from the Jersey shore. Not only wanted to tell me everything about herself that first night I imagined her, but also demanded to know everything about me: why I dye my hair, how my boobs got the way they are, why I always write about dissatisfied men instead of dissatisfied women. My politics. Why I fantasize about being a teenager when I have sex . . . all that. None of her beeswax. It's interesting . . . I wanted to know all that stuff about my mother . . . that must be why she ran away from me so much and hated me so often . . . It's like some natural principle . . . whatever you did to drive your parents crazy, there's someone waiting in the wings to do that to you . . . even if you have to invent them. I had a dream about this college girl. She was a lit major with a minor in theatre, by the way. *(Munching)* Mmm. These are delicious! And it says here: No Cholesterol. *(Turning package)* Oh, but there's fat! Eighty grams of fat! Imagine that! No cholesterol but a thousand blobs of fat! Fat and cholesterol are like Sacco and Vanzetti, everybody knows that. So this little lit major said:

I spin with my planet in deft, senseless earnest

She was quoting a poem. I thought the line was vacuous and stupid, I'm opinionated, I admit that. She defended the line, thought it was resonant and meaningful. When I woke up I realized maybe there's something to it; I mean, we are all spinning all the time, and that's probably very debilitating in its way: I mean, our TV dinners are spinning, our books, our papers, our clothes, our literary agents. I mean, you get on a plane and fly across the country; when you get off the plane you're exhausted when all you did was sit there; the involuntary movement was exhausting. Maybe that's why we're all so inexplicably blank and tired.

I couldn't stand that college girl character. She was smarter than I am and I don't suffer geniuses gladly . . . so I dropped her from the novel. Couldn't enjoy her, didn't want to listen anymore. It's so funny . . . that's what my mother did to me, only she wasn't a writer, she was my mother. Although in a way, a point could be made that we write our kids . . . you use DNA instead of ink, but the channeling aspect is the same. *(Munching)* These things are delicious!

(Eating.)

You know what these things remind me of? Those Bongos or Condos . . . Conchos . . . Those cheese things that have peanut butter stuffed up them! Combos! Those say no cholesterol too! I was in the library working, and there were these two boys eating them . . . I adored these little boys! They were about fourteen or fifteen, wearing hats . . . one of them had a baseball cap on backwards, the other had a rag tied around his head . . . these headdresses were acts of rebellion, intelligent, friendly rebellion . . . and they were laughing and laughing . . . so I stopped what I was doing and started eavesdropping . . . turned out they were talking about how when the atom bomb fell, it landed on this one particular girl! The first boy said: The Atom Bomb landed on this one girl! It was really funny! She went splat! Parts of her body were spread out for ten miles! Her hands were all cut off and everything! It was gross! And they laughed hysterically. So then the other boy said: I heard when you get shot in the head sometimes you don't even know it! I bet she didn't even know it! And they laughed again, but different. Then the first boy said: have you seen my sister? She has never cut her hair and it's four feet long, and she has a little triangle missing from her nose! My dad was giving her the beat and she fell and chipped a part of her nose! If you look you can see a triangle missing! And they laughed again.

I love these adolescent kids . . . I love the way they take the gruesome things they hear about and merge them with the details of daily life, and then laugh! That's adolescent humor! Mythic humor! Like that story I grew up with about the girl with a beehive hairdo who put honey in it and a thousand bees came and stung her to death! Mythic humor! It's a humor whose purpose is to try to understand horror, act real casual about it and establish a big distance from it, all at the same time . . . it was so cute. That gruesome story about the bomb falling on this one girl . . . what a nerd, eh? . . . and then combining it so casually with that story about his sister with the Medusan hair and the Bermuda triangle missing from her nose . . . I loved those boys!

I wrote nonfiction . . . it was beautiful, my nonfiction . . . it was beautiful the way novels are beautiful, because I used images from my own life . . . images I'd saved up from all places: here, there, little bits and chips of poetry I'd been collecting all my life. Makes me think of sea glass . . . you know, that's what they call those smooth, not quite but almost transparent slices of shell you find on the beach . . . they're clear colored, or nearly green, and smooth from who knows what years of compression and abrasion at the whims of the tide . . . sea glass. I collected that too, sea glass, found hundreds of pieces on thousands of sleazy beaches up and down the world, saved them up and finally put the pieces in a big glass jar with water. I loved the sound the pieces made as they clicked, they looked like trash, like beautiful pieces of a shattered something, only smooth from centuries of abrasion . . . or like the glass window people put up in the bathroom to keep people from looking in. That's what these images were like, but now I don't have any more images. They're all gone, I used them up, tossed them into fountains of other purposes, gave them away . . . people wondered why my work was beautiful. I'm out of them now, all I do is listen. So as you're leaving please speak extra loudly. I've got my notebook and pen out; this is how I make my living now.

Character Cut from the Novel

You're looking at me like there's something wrong with me. Something, like you're thinking, there's something "unnatural" about me and there is. See, I was in a novel, but I got axed. I'm out. I'm not in the novel, but that doesn't mean I just WENT AWAY. I'm still here, the bitch got up one night with a hangover, she thinks all writers are supposed to have a hangover. And she axed me. She's a fucking bitch. See, I was in the sketch. She did a lot of *sketches*, you know, character sketches, like the way the great painters did pencil sketches of the famous paintings before they painted them.

Fig. 20.2. "Character Cut From the Novel." Photograph by Donna McAdams. Reprinted by permission.

Kind of like a prenuptial agreement between the oil and the canvas. In the movies, that's called a treatment, but I think that's really stupid. To me a treatment is something you take for a disease. All these words. People just litter the streets with words. Like *sides*. When you're supposed to audition, and they give you the lines in advance, those are called sides. But to me sides is what you take in an argument. My character used to audition a lot on the college campus, and she always thought the word was—*sighs*—like (*sigh*). So there's some big symbolism right there! And all these words! Words, words! Like this dress! This table, this chair, my arms. Words. All this is just a bunch of words! You heard that bee before. That's a fear she gave me. Of *bees*. Writers are our mothers, they give us fears, phobias. Like, this one "sketch" she wrote me was about how afraid I am of bees. She wrote me a dream where a bee keeps painting itself bigger and bigger with strokes to its underbelly, first it became the size of a sparrow, and it goes stroke for stroke bigger till it's the size of a duck, the hum getting louder and louder, and finally I turn in the dream to the main character of the novel, a man who I'm supposed to want very badly, although he did nothing for me, a middle-aged married man with three kids and all of a sudden he realizes his life is still unlived, and his son is a pig, his daughter's a jerk, and I forget the third kid, and his wife's gone to fat and wears cold cream and curlers, so that's not very interesting anymore, so we fall hot and mad for each other, we meet at a college campus, mine of course, and we have an affair, although he *bored* me and I *horrified* him, so when she saw that, she axed me and gave him an African American woman, which is more interesting but less likely given what a racist sexist jerk he was, so anyway, in the dream this bee is getting larger and larger, and I turn to him and say WHAT IS THAT, and he says: I believe they call it DEFER-ENCE. And then I wake up. So there was some more big symbolism, my fear of bees is my fear of subservience, I guess, I mean she wrote me a college education as a lit major and I fucking well intend to use it. Al-though I never understood what the word POSTMODERN means, and now that I've been axed from the novel, there's no one I can ask, thank you very much.

So I'm out and about. A mutant. I've got a character and no ongoing circumstances. So I sit. I sit at this table. This is where she left me. It's nice, this table, I'm here a lot. To my right is a window, and there's a tree out this window, a young tree, and I'm on the second floor, and from this height, all you can see of this young tree is four feet of skinny bark, like the back of a young immigrant worker, shirtless; you can't see the roots at the bottom, or the leaves at the top, just the work in progress of ascension, of going up to offer leaves. You see just this, that's where the window catches the tree. I like that. That's like me. I liked the way she did that. That's reasonable symbolism. The only problem is the tree is still in the novel, and the window too, and the table, and the chair, and the main character with the wife with the curlers, so everyone's fine except for you know who. Sitting here in a black floral dress. Twenty-nine years old. I've been twenty-nine for forty-four years. It's starting to bore me. Like Cher. She's been twenty-nine for forty-four years too, but at least she has a bank account and a boyfriend.

So fuck O fuck O fuck these women writers, man. I prefer men: Hemingway, Faulkner, Milan Kundera, John Updike, Saul Bellow, Camille Paglia. I mean, this woman . . . the woman who wrote this novel I was cut from, she's not stupid! She's very bright! She teaches literature at a college in Connecticut, although that doesn't necessarily show how smart she is . . . but she can't plot! She can't deal with the plot . . . there's NO PLOT! I mean, she *had* a plot, in a way, but she seemed scared of it . . . like the way she put me up all scared of the bee . . . waiting to be stung by it . . . so instead of a story there's just a bunch of disorganized anecdotes . . . some of which are beautiful! She writes beautifully! She's got an ear for dialogue . . . like the way people don't always respond directly to what's said to them, but instead respond several lines later so it's like music. There's asking and answering but not directly, like life. Like that! She's good with that. But where's the plot? It's going along and all of a sudden you have to hear about her drug problem and her mother and her trip to Peru! See, I don't care about Peru! Just tell the story! Just tell the story! But no! She can't! Almost an apology, she has to apologize for having a story by developing some crippling, vision-obscuring problem! See, it's women! The problem is Women! Women! Having a story, it's too scary for them, it's too scary, it's like throwing a spear at an animal and having it hit, it's violent in some way, it's terminal, it *ends!* Stories end! So instead they throw the spear, and then, afraid it's gonna hit the good heart that they aimed it at, they run after it, *catch* it; the animal shrugs its shoulders and walks away, and then what? Where do you go from there? To *Peru!* Or get a drug problem. Or talk about your mother. Or, no, you know what it's like? It's like they write themselves roles as Greek heroines, walking in white togas, but they write themselves togas that are too long and they're walking along having deep philosophical conversations and they start to trip on them and fall, or, I don't know! I don't know what it's like! I'm not the writer! See, that's why I like Camille Paglia! He says that women are fundamentally inferior, and that the reason nature rendered them fundamentally inferior is so that men will find them sexy and we can perpetuate the race! And I like that! That makes sense to me! I mean, here I am, so fundamentally inferior that I can't keep my ass in a plotless grade-B third-rate novel, but am I sexy up here, or what?

But she did write me some nice moments, and those are for keeps, like when you don't win the grand prize on *Wheel of Fortune* but you get to keep the money from the first few games, right? She wrote me some nice moments. She wrote me this dress, and I like it. She wrote me on the verge of smoking, and I like that: here are the cigarettes, and here are the matches, O! I like that. I'm always about to light a cigarette, it's so lovely. Frozen, like a painting. And she wrote me two scenes that I love, that you can probably see in me, just looking at me. I'll tell you about those.

In the first one, I'm much younger, like fourteen. See, right now I'm twenty-nine. But then I was fourteen, and I'm living in this development complex. That sounds paradoxical, doesn't it: Development complex. I mean, y'can't develop so well if you have a complex . . . witness the main character, the businessman with the curlers wife . . . but anyway. I'm this teenager, with an awkward body but a beautiful face, if I remember my body, my legs were like thick sticks, the baby fat refusing to come off the ankles, the legs resisting womanliness, and then the hips and chest just the opposite, refusing to put *on* flesh, again resisting womanliness, but the face is all woman, all woman waiting to happen; a face that looks licked by candlelight all the time, with downy hair above the upper lip, blond; and hair that falls from the top of my head like "hopes in a spell of sadness." And I'm gawky and everything, but one summer they notice my face, the boys, they notice it, as if a shroud just fell away, which it did, and she goes on real nice about how beauty reveals itself in a single month, or in a single moment; suddenly beauty is present in a new way. And that one summer, every night in August, that summer I turned fourteen, I allowed the boys in the complex to push me up against the metal fence by the tennis courts and put lipstick on me . . . they take the top off the lipstick . . . it's gloss really . . . and then fight for who can turn the bottom and raise up the stick of colored gloss . . . they do it so slowly . . . it comes up above the metal rim, faint pink and glowing, and they take turns in the twilight growing dark, putting my lips on me . . . they apply it tenderly so as not to crush the stick . . . they laugh softly . . . we smell each other's breath . . . I open my mouth slightly . . . I tighten the lower lip to make it easier, but the upper lip I leave slack . . . it sits so soft above my two front teeth like a silk blouse above cleavage . . . and the boy who does the upper lip leans in close and works like Picasso . . . sketching an image . . . chest to chest . . . an image of desire . . . and the sky goes from blue to deep blue to black . . . and there's gruff laughter and talk but the work is gentle . . . and we do this every night in August that summer I turned fourteen . . . and every time we hear sirens we imagine the police are coming for us . . . that we've been found out . . . we feel so dangerous . . . and when I leave these lovemaking sessions there's lipstick on my chin, in the crack between my teeth . . . above my upper lip . . . I look like I've been necking furiously, making out passionately, and yet I leave that summer without so much as a single, simple kiss. Nice, eh?

The second nice bit she did for me was . . . right here, at this table by the window with the young tree in it. This one is my last image from that fucking bitch. It's nice. It's a still image, with just sound. No movement. Here's the background: I'm twenty-nine. I've just been swimming like a hundred laps in a nearby pool, tight at first, then loosening "like a dress that's come unzipped," and I'm in motion, all breath, and above me clouds churn "like muscles in use"! But it doesn't rain, and I finish, and I get out, dripping water like power, I dress quickly, go home, sit down at the table with the young tree. Coffee, I have hot black coffee, and in my body pure white joy. I've got a beautiful body by this time, it's perfect, in fact, and of course I'm about to light a cigarette. And inside me is health, silence. So here's the image: at the table, perfect; in fact, somehow, at the very needle's edge of my perfection, at the height of my power as a physical and sexual being. But there's a bee, buzzing behind the blind, caught between the screen and the blind, and I'm afraid of bees, like I told you before, I'm afraid because I've NEVER BEEN STUNG, and I'm waiting to be stung, because I'm twenty-nine and it's never happened. I've never felt that pain, never been surprised in that way by a creature I've frightened enough to commit suicide in order to hurt me for a moment, and it's bound to happen, and each day that passes and it hasn't happened, I feel more bound to the event, to how inevitable it is. So there's just me: still, beautiful, at my height, like when you throw a ball straight up in the air and it goes as far as it can go, there's a moment when it just hangs there, perfectly still, before it falls back down again; that's my moment. And there's the bee, furious and mixed up behind the blind, and my fear of it, I guess it represents the inevitable fall, I don't know, but there's just perfection and fear in one still image, and O God O Christ O God:

I wish she could just have told the story.

Secaucus, New Jersey, Monologue

At 1:20 in the morning on December 20th the year of 1991 I had a kid.

And I still have him, and it's almost three years later. It's the most shocking thing in the world that I ever did or will do. It is bizarre, ridiculous, otherworldly, and completely banal. It's exhausting, demented, exhilarating, refreshing, depressing, wretched, and queer. *And no one talks about it.*

I have had vomit on my shirt, poop on my pant-legs and spit-out carrots in my hair for two years, and NO ONE TALKS ABOUT IT. Now in a world where there are race riots and ethnic cleansing, where there are guns in the schools and asbestos in the synagogue bathroom and vice versa, having a kid doesn't seem too important, so NO ONE TALKS ABOUT IT. Everyone has kids, so no one talks about it. Very few people in the performance community have kids, so there's not much talk about it.

So Screw it! I'm not going to talk about it either! I feel alienated enough! I feel often enough like my behavior is odd in some way or like I don't blend in properly in some respect! Although I'm sure no one notices! So I'm not going out on a limb to discuss these things! I'm not going to talk about my theory that Dr. LaMaze was either a sexual sadist or a serial killer, or that laboring made me weep tears of oil during which I saw Jesus Christ and knew exactly how inconvenient the crucifixion must have been insofar as the thorns and nails were painful but the worst pain was the deep, unrequited love he felt for the people who were killing him, and he shrieked for help while the nurses gossiped in the hallway! Or how he cried out for God his father whose answer either never came or was inaudible; a lot of angry people speak too softly, it's called passive aggression! I'm not going to talk about how the tender flowers that grew up between my nerves took a shock-bath in ice water and couldn't move anymore, couldn't signal anymore; or how I sat for half a year with the beige curtains drawn and the sunlight coming through them like weak coffee while I curled up there with a hole in my abdomen the size of the Delaware Water Gap as this tiny predator yanked and gnawed and bit on my boobies fifteen, sixteen, seventeen times a day! Or how it became clearer and clearer with each passing moment that the child I had borne was a precise clone of his father in every respect, from his appearance to his mood to his sense of humor to the shape of his peepee like as if I had nothing whatsoever to do with his composition.

Obviously this is not what people talk about. So I'm not going to discuss it.

No, no. I think instead what I would like to talk about is how funny it is that all of a sudden, as soon as my kid was born, my sense of vision had no meaning! And I am a very visual person, not because I am an artist, but because I'm an atheist. I believe what I see, that's my religious belief. Like, I never saw a snake talking to some naked gal in a garden who then gave a piece of fruit to some bumbling guy and they ended up getting dressed, leaving that municipality and opening up a bodega or a farm or something. So I'm not so sure I believe that story! Whereas sometimes what you do see is so breathtaking that it's hard not to take it spiritually! I'm a visual person!

So it was so shocking when all of a sudden, I mutated from being a visually clutchy person to being someone who never used their eyes. My eyes became vestigial. I broke up with my eyes. There was no big scene, it happened quite suddenly. Suddenly it was my *ears* bringing in the critical information.

It began in the hospital with Bobby McFerrin on the headphones; the dirty, restless river for my eyes, but for my larger being, Bobby McFerrin stinging my soul through the headphones, singing I'M MAD O MAD! I'M ANGRY, ANGRY. And I just cried until they threw me out of that hospital. I came home, I came up the stairs.

Then there were thuds and gurgling. And there was crying, and within the crying, there were different cries: there was the crackling cry, like a knife, a cry of dumb need that didn't even know what it wanted; there was the soft, social cry to be held; the long, insistent, articulate cry of hunger; the short attenuated shrieks for diaper work, and the little croaks that were just games with sound.

(Each toy or device that follows is demonstrated by the actor. Toys and music boxes are set on stage on a table, and miked for sound.)

Then came the toy and TV cacophony. First, the tender little toy dad brought for him, a little clown that plays "Put on a Happy Face," which actually seemed to amuse the little tyke. Then came the white bear that played "Love Me Tender," while the animal moves its head like a junkie nodding out in an alleyway. Then came the croaking frog, then he learned to sit up.

Now once you can sit up, you're master of the Universe because it frees your hands! Your hands are free! The world around you is like Mission Control! So then comes the train sound toy, so digital, precise and mournful, the bells and whistles, and track sounds, and then the animal identification toy, screaming WHAT AM I? and urging the listener to identify the gobble with the picture of the turkey, etc. WHAT AM I? WHAT AM I? And then you can combine them! Wind 'em both up and play "Put On a Happy Face" with "Love Me Tender," or have the sounds of the train with the shriek of ontological confusion: WHAT AM I? WHAT AM I? I mean, which of us hasn't asked ourselves that question down at the train station from time to time, ladies and gentlemen?

Then pretty soon the TV starts vomiting purple sound into my life, with this low-IQ goody-goody dinosaur named Barney singing "I LOVE YOU! YOU LOVE ME! WE'RE A HAPPY FAMILY! WITH A GREAT BIG HUG AND A KISS FROM ME TO YOU! WON'T YOU SAY YOU LOVE ME TOO!" You could check right into a clinic with those lyrics! It brings up everything that went wrong! Everything that didn't happen in your childhood! You need a doctor!

Then the child hates getting his diaper changed so in order to do it, you have to get this SINGING TOOTHBRUSH! It's the only thing that works! You let him hold the fucking thing and press the button while you hose down his ass. Now if you ever wish someone was dead, you just invite him or her over to your house and you play them this song as many times as you can:

I'M YOUR FRIEND BRUSHY BRUSHY! I KEEP YOUR TEETH SHINY AND BRIGHT! PLEASE BRUSH WITH ME EVERY DAY, MORNING NOON AND NIGHT!

Now if your will to go on living is THE SLIGHTEST BIT TENUOUS, this will DEFINITELY finish you off! And, depending on whether he's made number one or number two, and how efficient you are at cleaning it up, you may have to listen to this song between fifteen and thirty times per diaper change!

Then the song from the Shari Lewis show that brings existentialism into the realm of Dr. Jack Kevorkian:

THIS IS THE SONG THAT DOESN'T END! IT JUST GOES ON AND ON MY FRIEND! SOME PEOPLE STARTED SINGIN' IT NOT KNOWING WHAT IT WAS! AND THEY'LL CONTINUE SINGING IT FOREVER JUST BECAUSE . . .

Now the thing I forgot to mention is that not only all this noise came in and collapsed in the center of my life, but at the same time I moved from West 76th Street on the island of Manhattan in New York City to SECAUCUS, NEW JERSEY! Now, SECAUCUS, NEW JERSEY! Think about it! It's something you used to make FUN OF and all of a sudden it's where your MAIL GETS DELIVERED, much less your child, the stigma of it! So instead of the familiar and comforting sounds of rapes and murders and car alarms I now have mah jong, karaoke, and car alarms.

There's something very weird about Secaucus. Okay it smells, but that's not it. The fact is, it's a swamp that got turned into a bunch of outlet centers. Secaucus is known for its outlet centers, and although it's just a swamp, people come there from very far away to buy things. But it's just a swamp and some alleged stores. And they call these stores OUTLET CENTERS. I find that so interesting. And although I have lived in Secaucus among these alleged outlet centers for three years, I've never seen a single center. You go looking for them, there are just these huge flat tracts of cement, with an occasional flattop building with a sign. It's just a scam built on a swamp! There aren't any of these stores! Although once I found one, because a Volkswagen Farvernugen full of Hasidim pulled up and asked me where Harve Benard was, they said it was a fashion outlet center. And I know there's a flattop building with a sign, so I pointed them that way. Then I went there myself, and it was a big room with a rack full of hideous mustard-colored plaid wool blazers and a man in a top hat talking on the phone. I don't know. They used to slaughter pigs here in Secaucus; now the main business is these outlet centers.

And there are highways. The whole town is highways. You have a feeling here the only thing that isn't a highway is your bathroom. This cab driver told me he moonlights as a toxic-waste disposal contractor man, he works putting toxic waste under the highways, they figure it's safe there because you drive right by, that's why the highways are always under construction, they're busy putting plutonium under them. And you wonder why you get so burned out by a traffic jam! You were being nuked there for half an hour while you listened to Lite FM!

Anyway, in the middle of these toxic roadways and bogus stores with hideous merchandise is this development complex where I live. It's called Harmon Cove. Harmon Cove! Isn't that a beautiful name? Harmon Cove! It implies music and resonance, gentle sailboats on a calm, clean tide! Harmon Cove! And it looks nice! Very nice! There's a pool, and some trees, and lots of different kinds of birds, and the landscaping is very meticulous, they sprinkle water all the time, even in the rain! Plenty of animals here! Unidentifiable rodents, as if all the gerbils escaped and mated with the water rats! And there are squirrels wandering around in a daze as if they just got back from Vietnam and can't find the Benefits Office! And suppos- edly benign snakes that grow to the size and thickness of your arm and sun themselves on top of the carefully carved bushes! And wild boars and mystical animals that wash up dead on the banks of the Hackensack River, which is a river to the same extent that these stretches of cement are outlet centers! It's very nice! Really, in a way! And precisely because it is so lovely, every plane taking off from the tri-state area flies directly over us! Little Harmon Cove! Wave if you ever take the red-eye! Since it's impossible to sleep with all that horrific, crashing din that sounds like the living apoca- lypse, I'm sure I'll be awake to wave back! It's a very attractive place! They take care of it very nicely! And in the center of town they have the Acme supermarket, where the bank recently gave me a mortgage to buy tampons!

And every night in front of the Acme the kids stand around with pimples and smoke cigarettes! These kids, they pull up alongside the two pay phones in the whole town, and break bottles and talk tough, and they've got pimples and raging hormones. And the pay phones ring, and they answer them, they're making arrangements all the time, and saying drop dead to people. That's important, man! They're climbing out of their skin, they're desperate and immortal! I call these kids the Acme Urchins. They're very very attractive! And they're always glad to have some farblungit matron such as myself sitting around in their midst waiting for a taxi! They never laugh until the car comes for me! It's the incredible allure of a town that's sinking. Literally, slowly, ineluctably sinking. It's so sexy, really, isn't it?

And the library! The Secaucus library! What a living testament to the value of erudition! First of all it's attached to the firehouse, so if your work ever gets the better of you, you can run across and slide down a pole! I went there one Thursday to try to find a certain John Donne poem called "The Funeral." It's a beautiful poem, full of strength and posture; I needed a copy of it to put in the program of some show I was directing. I drove over there, parked across from red engine number 12 and went in. Now for openers it's the only library I ever went in that has MUZAK blasting! I get through the door, I hear WALK ON BY! DUH DUH DUH . . . DUH DUH DUH! WALK ON BY! FOOLISH PRIDE! I WILL NEVER GET OVER LOSIN YOU! AND SO IF I SEEM! BROKEN AND BLUE! WALK ON BY! DUH DUH . . . etc. Now this is the fucking library! And people are standing around drinking iced tea! All I saw was a bunch of newspapers lying around and a few copies of *Valley of the Dolls* and a notice about how senior citizens can get free Xeroxes. So I said to the guy: Where is the poetry section? So he takes a sip, he was busy describing how he got stung by a bee on Saturday, and he says, Whatcha looking for, young lady? So I let that go, and I said: John Donne. So he thinks a second and he says: John Donne *what?* Eh, Pete? Ha Ha!

Now you're probably thinking I'm too snooty; that in reflecting on the snobbery of others, I've taken on an arrogance of my own. But I tried! I really tried! When we first moved to Secaucus, I made a real effort! I met my upstairs neighbor out by the mailbox, and WAS I CORDIAL! I fucking was! and she introduced me to her dog Jellybean and she said LOOK! JELLYBEAN GOT A LETTER! And she opened up a card, and made me hold the dog while she read him his Christmas card, and then she said: Everyone knows Jellybean. Even the mailman Earl knows Jellybean! And the mailman for some reason rolls back his eyes and goes into a trance-like state, and he says: OH YES! I KNOW JELLYBEAN! Couple days later I notice that her license plate says JELLY B! I mean what the hell is going to happen when that dog kicks the bucket? The sight of her car is going to shatter her composure!

But that's not the point! The point is, that first meeting went OK! I did very well! I mean, I played my part, I smiled, I held the dog, I read the card, I acknowledged the mailman, et cetera, but not two weeks later I blew the whole gig because I had been pulling up weeds in the front, and all of a sudden I felt something creeping on my thigh inside my pantleg, and I couldn't reach it and I thought it was a bee and I came tearing around the side of the house, kicked open the door with my foot and pulled down my pants but unfortunately my underpants came down too and my entire tushy and all its complements were hanging out there when Jellybean and the mother, the son and the father come up the stairs and see my whole predicament. So what can I tell you. We're on sitcom territory here, right?

They have a newspaper out here called the *Secaucus Reporter*. It comes out once a week whether it needs to or not, there's a limited amount of news over here. But it's free, they deliver it! And each resident gets about eight or ten copies, so it comes in handy if you're moving, you can wrap your glassware! It is a fine specimen of modern journalism! Whereas they can't get the movie times right at the local theatres, and once I had to watch *Rock-A-Doodle* because I was an hour and twenty minutes late for the adult feature, they certainly have drawn a bead on what matters in the news! For example, this compelling headline:

NO GO ON BASEMENT SWAP *(Holds up paper)*

This is a real scoop! I read it with such interest! It is a groundbreaking article concerning certain shocking shenanigans going on with regard to Mayor Anthony Just's basement! Just listen:

THE BOARD OF ADJUSTMENT VOTED TO DISAPPROVE A THIRD VARIANCE ON MAYOR ANTHONY JUST'S HOME THIS WEEK, AMID BUF-

FETING RUMOR, SPECULATION AND QUESTIONS ABOUT PAST PRAC-
TICES.

WHILE MAYOR JUST AND HIS SON SAID A SWAP OF BASEMENT ROOMS
FOR AN OUTSIDE BUILDING HAD BEEN DONE IN GOOD FAITH, SOME
BOARD MEMBER BELIEVED IT WAS A VIOLATION.

THE HOUSE MAYOR JUST PURCHASED IN 1963 WAS BUILT ON AN
UNDERSIZED LOT, BUT IT HAD A FINISHED BASEMENT IN WHICH
MAYOR JUST'S SISTER LIVED! A little Jane Eyre twist right there!

Here finally is a story worth following! This arresting piece of journalism
was written by staff reporter Al Sullivan. He is a very gifted man who
I'm sure lives somewhere here in Harmon Cove, perhaps in someone's
basement.

So you can see clearly that Harmon Cove is an incredible place, a little
haven in the filthy mist at the elbow of New York and New Jersey. The
women here are incredible, too! There's a pool, and they come to the pool
with diamonds, waterproof outline lipstick and gold chains BUILT INTO
THEIR BATHING SUITS! In other words, the gold chains are part of the
suit! The bra straps, the bikini g-strings! They have children but they
wouldn't be caught dead with them! And they play tennis all day, which
keeps them fit! These are healthy women! I am the only unhealthy example in the entire community. My gold collection is limited to the L'Chaim
pin I found on Yom Kippur at the Beth Emeth Synagogue in New Rochelle
twenty years ago, and I consistently commit the faux pas of being seen
with my child not only on weekends but on the weekdays as well.

So, since I have no gold and my neighbor saw my ass, I walk my child
alone. It's pretty here! We walk alone every morning, he in his stroller and
me pushing him along. He only knows two letters of the alphabet: the
letter B, because his name is Bennett, and the letter O, because it "goes
around and around." And, as with all pieces of his knowledge, he likes to
chant them out loud, as if they were a pin that could somehow pop the
bubble of all human knowledge and open up the world! So we plod down
the sidewalk, the child screaming B-O! B-O! B-O! most of the way, which
I'm sure doesn't make me seem too attractive to the neighbors, and I try to
act like I don't see anyone, since each person I ignore spares them the
trouble of ignoring me, and these people have enough to do, God knows!

And yet, it haunts me . . . Who are we at the moment we choose to ignore the presence of another human being? Who are we at that moment? I was walking Bennett, okay he's screaming B-O! B-O! And my watch has stopped, and it's important! It's important for me to know what time it is because I have to get him in position every day to see the 3:45 train go by, it's critical! It makes his day! Life with a child is a critical mass of routines and, if you miss one, you pay later! So I see this woman coming toward us, okay, she's one of those in-crowd kitty-cool gold-lamé life-is-gay tennis players, but . . . she has a watch! We're all human beings, we'll all be dead in fifty years, and we all measure the element that ages and kills us with the same chronometer! Okay, hers was gold and mine was stainless steel, had vomit in it and had ceased to function, but that's a technicality! It's all the same! So we're going by, Bennett's with the B-O! B-O! And I said to her, excuse me! Could you please tell me what time it is? And she . . . I can't even do it! She . . . she waved me away as if I was a bunch of bugs! You know those frantic clusters of summer gnats you encounter sometimes moving in a wild cloud around each other? She turned her head as if me and my kid constituted one of those blobs of bugs and waved her hands like this, as if to totally disperse us so she could get by! And she kept on walking.

Now look! We may not be the most appealing people! But this woman LITERALLY WOULD NOT GIVE US THE TIME OF DAY! Literally would not!

So anyway, we're out on one of these cordial morning jaunts when all of a sudden I hear a man's voice say:

I DON'T KNOW HOW YOU DO IT.

I was shocked, I mean, someone spoke to me, so I whirl my head around, and there's this guy. He's about 5'10", paunchy, light brown hair, fuzzy blue eyes, broken blood vessels in the nose, like he drinks too much and used to be good looking. So I said: I beg your pardon? and he says again:

I DON'T KNOW HOW YOU DO IT.

So I said, DO IT? And he says, I DON'T KNOW HOW ANY OF YOU WOMEN DO IT! YOU COOK, YOU CLEAN, YOU TAKE CARE OF KIDS

DAY AFTER DAY! So I said, well. I don't cook or clean and he says again: I DON'T SEE HOW YOU WOMEN DO IT! I'M A FEMINIST! YES SIR I AM! I STUDY FEMINISM! I STUDY FEMINISM IN A CLASS! AND FOR MILLIONS OF YEARS WOMEN HAVE DONE IT! AND I'M A FEMINIST! AND CAN YOU BELIEVE IT! AND WHEN THE TEACHER HAD TO BE ABSENT FOR A MONTH TO GET A HYSTERECTOMY, SHE ASKED ME TO TAKE OVER THE CLASS! I TOOK OVER! AND CAN YOU BELIEVE IT? YOU WOMEN ARE INCREDIBLE! I DON'T KNOW HOW YOU DO IT!

So I said thank you. And I walked away.

And then came the Summer, my second Summer at Harmon Cove. And the pool opened, and then came the exquisite, elongated, sensuous sessions between my body and the cool clean painted blue of that pool: afternoons clawing at that body of water like one might the body of a lover in a cheap motel; in the mornings, throwing myself in and clinging to that cold the way a sleeper in the middle of a beautiful dream clings to sleep; and then, in the evenings, my eyes clawing at the jagged edges of the rising moon, my fingers clawing at the edges of the pool, swimming back and forth and back and forth till they threw me out and locked the gate.

So then one day I'm walking my child after a particularly sensuous morning swim, when all of a sudden I hear, from behind me:

I DON'T KNOW HOW YOU WOMEN DO IT!

And I turn around, and it's the same guy! Launching the same rap! And of course at the same moment I realize he says this same thing to every woman he sees, and doesn't even remember the particular woman to whom he says it: a kind of social promiscuity, a new kind of sexism, even, ladies! So

I said, DO IT? And he says: I DON'T KNOW HOW YOU WOMEN DO IT! YOU COOK, YOU CLEAN AND TAKE CARE OF KIDS DAY AFTER DAY! So I said, I don't cook or clean, and he said: I'M A FEMINIST, I STUDY FEMINISM! YES SIR I DO! AND WHEN THE TEACHER HAD TO GET A LAPAROSCOPY, SHE ASKED *ME* TO TAKE OVER THE CLASS FOR HER! I DON'T KNOW HOW YOU WOMEN DO IT!

Now this whole thing was getting very tightly on my nerves. I mean, first of all, a disquisition on feminist thinking from a paunchy, pixillated white man at nine a.m. of the clock on a Wednesday morning was NOT my idea of what I had in mind for myself socially. So I said to him, Look! There are seven hundred and seventeen women living in this complex who would be *very glad* to clear this mystery up for you with hands-on training! I mean, it was a disgrace! This man was walking around with NOTHING TO DO! So he says: OH! ALLOW ME TO INTRODUCE MYSELF! MY NAME IS TIMMY "THE TIN-MAN" TARANTELLA! So I said, How do you do? or something. And he says, what do you do? And I said, cook, clean and take care of babies! So he says, how 'bout coming out for karaoke in the Harmon Cove Clubhouse this Friday! You deserve the rest! Take the night off! You can do something! You can do something! Want to be in it? C'mon! Give it a try! So I said, Well, as a matter of fact, I am a performance artist, and maybe I can do a little something. I mean, after the knife fight that broke out during my show at Cafe Bustelo, I figure a little upper-middle-class hostility isn't much to cope with. So he says GREAT! And he gives me this flyer, look! I kept it! Here it is! It says:

THE RECREATION BOARD
PROUDLY PRESENTS
THE HARMON COVE VARIETY SHOW
CO-HOSTS TIMMY "THE TIN-MAN" TARANTELLA
AND RHONDA B. REISBAUM

Scheduled to Appear: The No Tones! Mick & Co.!

The Harmon Cove Boy Toys! The Vinnettes

Whitey!

AND FEATURING SPECIAL GUEST STAR *MAYOR ANTHONY JUST!*

I thought I was going to die! A chance to dance karaoke with the guy who locked his sister in the basement!

And more Guest Stars and Surprises!
Call Tom or Anthony if you want to be on the bill!
This is the night your star can shine!
TELL THE BABYSITTER YOU'LL BE LATE!

See, there's that nice, feminist touch I've come to expect from the Tin-Man! And it finishes up,

STAG OR DRAG—YOU'LL HAVE THE BEST TIME IN YOUR LIFE

Isn't it interesting, Stag or drag, those are the only choices?

Anyway, I went to karaoke that night in the clubhouse. I was afraid but I went. I went forward with my knees knocking. I got dressed. I put on makeup. Who knew what I would find there at the clubhouse!

(Lighting change: disco lights up, general wash down.)
(Disco music up.)

When I arrived, boy, what a thrill! They sure knew how to do it up! The place looked great! And everyone was there . . . Oh, Jeez, there's Timmy the Tin-Man dancing with Rhonda B. Reisbaum! And there's Mayor Just and his son dancing with the woman from the basement! And there's Whitey up on the dais . . . he must be the DJ for tonight . . . Oh! And there's the woman who waved me away as if I were a bunch of bugs! HI! HON! *(waving frantically)* HI!

Then the performances began! Boy that Vinny sure can sing! And those Vinnettes! What backup! And there go the Harmon Cove Boy Toys! They really are on top of things! Rhonda looks so stunning in that silverleaf bathing suit! And that Whitey! He's got a voice like Sinatra . . .

Then all of a sudden it was my turn. I could feel the lights come up on me. Everyone was looking at me. I knew it was my turn to . . . I was supposed to perform . . . to perform . . . but I just . . . . I just . . .

(Fade up: I'm Mad O Mad . . . I'm Angry, Angry . . .)

End

ANOTHER END

TWENTY-ONE

What Is Performance Studies Anyway?

Richard Schechner

Is performance studies a "field," an "area," a "discipline"? The sidewinder snake moves across the desert floor by contracting and extending itself in a sideways motion. Wherever this beautiful rattlesnake points, it is not going there. Such (in)direction is characteristic of performance studies. This area/field/discipline often plays at what it is not, tricking those who want to fix it, alarming some, amusing others, astounding a few as it sidewinds its way across the deserts of academia. At present, in the United States, there are only two performance studies departments—full-fledged academic enterprises replete with a chairpersons, the ability to tenure faculty, an independent budget, and so on. One of these, my own home base, is at New York University's Tisch School of the Arts; the other is at Northwestern University. It is worth sketching the development of these departments.

In 1965 Robert W. Corrigan founded the New York University School of the Arts. Corrigan had been at Tulane University, where he was my dissertation advisor/mentor. He was also the founding editor of the *Carleton Drama Review*, later the *Tulane Drama Review*, presently the *Drama Review (TDR)*, which I edited from 1962 to 1969 and again since 1986. In 1965 I published "Approaches" in *TDR*, an essay in which I said that performance was an inclusive category that included play, games, sports, performance in everyday life, and ritual. In 1967 Corrigan invited me to head the Drama Department in the NYU School of the Arts. I came with *TDR* but declined the headache of administration, suggesting instead Monroe Lippman, who had resigned as chair at Tulane. In 1968, we brought to NYU Brooks McNamara, a Tulane Ph.D., theatre historian, and scenographer. His passion was for popular entertainments, mine for the avantgarde and Greek theatre (a combination that bore fruit in *Dionysus in 69*). In the early 1970s, adding Michael Kirby and Ted Hoffman to the faculty, we moved further and further away from a conventional drama department. I taught courses in ritual, using anthropological thinking and joining forces with Victor Turner.

In 1979, with the strong support of David Oppenheim, who became dean of the School of the Arts in 1968 (Corrigan having gone on to found the California Institute of the Arts), I began a series of courses entitled Performance Theory. These were the kernel of what was to become performance studies at NYU. As the flyer for the first such course proclaimed, "Leading American and world figures in the performing arts and the social sciences will discuss the relationship between social anthropology, psychology, semiotics, and the performing arts. The course examines theatre and dance in Western and non-Western cultures, ranging from the avantgarde to traditional, ritual, and popular forms." The visiting faculty for this initial offering included Jerzy Grotowski, Paul Bouissac, Donald Kaplan, Alexander Alland, Joann W. Kealinohomoku, Barbara Myerhoff, Jerome Rothenberg, Squat Theatre, and Victor Turner. Here, possibly for the first time together, were anthropologists, a Freudian psychoanalyst, a semiotician specializing in play and circus, a dance scholar, a poet and scholar of oral cultures and shamanism, and leading experimental theatre artists. The graduate assistant for the course was Sally Banes.

Over the next three years, Performance Theory counted among its visiting faculty Clifford Geertz, Masao Yamaguchi, Alfonso Ortiz, Erving Goffman, Eugenio Barba, Steve Paxton, Joanne Akalaitis, Yvonne Rainer, Meredith Monk, Augusto Boal, Colin Turnbull, Richard Foreman, Allan Kaprow, Linda Montano, Spalding Gray, Laurie Anderson, Peter Pitzele, Brian Sutton-Smith, Ray Birdwhistell, Edward T. Hall, Julie Taymor, and Peter Chelkowski. Victor and Edith Turner were frequent participants. Topics ranged from "Performing the Self" and "Play" to "Shamanism," "Cultural and Intercultural Performance," and "Experimental Performance."

By the end of the 1970s, we at NYU knew we weren't teaching "drama" or "theatre" in the ways it was taught elsewhere. Often we weren't teaching these subjects at all. So in 1980 we officially changed our name to Performance Studies. But we needed coherent leadership more than a name change. Enter Barbara Kirshenblatt-Gimblett, who came to NYU from the Department of Folklore and Folklife at the University of Pennsylvania with a Ph.D. in folklore from Indiana University. Kirshenblatt-Gimblett's far-ranging interests spanned Jewish studies, museum displays (from colonial expositions to living history museums), tourist performances, and the aesthetics of everyday life. She became chair in the spring of 1981 and remained in the post for twelve years. It was Kirshenblatt-Gimblett who crafted a singular department out of what had been disparate and sometimes quirky interests and practices.

In such a short essay, I can't detail what happened from then to now. At NYU we follow a dictum of having people teach what is most important to them. We resist abstract plans. PS goes where faculty and student interests take it. We know that such a small department can't do it all, so we exist as a conscious partiality, a knowing slice of the pie. With the arrival of Marcia Siegel in 1983, dance was folded into the mix. When Peggy Phelan joined in 1985, a strong feminist tendency, informed by psychoanalysis, became a PS mainstay. Michael Taussig was at PS from 1988 to 1993, teaching his own conjunction of Marxism, postcolonial thought, and anthropology. Kenyan writer and activist Ngũgĩ wa Thiong'o holds a joint appointment from PS and Comparative Literature. Younger faculty May Joseph, José Muñoz, and Barbara Browning bring with them particular interests ranging from queer theory to samba. As of this writing, Diana Taylor is set to become chair. Because PS is in New York, we are able to draw a rich panoply of adjuncts, with interests ranging from Asian performance to jazz, orality to Artaud and Valerina, and much more.

What happened at Northwestern is parallel to but different from NYU. NYU's performance studies is rooted in theatre, NWU's in oral interpretation. These are not only genres, but academic traditions. The theoretical and historical foundation of NWU's program is rhetoric, broadly understood. In a 1993 Internet discussion of "What Is Performance Studies?" Nathan Stucky of Southern Illinois University wrote (in part),

> By the late 1960s and early 1970s many (then Oral Interpretation) programs were really practicing what was called "Performance of Literature." However, the view of literature quickly broadened to include cultural performances, personal narratives, everyday-life performances, non-fiction, ritual, etc. . . . By this point in time, ethnographic work, as well as folklore and anthropology,

began to be of some interest. . . . So, along with the literary, theoretical, and critical models of performance that one might associate with "Interpretation" has been the emergence of interest in cultural and social elements, as well as interest in performance as a way of knowing. These threads connect logically and historically through relatively recent literary/critical foci to the oral tradition which has always been part of these approaches to performance.

In 1991 Dwight Conquergood, currently chair of NWU's Performance Studies Department and a major theorist of performance studies, raised what he called "new questions that can be clustered around five intersecting planes of analysis":

1. *Performance and cultural process.* . . .
2. *Performance and Ethnographic Praxis.* . . .
3. *Performance and Hermeneutics.* . . .
4. *Performance and Scholarly Representation.* . . .
5. *The Politics of Performance.* . . . (1991: 190)

Conquergood's questions indicate how closely related the NWU approach now is to NYU's. A further demonstration of this convergence is the collaboration between the two departments on the recurring Annual Performance Studies Conference(s). The first was held at NYU in 1995, the second at NWU in 1996, the third at Georgia Tech in 1997. Of course, by now many PS graduates—from NYU and NWU—are teaching, have authored dozens of books with a PS approach, and are disseminating PS ideas. A number of performance artists and theatre directors have also been influenced by PS.

But what is performance studies, conceptually speaking? Can performance studies be described? Performance studies is "inter"—in between. It is intergenric, interdisciplinary, intercultural—and therefore inherently unstable. Performance studies resists or rejects definition. As a discipline, PS cannot be mapped effectively because it transgresses boundaries, it goes where it is not expected to be. It is inherently "in between" and therefore cannot be pinned down or located exactly. This indecision (if that's what it is) or multidirectionality drives some people crazy. For others, it's the pungent and defining flavor of the meat.

PS assumes that we are living in a postcolonial world where cultures are colliding, interfering with each other, and energetically hybridizing. PS does not value "purity." In fact, academic disciplines are most active and important at their ever changing interfaces. In terms of PS, this means between theatre and anthropology, folklore and sociology, history and performance theory, gender studies and psychoanalysis, performativity and actual performance events, and more—new interfaces will be added as time goes on, and older ones dropped. Accepting "inter" means opposing the establishment of any single system of knowledge, values, or subject matter. Performance studies is unfinished, open, multivocal, and self-contradictory. Thus any call for or work toward a "unified field" is, in my view, a misunderstanding of the very fluidity and playfulness fundamental to performance studies. That sidewinder again, the endlessly creative double negative at the core of restoration of behavior.

Closer to the ground is the question of the relation of performativity to performance proper. Are there any limits to performativity? Is there anything outside the purview of performance studies? To answer, we must distinguish between "as" and "is." Performances mark identities, bend and remake time, adorn and reshape the body, tell stories, and allow people to play with behavior that is "twice-behaved," not-for-the-first-time, rehearsed, cooked, prepared. Having made such a sweeping generalization, I must add that every genre of performance, even every particular instance of a genre, is concrete, specific, and different from every other. It is necessary to generalize in order to make theory. At the same time, we must not lose sight of each specific performance's particularities of experience, structure, history, and process.

Any event, action, item, or behavior may be examined "as" performance. Approaching phenomena as performance has certain advantages. One can consider things as provisional, in-process, existing and changing over time, in rehearsal, as it were. On the other hand, there are events that tradition and convention declare "are" performances. In Western culture, until recently, performances were of theatre, music, and dance—the "aesthetic genres," the performing arts. Recently, since the 1960s at least, aesthetic performances have developed that cannot be located precisely as theatre or dance or music or visual arts. Usually called either "performance art," "mixed-media," "Happenings," or "intermedia," these events blur or breach boundaries separating art from life and genres from each other. As performance art grew in range and popularity, theorists began to examine "performative behavior"—how people play gender, heightening their constructed identity, performing slightly or radically different selves in different situations. This is the performative Austin introduced and Butler and queer theorists discuss.

The performative engages performance in places and situations not traditionally marked as "performing arts," from dress-up to certain kinds of writing or speaking. The acceptance of the performative as a category of theory as well as a fact of behavior has made it increasingly difficult to sustain the distinction between appearances and facts, surfaces and depths, illusions and substances. Appearances are actualities. And so is what lies beneath appearances. Reality is constructed through and through, from its many surfaces or aspects down through its multiple depths. The subjects of performance studies are both what is performance and the performative—and the myriad contact points and overlaps, tensions and loose spots, separating and connecting these two categories.

REFERENCE

Conquergood, Dwight. "Rethinking Ethnography: Towards a Critical Cultural Politics." *Communications Monographs* 58 (June 1991): 179–94.

Contributors

T A N Y A   A U G S B U R G teaches performance studies at Arizona State University. She is completing two manuscripts, tentatively entitled *Private Theatres Onstage* and *Self-Enhancements.*

J A N E   B L O C K E R is an assistant professor of art history at Georgia State University. She is the author of a book on performance and earthwork artist Ana Mendieta titled *Where Is Ana Mendieta? Identity, Performativity, and Exile,* forthcoming from Duke University Press.

J A M E R   H U N T is a visiting assistant professor of design and critical theory at the University of the Arts in Philadelphia. He writes on psychoanalysis, surrealism, and gender, and is currently finishing a book on Sylvia [Bataille] Lacan and absence.

M A Y   J O S E P H is an assistant professor of performance studies at New York University. She is the author of *Transnational Mediations: Postcoloniality and Cultural Pursuits* and coeditor of *Performing Hybridity,* both forthcoming from the University of Minnesota Press.

A M A N D A   D E N I S E   K E M P is a doctoral candidate in performance studies at Northwestern University. Her dissertation is entitled "The Americans Are Coming! South African Resistance and the Sign of the American Negro (1920–1940)." She coauthored "The New South African Feminism" for publication in *The Challenge of Local Feminisms.* She has worked with Amakhosikazi Productions and Dread Intimacy, a black women's poetry collective in South Africa.

J I L L   L A N E is a doctoral candidate in performance studies at New York University. She was the director of the First Annual Performance Studies Conference (March 1995). She is completing writing her dissertation on race and nationalism in Cuban popular performance during the anticolonial wars.

DEB MARGOLIN is a playwright, performance artist, author of six full-length solo performance pieces, and a founding member of Split Britches. Her most recent performance, *Critical Mass,* premiered in February 1997.

RANDY MARTIN is the chair of the department of Social Science at Pratt Institute and is the author of *Performance as Political Act: The Embodied Self* and *Socialist Ensembles: Theatre and State in Cuba and Nicaragua.*

JON MCKENZIE is the cofounder of VRcades, a group combining cultural theory and electronic media. He recently created StudioLab, a workshop exploring different performance genres, and uses it to teach courses at New York University (www.nyu.edu/classes/mckenzie).

MICHEL A. MOOS was educated at Yale University and Oxford University and has been Woodruff Scholar at Emory University. He works on comparative media, technology and literature, and his most recent book, *Media Research: Technology, Art, Communication,* re-presents the writings and work of Marshall McLuhan.

ORLAN is a performance artist and professor of art at the Ecole des Beaux Arts in Dijon, France. Her performances and videos have been widely exhibited throughout Europe and the United States.

PEGGY PHELAN is an associate professor of performance studies at the Tisch School of the Arts, New York University. She is the author of *Unmarked: The Politics of Performance* and *Mourning Sex: Performing Public Memory,* and the coeditor with Lynda Hart of *Acting Out: Feminist Performances.*

DELLA POLLOCK is an associate professor in the department of Communication Studies at the University of North Carolina at Chapel Hill. She is a coeditor of the journal *Cultural Studies,* the editor of *Exceptional Spaces: Essays in Performance and History* (in press), and the author of *In the Secret Divide: Performing Birth Stories* (forthcoming).

JOSEPH ROACH is a professor of English and theatre studies at Yale University. His publications include *The Player's Passion: Studies in the Science of Acting, Cities of the Dead: Circum-Atlantic Performance,* and *Critical Theory and Performance,* coedited with Janelle Reinelt.

RICHARD SCHECHNER is a professor of performance studies and a University Professor at New York University. His books include *Between Theater and Anthropology, Performance Theory,* and *The Future of Ritual.* He is the editor of *TDR: The Journal of Performance Studies* and the artistic director of East Coast Artists.

MADY SCHUTZMAN teaches in the School of Critical Studies at California Institute of the Arts, where she is also an assistant dean. She is the coeditor of *Playing Boal: Theatre, Therapy, Activism* and the author of the forthcoming *The Real Thing: Performance, Hysteria, and Advertising.*

EVE KOSOFSKY SEDGWICK is the Newman Ivy White Professor of English at Duke University. She is the author of *Between Men, Epistemology of the Closet,* and *Tendencies.* She has also written a book of poetry entitled *Fat Art, Thin Art* and is the editor with Adam Frank of *Shame and Its Sisters,* by Sylvan Tomkins.

ROBERT SEMBER is a member of the Special Projects of National Significance (SPNS) Evaluation and Technical Assistance Center (ETAC) at Columbia University's School of Public Health, where he works on issues related to the AIDS crisis. He is a doctoral candidate in performance studies at New York University and is writing a dissertation on the work of David Wojnarowicz.

THERESA M. SENFT is a doctoral candidate in performance studies at New York University. She recently edited a special issue of *Women and Performance,* where she serves on the editorial board, on sexuality and cyberspace. Her dissertation is entitled "Feminettiquette: Feminism, Performance, and the Internet."

MARCIA B. SIEGEL is the author of *Days on Earth: The Dance of Doris Humphrey, The Shapes of Change: Images of American Dance,* and three collections of dance criticism.

DORIS SOMMER is a professor of Latin American literature at Harvard University. She is the author of *Foundational Fictions: The National Romances of Latin America, One Master for Another: Populism as Patriarchal Discourse in Dominican Novels,* and a forthcoming book about the "rhetoric of particularism."

DIANA TAYLOR is a Professor of Performance Studies and Spanish and Chair of the Department of Performance Studies at New York University. She is the author of *Disappearing Acts* and *Theatre of Crisis: Drama and Politics in Latin America*. She has edited three volumes on Latin American, Spanish, and Latino theatre, and co-edited *Negotiating Performance: Gender, Sexuality, and Theatricality in Latin/o America* (with Juan Villegas) and *The Politics of Motherhood: Activists' Voices from Left to Right* (with Alexis Jetter and Annelise Orleck).

Index